Legislating Racism

Racism
THE BILLION DOLLAR CONGRESS AND THE BIRTH OF JIM CROW

THOMAS ADAMS UPCHURCH

THE UNIVERSITY PRESS OF KENTUCKY

Publication of this volume was made possible in part by a grant from the National Endowment for the Humanities.

Scholarly publisher for the Commonwealth,
serving Bellarmine University, Berea College, Centre
College of Kentucky, Eastern Kentucky University,
The Filson Historical Society, Georgetown College,
Kentucky Historical Society, Kentucky State University,
Morehead State University, Murray State University,
Northern Kentucky University, Transylvania University,
University of Kentucky, University of Louisville,
and Western Kentucky University.
All rights reserved.

Editorial and Sales Offices: The University Press of Kentucky
663 South Limestone Street, Lexington, Kentucky 40508–4008
www.kentuckypress.com

08 07 06 05 04   5 4 3 2 1

Library of Congress Cataloging-in-Publication Data

Upchurch, Thomas Adams.
   Legislating racism : the billion dollar congress and the birth of Jim
Crow / by Thomas Adams Upchurch.
       p. cm.
Includes bibliographical references and index.
   ISBN 0-8131-2311-9 (acid-free paper)
   1. African Americans—Civil rights—History—19th century.
2. Minorities—Civil rights—United States—History—19th century.
3. African Americans—Legal status, laws, etc.—History—19th century.
4. Minorities—Legal status, laws, etc.—United States—History—19th
century. 5. United States. Congress (51st, 1st session : 1889-1890)
6. United States. Congress (51st, 2nd session : 1890-1891)
7. Racism—Political aspects—United States—History—19th century.
8. United States—Race relations—Political aspects. I. Title.
   E185.61.U63 2004
   323.1196'073'009'034—dc22   2003020484

Manufactured in the United States of America.
Member of the Association of
American University Presses

To Billy and Rowena

CONTENTS

ILLUSTRATIONS

PREFACE

When Reconstruction met its inglorious demise in 1877, it died unmourned by most white Americans. The issue of the proper place and status of African Americans in southern politics and society lay dormant throughout the 1880s, as Democrats and Republicans split national political power and the collective attention of the American people turned toward Gilded Age economic issues. During that time, Bourbon political leaders cautiously reestablished Democratic control over the southern states, obviating the civil rights of their black denizens in various ways, including political disfranchisement, economic discrimination, and social ostracism. In 1889, however, with the inauguration of GOP President Benjamin Harrison and the convening of the Republican majority in the Fifty-first ("Billion Dollar") Congress, attention reverted to what most observers alternately called the "Negro question," the "southern question," or the "race problem." An influential group of Republican leaders hoped to reinstate full suffrage rights for black southerners by passing a strong federal elections law, which would soon come to life under the title of the Federal Elections Bill. Democrats wanted to prevent that possibility at all costs and to solve the race problem in ways of their own choosing, such as promoting a federally funded program to make it possible for black southerners who wished to leave the United States for new homes abroad to do so. If that idea failed, as a last resort they hoped to get away with rewriting southern state constitutions in such a way as to nullify or negate the impact of any new federal elections law the Republicans might pass without overtly violating the U.S. Constitution's Fourteenth and Fifteenth Amendments.

The Republican reformers would find their task complicated not only by the obstinance of the Democrats but also by infighting in the ranks of their own party, as half of the party's leaders pushed the continuation of a Gilded Age economic agenda that included everything from tariff and pension reform to silver coinage and regulation of trusts. Then there was the Republican wildcard, Senator Henry Blair of New Hampshire, who had his own agenda, which fit in neither the economic nor the racial reform category. Beyond those obstacles, the reformers had to contend with an American public that had grown increasingly apathetic to the issue of black civil rights over the dozen years since Reconstruction ended, as well as with a growing public awareness of the duplicity of the Republican Party in dealing with Native Americans and Chinese Americans vis-à-vis African Americans.

With such a host of problems facing the new Congress and administration, would the reformers be able to accomplish their goal of reenforcing the voting rights of African Americans? Or would they be consigned to compromising with their opponents and merely salvaging some marginal degree of civil rights for black southerners? Or would events unfold in ways beyond their imagination, such that the majority party would be totally and abjectly defeated in their quest for racial reform? The events in the South—beginning with the Mississippi disfranchising constitution of 1890—that relegated American blacks to the back of the bus are well known, but those happenings might not have become so entrenched in American society had they not been reinforced by the Billion Dollar Congress in the nation's capital. The parenting of the very un-American baby Jim Crow required the efforts of both southern and national politicians at the dawn of an era when the entire western world began to view itself as encumbered with what British writer Rudyard Kipling called "the white man's burden."

This book represents the culmination of more than five years of conceptualization, research, writing, and revision. It has been made possible because of the support, advice, encouragement, and constructive criticism of several fellow historians, all of whom I highly respect for their wisdom, experience, and knowledge. I thank Mark W. Summers of the University of Kentucky, a true scholar in the field of late-nineteenth-century American history, for freely giving his time to help me, a total stranger, by reading the whole manuscript and offering the benefit of his expertise. His thirty-page critique of my work was invaluable to the revision process. Reid Derr, a good friend and fellow laborer in the history department of East Georgia College, likewise read the whole manuscript and made some crucial observations that I incorporated in later drafts. Stanly Godbold, who is both a true friend and a mentor, as well as the former southern history specialist at Mississippi State University, read and re-read drafts of some chapters, helped me mold and shape the thesis, and, more important, gave me encouragement to press on (over delicious cups of coffee often served at his home by his lovely wife Jeannie), which is the contribution that I thank him for most. Bob Jenkins, my doctoral program advisor and specialist in African American history, had the dubious task of reading the earliest drafts of this manuscript. With the patience of a saint he did that thankless work, so I thank him now. It was also he who encouraged me to inquire to the University Press of Kentucky for publication of this manuscript, for which I am equally grateful. Many thanks also go to John Marszalek, Ren Crowell, and Jim Haug for serving as readers and critics, and to Bo Morgan for being the conduit through which I was introduced to some of the aforementioned readers of this manuscript. I also thank Jeff Howell for proofreading the final draft.

I am appreciative of the fact that I rarely had to make research trips alone, because some good friends and colleagues accompanied me: Steve Belko made trips to North Carolina, Missouri, and Arkansas with me; Tim Smith flew to Washington, D.C., with me; Ken Homer drove to South Carolina with me; Craig Piper met me in Jackson, Mississippi; and my beautiful and talented wife, Linda, served as my companion on trips to Colorado, Washington, Georgia, Alabama, and South Carolina.

I am indebted to numerous librarians and archivists around the country, most of whom I do not know by name. I thank David Hays, the archivist at the University of Colorado, for making my stay there especially enjoyable and fruitful. Those at the Mitchell Memorial Library at Mississippi State University, the Mississippi Department of Archives and History, the Library of Congress, the Southern Historical Collection at the University of North Carolina, the Perkins Library at Duke University, the South Caroliniana Library, the Missouri Historical Society, and the Georgia Southern University interlibrary loan office were also particularly helpful. Bill Stern of Press Express in Statesboro, Georgia, also earned my gratitude for his excellent work in preparing the illustrations for this book.

The faculties and staffs of the history departments of Mississippi State University, Delta State University, and Holmes Community College, as well as many former fellow graduate student friends, also merit recognition for helping me through the "starving times" of my college education. I also thank my friends and colleagues in the administration of East Georgia College for providing the funds and moral support that got me through two important research trips. And I especially appreciate my wife, Linda, my children, and my extended family for standing by me through all the challenges that life threw our way during the years this book was in gestation.

Finally, I thank the University of Alabama Press for use of excerpts from an article of mine called, "Senator John Tyler Morgan and the Genesis of Jim Crow Ideology, 1889–1891" *Alabama Review* 57 (April 2004). I also thank *Southern Studies* for use of excerpts from my article, "The Butler Emigration Bill of 1890 and the Path Not Taken in Southern Race Relations," IX (1998): 37–68.

INTRODUCTION

The Grand Old Party Faces the Grand Old Problem

Slavery restriction, emancipation, negro suffrage, civil rights, and fair elections are but the basic pillars of one political faith, and the stand men take upon them, independent of their personal interest, is the measure of their Republicanism.

—*Philadelphia Press*

For twenty years the Republican party has cracked the party whip with more arrogance over the negro voter, as its political owner, than ever their original owners did.

—*Charles H. Mansur, Democratic representative of Missouri*

As the 1880s gave way to the last decade of the nineteenth century, a new mood began settling over the United States. The nation buzzed with the excitement and anticipation that always looms in the air at the beginning of a new era of history. This new spirit of the times, or zeitgeist, signaled a change in the air. The nation was still deep in the throes of the Gilded Age of American history, in which the search for national economic growth, as well as personal opulence, held a generation captive. Voices of reform could be heard clamoring for regulation of the nation's corrupt corporations and political process, but the nation was not ready to abandon its collective quest for wealth. Politically, the nation was still led by many of the same men who had guided the country through the tragic and troublesome years of the Civil War and Reconstruction, but one by one they were gradually

1

retiring, dying, or subsiding in influence. Under their watch, the very soul of this mighty republic had been on trial, battling through the issues of slavery and abolition, secession and reunion, reconstruction and disengagement. Now on the horizon were the rumblings of various new forces, each of which vied for a spot in the national polity—Populism, Progressivism, new Nationalism, Imperialism, and Jim Crowism. Simultaneously, each of these forces would make its grand appearance upon the stage of national and world affairs. The 1890s would christen a new generation of Americans destined to reunite the North and South in support of the Spanish-American War, World War I, and, ultimately, the rise of this nation as a global superpower.[1]

The political leaders of the United States, caught up in the conflicting passions of the moment, failed to recognize and embrace the new zeitgeist of national unity. In Washington, D.C., the men of Capitol Hill and 1600 Pennsylvania Avenue had the responsibility of recognizing and welcoming the new era, yet many of them either could not or simply refused to do so. They had one last, great series of sectional battles to fight before they folded the bloody shirt and tucked it away. Control of the national destiny in the arena of race relations lay in the balance. The resulting clash of the titans at the nation's capitol would capture the attention of the country for more than a year, but it would leave a lasting imprint upon the fabric of American society and politics for the next seventy-five years.[2]

The elections of 1888 gave the Grand Old Party (GOP) both a majority in Congress and a president of the United States for the first time since 1874. Not since then had the GOP enjoyed majorities in both houses of Congress and the one-man majority that comes with control of the White House. The Democrats had controlled the House for fourteen of the previous sixteen years while Republicans had controlled the Senate for fourteen of the sixteen and the presidency for twelve of the sixteen. In the Fiftieth Congress, the Democrats had enjoyed a majority of nineteen in the House, while Republicans had held a two-man lead in the Senate. The Fifty-first Congress gave the Republicans a majority of nineteen in the House and ten in the Senate. Thus, from 1889 to 1891, a potential Republican juggernaut controlled Washington, D.C.—one party that, if it flexed its muscles, would enjoy hegemony over the federal government and would hold the power to do whatever it should choose.[3]

Together, the Republican tandem of the Fifty-first Congress and President Benjamin Harrison expected to resolve a host of long-running problems, not the least of which was the South's "race problem," or "Negro question," as politicians and the media alternately called it. The "problem" was that the proper status of African Americans had not been settled since the emancipation of the slaves in 1865. Conflicting views about what rights they should possess had caused outbreaks of violence and discrimination of all types against them. Native white southern Democrats, most of whom were ex-Confederates who had remained rebels at heart, controlled southern state and local governments. They deprived most qualified African Americans of the right to vote, and from that root grew all of the various civil rights abuses and racial injustices common in the South, such as segregation laws, lynchings, the convict lease system, educational deprivation, and job discrimination, to say nothing of rampant alcoholism, poverty, and despondency within the black community. The "question," which the federal government had ignored since the end of Reconstruction in 1877, was what to do about it. The American public and political leaders from both major parties were divided over the answer, and certainly no answer existed that would please everyone—black and white, northerner and southerner, Democrat and Republican.

The Republican experiment to incorporate black southerners into the national polity and the mainstream of American society had failed during Reconstruction for a number of reasons, including white southern resistence to such measures, opposition by the Democratic Party nationwide, disagreement among Republican leaders about party priorities, and public pressure to lay to rest issues leftover from the Civil War and move on to other business. As the famed southern egalitarian writer George Washington Cable put it: "The popular mind in the old free states, weary of strife at arm's length, bewildered by its complications, vexed by many a blunder, eager to turn to the cure of other evils, and even tinctured by that race feeling whose grosser excesses it would as gladly see suppressed, has retreated from its uncomfortable dictational attitude and thrown the whole matter over to the states of the South." Cable went on to say that nearly by consensus the American people of that day agreed that Reconstruction had been the most "dreadful episode" in the country's history. In the dozen-plus years since Reconstruction, however, the country—under divided Democratic and Republican leadership—had "set aside" the "compulsory" racial experiment and put "a voluntary reconstruction . . . on trial." The northern public at large had given "virtual" (if not actual) "consent" to this change of course.[4] The nation as a whole had prospered economically as a result. But now, the GOP had regained complete control of the federal government. Perhaps it could now finish the work it had started in the 1860s; perhaps it could now solve the southern race problem once and for all.

From the time of their election in 1888, many Republican leaders of the Fifty-first Congress had pledged to devote their attention to solving the race problem. Included among them in the House of Representatives were Henry Cabot Lodge of Massachusetts, Jonathan H. Rowell of Illinois, and Thomas B. Reed of Maine—who would be elected the new Speaker of the House. In the Senate, George Frisbie Hoar of Massachusetts and John Coit Spooner of Wisconsin would lead the charge. Other influential Republicans not in office at the time, including Chicago writer Albion Tourgee and New York election supervisor John I. Davenport, also threw the weight of their reputations and positions behind the reformers in Congress. They all agreed that the solution to the problem lay in electoral reform. Enforce the black voters' suffrage rights in accord with the Fifteenth Amendment, they said, and blacks could control their own destiny and put an end to all other forms of discrimination and mistreatment. Aside from the noble intention inherent in such a plan, the reformers also had an ulterior motive in wanting to enforce black suffrage. The disfranchisement of blacks prevented the establishment and perpetuation of overwhelming Republican majorities in at least thirty southern congressional districts. The GOP had managed to win control of Congress in 1888 without those districts, but, in order to maintain control, the reformers believed they would need to pass a strong federal election law authorizing supervision of congressional and presidential elections in the South. Thus they set out to solve the southern race problem with the stroke of a pen by passing a single law, which would come to be known officially as the Federal Elections Bill. As one Republican newspaper put it, the GOP had pledged itself to such a plan, and anyone who dared "to block the wheels of the party chariot will be crushed beneath its wheels."[5]

Yet there were numerous pebbles in the path of the oncoming "chariot" that lay as serious obstacles on the road to reform. Majority numbers do not necessarily equate to strength, and by no means was it a foregone conclusion that the crusade for southern electoral reform would succeed. Perhaps the most important obstacle standing in the way of the Republican reformers was resistance from white southerners, who rattled their sabers with frenetic desperation at the thought of a return to Reconstruction, even going so far as to threaten another Civil War to stop it. White southerners felt both intense anger and great fear and loathing at the very thought. They realized that the current practice of suppressing the black vote by fraud, intimidation, violence, and outright violation of the Fifteenth Amendment could not last much longer, but even so they opposed federal intervention in their local affairs. When, in his first annual Message to Congress, President Harrison hinted that the idea of state governments solving the

The Republican Party 'Chariot.' Another sort of presidential trip—not very agreeable, but the coach will get there all the same. (Puck, 1889.) What appeared to some observers as the Republicans' unstoppable party "chariot" appeared to others as a rickety stagecoach that could easily be thrown off course by Democratic obstruction.

problem themselves would be acceptable if only they would make some noticeable good faith effort to do so, white southerners knew the time had come to act. Harrison encouraged the South to be "at work upon" the problem and to suggest solutions, as if to say he would welcome the opportunity to forget the idea of supervising federal elections if only southerners would give him reason to. He warned that if southerners did not make some visible progress quickly, he would support whatever plan the Republican Congress passed to deal with the problem.[6]

White southerners thus began developing their own solutions to their region's race problem, which differed starkly, of course, from proposed Republican solutions. Mississippi Democrats took the lead in contemplating ways to disfranchise black voters without overtly continuing to violate the U. S. Constitution, options the reformers might at least tolerate if not embrace. South Carolina Democrats, meanwhile, began pushing the idea of helping fund a mass exodus of black emigrants out of the South to locations where they could enjoy the fruits of separation from whites.[7]

Besides resistance from white southerners, the reformers faced other obstacles as well. The same factors that had combined to put an abrupt end to Reconstruction still existed: Democrats from all sections of the country—not just the South—opposed any such attempt to resurrect the black voting rights issue, as did some influential Republican senators, including Matthew Quay and Donald Cameron of Pennsylvania, William M. Stewart and John P. Jones of Nevada, and Leland Stanford of California. Likewise, some leading Mugwump Republican journalists and pundits, such as E. L. Godkin and Carl Schurz, found the reformers' plan odious.[8] In addition, a very real possibility existed that in Benjamin Harrison the GOP would suffer the same type of weak presidential leadership that it had endured under Ulysses S. Grant, who lost the will to enforce the Fifteenth Amendment. A sizeable majority of the American public, as well as an influential contingent of political leaders and journalists from both parties, stood against the idea from the beginning, and that obstacle was compounded by the fear that Harrison might become more of a liability than a leader. The effect of this combination meant that in order to achieve their goal the reformers would have to fight on three fronts simultaneously—against (1) Democrats; (2) dissident Republicans; and (3) public opinion—and all quite possibly without strong leadership in the White House.

These fronts require a brief explanation. First, the Democratic opposition: the Democratic Party still claimed to be the torchbearer of Jeffersonianism in 1890; that is, the party that espoused state rights, local sovereignty, and the mythology that rural agrarianism was somehow more patriotically "American" than centralization, urbanization, and industrialization, all of which the GOP was more apt to espouse.[9] But it had, in fact, become little more in the minds of many observers than the party of white supremacy, low tariffs, unionization, alcoholism, and Roman Catholicism. Moreover, since the Civil War, it had been reduced in the estimation of bloody-shirt-waving Republicans to the party that once proudly committed three of the most heinous sins that can be committed in a democracy—slaveholding, secession, and treason. Therefore, it could not be entrusted with the reins of the national government. The party's chief function in national politics throughout Reconstruction and the Gilded Age seemed to be to prevent Republican legislation when possible and to make it difficult the rest of the time. As Massachusetts Senator George Frisbie Hoar put it, the Democratic Party had only managed to stay alive since the inception of the GOP by appealing to the basest elements of the American voting public. Democrats, said Hoar, sought to convince uneducated and ignorant voters that Republicans had the diabolical intention of increasing the power of the federal government at the expense of state and local sovereignty.

Hoar thus considered the Democrats the "against" party: against all of Lincoln's policies during the war, against all aspects of Reconstruction afterward, against giving blacks a fair chance in life, against the protective tariff, against national defense spending, against adding western states to the Union, and against the Homestead Act. What did the Democrats stand *for*? asked Hoar. A curious assortment of ideas, issues, and items, including unrestricted immigration, illiteracy, intemperance, and religious nonconformity. Moreover, they stood for allowing anyone to come to America and practice any kind of strange religion (he named Mormonism, specifically), practice any kind of deviant behavior—such as drunkenness, gambling, and reveling—and then keep them uneducated and ignorant so that Democratic Party bosses like those operating out of Tammany Hall could easily control them.[10]

Democrats denied all such charges. As former Democratic Speaker of the House John G. Carlisle of Kentucky explained, "It is easier to scold than to reason, and if epithets were as effective as arguments, the Democratic party would have been overthrown [by the Republicans] long ago."[11] He considered Hoar's charges ludicrous. The Democrats could hurl epithets equally well, however. They charged that the Republican Party represented nothing more than a reformulated version of the old Federalist Party of a hundred years prior with a new name. That is to say, both Federalists and Republicans represented elite groups of self-interested sectionalists who favored taxing the poor to their limit in order to continue building the central government in size and scope until it would ultimately evolve into a despotic leviathan under their own partisan control.[12] And with that control, the "imperialists," as many Democrats liked to call Republicans, would force their neo-Puritanical, neo-abolitionist views on the rest of the American people.[13]

Whether or not such charges were true, at least half of the American public agreed with the Democrats' assessment of the GOP. This same half of Americans also tended to accept the Democrats' pluralistic vision that the United States should welcome a variety of types of people and reject the self-righteous, exclusionary elitism of the GOP. After Reconstruction, a clear majority of the American public had repudiated the social engineering of the Republicans. They virtually demanded that the federal government, no matter which party controlled it, retreat toward a more conservative and less proactive type of governance. The Democratic Party definitely held the more conservative views among the two parties on virtually all aspects of government but most noticeably so on racial issues. They stuck much more firmly to the traditional American laissez-faire approach to government than did the Republicans. The GOP had always been more proactive legislatively, more prone to expand the scope of the federal government, and more willing to experiment socially and economically than the Democrats. By twenty-first-century standards this Republican activism does not look very progressive or liberal, but it looked radical enough to scare many Americans at the time. To many contemporary political pundits, the do-nothing attitude of Democrats came closer to fulfilling the intentions of the Founding Fathers than the "do something even if it's the wrong thing" attitude of the Republicans. Even so, these same pundits judged that the Democrats would lose the fight over racial reform, not because they were the minority party, but because the Republican Party had superior political leadership. The Republicans would prevail, they said, not merely because they outnumbered their opponents but because they would outwit them.[14]

The Democrats had grown accustomed to their role as the minority party through many years of practice. They had, after all, been the minority party almost continuously since Reconstruction, rarely controlling more than one house of Congress or the White House at any given time. The GOP pushed legislation while the Democrats resisted. This pattern often produced gridlock, but often it eventually led to compromise.[15] The election of the Republican majority in Congress and a Republican president in 1888 threatened to break this pattern of gridlock or this pattern of the opposing sides compromising and finding common ground where neither really wanted to stand. The Democrats perceived the Harrison administration and the Fifty-first Congress as intent upon crushing all minority opposition. They scrambled, accordingly, to find a foothold to brace themselves against the coming onslaught. They had only three possible weapons with which to stave off their political enemies: (1) public opinion, which they believed to be on their side and hoped would continue to favor their views on the southern race problem; (2) the filibuster, which could be used in either the Senate, the House, or both (so they thought) as a last-ditch effort if all attempts at compromise and reason failed; and (3) factionalism within the GOP, which could work to their advantage, particularly if they could convince a small number of Republicans to abdicate from the majority and join their side.

The second front on which the Republican reformers would have to fight loomed among dissidents within the ranks of the GOP. Democrats realistically hoped that the Republicans of the Fifty-first Congress would split. All political parties routinely experience factionalism, and the GOP had been notorious for its internecine disputes. Since gaining power in 1860 it had splintered into Radicals and Moderates, Stalwarts and Liberals (Half-Breeds), Regulars, Independents, and Mugwumps, and a variety of small fringe groups such as Prohibitionists and Greenbackers. Various factions fought for control after 1888 as well, and these factions were organic and ever-changing, with individual Republicans wafting in and out of alliance with them constantly as issues came, evolved, and departed. Some of the Republican migrants, such as Carl Schurz, at times seemed friendlier to the Democrats than to their own party because of hurt feelings and wounded pride engendered by years of infighting with the GOP leadership. And some even bolted and became Democrats, such as former Union general and leading Radical Republican during Reconstruction, Benjamin Butler of Massachusetts.[16]

The organic nature of these nebulous factions makes it difficult to prescribe clear definitions to them. But for simplicity's sake, two groups of Republicans may be identified. Those who favored helping black southerners in some way can be called the "reformers." Those who did not favor special legislation to help black southerners (because they did not wish to reopen the sectional wounds of Reconstruction, or because they sought political power for economic benefits and maintained power by graft for themselves, their constituents, or both) might best be called "money men." These rival and often conflicting factions made the challenge of racial/political reform difficult, because at least half of the GOP leadership was beholden to the machine and was thus just as concerned with economic issues as with solving the southern race problem.

Abraham Lincoln once remarked that the Republican Party stood for both humanitarianism and economic growth, but when the two conflicted with one another, Republican leaders would always choose the welfare of the poor and downtrodden over financial gain for themselves and the nation's business interests. But would the party of Lincoln remain true to Honest Abe's creed in 1890? Whether the party of Lincoln or even Lincoln himself had ever been true to the creed is in fact questionable. It seems more reasonable to conclude that four types of Republicans had always existed from the founding of the party in the 1850s up to the 1890s: (a) those mainly interested in humanitarian concerns; (b) those primarily interested in the almighty dollar; (c) those who felt torn between these competing forces; and (d) those who wanted merely to use blacks as pawns in their high stakes political game.[17] The GOP in 1890 contained a sizeable contingent of all four, and therein lay the seeds of a potential party schism that threatened to prevent passage of legislation for solving the southern race problem.

Although this division of the GOP into factions could be seen at all levels of government, nowhere did it appear more pronounced than in the U. S. Senate. Some Republican senators were genuine in their humanitarian concern for black southerners, and they could accurately be considered political philanthropists who believed it their duty to practice noblesse oblige toward the needy masses. They sincerely wanted to help the dispossessed black denizens of the South. In this group were George Frisbie Hoar of Massachusetts and Henry Blair of New Hampshire. Several others were not so easy to categorize, such as John Sherman of Ohio, William M. Evarts of New York, Preston B. Plumb of Kansas, Justin Morrill of Vermont, Leland Stanford of California, and Henry L. Dawes of Massachusetts, all of whom expressed interest in helping black southerners but rarely took noticeable action toward that end. Those who seemed mainly intent upon using blacks for partisan political gain included John J. Ingalls of Kansas, William E. Chandler of New Hampshire, and Joseph N. Dolph of Oregon. Many of those with longtime service in political office changed over time or vacillated between the groups, depending upon the specific issue in question. William E. Stewart of Nevada and Henry M. Teller of Colorado, for instance, abandoned their humanitarianism of the Civil War–Reconstruction period in favor of economic concerns in the 1890s.[18]

The Republican money men in the Senate included Matthew Quay and Donald Cameron of Pennsylvania, Nelson Aldrich of Rhode Island, William Boyd Allison of Iowa, and Philetus Sawyer of Wisconsin. Because of senators like these and their vacillating cohorts, throughout the Gilded Age and especially in the late 1880s, public opinion came to view the Senate as an exclusive society comprised mainly of millionaires. Although that belief exaggerated the wealth of the average senator, it contained more than a grain of truth. Indeed, many senators had vested interests in railroads and other corporations, having cashed in on the incredible wave of growth and expansion that occurred during the Gilded Age. Several gained personal fortunes in excess of $1 million in the process.[19] Iowa's senior senator William Boyd Allison, for instance, who had viewed the Civil War, in his biographer's words, "merely as a great opportunity for making some money," built a personal fortune in western railroads during and after the war. He had also entangled himself in the infamous Credit Mobilier scandal of the Ulysses S. Grant administration but managed to escape "more lightly than he deserved," for, despite what the rest of the nation thought of him, the Iowa legislature repeatedly sent him back to Washington to represent the Hawkeye State.[20]

Some of these money men in the Senate loved to show off their wealth, with the intention of making a statement about money equaling power and aristocracy. The public marveled at the lavish lifestyles and the gaudy displays of opulence of such senators. Wisconsin's senior senator Philetus Sawyer, for example, moved into a new custom-built Washington, D.C., mansion in 1890, where he regularly entertained guests, including constituents and political supporters and sometimes capitol city social elites and international diplomats and dignitaries. Similarly, Nelson Aldrich of Rhode Island held such wealth and power that some called his tiny state his personal "fiefdom,"[21] and Matthew Quay of Pennsylvania was said to be (metaphorically) the richest man in the world because he "owned a president, a Speaker of the House, and his own state"—the "Quaystone" state.[22] Railroad tycoon Leland Stanford really *was* one of the richest men in the world— a genuine self-made millionaire who in 1890 used part of his fortune to put the finishing touches on the university in Palo Alto, California, which bears his name.

Although the Senate affords a better view of the dichotomy of reformers and money men in the GOP than does the House, the same bifurcation of interests existed there. The preoccupation of half of the Republican leadership in both chambers of Congress with money and financial issues is clear, and the impact of this priority upon the overall party agenda cannot be overstated. So adept would this Fifty-first Congress become at passing economic legislation, in fact, that it would soon earn the opprobrious sobriquet of "the Billion Dollar Congress" from Democrats and independent pundits. But at the convening of this Congress in December 1889, no one yet knew just how much of a spending spree lay in store. As Congress prepared to do its business going into the new year of 1890, some of the most pressing items on the "Billion Dollar" economic agenda were the tariff, which had been a political football that both parties kicked back and forth throughout the 1880s and which most Republicans now wanted raised; the coinage of silver, which had also recurred as a bone of contention year after year and which now threatened to divide the party into factions; trusts, which had only begun to command the attention of the nation but which most Americans agreed needed regulating; and pensions for Union veterans of the Civil War, which, like the southern race problem, could now be addressed to the satisfaction of Republicans for the first time since Reconstruction because of their simultaneous control of the Fifty-first Congress and the White House.[23]

From the day the Republican majority won election in 1888, the reformers and the money men began fighting for control of the overall legislative agenda for the Fifty-first Congress. The two most important items on the Republican agenda—raising the tariff and enforcing the voting rights of southern blacks—alienated Democrats, but the black suffrage issue also caused internal friction between the reformers and the money men. These money Republicans did not oppose the idea of passing a new federal election law—they simply did not want to do it at the expense of their economic agenda. Most had few black constituents, so the suffrage issue never hit close to home. Economic issues did. The GOP leadership agreed that the tariff issue should thus be disposed of first.[24] Although the reformers wanted the Federal Elections Bill to be the party's flagship issue, the money men prevailed. The GOP leadership chose tariff reform over other economic issues, ostensibly because it affected the most voters directly. Most Republicans, no matter which clique they belonged to, believed that raising the tariff would increase the wages and improve the living standards of the nation's industrial workers, and by 1890, for the first time in American history, industrial workers outnumbered farmers.[25] The tariff was seen, therefore, as the least problematic of a number of unusually divisive issues.

The pension issue, however, had more staunch supporters than any other single economic issue, because the Grand Army of the Republic (GAR) had been lobbying for pension increases for a decade. The GAR originated in 1868 as a fraternal brotherhood of Union Civil War veterans. By 1890 it boasted 400,000 members, but because voting-age sons of the veterans also supported the cause célèbre of their fathers, the GAR actually controlled about one million votes. No Republican politician, therefore, dared cross the GAR, which gave the veterans' club power out of proportion to its numbers. Consequently, with the Republicans controlling both houses of Congress and the White House, the pension issue seemed sure to be near the front of the docket and sure to garner a great deal of attention.[26]

The reasons for the decision to raise the tariff before proceeding with the Federal Elections Bill made perfect sense to the GOP leadership at the time, but most African Americans bewailed the decision, the reformers soon came to regret it, and many historians have criticized it ever since. The decision was based upon the idea that there would be plenty of time to get the entire Republican agenda passed, so the order they took the issues in did not really matter. But since the agendas of individual Republican politicians generally reflected the will of their constituencies, the GOP leadership followed the dictates of public opinion as they perceived it, which leads to the third front upon which the reformers would have to fight their battle—public opinion. What the money men realized—and what the reformers could not yet see well or refused to acknowledge—was that between the end of Reconstruction and 1890 a change had occurred in the nation's collective thought processes about the race problem. Many white northern humanitarian leaders had withdrawn not only their vocal support for the idea of forcing racial equality on the South but even their tacit support. They had begun in earnest to seek some other solution to the race problem. They never second-guessed the necessity of fighting the Civil War to preserve the Union or to emancipate the slaves, but they had begun to wonder whether bestowing equal civil and political rights upon the freedmen had been a wise change and a prudent move. They had given the Republican leadership the benefit of the doubt on the issue initially, but now, with the knowledge of how troublesome Reconstruction ultimately became weighing heavily in their minds, the idea of Republican reformers reenforcing black suffrage on the white South certainly did not excite them.[27]

A prime example of this transformation can be seen in the First Mohonk Conference on the Negro Question, which met in June 1890 at Lake Mohonk in Ulster County, New York. Former Republican president Rutherford B. Hayes chaired the conference. Many of the leading educators, ministers, journalists, and political figures in the nation spoke and exchanged ideas, including the former Union general O. O. Howard; the influential novelist and political pundit Albion Tourgee; the Reverends Dr. Lyman Abbott and Dr. James Buckley of New York City; the president of Swarthmore College in Pennsylvania, Edward H. McGill; the former president of Cornell University in New York, Andrew White; the president of Rutgers College in New Jersey, Dr. Merrill E. Gates; the corresponding secretary of the American Missionary Association, the Reverend Dr. A. F. Beard; the editor of the *Independent* newspaper of New York, Dr. William Hayes Ward; and the U. S. commissioner of education, W. T. Harris. With the exception of Albion Tourgee, none of these leaders advocated civil rights or political or social equality as the answer to the "Negro Question." They could not even agree on the nature of the question, much less its answer. An exchange between Lyman Abbott and James Buckley reveals the extent of the disagreement. Abbott asked, "How much longer must we go on talking about the Negro problem? There is no Negro problem,—only the problem of humanity." Buckley responded, "Dr. Abbott proposes to ignore the Negro problem, and to make it one of the common problems of humanity. If there be no such thing as a Negro problem . . . we should not be here. But there *is* a Negro problem." Perhaps the most striking remark of the conference came from Abbott, who said, "So far as I can see, those that discuss the Southern problem may be divided into two classes,—those who know the facts and therefore have no theories, and those who have theories because they do not know the facts." Several speakers sought to refute that statement, but with little success.[28]

The First Mohonk Conference on the Negro Question ended with no answer, but it did end with some recommendations that a majority of the participants approved. The most notable was that the nation's emphasis should shift away from political solutions and toward educational solutions and, particularly, vocational education for blacks. As Rutherford B. Hayes put it, "the educational, the benevolent, and the religious side of the [Negro] question" is "hardly less grave and influential" than the political side.[29] The only other meaningful fruit to come from the conference was a Second Mohonk Conference on the Negro Question a year later, which showed a continuation of the philosophy adopted earlier of stressing vocational education as the best solution to the southern race problem. Both conferences offer important glimpses of northern humanitarian sentiment beyond the halls of Congress and outside the realm of politics at this critical, transitional period in American history. What they reveal is that, since Reconstruction, northern concern for the welfare of black southerners had increasingly begun to take the form of philanthropy, not political activism. The philanthropy of this era came to be embodied in a philosophy known as the Social Gospel—a combination of traditional Christian mission work and a secular brand of enlightened humanitarianism. It could be seen manifest in projects such as the establishment of Tuskegee Institute in Alabama in 1881, which appeared to represent the model school for black southerners and, to many observers, the wave of the future in helping uplift the African American race. The Social Gospel, along with the American laissez-faire political tradition, which frowned upon federal activism, caused the great crusade of the former abolitionists-turned-postwar-humanitarians to implode after Reconstruction. By 1890, the northern public had become almost completely silent, if not altogether unconcerned, about the federal government helping black southerners. Hence, if the reformers in Congress intended to address the South's race problem without incurring the wrath of their constituents, they would have to do so upon the basis of preserving and defending the Constitution rather than upon the basis of providing federal humanitarian assistance to blacks, and they would have to make a strong case for their action.[30] Protecting the Constitution—Reconstruction Amendments and all—would therefore be their rationale. This peculiar Republican sense of patriotic duty to uphold the new and improved Constitution thus served as the justification for bringing the southern race problem to the fore in 1890, more so than humanitarian concern for the welfare of blacks. With exceptions made for the few true-blue reformers, such as George Frisbie Hoar and Albion Tourgee, most Republican leaders could accept this compromise. Most were not willing to sacrifice their personal political ambition for the principle of supporting an unpopular measure. And many were not genuinely concerned about the welfare of African Americans nearly so much as about the partisan political advantage that could be gained from the black vote of the South, despite claims to the contrary that they sometimes made.[31]

This charge can be proven based upon the total of the evidence. It is clear, for instance, that this young administration and this new Congress faced other related racial issues which they had no intention of handling with any humanitarian concern. Trouble in the West with disgruntled and rebellious Native Americans represented a race problem just as old and irksome as the southern black-white problem, and the question of continuing the restriction or "exclusion" of Chinese immigration had likewise lingered since 1882 without an answer pleasing to everyone. But since both issues affected a comparatively small number of people—and it is important to add that none of the affected people were either citizens or potential voters—these race problems garnered little attention from Republican reformers. Since they could not hope to gain any political advantage for their party from worrying about such minority groups, they simply chose not to concern themselves with them. At the same time, something akin to a race problem had begun to develop in the Northeast as well, where an increase in immigration was rapidly changing the ethnic makeup of America's largest cities. Unlike the Native Americans and the Chinese, the millions of European immigrants landing on the shores of the great East coast cities represented potential voters in the eyes of politicians, and both major parties coveted their allegiance and raced to sign them up to vote. Frequent problems resulted from the new immigrants' use of the ballot, however, because, due to language and education barriers, they could generally be manipulated by unscrupulous politicos more easily than could old-stock Americans. Yet inasmuch as new immigrants tended to be white-skinned Europeans who lived in northern cities, Republican reformers did not expend their energy calling for federal intervention to fix voting irregularities associated with them like they did in regard to similar voting problems in the South. When they mentioned reform at all regarding their immigrant vote, it was in terms of correcting the problem at the state and local levels, not through an act of Congress as they were now calling for to help black southerners.[32]

Even if the reformers managed to succeed in the aforementioned fronts, they still had to contend with the possibility that they would have

Every Dog (No Distinction of Color) Has His Day. Red Gentleman to Yellow Gentleman. "Pale face 'fraid you crowd him out, as he did me." (Harper's Weekly, 1879.) The astute political cartoonist Thomas Nast could see the United States's multicultural dilemma as early as 1879. Still tossing in the wake of Reconstruction, however, most white Americans were unwilling to face the problem at that time.

weak leadership in the White House. Benjamin Harrison had won the presidential sweepstakes only in the electoral college, not in the popular vote. His credibility was thus in question from the beginning of his term. In order to lead the nation effectively, he would have to win the confidence of a resentful majority of American voters, who certainly had not given him or the GOP a mandate for making changes as radical as the one they envisioned regarding black voting rights. Political pundits questioned Harrison's leadership skills and doubted that he would be prepared for the challenges that his administration would face. They had good reason for skepticism. Prior to his election as president, Harrison had enjoyed something less than a sterling career in national politics. He lacked experience, having served only one term as a U. S. senator and otherwise having held only a few minor positions in Indiana state politics. This record inspired little confidence among the American people, even among those who voted for the Hoosier statesman.[33] In the campaign of 1888, Democrats had openly expressed delight with the GOP's choice of Harrison as its standard-bearer. They thought incumbent president Grover Cleveland could easily defeat this second-rate, unexciting Republican candidate. Democratic Senators James Berry of Arkansas and Alfred Colquitt of Georgia agreed that they could not be more pleased with the GOP's choice of Harrison as the Republican presidential nominee if they had picked him themselves. Alabama Senator James L. Pugh commented that Harrison must be undoubtedly the "weakest man in the Republican party. . . . He has more ways to make people dislike him than any man I ever met in Congress." South Carolina Senator Matthew Butler added, "If we can't beat Harrison, we can't beat anybody."[34]

Harrison had received the nomination for four reasons, none of which seemed very flattering to him. One, he hailed from the most important of all the "doubtful" or "swing" states, a place that fellow Indianan and Democratic Senator Daniel Voorhees called "the Belgium of [American] politics, the debatable land between great contending parties and opinions."[35] Harrison, the GOP assumed, could deliver this pivotal state into the Republican fold, which is ironic considering the fact that he could not win reelection to the U. S. Senate there in 1887. Two, the party's real thoroughbred, James G. Blaine, the "plumed knight" of Maine, who had lost the presidential contest in 1884—one of the closest in American history—by barely one thousand votes, chose not to run, citing lack of unanimous approval for his nomination within the party.[36] Three, the two rival factions of the party—the reformers and the money men—needed a candidate they could both agree upon. Harrison was a candidate that neither felt particularly excited about, yet both could tolerate for the sake of compromise. And four, he was the grandson of a president.[37]

The GOP's strategy to unseat the Democrat Cleveland with the uninspiring Harrison looks brilliant in retrospect. Since 1889 marked the one-hundredth anniversary of the U.S. Constitution and federal system of government, which gave us the presidency and the modern Congress, the Republican strategy relied on reminding voters that the next commander in chief would be the "centennial president." In the best tradition of bloody-shirt Republicanism, the GOP made sure voters understood that Harrison was a Union veteran while Cleveland was not. Only Harrison, therefore, was qualified to be the "new George Washington," the first president in the second century of presidents, and only Harrison had the right to represent the great United States at its centennial celebration. This plan of using the centennial, with all its patriotic sentimentalism, worked well in conjunction with their concomitant strategy of harping upon Harrison's impressive family tree. His grandfather, William Henry Harrison, had won the presidency in 1840 and had briefly served in 1841, before succumbing to pneumonia. His great grandfather, the first "Benjamin" Harrison, had signed the Declaration of Independence. The current Benjamin formerly held the rank of brigadier general in the Union army during the Civil War. His pedigree was clearly superior to his experience in high office, and the GOP hoped that it would be enough to lead the party to victory against the semi-popular incumbent president Grover Cleveland.[38]

Harrison stunned his detractors and pleasantly surprised his lukewarm supporters by winning the election and becoming the nation's centennial president. Once elected, however, questions about his credibility immediately surfaced. Besides not winning the popular vote, which was a major issue in itself, he was also unable to overcome the stigma that he was not the real standard bearer of the GOP, much less the leader of the whole U. S. government. On the issue of losing the popular vote, Democratic leaders and voters alike resolved to hold the Harrison administration in contempt from day one, not merely because of his weak electoral college victory, but because that victory resulted from some questionable, if not utterly fraudulent, voting irregularities in at least two states—Indiana and New York. The Hoosier and Empire states—the home states of the two candidates—were the only two that the GOP carried in 1888 that it did not carry in 1884, but they made all the difference in the outcome of both elections. The Democrats thus set out to derail the new administration from the start, to malign Harrison's leadership or lack thereof at every opportunity, and to poke fun at him personally whenever possible.[39] One southern Democrat achieved the latter two aims in one jibe, proclaiming before Congress: "Lincoln, I believe, was a great man; but has a party that started with [such] a great man and run to the present Executive not gone to seed? What better evidence of degeneracy would you have?"[40]

On the second issue, two leaders in the Republican Party overshadowed the president in the popular perception. One was Thomas B. Reed, who, as the Speaker of the House in the Fifty-first Congress, proved a stronger presence in the national government than Harrison. Besides Reed, Harrison's chief rival in the Republican hierarchy, the ever-controversial James G. Blaine, held enough sway over the party that he could essentially name himself to whatever position he chose in the Harrison administration, a fact that was not lost on the American public. He chose the office of secretary of state. Although his position placed him in charge of foreign policy and largely kept him out of the limelight during Harrison's term (because no serious foreign policy issues arose from 1888 to 1892), some Americans never ceased to consider him a more dominating presence in the Harrison administration than the president himself.[41] As one newspaper put it, compared to Blaine, President Harrison looked like a "Lilliputian." Concerning the jockeying for power in the GOP, the paper added that "it is dollars to doughnuts that when the smoke of battle clears away he [Blaine] will make a hole in the earth with his forefinger, drop . . . 'Harrison the small,' into it, and leave the country the pleasant task of shoveling the earth."[42]

While Harrison actually stood considerably taller than a mythical Lilliputian, he was still quite diminutive in stature, although not small in girth. Besides his size, or lack thereof, he also seemed to wear a permanent squint on his face, leading Theodore Roosevelt to comment once that he always looked like "a pig blinking in a cold wind."[43] Yet, this odd-looking little man now had the job of trying to unite the Republican Party after the election, to win the confidence of spiteful Democrats, and to guide the ship of state through the turbulent political waters that lay ahead. Could he do it? No one knew, but if so, his success would start with the wooing of the American public through his outstanding oratorical ability. Yes, fortunately for Harrison, he did have that one great redeeming quality. He was by all accounts an exceptional public speaker. Many contemporaries—Republican and Democrat alike—considered him to be among the best orators they had ever heard. Early historians likewise thought him among the best ever elected president. But even so, he quickly proved ineffective as the leader of his party, much less the commander in chief of the nation, because his executive actions rarely matched his eloquent rhetoric.[44] As one contemporary observed, Harrison "had a trick of turning a Republican into a Democrat that was almost sleight-of-hand. . . . If people could have just heard those splendid speeches, just heard Harrison, and then gone straight home and remembered how fine it was and never, never tried to shake the speaker's hand that was so like a wilted petunia—well, history might have been different."[45]

But try they did, not only to shake his hand, but to capture his gaze, to hold his attention, and to win his affection. Supporters, spoils seekers, and congressmen in need of political favors immediately inundated the new executive. The incredible volume and variety of citizens expecting presidential action overwhelmed him. On one occasion, Republican Senator John J. Ingalls of Kansas visited Harrison at the White House to seek a presidential appointment for a friend to a low-level post in the Sunflower State. Harrison rejected Ingalls's candidate, however, and told him he would appoint a friend of his own from Indiana to the post. Ingalls responded by declaring, "Mr. President, if you have any friends in Indiana or anywhere else for God's sake nominate them."[46]

African Americans found themselves among the most expectant and disappointed of Harrison's supporters.[47] When a delegation of bishops from the African Methodist Episcopal Church came pleading the case for civil rights legislation, which Harrison had already promised to support in every campaign speech as well as in his inaugural address, they left without satisfaction. Harrison assured them only that something would be done, but otherwise told them nothing to inspire faith and confidence in his administration. He realized that he could not please everyone, and he did not want to build hopes any more than he had already done. Onlookers immediately interpreted his vagaries and silences as aloofness and apathy.[48]

Harrison's personal racial views could sometimes seem just as erratic and puzzling as his presidential leadership, or lack of it, on racial issues. While he rejected the idea of inherent black inferiority to whites—an idea that had steadily grown in popularity throughout the 1880s—he did not award any more civil service jobs to blacks than had any other post-Reconstruction president. In fact, he appointed only ten blacks to office. African Americans nationwide voiced their disappointment, but northern blacks complained the loudest, because, whether intentional or not, Harrison appointed southerners almost exclusively when he appointed any blacks at all. The northern Republican press charged him with a much more serious discrepancy, however. The *Boston Herald,* the *Buffalo Express,* and the *Pittsburgh Dispatch* all reported that, shortly after moving into the White House, Harrison had fired all of the blacks on staff and replaced them with white workers. There is no confirmation that such a thing ever happened, but the fact that the northern Republican press reported it makes it at the very least plausible. The modern authority on the racial views of the presidents, George Sinkler, does not discount the possibility that such an incident occurred.[49] If it did occur, Harrison's action would by no means have been unique. Black-owned newspapers across the country constantly kept tabs on Republican leaders, and they routinely reported similar cases where professing humanitarians practiced racial discrimination.[50]

Since Reconstruction, African Americans had become increasingly aware of the duplicity of their supposed Republican friends. They had begun to grow wary and weary of political rhetoric that had promised them much and had given them little since the mid 1870s. Many had become disillusioned with their dismal situation. It increasingly appeared that the problem was not so much the Republicans' inability to do something about black suffrage as it was their unwillingness to act. For instance, the GOP had adopted the high protective tariff as its issue of choice during the first Cleveland administration, scarcely mentioning civil rights for blacks. Where were the party's priorities? asked African Americans. It should not be surprising that, by 1890, several thousand black voters had already abandoned the party that emancipated their race, and many others threatened to do so. Some of the defectors joined the Democratic Party, others became independents who hoped to force both parties to compete for their allegiance, and the rest stopped voting altogether out of disgust and despair. T. Thomas Fortune, the mulatto editor of the *New York Age,* for instance, expressed what many other blacks must have been thinking when he said, "I have served the Republican party, the Prohibition party, and the Democratic party, and . . . I declare that none of them cares a fig for the Afro-American further than it can use him. . . . We [blacks] have served parties long enough without benefit to the race. It is now time for parties to serve us some, if they desire our support."[51]

African Methodist Episcopal Bishop Henry McNeal Turner of Atlanta agreed, saying, "I have not deserted the Republican party, the Republican party has deserted me and seven millions of my race."[52] A few radicals in the black press even contemplated the chimerical idea of forming their own party. The majority within the black community, however, remained loyal to the party of Lincoln. These loyalists tended to ostracize those who bailed out of the sinking Republican ship, and some even committed acts of violence against the defectors. Although most blacks remained loyal to the Republican Party, the growing lack of accord about how to deal with the unfavorable circumstances only exacerbated their problems.[53]

Southern Democrats used the friction between the GOP and African Americans to justify their racist beliefs and actions. As Senator James K. Jones of Arkansas put it, "Oppressed and outraged people seek their friends; and the negro knows that, while the [white northern] Republican neighbor is his friend for 'campaign purposes,' for sympathy and help he must look to and rely upon the [white] people of the South."[54] Such charges would become one of the Democratic battle cries in the upcoming fight to solve the southern race problem.

President Harrison and the Republican leaders of the Fifty-first Congress faced serious challenges as they assumed control in 1889. Yet they made their decision to tackle the southern race problem before they took office, and they would stick to it, come what may. The only question was how to accomplish their goal of reforming the South. To the average Republican congressman or senator, the plan of implementing a massive new program of federal supervision of elections looked like a good one. At least, it seemed to be the best of the three possible solutions to the race problem that had been thought of so far and that would consequently come up for consideration. The other two—to uplift blacks through a federally funded education program, or to relocate blacks from the South to other parts of the nation or world through a federally funded colonization program— inspired less passion than ballot reform. The former came to life in the Blair Education Bill, the pet project of New Hampshire Senator Henry Blair, which had appeared before Congress twice already by 1890 without passing but was scheduled for another hearing in the Fifty-first Congress. The latter, an idea that many politicians and social leaders had advocated since the first African slaves arrived in the Americas, now seemed to be a good idea to almost every southern congressman, including its chief proponents Senators Matthew Butler of South Carolina and John Tyler Morgan of Alabama. It, too, would come to life, if only briefly, in the form of the Butler Emigration Bill. It would, in fact, be the first of the potential solutions to the race problem that Congress would debate.

Chapter 1

To Empty a Running Stream

The U. S. Senate Considers the Butler Emigration Bill

The South would be a great deal better off if it could get rid of a large part of its negro population.

—*Savannah Morning News*

The Negroes will never migrate. They are a race of strong local attachments. They are parasitic in all their tendencies. . . . I have not the slightest confidence in the idea of deportation.

—*Senator George Vest of Missouri*

Fully aware of Republican intentions to push a federal elections bill through Congress, Democrats sought to forestall that plan and, if possible, eliminate the need for it by introducing their own bill to deal with the southern race problem. Realizing that the Republicans would need a few days to organize and prioritize their legislative agenda, the Democrats hoped to take initial control of the business of the Senate and spark a debate that might catch fire in the American public as well as in Congress. Their plan was to introduce a bill that would make it possible for those black southerners who wanted to leave the South to do so at taxpayers' expense. The idea was neither new nor unique. The belief that Congress should appropriate funds for such a mass exodus of African Americans had a long history. Various schemes for removing blacks from the South had been attempted from time to time, as early as the colonial era and as late as 1879, with paltry results in each case.[1] Such attempts had failed each time because of the exorbitant expense involved and a general lack of interest among blacks in emigrating.[2] Although these early measures had most often been called "colonization" plans, the Democrats of 1890 called theirs an "emigration" bill because they wanted to stress the fact that they would not be forcing the removal of blacks from the South but would merely be giving them the option and the ways and means to leave voluntarily.

Since all previous attempts at colonization had failed, why did many Democrats believe that their new plan would be any different? The answer is complex, but it shows that the plan was not as foolish as it might appear on the surface. First, there had always been a large contingent of black southerners who wanted the option of leaving the South and were thus intrigued by such proposals. As black educator William H. Crogman explained it, "For the first ten or twelve years after the [Civil] war. . . . Every little politician, every crank, constituted himself a Moses to lead the Negro somewhere; and various were their cries. One cried, 'On to Arkansas!' and another 'On to Texas!' and another 'On to Africa!' and each had a following more or less."[3] Thus, many blacks expressed interest in leaving their current homes throughout the 1880s, if only someone would lead them and if somehow their move could be funded. By 1890, nothing had changed to diminish this interest, but several important developments had occurred to increase it. For one thing, the same economic hard times that caused the white agrarian revolt in the late 1880s had hit the black farmer as well, causing many, for the first time, to consider moving to greener pastures, whether Africa or somewhere else. For another thing, the gains blacks had made during Reconstruction had been almost totally lost in the 1880s because of various discriminatory practices in the South. Among these practices were: violence against blacks, which inexplicably escalated in 1889, particularly in the form of lynchings; disfranchisement, which had already robbed them of most of their political power in the South by 1890, even before Mississippi's new constitution started a wave of state usurpations of the Fifteenth Amendment; and forced segregation, which had become commonplace by this time. For a third thing, some blacks complained of taxation without representation, the old tried and true protest mantra of the American Revolution generation. They argued that without enforcement of the Fifteenth Amendment they could not be represented in proportion to their population in the federal and state governments, yet their tax dollars helped pay the governments' bills. Moreover, the state governments did not distribute government services, such as public education, equally among the races. Why should they remain in a nation which did not give them a fair return on their tax dollars? Finally, a sudden wave of propaganda promoting the idea of emigration swept over the United States in early 1890, convincing many blacks and whites alike that the best solution to the race problem lay in total physical separation of the races.[4]

This wave of propaganda, more than any other factor, caused Congress to take up the issue of federal aid to emigration in early 1890. The story of how it happened begins in Liberia. This small American-made nation on the malaria-infested coast of western Africa had suffered from poverty and government instability since its founding in 1817. The American Colonization Society (ACS) and various other colonization organizations had settled only a few thousand black Americans in Liberia in all those years. No one representing the ACS ever advertised Liberia as an inviting paradise. Most emigrants moving there could expect to trade one type of hard life in the United States for a different type of hard life in Liberia, which included fighting diseases without adequate medicines and medical facilities; making friendships, alliances, and trade partnerships with natives who did not always welcome new neighbors, suffering through poverty that would likely be even more abject than the worst sharecropping arrangement in the American South; and living under an unstable and sometimes oppressive government. Few black Americans wanted to make this trade, and, from a purely financial perspective, even fewer could afford to. The year 1889, however, brought a ray of hope to Liberia for the first time in many years, when European companies began exploiting the nation's lucrative, indigenous rubber plant. It seemed to Liberians and the ACS that the upstart rubber industry would be the panacea bringing economic development and the ways of civilization to the vast jungle hinterland. With signs of life in the Liberian economy, therefore, the ACS could begin anew its previously flagging efforts at recruiting potential emigrants.[5]

Leading this recruiting drive was Edward Blyden, a West Indies–born Liberian who spent much of his time in London. He toured the United States in late 1889 and early 1890, speaking and making acquaintances with Americans of wealth and means. His visit would not have caused nearly as much interest as it actually did without a connection that he established by chance with some influential white South Carolinians who favored emigration as the solution to the South's race problem. Blyden's visit to the United States just happened to coincide with the publication of a book called *An Appeal to Pharoah* [*sic*], written by an anonymous author, later revealed to be Carlyle McKinley, assistant editor of the *Charleston News and Courier.* Although McKinley and Blyden had apparently never met or corresponded before, they spoke essentially the same message—that the solution to America's race problem lay in black emigration. In December 1889, James C. Hemphill, McKinley's boss and chief editor of the *Charleston News and Courier,* invited Blyden to South Carolina for an interview. Blyden accepted, the interview went to press, and papers all over the country soon began broadcasting his startling views on emigration to a fascinated public. As a Liberian, Blyden's words seemed to validate the idea of emigration expressed in *An Appeal to Pharoah* [*sic*], which probably would not have generated much enthusiasm otherwise.[6]

As it turned out, its influence reached even to Africa itself, where British-American adventurer Henry M. Stanley, who had long been employed in mapping the Congo region, building roads and describing the natives of inner Africa for King Leopold of Belgium, read it with great approval. Stanley, who had caused quite a stir with the publication of his own books about the previously isolated inner reaches of Africa,[7] wrote the publishers of the book in early 1890 to thank them for its message. He favored emigration as the solution to America's race problem. He believed that if *An Appeal to Pharoah* [*sic*] could be widely distributed throughout the United States, it would spark a mass emigration movement within five years. But he predicted that it would never happen because "American capitalists . . . are more engaged in decorating their wives with diamonds" than with contemplating difficult racial issues.[8]

A few American capitalists, however, did prefer emigration for blacks to diamonds for their wives. Among them were some southern members of the U. S. Senate. Matthew Butler, the senior senator of South Carolina, took the lead in drawing up the emigration proposal, which called for a modest appropriation of $5 million per year to begin the enterprise. Butler, whose friends and family called him by his middle name, "Calbraith," had been a Confederate general who lost a leg in the Civil War. He became a Redeemer thereafter, and the South Carolina legislature sent him to the U.S. Senate in 1876. He was an archetypal Palmetto State hotspur who seemed to carry a perpetual chip on his shoulder when speaking about either the North, the Republicans, the war and Reconstruction, or the race problem. In the Senate, he generally avoided making long, impassioned speeches, but he would never allow his state, his section, his party, or his race to be disparaged without a fiery retort. Unlike some of his former Confederate colleagues, he never rose to the highest level of leadership among southern Democrats in the Senate.[9] Although he wrote the bill and introduced it to the Senate, he did not begin the discussion of it, nor did he ever advocate it as seriously and forcefully as another proponent of emigration did. Those distinctions belong instead to John Tyler Morgan of Alabama.

Morgan, a relative of former U. S. President John Tyler of Virginia, had represented the Camellia State in the Senate since 1876, when, during the "redemption" of Alabama, he won a close and contested race. Republican colleague and senior Alabama Senator George F. Spencer, who believed Morgan's election to have been fraudulent, accepted his seating only begrudgingly. In his younger days, Morgan had served as chief lieutenant of one of the most ardent fire-eaters of the Civil War generation, William L. Yancey. He had also risen to the rank of general in the Confederate army. To say that he loved the South—particularly the Old South—and that he believed in the old prewar state rights view would be understatements. While most of his colleagues focused on current Gilded Age concerns or looked ahead toward Progressive Era issues, Morgan favored retrenchment, regression, and restoration of the prewar status quo. Indeed, he must be counted among the most conservative men on Capitol Hill in 1890, and he could be arguably called the most outspoken racist ideologue of his generation. He was widely acclaimed to possess, as his biographer put it, "a wider range of information" on public issues than any other man of his generation. He was certainly among the most talkative men in national politics and was reputed to be the foremost "long-distance talker" or "jawsmith" in the U.S. Senate. One Alabama newspaper remarked of Morgan that "his fervid eloquence" could be compared to a "mountain torrent . . . dashing against the opposition," and that when he believed in something passionately, his beliefs were like "lightning . . . coursing through his veins."[10]

On January 7, 1890, Morgan called up the Butler bill for consideration. Sensing that Republicans would likely consider the bill a divisive, partisan, and sectional measure, Morgan tried from the start to prove otherwise. The bill did not propagate a radical new idea, he said, but an idea that had been around in various forms for more than a century. Summarizing his argument, many of the most respected leaders in American government throughout the nation's history had believed that the solution to the race problem lay in deporting or scattering the black population. Even some of the staunchest and most revered Republicans and Whigs of earlier generations favored this approach, including Abraham Lincoln, Henry Clay, and Daniel Webster. The current Secretary of the Treasury in the Harrison administration, William Windom of Minnesota, whose credentials as a partisan Republican and a genuine humanitarian no one questioned, also advocated emigration. Why should the idea not be taken seriously then? If the main source of the race problem came from the concentration of blacks in one region, what could possibly be wrong with diffusing the population? If the federal government simply shuffled blacks around in the United States, it would spread their voting strength thin enough that there would be no danger of them controlling any state government. The specter of black control of state and local governments was, after all, what white southerners feared so much, causing them to disfranchise blacks and otherwise to try to keep them down socially and economically. Eliminating that threat by scattering blacks in America would be an improvement over existing conditions, but removing them from the United States altogether would be even better.[11]

Morgan believed that the technological advancements of the industrial revolution in Gilded Age America had made the logistics of mass emigration possible for the first time. He claimed that more blacks could now be shipped abroad in one year than had been shipped in the first twenty years of the American Colonization Society's existence. Even though the population of blacks had reached almost eight million by 1890, through a long-range, federally funded program, every one could conceivably be helped to return to his or her ancestral homeland. Morgan then changed the thrust of his argument, asking, if there never had been any Africans in America and suddenly eight million of them wanted to immigrate to America, would the federal government allow it? "No! Never!" he exclaimed. Why, then, should they be allowed to stay now?[12]

Morgan next invoked the old pre–Civil War southern argument of white paternalism toward blacks, claiming that he and his fellow supporters of the Butler bill all cared deeply for the welfare of their black friends and neighbors, even to the point of considering many of them as family members. And while it would be difficult to break their long-term bonds of affection, these Americans of African ancestry would ultimately be better off in the land of their forefathers than in the United States. They were now, for the first time, psychologically and intellectually prepared for the move en masse because they had gained education, political experience, Christianity, and social civility from having enjoyed a generation of freedom in the United States. If anyone seriously thought that by moving to Africa, black Americans would lose these attributes of civilization, white southerners would never try to encourage them to leave. But the opposite would surely happen—black Americans would help lift the whole African continent out of barbarism and backwardness. If Africa could be so converted, it would only happen through the work of blacks themselves, because most native Africans had "a marked aversion to the white race." Certain parts of Africa were among the only places on earth where the white Catholic church, which for centuries had built its reputation upon dogged determination to proselytize reluctant peoples, had given up its missionary efforts. Therefore, black Americans must become the missionaries, a privileged elite in Africa who would do what white men could never do. But, to be successful, they would have to learn to "be as kind and patient and generous towards their own kindred as we [white southerners] have been to them." Morgan read from the publications of the British Zoological Society and the journal of Henry M. Stanley to prove just how badly Africa needed this civilizing influence and to prove that the interior of the dark continent, particularly the Congo region, would make a suitable habitation for the emigrants.[13]

Morgan reasoned that a mass expatriation to Africa would affect blacks the same as the American Revolution had affected the patriots in the colonies: it would give them "independence, liberty, and power," but, unlike the founders of the United States, they would gain all of this "without a sacrifice." If they remained in America, they would never enjoy these blessings, but they would waste their lives trying to obtain them, for no matter how intelligent, talented, and determined a black man may be, said Morgan, "he cannot find a place suited to his worth in any part of the United States. The more conspicuous his abilities may be, the less chance he will have for a position where he can make them felt. All of us, in every part of the Union, with one accord refuse to the negro the power and influence for which we have endeavored to qualify him. How many blacks hold positions of power and influence in the North? None! What northern state had ever sent a black man to either house of Congress? None!"[14]

Considering the nature of the situation, it would be more humane, Morgan continued, to stop building the hopes of black Americans through the drawing of them into the vortex of party politics and making them the spoils. Removing them from the political equation by encouraging and helping them to emigrate would be in the best interest of everyone: it would restore peace between the North and South, remove a stumbling block from the path of both Democrats and Republicans, uplift the continent of Africa, and give the emigrants opportunities for self-fulfillment that they would otherwise never know. He concluded by asserting that "pride of race will cause the African negro to rejoice in his coming as the redeemer and regenerator of his fatherland. . . . Their light shall be as a city set upon a hill."[15]

Following Morgan's lengthy opening remarks, Matthew Butler spoke briefly on behalf of his emigration bill. He began by explaining that the bill did not call for involuntary deportation of blacks, but only voluntary emigration. His argument thereafter quickly degenerated into a rant about his perception of the race problem rather than an explanation for why the best solution could only be found in emigration. Whereas Morgan had made a strong case for how emigration would benefit everyone in America and Africa, Butler mainly just attacked what he considered to be the hypocrisy of northern Republicans and philanthropists who loved "the negro at a distance" but wanted to keep blacks in the South for political purposes.[16] Similarly, whereas Morgan truly thought emigration represented the best solution to the race problem, Butler seemed insincere in advocating his own bill. His true intention behind the bill appeared to be only to antagonize the Republicans with a measure that he knew would irritate most of them. Indeed, according to one northern newspaper, Butler later admitted that he did not really expect anyone to take his bill seriously and had only introduced it as "a piece of sarcasm" to make the Republicans do some soul-searching before they launched their Federal Elections Bill.[17]

If Butler hoped to antagonize the Republicans, his plan worked. If he wanted to cause soul-searching among them, it failed. Three Republicans briefly answered Butler's attack. George Frisbie Hoar of Massachusetts pointed out that most blacks did not wish to abandon their belief in the American dream, and they never would. Why would they possibly want to leave this "paradise of labor?" he asked.[18] Henry Blair of New Hampshire contended that it would be much cheaper and easier to keep them here, educate them, and help them gradually to assimilate into white society than to ship them off to Africa. He also doubted that emigration could work because, for every one black American who boarded a ship bound for Africa, two native Africans would board the same ship for the return voyage to America. In other words, most Africans, given a choice, would gladly trade the hardships of life in their native land for the difficulties of life in the United States.[19]

John J. Ingalls of Kansas next rose to answer Butler. Ingalls was almost as much a partisan, sectionalist, and hotspur as Butler, despite being the current president pro tem of the Senate, and a three-term member. He had a habit of launching into both bloody-shirt tirades and racist diatribes that could leave listeners flabbergasted, which he did in his response to the Butler bill—a speech he called the "Fiat Justitia."[20] He also committed egregious plagiarism in this well-prepared but rambling reaction to the Butler bill. Opponents charged, and Ingalls's biographer has verified, that the main ideas and many of the words of this speech came from a book called *Justice and Jurisprudence* by John Philpot Curran, although Ingalls never gave him credit.[21]

The "Fiat Justitia" reads more like an incoherent, rambling racial tirade than a well-conceptualized and scholarly case against emigration. For the historian, it is in fact difficult in places to determine whether Ingalls favored or opposed emigration. But oppose it he did, because he wanted the black vote to remain in the South and be protected by the provisions of the coming Federal Elections Bill. In essence, Ingalls argued that, if Butler, Morgan, and other white southern emigration advocates really cared about blacks, they would give them equal voting rights in the South rather than try to deport them to Africa. As long as blacks stayed in the South and did not venture northwestward to Kansas, Ingalls favored a large black population remaining in the United States. He did not favor racial mixing, however. Indeed, he found the idea absolutely repulsive and wanted to make perfectly lucid the fact that, while he favored political equality for blacks, he drew the line at social equality. For an illustration of just how strongly he felt about the issue, he recalled a recent conversation with Frederick Douglass. The venerable old black civil rights leader had told Ingalls that he believed the different races would eventually amalgamate in the United States. Ingalls scolded Douglass for the assertion, proclaiming defiantly that whites would never amalgamate with an "inferior" race. (Douglass later responded to the Kansan's speech saying, "I have always entertained for that gentleman the highest respect. When he is right he is very right and when he is wrong he is very wrong. There is no halfness in his character and composition. He is either all or he is nothing. In this present instance he happens to be not only wrong but very wrong."[22]) Ingalls thought his own brand of racism somehow a great degree better than the brand his southern Democratic colleagues espoused. He accused white southerners of actually favoring "extermination" of blacks to either amalgamation or emigration. He ended the "Fiat Justitia" with a barrage of bloody-shirt South-bashing, which included, among other things, several uncomplimentary descriptions of the recently deceased leader of the Confederacy, Jefferson Davis, and a pronouncement of judgment against the state of Mississippi for its backwardness.[23]

Thus closed the first round of verbal sparring over the Butler Emigration Bill. Even though it had accomplished nothing, advocates of the bill continued to try to generate support for the plan. On January 30, Zebulon Vance of North Carolina, one of the recognized southern Democratic leaders in the Senate, spoke on its behalf.[24] Vance gave a long and well-conceived response to Ingalls's charges. In it, he proved that he not only supported the emigration idea, but also that he could articulate the southern position on racial issues in general as well as anyone in Congress. While the "iridescent" Kansan had succeeded in shifting the focus of the debate to put the Democratic sponsors of the bill on the defensive, Vance countermanded in such a way that his side regained the initiative, forcing Ingalls and the Republicans back into the role of spoiler. The North Carolinian began by citing the latest statistics of demographic change among the black population in his home state, showing that in 1889 a huge migration of blacks to Mississippi had begun, which continued into early 1890. The migrants chose to move to the cotton kingdom of the Yazoo Delta by the thousands, he determined, because it was one of the few places in the United States where the demand for agricultural labor currently outstripped supply. Vance saw two interesting points to be made about this movement of blacks to Mississippi. First, it proved that blacks in large numbers would indeed pack up everything they owned and travel a long distance to find a better life, which lent credibility to the emigration idea. Second, these migrants willingly chose to take up residence in a state in the deep South which, according to Ingalls, set the standard for committing racial injustices. If race relations were really so bad in Mississippi, he asked rhetorically, why would so many blacks want to move there? Why did they not instead choose to migrate to Ingalls's state, Kansas, or some other northern state? Could this perhaps be a commentary on how badly white northerners treated blacks? Perhaps black southerners had heard of the discrimination that greeted the Exodusters in Kansas. Clearly, said Vance, either blacks did not see the North as a region where they could find better economic opportunities than existed in the South, or else they did not think they would be welcomed there socially. Either way, it meant the North had problems and prejudices of its own and should not be casting stones at the South.[25]

Vance used this preliminary argument to set up his main point: he did not support Senator Morgan's opinion that Africa should be the destination of choice for black emigrants. Rather than emigration, Vance favored the dispersal of blacks throughout the United States. Particularly, he hoped to spread them evenly throughout all of the northern and western states. He complained that the South should not be allowed to hold a monopoly on blacks since white northerners claimed to love them so much. In making such a sardonic comment, he tried to sting Ingalls and fellow Republicans with a charge of racial hypocrisy and thus make them defend their reason for wanting to keep blacks exclusively in the South, which he believed was purely so that the GOP could exploit their votes. Republicans,

Exodusters and the Excluded Ethnics. (*Harper's Weekly*, 1879.) Thomas Nast again showed a clarity of thought on the subject of racial migration and immigration that most white Americans and their political leaders could not grasp during the Gilded Age.

however, saw no benefit in arguing with Vance over a bill that they knew would never pass, and they refused to be drawn into his snare.[26] Wade Hampton, South Carolina's junior senator, delivered the next and final speech on behalf of the Butler bill, which turned out to be an anticlimactic conclusion to the debate.[27] He made a defense of the Butler bill using the biblical analogy of Abraham and Lot separating from one another for the good of both (as recorded in Genesis, chapter 13)—an argument that made as much sense as any other pro-emigration argument—but no one listened. Thus ended the brief but suspenseful debate over the Butler bill. The Senate never voted on the bill but simply laid it aside, which is, of course, the fate of the majority of bills that ever come before either house of Congress in any session. Both the bill and the idea of emigration in general continued to surface, however, in impromptu discussions in both the Senate and the House periodically during the remainder of both sessions in 1890–1891. Republican Senator Henry Moore Teller of Colorado even introduced a bill in the second session that would have appropriated a $50 million federal loan to the Afro-American Colonization Society to buy land from Mexico in Baja California, but the Senate never considered it.[28]

In the midst of the Federal Elections Bill debate, a year after the Senate had laid aside the Butler bill, several Republicans took pleasure in bringing up the southerners' "negro-deportation-by-emigration scheme," as Senator Shelby Cullom of Illinois called it. He found it odd that the same southern Democrats who advocated a federally funded program of emigration argued against the Federal Elections Bill on the basis that it would increase the power of the federal government and cost too much.[29]

Senator William M. Evarts of New York found the same hypocrisy evident in the southern Democrats' position on emigration, noting how they demanded to be left alone to work out their own destiny on racial issues such as black suffrage and segregation, yet they conveniently changed their tune now to ask for federal money to help them get rid of blacks through an "expatriation" project. John Tyler Morgan answered Evarts by pointing out that the only senator who ever advocated a "forced removal" of blacks was William Windom, a northern Republican currently serving as Secretary of the Treasury in the Harrison administration. Windom, like Zebulon Vance, favored dispersion of blacks throughout the United States over deportation abroad, but thought that the federal government should not give blacks a choice in the matter. Morgan admitted that the idea would be an acceptable alternative to voluntary emigration, bellowing, "I want them scattered. I want the senator from New York to have thousands and hundreds of thousands of them if he would like to have them."[30]

Democratic senators from the deep South favored the Butler bill almost unanimously, with the lone dissenting voice coming from Alfred Colquitt of Georgia. Colquitt did not oppose the bill in principle. He simply thought it an unrealistic option considering that all previous colonization programs and schemes had failed. As he put it, "All forms of colonization to any part of this country, to Africa, or anywhere else must be absolutely and finally discarded. Such a thing is out of the question. It is a chimera. It is not possible."[31] No Democrat outside of the deep South expressed opposition to the Butler bill except George Vest of Missouri. Vest, a diminutive Democrat with neo-Confederate views, would go on to enjoy a long, distinguished career in American government (yet somehow is remembered in history only for eulogizing dogs as man's best friend). During the Democrats' filibuster of the Federal Elections Bill in January 1891, he and John Tyler Morgan killed a fair amount of time disagreeing over the feasibility of emigration as a solution to the southern race problem. Vest argued that blacks were not a pioneering people, as were whites. They would never voluntarily venture into the great unknown but would rather choose a degraded status in the United States because they had a childlike dependency on whites. If that were true, asked Morgan (reading from the *Washington Post*), why would two thousand blacks from Texas and Mississippi be converging upon Savannah to await transportation to Africa from the Congo National Emigration Steamship Company? Vest responded that they would only sit there in Georgia waiting to be told what to do because they would not have the capacity to figure it out for themselves.[32]

Vest then recalled an incident that he claimed to have personally witnessed and participated in involving would-be Kansas Exodusters in 1879. He said that a large group of blacks had been "seduced" into moving to Kansas by fictitious portrayals of the Plains state as a land flowing with milk and honey. He went down to the railroad depot in his hometown of Kansas City, Missouri, on a cold autumn day, when the bone-chilling prairie wind turned the landscape into a virtual frozen tundra, to witness the arrival of these migrants from the deep South. "There were one hundred and fifty of those poor, deluded creatures" who waited to "be taken where they could live without work, and where, under cloudless skies, there would be perpetual flowers and sunshine." These Exodusters told him they were scared to be in Missouri because they had heard stories about the Border Ruffians of old. They wondered when they could cross over into Kansas. Vest complained that the "scoundrels" who had lured them there never showed up to lead them on into Kansas, whereupon he and other compassionate white Missourians had no choice but to take them in and feed them lest they starve and freeze to death.[33]

The emigration debate also spread from the Senate to the House of Representatives. In the House debate over the Federal Elections Bill in July 1890, Henry Cabot Lodge of Massachusetts declared that talk of emigration among white southerners "is a confession of failure and a cry of despair" in trying to solve the race problem without federal help.[34] Other House Republicans found comic relief in presenting a resolution passed by the Afro-American Congress, an organization that had coincidentally assembled in Chicago at the same time that the Senate took up the Butler bill. It asked Congress to appropriate $100 million for the relocation of every "unhappy" white citizen of the South to the North. It added that Senators Morgan, Hampton, and Randall L. Gibson (of Louisiana) should be jointly appointed "the Moses[es] to direct the unhappy people out of the States of their misfortunes."[35] Although the Afro-American Congress poked fun at those it perceived as the leaders among southern racists, it did, in fact, favor what it called "emigration" (by which it meant only "migration") "to more law abiding sections" of the United States.[36]

Most House references to emigration, however, contained no such humor. Representative Charles E. Hooker of Mississippi contended, very seriously, as did many other Americans, that God had ordained African slavery in the United States because He wanted to civilize and Christianize a portion of the race in order to send them back to Africa someday to evangelize the gigantic, pagan continent. Hooker thus favored emigration and believed fully that there would come a time in the not-too-distant future when God would lead his chosen people out of the land of their captivity back to their ancestral homeland. In the meantime, he thought it paramount that whites instill them with education and morality to prepare them for the work ahead. He named Bishop Henry McNeal Turner, who had only lately become recognized as a leader of the black race in America, as the probable "Moses" of the emigrants. Hooker's ideas, to some extent, proved prophetic. Indeed, Turner did become the most vociferous and visible leader of the emigration movement throughout the 1890s.[37]

Turner was born in South Carolina in 1834 to a free family. He claimed that his maternal grandfather had been an African prince before becoming a slave, but there is no evidence to support that claim. What is certain is that his maternal grandmother was white, which gave Henry an unusually light complexion and Caucasian facial features. Self-educated, articulate, and ambitious, Turner rose through the ranks of the African Methodist Episcopal Church, serving as a chaplain to black Union troops in 1863 and gaining ordination as a bishop in 1880. He came to national prominence as a spokesman for emigration in 1890, despite the fact that he did not personally make a pilgrimage to Africa until the latter part of 1891. During the debate on the Butler bill, Turner wrote an open letter to former U. S. Senator Blanche K. Bruce of Mississippi, published in the *Washington Post*, strongly supporting the bill. Turner wrote with complete sincerity and conviction that, if the bill passed, blacks would be fulfilling their destiny in the service of Christ, for which generations of bondage and hardship had prepared them.[38] This letter catapulted him into the role of leading spokesman for the cause of black emigration. Consequently, his stature grew over the next few years, and he became the heir apparent of Frederick Douglass as the most visible, respected spokesman for African Americans. A much younger man, however, one Booker Talifero Washington, who did not favor emigration, eventually achieved that distinction after delivering his famous "Atlanta Compromise" speech in 1895.[39]

Even after the Butler bill had been laid aside, Turner continued to press for its reconsideration. He wrote a long letter to Butler thanking him for his interest in helping black Americans and calling him the "Providential instrument" for carrying out God's plan. He realized that Butler wanted to rid the South of its high black population rather than to help blacks fulfill their divine destiny, but Turner praised him anyway, saying, "Some may hiss and condemn your course for the present, but unborn generations will commend your courage and honor your memory." Turner found only one fault with the bill, that the proposed appropriation of $5 million "would be but a drop in the bucket" compared to the need. He urged Butler to reintroduce the bill with the appropriation increased at least "ten times," because "hundreds of thousands" of black Americans desired to emigrate.[40]

Such religious interpretations of the history and destiny of African Americans did not originate with Turner. Alexander Crummell, also a black religious leader of national stature, preceded Turner by many years in preaching that God's divine plan for black Americans included sending them back to Africa. In fact, he had been preaching this message even before emancipation, which means he had been competing against the egalitarian ideology of abolitionists and neo-abolitionists, with little success, for most of his lifetime. Crummell considered the years since 1865 to be, for African Americans, analogous to the biblical story of the Hebrews wandering in the wilderness for forty years, when all along the promised land lay within their reach. The ancient Hebrews needed only to cast fear aside and simply go forth in faith and claim their prize. He also believed that the Liberian experiment had failed thus far because 90 percent of the settlers there had no education and thus little understanding of how to conduct a civil government or society. He also pointed out (incorrectly) that not a single scholar or statesman had emerged from Liberia in the nation's existence.[41] Evidently, he did not think Edward Blyden qualified as a scholar or statesman. Or perhaps Crummell refused to recognize Blyden's accomplishments because he believed him to be a Moslem, as did many other contemporaries, a notion that the renowned Liberian emigrationist neither admitted nor denied.[42]

Some white religious leaders noted the propensity of black American Christians for evangelizing and proselytizing in the United States while making little effort to spread the Gospel abroad. They complained, too, that these black clergy tended to focus more upon gaining equality for their people in America than upon saving their souls. They thought it hypocritical that black Christians would favor spreading the ideology of egalitarianism in the United States over heeding the real call of God's people—mission work. They thus spread a message that black Americans had an obligation to become missionaries to one of the largest non-Christian populations in the world: Africans. One commented that the "development of Africa excites in the Christian world to-day a more common and widespread interest than any other subject," but, sadly, the "educated and well-to-do American negro alone seems to be apathetic and indifferent" about it. Meanwhile, "tens of hundreds of white men" have died in the "forests and swamps" of Africa fulfilling their Christian duty. He added that black Christians could not claim that lack of funds kept them from the mission field, because white mission societies would gladly support them with generous contributions.[43] At the time this criticism arose, the African Methodist Episcopal Church had only just begun to launch a serious evangelistic effort in Africa, and Turner, in fact, made his impact felt in Africa immediately thereafter.[44]

Besides stirring the Christian community, the Butler bill also sparked a tremendous discussion of the emigration idea in the forum of secular public opinion. Although no public consensus on the subject ever emerged, the amount of white support for it was unusual. Unlike earlier and later waves of emigration fervor, the one that the Butler bill sparked did not produce a great outcry from white southern employers, who usually feared a labor shortage resulting from a mass exodus of black workers from the fields. Whereas the 1879 exodus to Kansas created quite a disturbance among employers throughout the South, the threat of an even larger loss of workers in 1890 elicited no comparable response.[45] There are two obvious reasons for this change. First, the black population had been in a constant state of migration from the hill and Piedmont sections of the South to the cotton belt throughout the late 1880s in search of better economic opportunities, and many white employers had already adjusted to the loss and prepared for the eventuality of even greater losses. Second, the agricultural economy of the South had become so depressed by 1890–1891 that a superabundant labor supply existed, allowing white employers to absorb the losses more easily than ever before.[46] By contrast, in the next large black movement out of the South after 1890—the great northern migration of the World War I years—the traditional pattern of white opposition resumed, indicating that the years surrounding the time of the Butler bill's consideration were the ideal time, and perhaps the only time, in American history when a majority of white southerners would have accepted black emigration as a serious possible solution to the race problem.[47]

Many northern newspapers—including the *Leavenworth Advocate,* the *New York Independent,* and four Philadelphia papers (the *Inquirer,* the *Examiner,* the *Star,* and the *Transcript*)—expressed their customary opposition to all emigration and colonization plans, lambasting the Butler bill as a foolish and racist proposition. Open-mindedness and ambiguity of opinion, however, characterized the views of other traditional opponents of emigration, such as the *Detroit Tribune.* At the same time, other major northern newspapers uncharacteristically supported the emigration idea, including the *New York Times,* the *Philadelphia Telegraph,* the *Pittsburgh Post,* and the *Chicago Tribune.* Most major southern newspapers—including the *Atlanta Constitution,* the *Charleston News and Courier,* the *Savannah Morning News,* the *Jackson Clarion Ledger,* and the *Arkansas Democrat*—favored black emigration in 1890. Although a few southern papers, such as the *Memphis Appeal-Avalanche,* remained neutral on the issue, virtually none opposed the Butler bill.[48]

One of the largest and most influential periodicals to support emigration was the *Nation,* published in New York by Republican editor E. L. Godkin. This leading Mugwump Republican organ proclaimed a similar message to that of the religious leaders, that black Americans had an obligation to go back to Africa. Its message differed, however, in that it emphasized infusing the dark continent with "civilization" (meaning, ostensibly, education and technology) rather than the Gospel. Moreover, it deduced that if blacks refused to go back to Africa, it proved that they lacked courage, as well as confidence in their ability to apply the knowledge in Africa that they had learned from white Americans without the help of white Americans. If that were the case, said the *Nation,* there could be no other explanation than that they realized their inferiority to and dependency upon the white man. Thus, logically, if they would not leave, they deserved their second-class American citizenship.[49]

Many of these supporters of emigration harped upon a common theme: the need for a Moses figure to arise and lead the blacks to their promised land, whether that be in Africa or somewhere else. One supporter, who had traveled extensively in the interior of Africa, believed that the Congo basin would be the promised land, calling it "another Canaan for our modern Israelites." He asked, "When is the new colored Moses to arise for this exodus and lead his people home?"[50] Another favored the migration of blacks to the American West, stating matter-of-factly that the migrants needed only two things that they did not yet have: a "Negro Moses" whom other blacks would respect and follow as a spiritual leader, and "Emigrant Aid" companies to help them with more earthly problems, such as dealing with land speculators, railroads, and unscrupulous traders.[51]

Others thought that neither Africa nor the western United States could be a promised land for the black sojourners because both places had been tried already without favorable results. Cuba, Mexico, Brazil, Argentina, or some Central American nation, they thought, would make the best promised land. The problem with such areas, however, was that, unlike Liberia, which had always existed essentially as a protectorate of the United States, the Latin American nations all possessed sovereignty. Black Americans could only settle in them by permission of the various governments, and in some countries protest against such settlement would be fierce.[52] This fact did not deter advocates of the plan, however, but merely prompted them to say that black emigrants did not need a "Moses" so much as they needed a "Cromwell" to take charge of the situation and force the issue upon the government, regardless of the protest of the people.[53]

Talks had in fact already begun in late 1889 between blacks in San Antonio, Texas, and the Mexican government for establishing a colony in Mexico.[54] Many blacks and whites alike hoped that the project would come to fruition, but most did not really expect that it would. One southern newspaper commented that, even if the Mexican government did pass the bill allowing the colony, few blacks would accept the invitation to move there, because: "The Negro knows when he has a good thing. He knows he is better treated and respected right here in the cotton region of the South than he ever has been or ever will be anywhere else in the world. . . . The Negro is well satisfied, prosperous, and as happy as a woodchuck."[55]

This assessment of the contentment of blacks made sense to many white Americans at the time because of the huge influx of black sharecroppers into the cotton states around 1890. Indeed, as Zebulon Vance had pointed out in his speech on the Butler bill, far more blacks had recently moved into the cotton region and the American Southwest for economic reasons than had contemplated moving out because of racial discrimination.[56] This fact forced some observers to view the emigration idea as tantamount to trying "to empty a running stream with a ladle."[57] Indeed, large numbers of blacks began migrating into the Yazoo Delta of Mississippi, into western Arkansas, and especially into Oklahoma in 1890. The Oklahoma Immigration Society was created especially to recruit blacks to the former Indian territory. In the case of both Oklahoma and Arkansas, however, black newcomers immediately discovered that their new white neighbors did not appreciate their presence. In Oklahoma, which had only been open to non-Indian settlement for one year, even the Choctaws refused to live alongside black settlers. Many Native Americans, despite their own degraded status in American society, looked down upon blacks as inferior because some leaders of their tribes had once held black slaves just as white Americans did. They thus tried, with temporary and limited success, to drive the black settlers out of Oklahoma. Consequently, as a last resort, many of the black migrants who had only recently moved from the eastern states to the inhospitable West now found themselves appealing in desperation to the American Colonization Society (ACS) for passage to Liberia.[58]

Most of these desperate souls took the obvious first step of writing letters to the ACS, notifying the organization of their interest in emigration and inquiring about the cost and logistics of a move to Africa. Few took the next step, however, of actually filling out official applications with the ACS in hope of being chosen for colonization in Liberia. The ACS, a privately funded New York City agency founded in 1817, could not afford to accept many applicants and thus weeded out the weak from those it considered most likely to survive and prosper in Africa. From its inception until 1890, the ACS had succeeded in helping only a few thousand blacks move to Africa, because it had always required that the emigrants contribute some portion of their own fare. In most years since emancipation, the ACS had received only a few dozen applications, or a couple hundred at most.[59] It frequently rejected applicants because they lacked the financial resources and often, by the organization's judgment, the know-how to start from scratch in the wilderness of Liberia and earn a living there.[60] In 1890–1891, the ACS received a record number of letters expressing interest in emigration, applications for passage, and money forwarded by hopeful emigrants as down payments on their moving expenses. It claimed that twice as many people as ever before currently wanted to emigrate—based upon letters of inquiry written mainly by male heads of household. It conservatively estimated the number at one million, a figure that included all family members of the heads of household.[61] While this interest caused great excitement in the ACS organization, most of these would-be emigrants lacked the ways and means to procure the necessary $100 to $200 per person to make the move. Moreover, in the judgment of ACS officials, many more did not possess the self-starting pioneer mentality required to carve a livelihood out of the African wilderness. Most of the blacks expressing interest, therefore, never even got past the initial inquiry stage to make it to the next and more important stage of completing the actual applications for passage. Thus, for all of the hype about emigration in 1890–1891, the ACS helped no more blacks relocate to Africa in those years than in any average year.[62]

Although interest in emigration arose among blacks throughout the United States in 1890–1891, in some areas of the country, the emigration fervor swept across the landscape like a brush fire or a religious revival. Conway County, Arkansas, was one such place. More than two thousand applications to the ACS came from this location alone in 1890–1891. The ACS chose only a small group of these Arkansans for passage, however—picking those it considered the most likely to succeed as African transplants. The Reverend James Dargan led in organizing this group and accompanying them on their overseas voyage. Both Dargan and his band of emigrants actually turned out to be quite ill-prepared for the move. The reverend embarked upon his journey abroad intending to stay in Liberia himself, but after arriving and surveying the deplorable living conditions there, he immediately decided to come back to the United States. He decried that the place was "not fitting for a horse to live much less a person." He left the other eighty-five emigrants there, however. As he departed, so he claimed, those he left behind began "holering and cring [sic] wanting to come back." Dargan's disturbing report captured the attention of many other blacks who hoped to emigrate, giving them serious second thoughts about leaving behind their American homes. Letters from the new Liberian transplants soon arrived, however, which reported that, after the initial shock of the move wore off, life was better in Liberia than in the United States, and they were glad they had made the decision to emigrate. One of the newly settled Africans even boasted that he would not move back to Arkansas if the state offered to give him free land and stock. The Arkansas emigration craze then resumed, with more people interested than before, although the number of qualified applicants did not increase.[63]

Propaganda inviting blacks to emigrate did increase, however, largely as a result of Bishop Henry McNeal Turner's work. After finally visiting Liberia himself in 1891, he wrote with assuredness that "anybody, white or colored, from America is welcomed out here in Africa, either on the coast or back in the interior, while Englishmen, French, and Germans are mostly hated. . . . Americans are looked upon as the guardians of Liberia and the friends of her blacks, and it modifies the prejudice somehow. I do not understand it yet." He added that the African people wanted black Americans to move there. A particular tribal king, he said, expressed a deep and sincere concern "about the colored people in America. He wanted to know when we were coming home. . . . He will give his kingdom to his children in the United States." Turner also cautioned, however, that "This is no place for fools or paupers. . . . Persons should not come here and expect to be hirelings; for the native African stands ready to do all kinds of work much cheaper and better than we can, except [for] skilled labor."[64]

Many black Americans criticized both Turner and the emigration movement in general. Bishop Benjamin F. Lee said that Turner "speaks of the United States as Hades and of Africa as Eden; yet even he still holds his residence in Hades, only paying Eden a brief visit once a year."[65] The most outspoken black leader to oppose Turner and emigration, however, was C. H. J. Taylor, an Atlanta lawyer who had served briefly as U. S. Minister to Liberia during Grover Cleveland's first administration and later became a Kansas City newspaper editor. Taylor thought of the little coastal nation in the same way that the Reverend Dargan of Arkansas had described it, saying all the hype about Liberia painted a misleading portrait of the true conditions there. He accused Turner of having an ulterior motive in soliciting for Liberia. Turner had a vested interest in the economic development of the African nation because he currently served as the Liberian consul to the United States.[66]

Other black leaders, such as the Reverend E. K. Love of Georgia and Virginia Congressman John Mercer Langston, a former U. S. Ambassador to Haiti, opposed emigration not because of Turner's leadership but because of either their principles or their pragmatism. They believed that, after centuries of slavery in America, during which they helped carve a civilization out of the wilderness for the benefit of whites, blacks now deserved the opportunity to fulfill the American dream, too. They should accept nothing less, they said, but should keep the pressure on the federal government until it finally capitulated and enforced the Fourteenth and Fifteenth Amendments.[67] Robert Smalls, a Republican politician from South Carolina, explained that African Americans had contributed 186,000 soldiers in 250 battles for the defense and interests of the United States in various wars, and, therefore, they "do not intend to go anywhere."[68] Frederick Douglass complained that most blacks could not leave even if they wanted to because their debts incurred from years of sharecropping locked them to the land and to their creditors. He noted that whites in North Carolina had tried to prevent blacks in their state from migrating to Mississippi recently because they wanted the migrants to stay and work off their debts.[69]

W. E. B. DuBois, an idealistic young graduate of Harvard University in 1890 who would later renounce his American citizenship and take up permanent residence in Africa, opposed emigration because he, too, had succeeded in America, thanks to his ivy-league education and natural ability. If only more blacks could become as educated as he, surely they would earn the respect of white America, he thought.[70] Booker T. Washington tacitly opposed emigration on the grounds that blacks, despite the best efforts of racist whites to keep them down, had made extraordinary progress between emancipation and 1890, and since the long-term economic prospects of the race appeared to be improving, African Americans should be patient and should not abandon their American homes.[71] T. Thomas Fortune, founder of the Afro-American League and editor of the influential black newspaper the *New York Age,* held a mixed view on emigration. He preferred protest, and even revolution, to leaving the United States, but he did propose in 1890 that African Americans leave the South. He urged that they "scatter . . . more generally throughout the republic" and thereby no longer constitute a "race problem" for any particular section of the country.[72] Clearly, black public opinion managed no consensus over the emigration issue.

Although the controversial Butler bill never became law, the interest in emigration it helped reignite blazed for more than a year before dissipating. Not only Butler, but at least one northern Republican senator, William E. Chandler of New Hampshire, a leading member of the Senate's committee on naval appropriations, continued to receive letters long after the Fifty-first Congress had adjourned from interested citizens offering their support for some amended version of the Butler bill.[73] Bishop Henry McNeal Turner thought it would eventually pass in a later Congress and that the bill's author, Senator Matthew Butler, would "go down in history as the pioneer of the grandest measure in the closing days of the nineteenth century."[74] Considering that (1) *perhaps* as many as one million (but certainly many thousands of) African Americans seriously entertained the notion of leaving the United States permanently in 1890–1891; and that (2) the Billion Dollar Congress had the money at its disposal and therefore could have afforded to fund such a mass exodus of blacks; as well as that (3) millions of white Americans would have either approved of or at least allowed their departure, the Butler Emigration Bill was not necessarily a quixotic pipe dream.[75]

From our post–civil rights movement vantage point, it is difficult to understand how the emigration idea could have ever been taken seriously as a potential solution to the South's race problem. Most African Americans in 1890, however, found it even more difficult to muster optimism about their future in the United States. What did they have to look forward to in this country? Thus, the emigration idea certainly seemed to be a legitimate alternative to their staying in the United States and watching their civil rights erode until they finally disappeared into oblivion.

Why, then, if so many African Americans took the Butler bill seriously, did Congress not give it the consideration it deserved? Some southern Democrats believed that most Republicans could never support such a solution, "because it would imply a confession" of failure on the part of those who had emancipated the slaves and begun the Reconstruction.[76] Although that explanation may contain a grain of truth, the real answer is probably that most Republicans could not bring themselves to contemplate sending away a race of people to whom the United States owed such a debt of gratitude. As Republican leader James G. Blaine once said, and many white Americans agreed, the nation "owes something to the negro."[77] African Americans had helped build the United States. Surely, the U. S. government owed them more than mere passage back to Africa. Emigration, in fact, must have seemed to many Republicans like a cruel end for a group of people who deserved so much better. Why should white Americans add to the injustices already committed against this unfortunate race and thereby saddle their consciences with an even greater degree of guilt than they already felt? Thus, even though money was available and interest among blacks abounded, the majority of the GOP—the party which represented humanitarianism, enlightenment, and progress—was not, nor would it ever be, prepared to support emigration. Such a potential solution to the race problem seemed to be just too extreme. Northern Republicans, and indeed the nation as a whole, therefore, accepted by default the unbridled growth of racial segregation—a milder form of physical race separation that had begun years before—as the best social arrangement for the racially bifurcated South. Segregation thus became, as one historian has put it, "the maximum oppression to be tolerated from racist Americans" by ambivalent and non-racist Americans.[78]

The adoption of full-scale segregation, however, was merely a social measure—it did not directly touch the issue of political rights for blacks. The American people and government still had to deal with the issue of the black man's place in the American polity. The Federal Elections Bill would soon address it, and many fair-minded Americans were ready. As the *Independent*, a New York periodical, put it, forget the emigration bill—bring on the Federal Elections Bill.[79] Bring it on the Republicans would, but not before they first considered another potential solution to the race problem, the Blair Education Bill. The issue of education for African Americans thus becomes the focus of the next chapter of this study.

Chapter 2

To Drain the Infinite Oceans

The Swan Song of the Once-Great Blair Education Bill

When education is universal, the question of race distinction will be obliterated, justice will prevail, and people of different color will live beside one another in all parts of our country with mutual respect.

—Senator Leland Stanford of California

It cannot be said that Congress has the power to tax the people for the purpose of handing the money back to them as a gift.

—Senator Richard Coke of Texas

Once the Senate brushed aside the idea of emptying a running stream with a ladle, it next sought to alleviate the race problem by draining the "oceans of illiteracy," as Senator Henry Blair of New Hampshire put it, with the Blair Education Bill.[1] Black southerners, more than any other group of Americans, faced the danger of drowning in a sea of ignorance, and the Blair bill was intended to be the life buoy for rescuing the victims and towing them to safety upon the shoreline of American society. The idea was that blacks could catch up with whites in education and that their ability to function and compete in the white-dominated society would soon eradicate the prejudice that created the race problem.

Like the colonization scheme, the idea of educating black southerners did not originate in 1890, nor did Blair pioneer it. From the outreaches of the Freedmen's Bureau and the American Missionary Association to the writings of Albion Tourgee and to the philanthropic efforts of George Peabody and Andrew Carnegie, black southerners had been the recipients of educational attention ever since their emancipation in 1865. Yet, compared to the need, all educational efforts before 1890 had amounted to little more than a drop in the bucket. Episcopal Bishop Thomas U. Dudley of Kentucky explained the problem in 1885 by saying, "in spite of all their boasted progress, the Negro possesses an ignorance which is simply abysmal."[2] Something more needed to be done. Blair's proposal differed from all of the previous education bills in that it called for the creation of a permanent, uniform, national, public school system in America supported with federal funds. The public schools would thus necessarily operate under federal supervision. This plan, first introduced in the Senate in 1881, produced some of the most highly charged debates in the history of Congress and in the history of public education in the United States.[3]

Actually, various congressmen introduced ten separate bills for federal aid to education in the decade of the 1880s, but the Blair bill alone received serious consideration. It was superior to all of the others, the result of Blair's extraordinary degree of research concerning the needs of public schools. It identified and explained the nation's educational problems using statistics that critics could not easily refute, and it proposed what seemed to be a sensible, though constitutionally questionable, solution to those problems. The Blair bill passed the Senate in 1884 by a vote of 33 to 11, again in 1886 by a vote of 36 to 11, and a third time in 1888 by a vote of 39 to 29. Unfortunately, it never came before the House for consideration because Democratic Speaker John G. Carlisle of Kentucky intensely opposed it and refused to squander the House's precious time on it.[4]

In each case, bipartisan and trisectional coalitions both supported and opposed it, and in each case a significant number of senators did not vote, although most made their opinions known. No clear pattern emerges regarding how northern, southern, western, Democratic, or Republican senators voted. Each voted his conscience or voted according to the dictate of his state legislature, and no consensus existed even among neighboring states in any given region. For instance, in the South—the region where the Blair bill would have had the greatest impact—North Carolina and Virginia supported it, South Carolina and West Virginia opposed it; likewise, Georgia and Mississippi supported it, while the state sandwiched between them, Alabama, opposed it.[5] By 1890, with the incipient Farmers' Alliance set against the bill, Democratic senators who favored the bill did so at the peril of losing their seats. James L. Pugh of Alabama came closer to that ignominious end than any other U.S. senator, but his extremely rabid opposition to the Federal Elections Bill throughout 1890, an election year, pleased enough constituents and members of the state legislature that he managed to keep his seat.[6]

Because the Blair bill had already been debated in three previous congresses, the arguments for and against it had already been made thoroughly manifest by the time the Fifty-first Congress considered it. Many senators who spoke on the bill in earlier debates thus chose not to speak in 1890. They simply awaited the end of the debate, so they could move on to other business. In this group were John Tyler Morgan of Alabama, William B. Bate of Tennessee, and James B. Beck of Kentucky (all of whom had consistently and outspokenly opposed the bill), William M. Evarts of New York (who had just as consistently and earnestly supported it), and John Sherman of Ohio (who had made a total reversal from initial opposition to strong support). Others, however, such as Richard Coke of Texas, never seemed to tire of finding new reasons to dislike the Blair bill. As one colleague remarked, Coke "finds so much vitality in this bill that he has to kill it every session by [making] a long speech."[7]

The final debate on the bill, which occurred in early 1890, would have been anticlimactic if not for three factors. First, the scheduling of debate on the bill fell, by chance, between the debates on the Butler Emigration Bill and the Federal Elections Bill. This fact made it a vital component in the larger discussion of the race problem at the beginning of the Jim Crow era. Understanding it now from the historical perspective is, therefore, essential for a clear comprehension of the greater issue. Second, Henry Blair's passion for his education bill did not abate in eight years of relentless work. Blair nurtured his bill, constantly updating his data and otherwise perfecting it, and he presented his case for the fourth time as though it were the first. The energy he spent and the time he consumed advocating this previously doomed measure commanded the public's attention, though sometimes it was only negative attention. This public fascination compels the historian to give Blair the consideration he craved for himself and his beloved education bill. Finally, this last debate on the Blair bill in 1890 represented the only real chance in four tries that Blair had to get the measure approved. He had presidential support and a Republican House that would certainly deliberate upon the bill should the Senate pass it again. It seemed to be a foregone conclusion, therefore, that it would finally become law under the auspices of the Billion Dollar Congress.

Blair was a native of New Hampshire, born into a poor and undistinguished family, but he became a self-made man, working his way through law school. He served as a colonel in the Union army during the Civil War, which helped him develop his leadership skills. The people of New Hampshire elected him to the House in 1875, and the legislature sent him to the Senate in 1879. Once in the Senate, Blair formulated his education bill, which consumed virtually his entire twelve-year career in that august body. His poverty and the difficult circumstances that he faced in his youth no doubt caused his great desire to see the disadvantaged receive adequate educational opportunities. Yet, despite such idealism, he understood that most congressional bills, no matter how noble or necessary, would never pass. Had his bill not passed the Senate, therefore, upon its first or second introduction, Blair probably would have accepted that fate and moved on to other issues. As it happened, however, the bill did pass the Republican-controlled Senate three times only to be subsequently tabled in the Democratic House, leading Blair to believe that the Republican majority elected in 1888 would break that pattern without the slightest hesitation. He had already secured President Harrison's endorsement of his plan, so the road toward passage of the bill seemed smooth.[8]

Impediments quickly arose, however, that Blair never foresaw. First, talk of the impending Federal Elections Bill threatened to destroy whatever goodwill existed between Democrats and Republicans, including the bipartisan coalition that had previously supported the Blair bill.[9] Second, the New South's post-Reconstruction industrial thrust had made the 1880s the most prosperous decade for the region since before the Civil War, as the *Manufacturer's Record* of Baltimore and similar journals revealed. Such economic recovery seemed to show that the southern states no longer needed federal money to rejuvenate their public school systems. The 1890s portended great growth and development for the region of the country that lagged the furthest behind in education and, at the same time, remained the most entrenched in the dogma of local government sovereignty. Third, by 1890, a turning point had been reached in the way many American education leaders viewed the educational needs of black southerners. The First Mohonk Conference showed that the standard type of education that the Blair bill espoused was not as suitable for African Americans as was vocational education, a fact that the bill did not particularly address.[10]

Finally, free-thinking northern news media, particularly E. L. Godkin's highly influential *Nation* news magazine, opposed the bill and increasingly waged war in print against it after 1886, calling it "A Bill to Promote Mendicancy." This phrase implied that federal funding and congressional supervision of education were steps in the direction of socialism, which would ultimately make all children educated under such a system wards of the state, thus destroying the initiative of the intellectually gifted. As the *Nation* explained it, placing education under federal control would take America's social structure, which had been "specially created for the benefit of valor, foresight, industry, and intelligence," and make it fit "the special needs of the ignorant, the weak, the lazy, and the incompetent. It is somewhat like a proposal to make such alterations in the house of a decent and prosperous mechanic so that tramps may feel at home in it." By 1890, newspapers all over the country (and especially in the South) had picked up this argument, including James C. Hemphill's *Charleston News and Courier,* Hannis Taylor's *Mobile Register,* and Henry Watterson's *Louisville Courier-Journal,* each of which could hardly contain its contempt for the Blair bill. Likewise, congressmen who opposed the bill but lacked original reasons to explain why, also embraced this argument. Between the press and the politicians, this mendicancy argument had made a tremendous impact on public opinion by 1890.[11]

Not surprisingly, the black press, including T. Thomas Fortune's *New York Age* and H. C. Smith's *Cleveland Gazette,* lined up in solid support of the bill, as did an overwhelming majority of their readers.[12] African Americans stood in no position to reject any offer the federal government might make for their welfare, especially one promoting educational advancement. Venerable statesman Frederick Douglass assessed the value of the Blair bill by declaring that "It will be at least a recognition of a great national duty towards a people to whom an immeasurable debt is due."[13] All black leaders, however, did not agree on every specific measure within the Blair bill. Fortune, along with Pan-Africanist Alexander Crummell and leading educators J. C. Price of Livingstone College in North Carolina and Booker T. Washington of Tuskegee Institute in Alabama, believed that an education equal in every respect to that which white students typically received would not benefit blacks as much as a special type of education of their own—namely vocational education. With the ideological support of esteemed white humanitarian leaders—such as the Reverend A. D. Mayo of Massachusetts, the Reverend R. H. Allen of Pittsburgh, and Samuel Armstrong of the Hampton Institute in Virginia—and with the financial backing of white philanthropists—such as Andrew Carnegie—many black leaders trumpeted vocational education as the salvation of the race.[14]

The first mention of the Blair bill in the Fifty-first Congress came in January 1890 as a response to the Butler Emigration Bill. In an impromptu remark that showed his disdain for Butler and the emigration idea, Blair complained that the race problem in America existed only in the "imagina-

tions and ineradicable prejudices of a few white men." Education, not emigration, would be the solution, he said, adding that reeducating some white
southerners to think like northerners would go a long way toward solving
the race problem.[15] Blair's off-the-cuff remarks did not further his cause,
but he, like so many of his Senate colleagues, could not help himself. Whenever he saw an easy opportunity to criticize the men across the aisle, he
took it, with no apparent regard for the consequences.

When, on February 6, Blair began formal deliberations on his bill in
the Fifty-first Congress, he exhibited much more caution about his choice
of words. He recognized that many of his Republican cohorts wanted to
dispense with his bill quickly, or forgo it altogether, in order to move on to
economic legislation—the tariff being at the head of the list. He hoped to
give them something to think about in the meantime by pointing out that
if the South as a whole was as educated as the North, southerners would
understand the logic of a high protective tariff, which would turn many
southern Democrats into Republicans. An educated South would be good
for the GOP, the national economy, and, ultimately, race relations in America.
Blair proceeded then to give a lesson showing the inextricable link between
education and economic prosperity. The North was wealthier than the
South, he explained, because it enjoyed the two complimentary traditions
of free labor and an educated working class. Educated workers, he opined,
would not work cheaply. Their demand for high wages would create high
consumer prices and thus keep the economy under constant stimulation.
The South possessed neither of these traditions. Slavery, he said, had retarded the South in both economics and education. Since the 1860s, southern labor had remained cheap because the workers were uneducated and
thus unable to understand the economic forces that kept them in poverty,
which, in turn, kept them from organizing or demanding higher wages.
This fact kept agricultural commodity prices low, which depressed the overall economy of the South. This retarded economic system caused a self-
perpetuating cycle in which the southern states could not afford to fund
their own educational institutions adequately. The only way to break the
cycle, asserted Blair, would be to infuse the South with federal funds. The
resulting economic stimulation would redound to the benefit of blacks and
whites alike.[16]

Since his argument rested upon ten years of research and three rounds
of practice prior to 1890, the only issue for this Congress to address, in
Blair's opinion, was that of appropriating the money. The question that
begged to be asked, therefore, was "Have we the money?" Blair answered,
of course, with a resounding "yes." The surplus stood at a record level, just

waiting to be spent on various projects both great and small. Would it be spent on such amenities as river and harbor improvements valued at $10 million per year, when there were "oceans . . . of illiteracy flowing over our land?" Or perhaps a new navy, valued at $350 million? "Educate the world," said Blair, "and there will be no need of a navy." The military analogy served him in another way when he compared the need for a national education system to the need for a national army, saying that, in war, if one part of the army is defeated, the whole nation may lose. In the war against illiteracy, likewise, the northern part of the army could not afford to let the southern part surrender in defeat, or the whole nation would lose. The price, measured in dollars, for a war against illiteracy would not be great compared to the cost, measured in the long-term interests of American society, of not waging the war. Consider, he said, the fact that the value of penal institution property in many states exceeded the value of property set aside for education. Perhaps "with the proper number of schools jails would disappear."[17]

Blair then read the keynote address from the annual meeting of the State Agricultural Society of Georgia. The address emphasized education as the greatest need among the poor people of Georgia, blacks and whites alike. To illustrate this point, Blair read an interview, conducted by an Atlanta institution of higher learning, of an unnamed, illiterate, thirty two-year-old black man. The interviewer asked the man if he had voted in the last presidential election. He replied that he had voted, but he did not know for whom he had voted. When asked if he had ever heard of James A. Garfield, Chester A. Arthur, or Grover Cleveland, he said Garfield sounded vaguely familiar, but he did not know the others. He could not identify Benjamin Harrison as the current president. He also did not know that England and France were not located within the United States.[18]

Blair also showed that white southerners needed better educations just as badly. He read a long statement from a missionary named Frank E. Jenkins who had lived and worked among the white population in Appalachia. Jenkins lamented the condition of these "poor white trash" who lived "almost untouched by the currents of modern life." These people resided in a seven-state region, a land area so vast—twice the size of New England—that state funds and resources never reached them. A national system of education, said Blair, represented their only chance to enter the mainstream of American society. Hoping to capitalize simultaneously upon the Senate's penchant for humanitarianism and its love for democratic principles, he complained that Appalachia whites could read neither the Bible nor the ballot.[19]

Opponents could not accuse Blair of focusing on the South to the

Ignorance Exposed. *"What ye readin' in the newspaper, Uncle Poke?"* *"Dis heah article 'bout dat man walkin' on de ceilin'."* *"Turn the paper 'round an' let me see't. Why, you've got it upside down!"* (*Harper's Weekly,* 1889.) By the time the Billion Dollar Congress convened in 1889, cartoons such as this one in the New York periodical *Harper's Weekly,* which made fun of the supposed ignorance of African Americans, had become all too common.

exclusion of all other regions of the country, because he also showed that there was much room for improvement in his native New England. He looked at fellow Senator Orville Platt of Connecticut, who opposed his bill, and commented, "it would be wise if we could get over this self-righteous notion that we are much better off than our neighbors in the Southern States." He pointed out that Charleston, South Carolina, currently spent more money per capita on education than did Boston, Massachusetts.

Moreover, even his own state of New Hampshire, he argued, could benefit from a national education system because, even in good school systems, there was room for improvement. Blair added that virtually all state Superintendents of Education supported his bill. He made the most of their support, reading aloud many of their letters addressed to him that emphatically endorsed his plan. He also read newspaper articles from all over the country to prove that illiteracy still pervaded every region of the United States in 1890.[20]

Although one senator or another interrupted him from time to time disputing his facts, Blair continually pounded away with charts and tables full of statistics. He also read even more letters of support, many of which came from various well-known and respected leaders in society, such as Frances Willard, president of the Women's Christian Temperance Union, and J. L. M. Curry, agent of the Peabody Fund. Curry was as respected as any educator in the nation, and his support of the Blair bill was thus quite important. At the time of the bill's initial introduction in 1882, he had written: "Here we stand face to face with necessity. All over this State the taxes of the white people cannot be made to suffice for the education of both white and colored; with the utmost goodwill, the resources are deficient. Nothing but national aid can solve the problem."[21] In 1890, Curry still publicly favored such a remedy to the country's education ills, but privately he favored emigration as the best solution to the southern race problem. As the administrator of the Peabody Fund, however, he continued to make annual public pronouncements on the woeful condition of education among blacks in the South, which provided Blair with much fuel for argument.[22]

After two weeks of tying up the business of the Senate, Blair ended his speaking marathon. He concluded with the two arguments he considered the most likely to produce an emotional reaction in his colleagues. He compared the literacy rates of the United States as a whole to various European nations that led the world in industry, technology, and military power, showing how severely the United States lagged behind. Should this not strike fear in the hearts of Americans, asked Blair? In his final argument, he turned to the Bible and made his case for a national education system based upon one of the parables of Jesus. He compared those educated people who opposed his bill to "Pharisees" who "go to church on Sundays and worship the Nazarene carpenter" but "stand erect before Almighty God and thank Him for one thing only: that He made them (as they are simple enough to imagine) better than other people." He aimed his remark particularly at southern Democratic leaders who he believed represented an aristocracy that capriciously doled out education to some and withheld it from others. He named randomly Senators James L. Pugh of Alabama, J. Z. George of

Mississippi, Randall L. Gibson of Louisiana, and the U. S. Supreme Court Justice from Mississippi, Lucius Q. C. Lamar, as typical of the southern aristocracy. Appealing to the Protestant religious faith of most fellow senators, Blair also compared these southern Democrats to the Jesuit leadership in the Catholic Church in America. Both elite groups held the education of millions of common people in their hands, and both opposed his bill. Contrary to the delusional thinking of the Jesuits, said Blair, in an obvious play on words, "The Catholic masses are for free schools," and, he concluded, so were the poor people of the South.[23]

Actually, the Catholic church in general, not merely Jesuits, opposed the Blair bill and took an official position to that effect. The Church feared that one of the underlying goals of a national education system was to destroy its autonomy and to indoctrinate Catholic youth with Protestant ideas and values. That fear is understandable from a historical perspective, considering that, in 1890, the Protestant majority in the United States still expressed an aversion to Catholicism almost as vigorously as they had done in colonial and antebellum times. Although it is ridiculous to say that a conspiracy to reeducate Catholic children existed among Protestant lawmakers, the idea that a national system of public education might undermine religious education certainly seems, on the one hand, to have been a rational fear. On the other hand, Protestant American society as a whole had not yet agreed upon a single, uniform purpose for educating the working classes. Preparing young people for the job market, for college, or for voting had not yet displaced religious training as the primary reason for emphasizing education as a social necessity. Thus, most Americans—regardless of their religious affiliation—saw education as a family concern or, at most, a local government concern. Blair ran ahead, therefore, even of Protestant public opinion, which makes the Catholic phobia of Protestant indoctrination seem irrational in the final analysis. To underscore just how disjointed the American public education system was at this time, not until 1889 did some Midwestern states, which were heavily populated with Germans, make English a compulsory subject in the public schools. At the same time, some southern states had only begun to adopt standardized textbooks.[24] Blair's idea of creating a national education system thus appears to have been far ahead of its time.

Blair reached out to Catholics by trying to convince them that the Protestant majority of the North would be more apt to accept them as social equals if only they would support his bill. Their support would ostensibly show their loyalty to the United States and thus discredit the idea that the Catholic people could not think for themselves because the Pope and the church hierarchy told them what to think. Blair's effort was not successful. Neither the Church nor a majority of American Catholics came to support the Blair bill, but they did praise the senator from New Hampshire for being a pioneering humanitarian in the field of education for the common man.[25]

Blair's odd way of reaching out to detractors by criticizing their religious, political, and socioeconomic views may or may not have been a wise strategy, but his choice of individual southerners to compare to the Jesuits definitely was not propitious. Both of the Mississippians mentioned, as well as the Magnolia State's other senator, Edmund Cary Walthall, actually favored the bill.[26] J. Z. George even spoke on its behalf a few days later, calling it (with all apparent sincerity) "a generous offer made by the Northern States to the Southern States."[27] Blair needed George on his team and very easily could have alienated the Mississippian by his ill-timed remarks about southern Democratic opposition.[28]

Once Blair had completed his speaking marathon, Charles Faulkner, a first-term junior senator of West Virginia, rose to initiate the verbal opposition. His state occupied the foremost position among those that Blair had mentioned as being heavily populated by uneducated "poor white trash." Unquestionably, West Virginia needed federal aid to improve its education system as much as any other state, yet Faulkner had shown no interest in fixing the state's pedagogical woes since joining the Senate. He had focused instead upon obtaining national regulation of the food and drug industries, a personal—and successful—crusade that foreshadowed the coming Progressive Movement of the early twentieth century. Regarding the Blair bill, he merely reflected the will of his constituency, arguing that it was unconstitutional. He declared that the only correct interpretation of the Constitution was the strict interpretation, which disallowed the growth of federal power through the "general welfare" clause. In taking this position on the establishment of a national system of education, Faulkner showed a double standard with regard to increasing the federal government's scope, for only by interpreting the general welfare clause broadly could he say that the federal government had the constitutional authority to regulate the food and drug industries. He believed that education was a different matter, however, not comparable to other issues, because the Founding Fathers had specifically forbidden federal interference with it. For emphasis, he invoked the names and writings of early national leaders James Madison, John Marshall, and Alexander Hamilton, who had all discussed education and had determined that it lay outside of federal jurisdiction. Moreover, he complained that the bill stemmed from socialistic roots. He noted accurately that a plan for redistributing the wealth of rich Americans to their poor neighbors lay at the heart of the Blair bill. Moving on to the next generation of venerable Americans of the past, Faulkner then quoted Andrew Jackson, Henry Clay, and Daniel Webster, who all agreed that the national government had power to collect taxes for national or interstate projects, but not to redistribute the money to the states or to the people. Most early American leaders had, therefore, forbade socialism or such socialistic schemes as this bill represented.[29]

Faulkner also complained that the Blair bill contained no provision for an equal distribution of funds to the races. Rather, it gave preeminence to black schools because they generally had the greatest need. He argued that such a policy violated the Fourteenth Amendment by showing favoritism based on race. He opposed what essentially is called today affirmative action. Not only was this policy wrong, said Faulkner, but if actual numbers of illiterates throughout the United States were taken into consideration rather than percentages of illiterates within each racial group, whites would be the main beneficiaries, for white illiteracy dwarfed black illiteracy in sheer numbers. Faulkner then concluded his speech with a glaring contradiction, proclaiming the Caucasian race the "superior and more intelligent race," adding that the black population represented nothing more than a "mass of ignorance" concentrated in the South.[30]

Senator Joseph Hawley of Connecticut, one of several curt but courtly New England Republicans in the Senate, answered Faulkner briefly. As a senator, Hawley focused mainly upon economic issues and thus never entered the ranks of the humanitarians within the GOP. He agreed with Faulkner's history lesson and conservative interpretation of the Constitution. He noted that many of his fellow Republicans, including Henry Blair, routinely misquoted Alexander Hamilton, the foremost broad constructionist among the Founding Fathers, using his interpretation of the "general welfare" clause to grow the power of the federal government in ways that neither Hamilton nor any of the other Founders ever envisioned. Hawley contended that Hamilton "never dreamed that the Federal Government should control the common schools."[31]

Richard Coke, the former Redeemer governor of Texas and current three-term U.S. senator, next declared his opposition to the bill. Coke, speaking with a distinctive lisp that made him pronounce the letter "s" as "th," mirrored Faulkner and Hawley's constitutionality argument, saying, "The powers delegated to Congress and those reserved to the States are absolutely fixed by the Constitution.... The States can not consent to a usurpation of their jurisdiction and powers by Congress." The lisp made it difficult for other senators to understand Coke and perhaps to listen intently enough to give any serious contemplation to his argument. Yet, Coke was more serious about conservative government than most of his peers. As governor of Texas he had dismantled the state-supported public school system that the Republicans built during Reconstruction, putting the schools back under county supervision. If he could have, he would have done the same for every state in the Union. There was no chance, therefore, of his accepting the Blair bill. He quoted Thomas Jefferson, who, like the other Founding Fathers, also excluded education from the powers granted to the national government. Coke noted that, as founder of the University of Virginia, Jefferson showed a more zealous passion for universal education than any other American who ever lived. If he did not support a national education system, what more needed to be said? What more was there to debate? How could any good American possibly support this bill? Could it be because some senators favored the United States imitating the European powers that provided national education systems? Indeed, thought Coke, because they favored the United States adopting the European model of "imperial centralization" and monarchical "paternalism" rather than living within the federalized framework of the Constitution.[32]

Leland Stanford of California, who was nothing if not the exact opposite of Coke in oratorical ability and leadership skills (one contemporary even called him the "greatest man in the world today"[33]), answered the Texan's charges. He countered that the people of northern Europe currently represented the vanguard of educated civilization. Criticizing the leading European education systems thus did not make sense. Perhaps the United States could learn from the European example in one way: during the time of the Roman Empire, the Latin leaders of Rome considered the Germanic tribes to be "so low down in the scale of humanity that it was almost impossible to think of civilizing them." Yet, once given the opportunity, they rose to a greater degree of civilization than the Romans ever imagined. Could history now be repeating itself, as white Americans pronounced judgment upon black Americans for being so far behind in the steps of human progress that they could never catch up? Stanford believed that with equal opportunities, any group of people could rise above its present condition. He not only favored the Blair bill, which would redistribute the wealth of his own class to the lower classes, but he also advocated that individuals take the initiative to make the world a better place by setting examples of personal sacrifice for the public good. Stanford, a multimillionaire railroad tycoon stood in a good position to lead by example and take such an initiative in education. He was putting the finishing touches on his own institution in

Palo Alto, California, even as he spoke. Stanford University would open in 1891. Yet, had he not been a rich man, he likely would have still favored education for the working man so that all could come to recognize and appreciate, as he put it, "the beneficence of God."[34]

Not everyone in the Senate could appreciate Stanford's lofty humanitarian rhetoric. Democrat John R. Reagan of Texas followed the Californian and rejected his comments as sentimental nonsense. He had spent his Senate career focusing on such economic issues to the exclusion of everything else, trying to lay the groundwork for the industrial development of Texas and the rest of the postwar South. He considered race questions to be an impediment to taking care of the more important economic business of the country.[35] His opinion of the Blair bill, therefore, was not generous. He charged that Blair portrayed the United States as being so illiterate and ignorant that it stood "in danger of going back into a state of barbarism" unless his bill passed. But who created this great republic, Reagan asked? Was it men who had attended a compulsory national school system, or was it men who had gained the free and liberal educations afforded by the family, the churches, and by self-help?[36] "What right has Congress to tax the people of Pennsylvania to educate the children of South Carolina, or the people of Ohio to educate the children of Mississippi, or the people of Iowa to educate the people of Texas?" Reagan concluded by cleverly criticizing the millionaire railroad tycoon Stanford without stepping beyond the confines of gentlemanly parliamentarianism and calling him by name. He instead used another railroad magnate, the notorious "robber baron" Jay Gould, as an example of someone who, although one of the richest men in the country, would pay the same amount of taxes to support public education under the Blair bill as the men who shoveled coal on his locomotives.[37]

Ephraim K. Wilson, a one-term senator from Maryland, who had an otherwise undistinguished career both before and after his six years in the Senate, followed Reagan in denouncing the bill. In his brief discourse, he quoted perhaps the most venerable educator in American history to that time, Horace Mann of Massachusetts, generally considered the father of the public school system in the United States. Mann believed that the Founding Fathers' exclusion of education from the Constitution left progressive-minded educators such as himself with no recourse but to work through the states, for only an amendment to the Constitution could change the situation. Wilson agreed, asking, if Congress succeeds in this attempt to defy the Constitution and tamper with education, what will be next? Such a small step might start a process that would ultimately lead to the evolution of a federal leviathan that forces its will upon the masses. He also asked, would American children eventually be indoctrinated with only that type of education which Congress authorizes? Could this seemingly small, innocuous step lead to other usurpations of the Constitution as well? What if Congress later came to disregard the constitutional prohibition on establishing a national public religion? Why should it be so unbelievable that such a thing could happen? Congressmen could argue that the nation would be better off if all Americans practiced the same religion. It would bring peace and stability to a chaotic system that currently sees some religious groups prosper while others struggle. Is not this analogy valid, the comparison appropriate, and the logic rational?[38]

John Coit Spooner, a second-term senator from Wisconsin, followed Wilson in declaring his opposition to the bill. The first Republican to denounce the bill, Spooner seemed an unlikely antagonist of federal aid to education because he identified with the reformers on most other issues, as the Federal Elections Bill debate would soon prove. A corporate attorney by vocation, he could wage a stiff battle in debate, and he certainly did so in opposing the Blair bill. He based his main objection upon the fact that his own state and several others provided quite adequately for education already. He saw no reason to change the present system—a system that worked well in states that stressed the value of education. In addition, the South was beginning to prosper materially to the point that it would soon need no outside help to catch up. Almost one million blacks attended the public schools in the South in 1890, which showed tremendous progress in southern education. Spooner agreed with Reagan, therefore, that taking money from his state of Wisconsin to educate the children of the South seemed neither fair nor necessary.[39]

Spooner habitually spoke kind words in Senate speeches and in the press about helping African Americans, but now that he had a genuine opportunity to help them get a better education, he balked. He justified his opposition by pointing out that public disapproval of the Blair bill had grown every year since the measure's initial introduction. He read from several leading newspapers to illustrate his point and commented that it would be foolish "to contend that the newspapers have entered into a conspiracy in favor of ignorance." Interestingly, one of his main sources was the *Charleston News and Courier,* which made a strange bedfellow for the Wisconsin Republican. It was the primary Democratic organ pushing the Butler Emigration Bill, which Spooner vehemently opposed. The South Carolina paper loathed the Blair bill with almost as much fervor as it supported the Butler bill. Throughout Blair's speaking marathon, it daily urged the New Hampshire senator to stop talking, for no one cared to hear what he had to say.[40]

Following Spooner, John S. Barbour of Virginia took the floor and gave his undivided approbation to the Blair bill, expressing incredulity that any sane southern senator would not do the same. He said that the argument over the strict versus broad construction of the Constitution was much ado about nothing. He pointed out how Thomas Jefferson, whom Democrats considered the father of their party, transgressed against his own political creed with the purchase of Louisiana, and how a southern Democratic Congress and president annexed Texas with equal disregard to strict construction of the Constitution. The fact is, Barbour propounded, southern Democrats had always abandoned the strict construction argument whenever it seemed in their best interest to do so.[41]

Midway through his talk, the old Virginia statesman turned and addressed the fiery young Charles Faulkner of West Virginia, no doubt giving him an icy stare. He pronounced with utter disdain his resentment of a West Virginian claiming to speak on behalf of the South. How could anyone from that state, which had sold out its fellow Virginians to the east in the Civil War, possibly claim to represent the southern point of view on any issue? Barbour then turned in the direction of John Coit Spooner on the Republican side and stated grimly, "This talk about the great wealth of the South is a delusion and an exaggeration. Where is it and in what does it consist?" He could not see it. All he saw was poverty, illiteracy, tenant farming, soil erosion, and a one-dimensional economy in the South. He pointed out how his own state of Virginia needed all the help it could get, federal or otherwise. He explained that when the Old Dominion gave up its claim to the Northwest Territory under the Articles of Confederation, it did so out of patriotic duty alone—it got nothing in return. Now that his state was inundated with a "mass of ignorance," caused, he said, by the emancipation of the slaves (the action of a president from one of the states created from that old Northwest Territory), it must be the patriotic duty of the emancipators to help educate the liberated blacks. It is nothing less than sickening, he added, that the state that gave the country George Washington, Thomas Jefferson, James Madison, and John Marshall had been reduced to the status of "a beggar."[42]

After Barbour, a few senators rose in short order to express either their support for or opposition to the bill, but none added any substantively new remarks. Closing the debate was the "iridescent" Republican John J. Ingalls of Kansas, who came out in opposition, saying that education would do southern blacks no good if they did not first have simple

Eulogy for the Blair Bill. Their only utility. . . . Good figures as Puck ever drew, He hates to bid farewell to you—And yet he stoutly must maintain That Puck's loss is the country's gain! (Puck, 1890.) The failure of the Blair Education Bill in the Fifty-first Congress marked a victory for the conservative approach to American education and arguably a defeat of social justice for African Americans.

justice. Therefore, forget the Blair bill, he said—bring on the Federal Elections Bill.[43]

The Federal Elections Bill was indeed on its way, but it would not be ready for the Senate's consideration for another nine months. In the meantime, the Senate voted to table the Blair bill, and the last hope for creating a national education system to benefit black southerners, not to mention poor whites in rural areas of the South, vanished for the next three decades. Blair, at every opportunity, perfunctorily reminded his opponents in the Senate of their coming eternal damnation for not passing his bill. When, in July 1890, the Senate debated a large appropriation for educating Native Americans in the West, Blair poignantly commented that "one cannot in listening to this debate fail to be struck with the fact that it is very much better to be an Indian [in terms of education] than to be . . . a citizen of the United States."[44]

Besides a few state Superintendents of Education, scattered educators, and Blair himself, African Americans were the primary mourners at the Blair bill's passing. T. Thomas Fortune urged his people not to grieve, however, but to consider the defeat of the bill as a wake-up call for self-help. He wisely urged his race not to wait for the federal government to endow them with education, but to educate themselves the best way they could. Booker T. Washington, among others, had already set this policy in motion and could now continue, undisturbed by competing ideas, educating black southerners. Three months after the Blair bill debate ended, the First Mohonk Conference on the Negro Question convened in New York state, and vocational education became the main topic of conversation there. The defeat of the Blair bill had basically served as a point of departure for the conference, as most participants seemed to know instinctively that there was no point in hoping for a renewal of interest in the type of plan that the Blair bill espoused. Most accepted the inevitable shift in the nation's focus on education toward vocational and moral instruction for blacks. As the Reverend R. H. Allen of Pittsburgh put it, "We speak of the Negro problem; . . . the solution of this problem is in the education of the hands and heads and hearts of this people. This will solve the problem of any race on the face of God's earth." To him, academic education was one of only three forms of instruction, and not more important than the other two, vocational and moral.[45]

In retrospect, T. Thomas Fortune's advice seems prophetic, Booker T. Washington's action appears appropriate, and the Mohonk Conference's focus looks right on target, because not until 1919 did a similar bill for federal aid to the public schools come up again in Congress. Other education bills did come up in the meantime, however. Justin Morrill, the elder statesman of Vermont, who had paved the way for subsequent congressional education legislation with his Land Grant Act of 1862, continued to advocate federal funding of colleges, even in 1890. The money would be divided between white and black colleges, but Morrill designed the bill mainly to support the latter. The debate over the Morrill bill was brief. The Senate did not want another long education debate in the same session. It passed the measure with haste. This Second Morrill Act, as it is now known, provided little consolation for supporters of the Blair bill, but it represented an important step in the forward march of America's educational development.[46]

Despite the failure of the Blair bill, Henry Blair's efforts to improve the nation's public education system forced a normally apathetic society to see the embarrassingly deplorable educational conditions that existed in many parts of the country. His work at the end of the Gilded Age thus ultimately provoked an overhauling of the education systems of the United States at the state and local levels during the coming Progressive Age of the early twentieth century. History has vindicated this senator from New Hampshire, therefore, as a visionary—a leader whose idea was ahead of its time.[47]

The defeat of the Blair bill marked a tragic turning point in both African American history and the history of education in America. Education simply did not garner the interest of the American public in 1890 that other issues did. More important, the idea of educating black southern children did not provoke the same level of public discussion and controversy as did other racial issues—namely emigration and enforcement of black voting rights. Specialists in the history of African-American education generally admit that the average black citizen at that time did not even care as much about education as they did about suffrage.[48] Only professional educators seemed to get excited about the issue. Black educator J. C. Price of Livingstone College, speaking at the National Education Association's Annual Convention in Minneapolis in July 1890, did not take a stance on whether vocational, religious, or academic education was the best solution for his people, but he took a strong stand on the belief that *some* kind of education was absolutely essential. "I do not argue," he said, "that increased intelligence, or multiplied facilities for education, will, by some magic spell, transform the negro into the symmetry, grace, and beauty of a Grecian embodiment of excellence. It is certainly not my humble task to attempt to prove that education will, in a day, or a decade, or a century rid the black man of all the physical peculiarities and deformities, moral perversions, and intellectual distortions which are the debasing and logical heritage of more than two and a half centuries of enslavement." But education would still be the solution to the race problem, he believed, because in it "an answer is to be found to all the leading objections against the negro which enter into the make-up of the so-called race problem." He continued:

> The great work of education among negroes consists in leading
> them out of the errors which centuries of debasing servitude

fastened upon them; but even when this is done, the negro will not be an embodiment of every moral excellence, but he will at least stand on the same plane of morals with the other representatives of our common and fallen humanity, and whatever is the possibility of one will be the possibility of the other, so far as education is concerned; for under it, we believe that the negro can be and do what any other race can be and do.[49]

For the Republican leadership of the Fifty-first Congress, both the education and emigration issues were merely unwanted distractions taking attention away from the most pressing item on their racial agenda, the Federal Elections Bill. Thus, in a matter of barely three months, the Fifty-first Congress had jettisoned two of the three potential solutions to the southern race problem. Federal supervision of elections, not education, said most GOP leaders, would be the salvation of black America. Both houses of Congress and the American public bid adieu to the education issue and girded up for the coming battle over the most controversial bill of its kind up to that time in the nation's history—the Federal Elections Bill.

Chapter 3

CHARTING NEW WATERS

The Race Problem and the "Reed Rules" in the House of Representatives

The "rights of the minority" have been so well protected that the rights of the majority have disappeared. . . . The contest over the rules is the first thing with which the Fifty-First Congress will be called on to deal.

—*Henry Cabot Lodge, Republican representative of Massachusetts*

The demand for the removal of the limitations in the rules means that the party in power is fatally bent on mischief.

—*Roger Q. Mills, Democratic representative of Texas*

While the Senate debated the emigration and education issues, House Republicans, led by new Speaker Thomas B. Reed of Maine, prepared to chart new waters in parliamentary procedure, changing hundred-year-old rules of debate. Although Reed did not design his new rules solely to ease passage of the humanitarians' racial agenda, the "Reed Rules," as they were known, had an immediate and dramatic impact on the House's attempts to solve the race problem. Understanding Reed's preliminary winter and spring cleaning of the House, which washed away the dusty old traditions, is thus central to establishing the context for the fight over the capstone of the humanitarian legislative agenda, the Federal Elections Bill.

Simply stated, the Reed Rules eliminated filibustering and other tactics of obstruction, such as disappearing quorums and endless roll calling, in the House. They allowed the majority party to secure passage of partisan bills, unimpeded by minority opposition.[1] The tradition of minority obstruction against partisan legislation was as old as Congress itself. Rarely did it impede legislation to the extent that it jeopardized the democratic process, although a notable exception occurred in the Fiftieth Congress. James B. Weaver of Iowa, who later became the first presidential candidate of the People's Party, blocked "the wheels of legislation for two weeks at a time," said one newspaper, in "an absurd recognition of the rights of a minority of one." Weaver's extremism in filibustering prompted much public discussion about changing the rules.[2]

The Republicans knew well that the minority could derail a majority's legislative agenda, because they had been the minority in the House almost constantly since Reconstruction, during which time they had become quite adept at filibustering on tariff issues. Before the convening of the Fifty-first Congress, therefore, a group of leading Republicans, which included Reed, future president of the United States William McKinley of Ohio, and future Speaker of the House Joseph Cannon of Illinois, agreed behind the scenes that their agenda was so important to the welfare of the country that they could not risk a Democratic filibuster. Moreover, they realized that the Democrats—particularly those from the South—would consider any bill for providing federal supervision of congressional elections to be highly partisan, sectional, and racially divisive and that such a bill would probably provoke a filibuster unlike any seen in the history of Congress. By passing the Reed Rules immediately upon convening, the House leadership could eliminate that threat before it could materialize. In so doing, however, they also created a storm of protest even before they introduced their highly controversial Federal Elections Bill, which made their racial agenda even more inflammatory than it would have otherwise been.[3]

Looking at Thomas B. Reed's background and record before 1890, the new Speaker seemed an unlikely candidate to lead the revolutionary reorganization of House rules. He grew up in a middle-class family in Maine. He had no distinguished record of military or political service before his election to the House in 1876. More important, during his twelve years of congressional service prior to his selection as Speaker, Reed had filibustered Democratic bills on several occasions, as had many other Republicans. He never expressed any compunction about his actions, however, despite the fact that his new rules now withheld the same tool from the opposition party that he and the GOP had often used when they were in the minority. How did he explain this double standard and apparent reversal of opinion on filibustering? He rationalized that, technically, each Congress had always established its own rules for conducting business. Just because previous congressional leaders had chosen to adopt the same rules as their forebears did not mean they were bound by the Constitution to do so. Likewise, each Congress voted on the rules it would adopt, and, therefore, the majority party in the House always chose the rules by which it would govern. If the Fifty-first Congress now chose to govern under new rules that would streamline the legislative process and bring greater efficiency to the operation of the federal government, why should anyone complain? Such an action lay completely within the constitutional authority of Congress.[4]

Moreover, each newly elected Congress established its own rules through a vote taken upon its first convening, which meant that the Speaker had no power to force rules arbitrarily upon the House. The Reed Rules, too, would be adopted only if a majority of representatives agreed to them. The power of the Speaker was thus limited. Each successive Speaker had, however, always been in a position to fine-tune the legislative process, and many had done so in one way or another. From 1811 to 1825, Henry Clay of Kentucky transformed the Speaker's role from that of a mere moderator of debate to that of a manipulator of partisan legislation, although he never abrogated the rights of the minority to hold the floor, as Reed now proposed. In 1836, Speaker James K. Polk, a Democrat from Tennessee, presided over his party's adoption of a controversial Gag Resolution that forbade the introduction of abolitionist legislation in the House. Both the Speaker's role and House rules remained fairly static thereafter until 1877, when, at the behest of Democrat John Reagan of Texas, who later became a senator, the House suspended the rules temporarily in order to pass a single railroad appropriation bill. In 1880, Democratic Speaker Samuel J. Randall instituted a series of special rules to regulate debate only on certain specified bills.[5] Precedents thus existed for the action that Reed planned to take as Speaker of the House.

More recently, Democrat John G. Carlisle of Kentucky, who served as Speaker from 1883 to 1889, increased the power of his position by refusing to hear debate on bills he opposed, such as the Blair Education Bill. Carlisle also believed adamantly in allowing the minority party to filibuster any bill at any time until compromise could be reached. This practice, which Republicans employed every time Democrats sought to lower the tariff, produced gridlock in the House. Indeed, the House passed few bills under Carlisle's watch except uncontroversial bipartisan measures.[6]

Carlisle, unlike Reed, never incurred the wrath of the minority party or the American public. His stoic demeanor, his ability to choose his words wisely, and his generally even-handed rulings from the chair contrasted sharply with Reed's personality and style of leadership. Whereas Carlisle had followed the custom of genteel parliamentarianism, "under which it is thought everything that is courteous is due to your adversary," Reed frequently found himself defending both his poor choices of words and the arrogance with which he expressed his opinion. Southerners, particularly, thought Reed guilty of what they perceived to be stereotypical northern "rudeness" in the Speaker's chair.[7]

Personalities aside, Reed believed that Carlisle took an overly conservative approach to the speakership, which perverted what the Founding Fathers had intended for the position. The Democrats had taken the old "tyranny of the majority" argument too far, he thought. As an avid student of history, Reed looked at the actions of the English Parliament at the time of the American Revolution to frame his opinion of what constituted tyranny. In his opinion, absolute rule by the majority did not automatically equate to tyranny. Rather, majority rule was the very essence of democracy. He also looked with equal interest at the contemporary procedures of the English democratic system in contrast to the American. Reed in fact used the English House of Commons, which did not allow obstructionist tactics, as a model for his future reformation of the American House of Representatives. He observed that the English custom required the minority party to sit in silence as the majority party legislated. This practice proved much more efficient than the American tradition of unlimited debate. "If time were eternity, or men were angels," said Reed, "there should be no limit to debate." But since neither was the case, limits should be set, and legislation should proceed with all due speed.[8]

English writers typically minced no words in berating American parliamentary procedures, and their opinion strongly influenced Reed as Speaker. Reed realized that, to Englishmen, the American House of Representatives had become something of a laughing stock. The Clerk of the English House of Commons, Reginald F. D. Palgrave, considered the minority party in America to be little more than a group of "jesters" who toyed with the majority party to the detriment of the nation. If such a thing occurred in Parliament, said Palgrave, "the national force which created the House of Commons would not for a moment tolerate such conduct."[9] Another English observer commented that "Legislation is government," and that the American minority should allow it to proceed. The minority party would simply have to console itself with the creed that "We are chastised with whips now, but when we become the majority, we will chastise them with scorpions."[10]

The day would surely come when the Democrats would be able to find solace in that motto, but at the moment, they refused to be consoled. Instead, they favored "twisting the lion's tail" and expressing their intense resentment of the British influence that Reed invited and welcomed into American politics. Some paranoid Democrats saw a nexus between the political philosophy of New England Republicans such as Reed and the Federalist Party of old, which called the infamous Hartford Convention during the War of 1812. The fact that many of Reed's New England contemporaries, including Henry Cabot Lodge of Massachusetts—whose great-grandfather, George Cabot, presided over the Hartford Convention—rushed to the new Speaker's support, exacerbated the Democrats' suspicion that the Republicans wanted to inch America back into the British Empire.[11] As did the musings of Massachusetts Congressman Benjamin F. Butler, who actually made a public speech in 1889 arguing that all English-speaking peoples of the earth should unite into one nation (whereby they would find it easier, essentially, to rule the world).[12]

Although Lodge, as the primary author of the House version of the Federal Elections Bill, would become the main beneficiary of the Reed Rules, midwesterners such as William McKinley of Ohio, author of the McKinley Tariff of 1890, and Jonathan H. Rowell of Illinois, a coauthor of the Federal Elections Bill, held just as much responsibility for pressing and sustaining the Reed Rules as any New Englander. McKinley, who would become president of the United States in 1896, made himself an easy target by supporting the new rules while simultaneously admitting that he had filibustered silently in his House seat for the past twenty years. He claimed in 1890 to have suddenly seen the error of his ways, declaring, "I cannot now recall that I ever did it for a high or noble or worthy purpose." Democratic representative "Private" John Allen of Mississippi, ever ready to turn a phrase for entertainment and dramatic effect, answered spontaneously, "Then he must have done it for a low, ignoble, or unworthy purpose.... I want to say to the gentleman that when I have filibustered it has always been for a high and worthy purpose."[13]

Public opinion was divided over the wisdom of Reed's new House rules, but the critics vocalized their opposition far more than the supporters proclaimed their views. To most observers, the whole idea of the majority forcing its will upon the minority seemed somehow un-American. The fact that such a numerical parity existed between the two parties, both in Congress and in the electorate, made the Reed Rules look especially unfair. In fact, the Democratic minority in the House actually represented 100,000 more voters than the Republican majority.[14] Many Americans, therefore, incredulous of the nerve of Reed and the rest of the GOP leadership in the House, complained, as did one New England newspaper, that "To all intents and purposes, a half-dozen men are making laws for sixty millions of people."[15]

That statement contained a grain of truth, but it exaggerated the ratio. The number of men making the laws was closer to a dozen than a half-dozen, because the Reed House could affect national policy only by working in conjunction with the Harrison administration and leading Republicans of the Senate. Yet, the sheer volume of business that the House conducted in 1890 gave the appearance that Reed and his lower chamber cronies possessed more power than the president and the Senate combined. Indeed, the House passed so many bills, thanks to the Reed Rules, that the docket in the Senate quickly became backlogged beyond all hope of being emptied before the Fifty-first Congress adjourned. The Reed House proved to be, without a doubt, the most active legislative body in United States history to that point.[16]

The Reed Rules directly and instantaneously affected the course of legislation regarding the southern race problem. The House applied the new rules, with dramatic results, to settle seventeen contested elections, ten of which involved African American candidates or ballots. One of these cases, in fact, provided the first opportunity for Reed to implement his new rules, because it arose on the first day of business in the first session. In each of the cases, a Republican candidate had lost a congressional race in 1888 and had challenged the results based on corruption or intimidation of Republican voters by Democrats, Independents, or Farmers' Alliance candidates (whose party allegiance was unascertainable). In three cases, the defrauded Republican was black, but in at least ten of the cases, the victor had won by disfranchising blacks or discounting their ballots. The rest of the cases originated in northern or border states where race made little difference in the outcome. In all cases, however, the Republicans stood to gain an even greater majority by unseating the victorious Democrat. Reed, therefore, set strict time limits for debating each case, and in most instances, the evidence seemed clear enough on the surface that Reed allowed only one day for testimony and the vote. The House resolved the first case, *Smith v. Jackson*, which involved two white West Virginians, in one day. Much to the dismay of the Democrats, Reed called for a vote and

Czar Reed. Her new champion—another case of 'elective affinity.' (*Puck,* 1890.) The man chosen Speaker of the House for the Fifty-first Congress, Thomas B. "Czar" Reed (R-Maine), is shown here as the new "plumed knight of Maine," having out-jousted James G. Blaine for the honor. Indeed, Reed became a much more powerful Speaker than Blaine had ever been.

counted Democrats present but not voting. This ruling caused pandemonium on the Democratic side of the chamber, as various representatives wailed and gnashed their teeth in protest, but the minority had no power to stop the vote.[17]

Reed justified the decision to implement his new rules in the *Smith v. Jackson* case by commenting quite insouciantly that it would be impossible to "conceive anything more dreary" than hearing protracted election cases in the House. Moreover, no one listened to the testimony anyway, he explained, because contested election cases represented the only truly and absolutely partisan issues that the House ever voted upon, and members almost invariably voted along party lines. Besides, he added, there had been about seventy-five such contested elections since Reconstruction, costing taxpayers a total of $318,000 and a full six months of wasted time. In Reed's opinion, only those cases that involved something more than the usual degree of corruption or intimidation, such as criminal misconduct on the part of one of the candidates or the death of one of the candidates, deserved that kind of time and expense.[18]

Two such cases came out of Arkansas, and both involved murder. In the case of *Featherston v. Cate,* the winner William H. Cate, a regular Democrat, had, through alleged misconduct, defeated the incumbent L. P. Featherston, an Arkansas Wheel Democrat backed by the Farmers' Alliance and the Republicans. This case also involved the murder of three of Featherston's supporters. After three days of testimony, Reed called for a vote, whereupon the House unseated Cate and seated Featherston in his place.[19] In the case of *Clayton v. Breckinridge,* the Republican John Clayton had been mysteriously murdered after the election while gathering evidence to prove that his opponent, Clifton R. Breckinridge, had won by fraud. Breckinridge took his seat in the House, after which he spoke and voted freely for nearly the entire first session while his case dragged on. The House took up his case and laid it aside several times for lack of conclusive evidence. In the end, however, the Republicans finally unseated Breckinridge, although they never proved that he had any direct involvement in Clayton's murder.[20]

One of the most spectacular of the contested election cases, *Langston v. Venable,* came, as did the vote on *Clayton v. Breckinridge,* after the Federal Elections Bill had already passed the House. It thus had no impact on the outcome of that bill, but the humanitarians hailed it as a great triumph nonetheless because it replaced a white Democrat with a black Republican. The House unseated the Democrat Edward C. Venable and awarded the contested seat to black Republican John Mercer Langston of Virginia. In a show of protest against this verdict (which was based upon sketchy evidence of Democratic vote fraud), the Democrats completely vacated the House on the day Langston was sworn in.[21]

The Reed Rules in general, but particularly the use of them in unseating Democrats in the early contested election cases, made the acrimony between the parties much more pronounced than it would otherwise have been going into the Federal Elections Bill fight. Reed and company cared not what the minority party thought, however. They knew they had a unique opportunity to rectify problems with black voting rights that had gone unaddressed for fifteen years and that could not be addressed successfully in any other way than by the use of political force. Experience proved as much. Voting fraud and political corruption had been rampant in the United States throughout Reconstruction and the Gilded Age. The Fifteenth

Amendment had been violated and practically rendered impotent in the parts of the South where it was most sorely needed. Although it was universally understood that the Republicans had passed the Fifteenth Amendment especially to benefit southern blacks, the South did not possess a monopoly on hatred of the new law. Court cases had also arisen in Kansas and Oregon to test the Amendment within weeks of its ratification in 1870.[22]

Although discrimination against black voters in the South was common knowledge, the Republicans lost the ability to do anything about it after losing their hegemony in the federal government in 1874. The federal courts, meanwhile, continued to rule upon cases that clarified and, in effect, limited the applications of the Fifteenth Amendment. The Radical Republicans still tried, however, to enforce the voting rights of blacks in the South. They managed to pass Charles Sumner's Civil Rights Bill postmortem in 1875 and at the same time passed a Federal Elections Bill in the House, which did not pass the Senate as a result of a Democratic filibuster. Thereafter, with Democrats in charge of one or more branches of the federal government, nothing substantial had been done to protect black voting rights.[23]

Sensing a golden opportunity to end a dozen years of Democratic resistance to Republican prerogatives, Reed and the GOP leadership in Washington, D.C., decided that they could solve the race problem with a Federal Elections Bill and push their economic agenda through in the same Congress. Using the Reed Rules, such a course of action would certainly be possible, and seemed likely to prove successful. Yet, serious complications immediately surfaced that GOP leaders evidently neither foresaw nor considered very carefully thereafter. The main one was that public opinion overwhelmingly favored leaving the issue of black voting rights alone. This sentiment had begun toward the end of Reconstruction and had continued to grow. In fact, by 1890, the pendulum of public opinion had swung so far away from protecting black voting rights that many newspaper editors and pundits began seriously discussing repealing the Fifteenth Amendment. While such a measure seemed too radical for most Americans' taste, lack of federal action to fix the nation's ailing political system between 1875 and 1890 nonetheless enjoyed a tacit popularity within white America on the eve of the Federal Elections Bill debate.[24]

There are at least seven reasons for white America's popular, albeit silent, approval of the so-called let alone policy. The first reason—and most commonly cited at the time—is that the vast majority of the American people, regardless of party affiliation, were weary of Reconstruction and ready to move on to other issues, particularly those involving the economic growth and development of the nation. In powerful, poetic language, one disgruntled Democrat summed up the feeling of a majority of Americans about the tired, worn-out issues of Reconstruction, reminiscing that "the years unfolded reconstruction to the astonished gaze of civilization. It came grinding across the face of the earth for seven dreary winters, for seven desolate summers, for seven blighted springs, and seven barren autumns, before it pulled its slimy length away."[25] Democratic voters in neither the North nor the South had ever wanted the type of Reconstruction that the Radical Republicans seemed determined to bring about, which granted citizenship and voting rights to blacks. Likewise, only about half of the Republicans ever truly committed themselves to Reconstruction for genuine humanitarian reasons. The other half of the party had merely found it expedient to protect blacks temporarily in order to prevent the freedmen's reenslavement, and they were more than glad to abandon blacks once they thought that danger had passed. By 1890, only a small, frustrated group of humanitarians remained to continue advocating racial equality, and even the most dedicated of them had begun to second-guess the wisdom of their egalitarian policy. Virtually every Republican, no matter which wing of the party he belonged to, could agree on economic growth, however, as the issue to bring sectional reconciliation to the bitterly divided nation. The American public concurred.[26]

Because of the widespread public disdain for the memory of Reconstruction, a major part of the Democrats' strategy to combat the humanitarians' racial agenda rested upon a plan to bewail the evils of that odious twelve-year span of American history at every opportunity. Some southern Democrats feared that an entire generation of northerners had come of age since Reconstruction who had no knowledge of that dreadful period and were otherwise completely ignorant about the issues of recent American history. A campaign of education (propaganda) was thus in order. As one Georgian explained to John Tyler Morgan, "I never met a northerner who had any conception of the doings of the carpetbagger. What we need is for you to tell 'the story over again' to unfamiliar ears. It needs to be a revelation."[27] Morgan happily obliged, as did many other Democrats, during the Federal Elections Bill debate, rambling for untold hours about the horrors of black and Republican rule in the 1860s and 1870s in the deep South.

Another reason for the general public's acquiescence to their nation's broken political system was that, oddly, many Americans of this generation viewed politics as some type of high stakes game. As such, campaigns and elections were supposed to be fun. Politicians, especially in the House, certainly seemed to enjoy making light of serious national problems on occasion. For example, when Democratic Congressman Roswell P. Flower of New York declared nonchalantly in a routine speech that the Democrats favored a "free ballot and a fair count," the Republicans chuckled in unison, amused that the Tammany Hall New Yorker had the gumption to make such an absurd statement while keeping a straight face. Flustered by the irreverent response, Flower reiterated the same statement more earnestly and forcefully. The chuckles grew to loud laughter. Becoming utterly embarrassed and trying to stave off complete public ridicule, Flower attempted a third time to prove his sincerity, adding volume and histrionics for dramatic effect. The laughter on the Republican side turned into a deafening roar. As Flower struggled to salvage his dignity, the Republicans goaded him on. They loved watching a member of the other party wither under the pressure of national humiliation. Finally, after Flower had apparently become visibly shaken and seemed to have reached his lowest ebb, a voice from the crowded chamber exclaimed, "I ask unanimous consent that his picture be taken." The Republicans erupted with side-splitting laughter. This game of politics was clearly good entertainment. The fact that the nation's leaders could laugh and joke at one another's expense about the corruption in the political system as it stood must have only increased the ambivalence that most Americans felt about changing it.[28]

Some people, however, did not see politics so much as a game of entertainment as a game of war. If, occasionally, someone got injured or killed in a war game, such misfortune was to be expected. It seemed to be a natural, unavoidable by-product of the system that some people would cheat at the game and others would be hurt in it. This cynical rationalization led many otherwise honest and upright citizens to conclude that there was nothing criminal or even unethical about guile and treachery within the realm of politics. Winning elections involved matching wits with the opponent and outfoxing him, not only in debates on issues, but also in underhanded electioneering when necessary. The party that could lie, cheat, bribe, or steal the most efficiently without getting caught would win, and it deserved to win. In essence, therefore, the Social Darwinist philosophy that pervaded this age was applicable to politics as well as to society. The smartest (most conniving) candidate would—and rightfully should—prevail, and the strongest (most impervious to criticism and investigation) would—and rightfully should—dominate.[29]

Although only a small percentage of Americans consciously believed that this natural order should not be disturbed, more expressed uncertainty about whether it should be, and most did not care one way or another. Apathy was thus a third reason for toleration of the decrepit political system. Most Americans simply did not feel directly threatened by crimes against the ballot because such problems always seemed to appear in other people's districts, not in their own. They saw that the main region suffering from this political infection was the South, which made it distant and, in a sense, foreign to most non-southerners. Only in the rare cases where a large number of white people in a given district in the Northeast or Midwest felt betrayed or defrauded in an election would there be a public outcry to change the system. Indeed, electoral depravity was not ubiquitous nationally, although all states suffered from it occasionally. It arose only in certain pockets and boroughs in some states, and different states experienced it from one election to the next. Between 1888 and 1890, Indiana, Michigan, Nebraska, New Hampshire, New York, and Ohio, as well as more than half of all southern and border states, caught the contagion of ballot corruption. More often than not, the voting fraud virus in the northern states was quarantined within the cities and rarely infected the rural areas. As a rule, the abuses in the South were confined to particular congressional districts that may have been either rural or urban, but usually those districts contained large black populations. Later in the 1890s and early 1900s, most of these heavily black districts would see their African American voters disfranchised across the board.[30]

A fourth reason for the tacit approbation was that not all of the manipulation of the system came in the obvious forms of buying and selling votes, miscounting and discounting ballots, driving voters away from the polls, or other such egregious abuses. More subtle methods of changing the outcome of elections could be just as effective. For example, gerrymandering, a milder and less offensive form of political decadence, ran rampant in both the North and the South, and both major political parties practiced it equally. This partisan maneuver of state legislatures drawing or redrawing congressional districts to give advantage to the party already in power did not emerge as a post-Reconstruction development, of course. Founding Father Elbridge Gerry gave the practice its name by promoting such redistricting in Massachusetts in 1812 to favor the Jeffersonian Republicans. In 1888, Massachusetts was still gerrymandered, only now in favor of the GOP.[31] One Democrat went so far as to make the distorted claim that, "No such Congressional and legislative gerrymandering has been continued or enforced elsewhere in the world as that existing in New England for Republican benefit. . . . Republicans have all of the twelve senators from New England and twenty-three out of twenty-six representatives," despite the fact that two-fifths of the electorate voted Democrat. How could that be so, charged Democrats, without gerrymandering?[32] Indeed, in Massachusetts in 1888, 178,000 Republicans elected ten congressmen while 151,000 Democrats elected just two. Actually, the reasons for this oddity are much more complicated than merely deliberate redistricting to favor the GOP. The fact that the vast majority of those Democrats were concentrated in Boston while the rural parts of the state contained more Republicans mainly accounts for the lopsidedness in Massachusetts.

Many other states and regions showed even more seriously skewed districts in favor of one party or the other. In Kansas, for instance, 182,000 Republicans elected seven congressmen, while 105,000 Democrats elected none. Pennsylvania and Illinois both appeared similarly skewed in favor of the GOP, while Indiana, Ohio, Mississippi, and South Carolina seemed just as unfairly twisted in favor of the Democrats. Tennessee and Maryland looked partially disfigured, while Iowa had extremely and egregiously irregular districts. Because the practice of carving up states in such ways had become so widespread, federal lawmakers began to discuss the possibility of taking redistricting power away from the states and giving it to Congress. But as one contemporary authority noted, doing so "would only exchange State gerrymandering for national gerrymandering" at the hands of whichever party happened to be in power in Washington at the time. Since there seemed to be no solution to this problem and since both parties were equally culpable, many Americans must have rationalized that they might just as well remain indifferent to the problem and let the parties battle it out in elections.[33]

The fifth reason for public reticence about changing the system was that the Republicans, who were the ones calling for reform, lacked credibility as reformers in the eyes of more than half of the American electorate. To most Americans it was clear that Republicans had been guilty of demagoguery on racial issues in the past. Democrats preferred, of course, to call it hypocrisy. At the same time that the GOP busied itself with forcing black suffrage on the South during Reconstruction, several Union states engaged in internal struggles that resulted in their rejection of black voting rights. Moreover, California, Delaware, Indiana, Kentucky, Maryland, Michigan, Pennsylvania, Ohio, and Oregon, all found it more difficult to ratify the Fifteenth Amendment than did any former Confederate state. Even after ratification, many white northerners and westerners continued to resent black suffrage. Some abolitionists-turned-humanitarians even came out publicly in second-guessing the wisdom of passing the amendment.[34] Moreover, after one Republican Congress gave the right of suffrage to blacks in Washington, D.C., a subsequent Republican Congress rescinded that right. Democratic Congressman William McAdoo of New Jersey marveled at this action-counteraction, which appeared to him to be a brazen example of Republican duplicity, declaring:

> If the colored citizen has the virtue which his friends claim for him and which I trust he possesses, then there is no better theater in the world for him to vindicate his right to rule and to wisely administer government and to show his power, wisdom, and self-restraint than to give him the ballot, surrounded, as he is, by the best environments, in this city. There is no claim that the negro is bulldozed in the District of Columbia. He is given every facility for education. He is surrounded with colleges for his special benefit; the most intelligent of his race are here.[35]

In addition to Republican duplicity on racial matters, the Democrats could criticize with equal truth and effect the many financial scandals that occurred under Republican auspices at the national, state, and local levels during Reconstruction. Southern Democrats could also rail against northerners of both parties for numerous instances of horrible political corruption in the big cities above the Ohio River and the Mason-Dixon Line.[36]

Moreover, the would-be reform party reeked from the stench of corruption at the ballot box after the 1888 elections. Besides the gerrymandering that, in part, helped produce the Republican majority in the House, Benjamin Harrison had won his electoral college victory (as Democrats saw it) only because of frauds perpetrated in Indiana and New York, the same two states that, incidentally, had propelled Grover Cleveland into the White House in 1884 through Democratic fraud. If the GOP indeed won in 1888 only because of fraud, as Democrats charged, this retaliatory strike was certainly the choreographed workings of the chairman of the Republican National Committee (RNC), Senator Matthew Quay of Pennsylvania. His only job as RNC chairman was to place as many states in the GOP column as possible, one way or another. Quay expected the Democrats to perpetrate their usual frauds in the election, so he must have rationalized that the Republicans should do the same, but do it more efficiently.[37] In fact, that seems to have been the case.

In the most shocking incident of apparent fraud in 1888, Democrats accused RNC treasurer William W. Dudley of Indiana, a close, personal friend of Benjamin Harrison, of buying the votes of "floaters" (uncommitted voters who sold their votes to whichever party bid the highest for them) with money donated by wealthy Pennsylvania businessman John Wanamaker.

Upon his election as president, Harrison immediately rewarded Wanamaker with the office of postmaster general of the United States. Dudley was tried in federal court, but the judge resigned amid the trial, allegedly under pressure from Quay and Harrison, and his replacement, a Harrison friend and appointee, dismissed the case on a technicality.[38]

In two other cases resulting from the 1888 elections, Mississippi Democrats caught local Republicans allegedly tampering with ballot boxes, but rather than being reprimanded by the RNC, the Republican Congress, or the Harrison administration, they were rewarded with government jobs. In one, Democrats accused a Republican operative named J. M. Little of rigging a ballot box to favor his party's candidate. Upon Harrison's victory, Little quickly moved to Washington, D.C., where the new president appointed him to an undisclosed, low-level civil service job, which he held throughout the remainder of the Harrison administration. In the other case, a newspaper editor identified only by his surname Sansby allegedly stole confidential documents from the Democratic executive committee in Mississippi, took them to Washington, and handed them over to Matthew Quay in exchange for an appointment as consul to Equador.[39]

Quay's political tactics were, therefore, if not altogether illegal, at least highly questionable. They appeared so detestable that even some fellow Republicans, such as Carl Schurz, a Missourian who had served as President Rutherford B. Hayes's secretary of interior, caustically criticized them. Schurz accused Quay of borrowing $200,000 from the Pennsylvania state treasury in order to speculate in the stock market for his own personal gain. The money evaporated in the market, leaving Quay unable to repay the treasury. He would have gone to jail except that wealthy friends came to his rescue, replenishing the depleted treasury. To Schurz, Quay had acted shamefully and had disgraced the GOP. Indeed, he lamented the fact that Quay represented his party, "the party of great ideas . . . the party of Lincoln and Sumner."[40]

Throughout 1889 and 1890, the press, needless to say, made fodder of Quay's dirty deals, but the Republican boss refused to answer his critics publicly. "The charges were made months ago . . . by entirely responsible parties," said the *New York World,* a Democratic organ, but Quay "remained silent in face of the fact that a distinguished man of his own party declared in Congress that his silence was confession. After all these months he offers the Senate and the country only his unsupported word that he is innocent, and his declaration that the crimes alleged were committed by his partner, who is now dead and therefore unable to answer."

A Republican organ, the *Philadelphia Inquirer,* answered on behalf of the Keystone State senator, however, saying, "The attacks were begun in the *New York World,* a newspaper that lives on sensations and cares nothing for their truth or falsity." An Independent paper, the *New York Herald,* not surprisingly, took the most objective view of Quay's personality, politics, and possible perjury, saying, "Quay is no better and no worse than others of his class, Democratic and Republican. He is a professional trickster and wire-puller, chosen to lead because he is untroubled by scruples and undisturbed by conscience."[41]

Of the three editorial opinions, the latter seems most likely the correct one. Quay merely exemplified and personified the corruption that ran roughshod throughout the American political scene during the Gilded Age. Yet, he tarnished the Republican Party more than it could bear at a time when its purity was most necessary. His actions on behalf of the GOP left pundits asking, rightly, could a party guilty of such crimes against democracy possibly clean up American politics? Could a party so notorious for its money scandals reasonably pass judgment upon the party of civil rights violators? This party had, after all, been racked by scandals and imbroglios of one type or another off and on since Abraham Lincoln's death. Now, under the backstage leadership of Matthew Quay, the corruption appeared to have reached an all-time high. Many, if not most, fair-minded observers did not deem this party qualified to sit in judgment of the Democrats. As one northern newspaper put it, the Republican Party talking about purifying the ballot was like "the devil quoting scripture."[42]

The sixth reason for the national public acceptance of the status quo can be identified, in a name, as Henry Woodfin Grady. If any one person influenced northerners to accept the southern racial point of view it was this unlikely young newspaper editor from Atlanta. Like a shooting star, Grady appeared on the scene of history only briefly before burning out in a tragic blaze of glory. Before 1886, he had been known only regionally, and then simply as a typical southern Democratic newspaperman. He became an instant national celebrity in December 1886, however, when he gave his first major after-dinner speech outside of the South. That speech, delivered at the New England Society meeting in New York City, he entitled "The New South." It contained a twofold message: first, that northern investors should continue to help promote the rapid industrialization of the South, which had begun in earnest after Reconstruction; and second, that the South should be left alone to deal with its race problem in its own way. Neither message was new, and neither originated in the mind of this young Atlantan, but Grady had an uncanny way with words and audiences. He wooed the wealthy, elite, Republican crowd with praise for all of their virtues of thrift, enterprise, intelligence, and humanitarianism, and with a call for sectional reconciliation and brotherly love between northerners and southerners. He convinced listeners with his calm, tactful, and often humorous style that the race problem would solve itself once the South attained its economic goals.[43]

Although a few northern skeptics challenged Grady's racial assumptions, none questioned the correctness of his economic agenda. Among the skeptics were William Tecumseh Sherman, who also spoke that night in New York, and the "iridescent" Republican bloody-shirt-waver Senator John J. Ingalls of Kansas, who later lambasted excerpts of Grady's speech on the floor of the Senate. Some prominent southerners, including the South's most famous editor, Henry Watterson of the *Louisville Courier-Journal,* also criticized Grady, accusing him of selling out his people by inviting more "carpetbagger" industrialists to move to the South. Despite these few notable exceptions, the general public immediately accepted Grady's message as gospel and quickly hoisted him above his peers to become the "Spokesman of the New South." He was only thirty-six years old.[44]

Active in Georgia politics, Grady could have easily won office at some high level in the state had he chosen to run. He reasoned, however, that he could have more impact on public opinion as a writer and orator than as a lawmaker. He was probably correct. He declined the opportunity to be considered by the national Democratic Party as a potential running mate for Grover Cleveland in 1888. Yet, had he lived until 1892, he might very well have become the vice president of the United States. But Grady died unexpectedly in December 1889 at the age of thirty-nine, shortly after delivering his finest public address. He spoke at the Boston Merchants' Association annual banquet to an audience that included Grover Cleveland and Andrew Carnegie, among other national celebrities. Despite suffering from a severe case of pneumonia, Grady made the trip from Atlanta to Boston in the dead of the New England winter. As contemporary writer Joel Chandler Harris observed, "he stood beneath the shadow of Bunker Hill," where resided the nation's strongest bulwark of civil rights sentiment, and made a final passionate plea for the North to leave the South's race problem alone. In anticipation of the coming Federal Elections Bill, and in what amounted to his dying breath, he justified the suppression of the black vote as a necessity rather than a choice. In essence, Grady explained that the South must first make some major economic progress, even catch up with New England in industrial development and diversification, before it could worry about elevating the condition of its black population. The overwhelmingly Republican audience, whether out of agreement with his message or out of appreciation for his courage and determination to deliver it in spite of his illness, cheered and applauded the Georgian. Some even wept.[45]

Grady's last speech, like his first, invited immediate protest from true humanitarians, yet when this southern star died on his trip home to Atlanta, even his most adamant critics mourned. As is so often the case with controversial public figures, his reputation in death became greater than his accomplishments in life. The money-minded Republicans of the Billion Dollar Congress, some of whom had been among those who first instituted the "let alone" policy in the South that ended Reconstruction, embraced Grady's memory by letting his message be the final word on the South's race problem. Many northerners quietly acquiesced, while many others expressed their outright and emphatic approval.[46]

The seventh reason for the tacit acceptance of the ailing American political system in 1890 was that, despite all of the problems associated with the use of the ballot, the United States still enjoyed by far the most democratically representative government in the world. In the national electorate as a whole, only 14 percent of the total male voting age population was denied the right of suffrage. While blacks comprised the largest single group counted in this 14 percent, Native Americans, Chinese and other new immigrants, criminals, and the mentally ill comprised the rest. Furthermore, black disfranchisement was not nearly as pronounced at the beginning of the decade of the 1890s as it later became. In fact, four southern states—Georgia, North Carolina, Tennessee, and Virginia—had actually experienced growth in the number of black voters between 1876 and 1890. More curiously, the number of Republican congressmen representing former Confederate states had grown from three in 1880 to thirteen in 1890. Such trends did not go unnoticed by the American public. Who could have known in 1890 that these trends would suddenly be reversed in the coming decade? Considering such patterns and taking all other factors into consideration, no other nation came close to accomplishing what the United States had done in building a representative democracy. The next closest nation, England, by comparison, still disallowed some 40 percent of voting age males the right to vote in 1890. When viewed in this respect, it becomes more understandable why the American people did not give their representatives in Washington a mandate to change the system.[47]

Without a popular mandate, Czar Reed and the Republican House had no hope of creating a bipartisan coalition to pass a Federal Elections Bill that everyone could tolerate. If change was to be made, therefore, it would have to be accomplished by Reed and the GOP acting unilaterally and forcing the issue, not by following public opinion. Urged on by President Harrison and a small contingent of humanitarian politicians and writers, Reed and company in the House thus determined to mount a crusade to clean up the system, particularly to enforce the Fifteenth Amendment in the South. Enforcing black voting rights would salvage the dignity of the party that had passed the amendment, and it would instill in the American public a renewed respect for the U.S. Constitution, which had been rapidly waning as a result of violations of the amendment. More important, said the humanitarians, it would simply be the right thing to do ethically. It would finish what the Republican Party had started some three decades before. Most important of all, however, black southerners represented by far the largest bloc of potential Republican voters in the nation, and with the full power of their vote behind the party's white vote of the North, the GOP's majority would be perpetuated for the foreseeable future. This, of course, was a fact that the reformers did not usually want to admit, but which was indubitably true.[48] Thus came one of the most remarkable showdowns between opposing parties and ideologies in America's political history, the epic fight over the Federal Elections Bill, and the House of Representatives would be the first theater of war in this great clashing of minds.

Chapter 4

THE VERY INSANITY OF DEMOCRACY

The Federal Elections Bill and the Return to Reconstruction in the House of Representatives

They say it is a force bill. . . . If things are crooked, a little force possibly will not be hurtful.

—*Edmund Waddill Jr., Republican representative of Virginia.*

It should be entitled "An act to stir up strife and cause bloodshed in the South."

—*Samuel W. Peel, Democratic representative of Arkansas.*

The formulation of the Federal Elections Bill did not originate with the convening of the Fifty-first Congress. Since the election of Grover Cleveland to the presidency in 1884, Republicans had considered sundry plans by which Congress might best protect the voting rights of black southerners. Leading the effort was William E. Chandler, a first-term senator from New Hampshire who had previously worked closely with the Hayes, Garfield, and Arthur administrations to find a remedy for suffrage abuses in the South. The solution that GOP leaders agreed upon during that eight-year period was to keep a watchful eye on the South but not to intervene. It would essentially be a time to test the South to see how much, or how little, white

85

southerners could be trusted to play fair in elections. Chandler, like many of his northern Republican colleagues, greatly doubted that such a gesture of goodwill toward the South would produce the desired outcome. The Cleveland victory in 1884, which resulted at least partly from black disfranchisement and ballot box fraud in the South, convinced Chandler that this soft approach would not work. He, in turn, helped convince many of his fellow Republicans who were vacillating between humanitarianism and economic concerns that controlling southern elections was an absolute necessity. Chandler took the moral high road and told his colleagues that no one could rightly consider himself a Republican if he did not support enforcing the Fifteenth Amendment. He also convinced many of his colleagues, including presidential candidate Benjamin Harrison, to campaign on the issue in 1888. By the beginning of the Harrison administration, the New Hampshire firebrand had already begun applying pressure to southern Democrats to clean up their act. He documented the abuses of the black vote in the South with a massive amount of evidence, which he dutifully presented to the Senate.[1] Republicans from all over the South eagerly helped Chandler in his quest to document the abuses. Dozens wrote to him, supplying him with eyewitness accounts and local newspaper reports of racial atrocities. African Americans appreciated Chandler's efforts immensely. One even went so far as to call him "the greatest man in the United States" because of his incessant labor on behalf of the downtrodden black race.[2]

In addition to the efforts of Chandler, writer Albion "Judge" Tourgee, a former carpetbagger justice of the Superior Court in North Carolina during Reconstruction, also worked behind the scenes to stir the humanitarian element of the party to action in 1888. Tourgee stood among the few Republicans who remained unshakeably radical in their racial views throughout their lives. He had never allowed the bloody shirt to be put away and had never accepted the "let alone" policy after Reconstruction. After the election of the Republican majority in 1888, however, he made an even stronger stand against southern ballot injustices. He wrote widely read articles in newspapers and magazines and met frequently with President Harrison, Speaker Reed, and other Republican leaders to help them formulate a uniform policy on the race problem.[3] He felt great anticipation about the work to be done by the Republican Congress, saying with all confidence, "For the Negro in the United States, the year 1890 is destined to be the most important . . . since the black man first touched . . . the ballot."[4]

Joining the crusade with Chandler and Tourgee were Murat Halstead, a Cincinnati newspaper editor, and southern writer George Washington Cable, both of whom hoped to rekindle the dying embers of humanitarianism in the Republican Party. Together, this small group of activists sold the idea of electoral reform to the inner sanctum of the Republican Party and publicized it in the news media at a time when most Americans had deliberately chosen to ignore the problem. They succeeded in stirring the righteous indignation of the GOP and public opinion in the North to such an extent that 1889 to 1891 became the high-water mark of interest in the race problem in post-Reconstruction America (excluding, of course, the civil rights movement of the 1950s and 1960s). Even Frederick Douglass, who had lived through the slave era, the Civil War, and Reconstruction, recognized that at no other time in his life had the race issue been more acute than during and immediately after the election of 1888.[5]

Once Chandler and his fellow crusaders succeeded in restoring public interest in the race problem, others quickly joined their cause. In his inaugural address, President Harrison came forward and urged, with characteristic ambiguity, that Congress write a bill of some kind for reforming the franchise in the South and thereafter remained silent on the issue for more than a year, allowing Congress to do the work.[6] Several congressmen from each side of Capitol Hill then raced to the table to draft competing proposals for a Federal Elections Bill. Each proposal disagreed with the others over the nature and severity of the measures to be adopted. Among the initial drafts that Congress considered, second-term Wisconsin Senator John Coit Spooner's came to predominate. Spooner had been among the first would-be reformers to follow Chandler's lead in the recent Fiftieth Congress. When Chandler fell seriously ill before the beginning of the Fifty-first Congress, Spooner became the recognized leader of his crusade in the upper chamber. In the House, the proposal of Jonathan H. Rowell of Illinois, a Union veteran who had been wounded in the Civil War and who had a gift for abrasive language when discussing the southern race problem, initially predominated. Although the Spooner and Rowell proposals were only rough drafts of what would evolve into the Federal Elections Bill, the ideas of both men remained deeply embedded in the bill even after their respective committees refined and reworded their proposals. In the end, however, George Frisbie Hoar and Henry Cabot Lodge, a tandem from the Bay State, emerged as the leaders in their respective chambers, writing the final drafts of the Senate and House versions of the bill and initiating the debate on each.[7]

Hoar, with his small glasses, his nearly bald head, and his seemingly constant frown, appeared physically like a caricature of the average Puritan-abolitionist-humanitarian from Boston. Democratic editor Henry Watterson of the *Louisville Courier-Journal* liked to call him "Grandma Hoar . . . a man of the most equal temper, for he is mad all the time. If he should chance to catch himself smiling, he would go off somewhere and kick himself."[8] Hoar completed his Senate version of the Federal Elections Bill before Lodge finished his House version and introduced it, quite prematurely, in the upper chamber in April, without the prior knowledge or approval of House Republicans. Lodge and Rowell expressed their dismay at Hoar's action, citing the fact that a bill for controlling congressional elections should originate in the body whose membership it was to affect directly (state legislatures, rather than the people, elected U. S. senators, of course, so the bill would not affect membership in the Senate directly). Hoar could not resist that logic, and he thus acquiesced, tabling his own bill in lieu of Lodge's forthcoming bill. Even so, Senate Democrats blasted the Hoar bill immediately, as if practicing for the showdown coming later in the year. Alabama Senator James L. Pugh, who had been a rabid secessionist before the Civil War and afterward became one of the most adamant white supremacists in the nation, took the lead, denouncing the bill as "revolutionary" and "subversive." Moreover, he predicted that it would "insure the shedding of blood" in the South. Senate Republicans, who would have plenty of chances for rebuttal later, could only listen to Pugh, bite their tongues, and bide their time, for Hoar remained determined to honor his commitment and let the House schedule debate on its own version of the Federal Elections Bill first.[9]

Hoar's commitment did not, however, prevent Republicans from voicing disapproval of Pugh's speech outside of Congress. William E. Chandler appealed to public opinion, writing in the widely circulated periodical *Forum,* "Giving the South before the war representation for three-fifths of its slaves was degradation enough for the North," but giving it full representation now that blacks were citizens but were not allowed to vote was the ultimate humiliation. He matched Pugh's saber-rattling by reminding fellow northerners that the North had whipped the South once already, and that it could do so again.[10] Chandler's acidic article elicited a response from Pugh's fellow Alabamian John Tyler Morgan, who called Chandler a self-appointed judge, jury, and "public executioner" of white southerners. He informed Republicans that their plan to control southern elections "has been more bitterly condemned" by the American people than any other partisan bill in the history of Congress.[11]

Morgan's statement about the unpopularity of resurrecting the black voting rights issue was certainly true. Indeed, by the time Henry Cabot Lodge introduced HR 11045, the Federal Elections Bill, in June 1890, a rather acrimonious discussion of the idea of nationalizing control of congres-

Fanning the Flames of Sectional Strife. "*Base and Unpatriotic. . . . It will fan into life the smouldering embers of the race question, which time and education are gradually extinguishing.*"—Protest of New York Business-Men against the Lodge Force Bill. (*Puck*, 1890.) Democrats repeatedly accused the Republicans of fanning the flames of sectional strife through their determination to pass the Federal Elections Bill.

sional elections had been going on for several months in Congress, in the press, and in American society at large. Following party lines as well as the Mason-Dixon Line, people began to form their opinions about the Federal Elections Bill before the Republicans had even written it. To Democrats and most white southerners, it would be a "force bill" no matter what it actually said, for by their preconceptions it would be written strictly to force black government and Republican rule upon the South—a region that still suffered from the aftereffects of the Civil War and Reconstruction all these years later. Any Federal Elections Bill would thus be by definition partisan and sectional. That belief seemed quite rational considering the conduct of the Republican majority in the Billion Dollar Congress to that point. The Reed House had already sent the Democrats reeling from the dizzying speed with which it had passed the McKinley Tariff and ruled upon more than a dozen contested elections. Now, for good measure, the Democrats would be forced to try to defend themselves against a bill they felt certain would destroy the balance of power between the two parties in national politics. Even worse, they would have no weapon with which to fight their battle except the voice of protest. The Democrats could only hope that by making a strong case against the idea of federal supervision of elections, public opinion—which already leaned toward the Democratic side on this issue—would turn against the Republicans to such an extent that they would be forced to abandon their plan.[12]

The first step in implementing this strategy to win the support of the American public was for southern Democrats to plead with northern Republican voters openly for empathy, and to beg them to try to imagine themselves in the unenviable position of white southerners. If the roles were reversed, they asked rhetorically, would northerners want to be robbed of the right of local self-government for which their forefathers had fought and died in the American Revolution, in order that an inferior, servile race (as they saw it) might control their region of the country? No, of course not. And if New England, rather than the South, were populated by an "ignorant race wanting to vote," said one southerner, "rivers of blood" would run there.[13] Given the fact that the North did not have a race problem like the South's, and never would, southerners did not realistically expect empathy from northern politicians, but they did hope that their appeals would bother the collective conscience of the northern public. The southern Democratic strategy of trying to make northerners feel sorry for the South had merit, but by itself, it would not be enough. If the majority of white Americans were to rise in condemnation of the "force bill," they would need other reasons besides mere empathy. To the white South's delight, the free-thinking northern press supplied several of these reasons.

To independent-minded northerners, a Federal Elections Bill, no matter how noble the intentions of the authors, would be the wrong idea for America at the time. Since it would appear to be strictly a northern measure passed against the South, it would rekindle the flames of sectional hatred that seemed to have largely burned out in the 1880s. As E. L. Godkin explained, "in resisting a repetition of the experiment [of unrestricted black suffrage] the southerners are resisting with full knowledge the probable consequences of failure." That is, it would return the South to the unstable situation that prevailed during Reconstruction. Echoing the southern appeals for northern empathy, Godkin added, "There is no reason to suppose that any State at the North would be willing, for the sake of the southern Negro, to commit the election of its State legislature to the charge of federal officers."[14]

Moreover, some independent-minded northerners reasoned that the supervisory law already in effect had never worked efficiently. There had always been a problem of finding good men to serve as supervisors, especially in the large cities, and that would no doubt continue to be the case under any new supervisory law. Supervising elections was a thankless job that required thick-skinned, highly principled individuals willing and able to accept temporary employment. Although the job paid well, most gainfully employed people would not want it. Some critics likened becoming an election supervisor in the 1890s to becoming a British tax collector in the American colonies on the eve of the Revolutionary War. Who wanted to be tarred, feathered, and rode out of town on a rail or worse? Honest civilians willing to serve as supervisors were thus always difficult to find, leaving many polling stations under the watchful eye of unscrupulous, and often criminal, caretakers. Consequently, the idea of using the U. S. Army to supervise elections invariably emerged. But, as the *Nation* explained, the Army, numbering only twenty-eight thousand in 1890, could not handle the job—and would not want the job, either. It already had its hands full patrolling the vast western territories and trying to bring thousands of recalcitrant Native Americans under the subjection of the U. S. government.[15]

Besides the pragmatic reasons already named, other, more philosophic, reasons for opposing the Federal Elections Bill emerged, which, to the delight of southern Democrats, sprang from the minds of some unlikely allies: northern humanitarians. The Reverend Henry Field, a former missionary to the freedmen during Reconstruction, was one northerner and professing humanitarian who helped legitimize opposition to the bill. Field proclaimed that the idea of reenforcing the Fifteenth Amendment in 1890 could only be considered "the very insanity of democracy." He based his opinion upon the concept of natural and inalienable rights, which the Founding Fathers had written into the Declaration of Independence more than a century earlier. Believing that each American state possessed an "inalienable right" to have "good government," Field favored disfranchisement of blacks in the South by both a literacy test and a property requirement. He explained that "Personal liberty may be a natural right, but the privilege of voting certainly is not. . . . Americans are wont to hail as movements in the direction of liberty" all laws extending the right of suffrage to those previously deemed unqualified to vote. "But whether they are in the direction of good government is another question." If those given the right to vote are not "fit to use it," he argued, it "is a step toward barbarism . . . a crime against civilization," for "self-preservation is the first law of nature."[16]

Other northern humanitarians, such as Charles H. Levermore, a history professor at the Massachusetts Institute of Technology and an avowed neo-Puritan, agreed. After recently visiting the South for the first time, he sighed that he could now "appreciate more fully and more kindly the terrible burdens" under which white southerners "stagger." He argued that they should be commended for the progress they had made in race relations since the war rather than condemned for their failure to catch up with the North. Enforcing the Fifteenth Amendment, Levermore insisted, would not help them catch up; rather it would drive them further behind.[17] Moorfield Story of Boston, who would later become the first president of the National Association for the Advancement of Colored People, also agreed. He philosophized that Reconstruction turned out to be nothing more than a failed experiment in American race relations and that "the strain proved too great"—both upon blacks, who, as a race, were not prepared for the responsibility, and upon the American democratic system, which was too fragile to support suffrage for minorities.[18] Former carpetbagger governor of South Carolina, Daniel Chamberlain, likewise agreed. After having presided over a state with a majority black population during Reconstruction, he now had a change of heart about the wisdom of black suffrage because, he said, it had taken Anglo-Saxons "at least eight centuries" to develop their political rights. Why should American "negroes" have rights suddenly thrust upon them with no preparation?[19]

Lending moral, if not vocal, support to the southern Democrats' cause was the fact that even some leaders of the black community opposed the Federal Elections Bill. Most prominent among them was Booker T. Washington. In his usual, cautious way, he carefully avoided making any controversial public pronouncements on the subject, but privately he hoped the bill would not come to fruition. He believed it would merely give white southerners more excuses to commit atrocities against blacks than they already had and would thus do more harm than good.[20]

Despite the fact that the idea of enforcing the Fifteenth Amendment had little public support, Rowell introduced HR 10958 for federal supervision of elections on June 14, 1890, anyway. It went to the Committee on Election of the President, Vice President, and Representatives in Congress, where various committee members promptly dissected and revised it. Five days later, it emerged as Lodge's HR 11045. On June 21, the Government Printing Office published it and distributed it to every member of the House. Allowing only five days for congressmen to study the mammoth bill, Speaker Reed scheduled the House debate to begin on Thursday, June 26.[21]

Reed recused himself during the debate, placing a four-term representative from Kansas named Samuel R. Peters in charge as Speaker Pro Tempore, ostensibly to remove some of the partisan appearance of the bill. Peters had lived in Memphis where he had earned his livelihood as a newspaper editor from 1868 to 1873 and, compared to other former carpetbaggers, had since enjoyed an above-average amount of respect among southerners in Congress. Although Reed showed prudence in appointing Peters as his stand-in, the move hardly put the Democrats any more at ease in the debate than they would otherwise have been. Under the floor management of former Senator Charles Buckelew of Pennsylvania, one of the eldest and most venerable members of the House, the Democrats tried, not surprisingly, to prevent consideration of the bill. But Reed's schedule allowed no flexibility. The new Speaker would utilize his radical rules to their fullest potential, initially allowing only forty minutes per speech. Midway through the debate, to expedite the impending vote, he cut the allotted time to five minutes per speech.[22]

Lodge, the Republican manager of the debate, introduced the bill over the objections of the minority. Since his Republican colleagues would support it without an extensive explanation of the contents of its seventy-plus pages, he did not need to go into the minute details of the bill in order to secure its passage. Instead, he touched on its basic features and explained why he thought it necessary for the improvement of the national polity. He noted that, fundamentally, the bill called for election supervisors to be chosen by the local circuit court judge in congressional districts only where a complaint of vote fraud was filed by at least one hundred citizens in an entire district, or by at least one hundred in a city with a population of twenty thousand or more, or by petition of at least fifty citizens in a county. In cases where a local judge suspected corruption throughout the entire district, the court would appoint canvassers to collect the ballot boxes from the various supervisors at each polling station. Lodge cited Article I, Section 4, of the U. S. Constitution, James Madison's constitutional convention notes, George Tickner Curtis's *Constitutional History of the United States*, and Supreme Court cases *Ex Parte Yarbrough* and *Ex Parte Siebold* to prove that Congress has power to regulate federal elections in such a manner.[23]

Had Lodge stopped there or stuck to the legal aspects of the issue, he would have done well. He could have perhaps made the debate over his bill more congenial, even if he couldn't make the bill itself more palatable to the opposition. Instead, he could not resist taking the opportunity to wave the bloody shirt and to express his neo-abolitionist racial views. Contemporaries knew to expect such inflammatory rhetoric from "Cabot," as friends and family called him. It should not be considered strange, therefore, that historians have tended to point out his notable character flaws as well. Lodge's biographers and other scholars who have looked closely at the man agree that he had an uncanny ability to rub people the wrong way. His abrasiveness stemmed from the fact that, while he possessed a brilliant intellect, he could not seem to bridle his tongue, making him seem unusually arrogant, even amid the ego-center of the nation that was Capitol Hill. Considering his background, Lodge had a right, however, if any congressman had a right, to consider himself an authority on certain subjects and thus to speak his mind without fearing the consequences. He was a forty-year-old Boston "blue blood" with a doctorate degree in history from Harvard. He had previously been employed as an editor of one of the most popular monthly news magazines in the country, the *North American Review*, and, in 1890, he served on the board of Overseers of Harvard. Brought up in the New England traditions of both Puritanism and abolitionism and surrounded all his life by educated, liberal politicians and literary giants, Lodge appeared to many observers to be a self-righteous humanitarian who was determined to live up to the expectations of Boston's social elites on the issue of civil rights for black southerners. He liked to think of himself as having inherited the mantle of radical progenitor Charles Sumner, and he certainly did in the sense that he became the undisputed leader of Massachusetts politics during and after the 1890s.[24]

In other ways, however, Lodge's words, actions, and demeanor typified what unabashed racists of the day saw as the hypocrisy of the Republican Party in 1890, making him an easy target for Democratic lampoons. In personality, he was a snobbish, serious-minded scholar who did not accept criticism well, who always had to be right and win every argument, and who seemed to possess no sense of humor. More educated than any other member of Congress and wealthier than most, he did not fit in among the boisterous, often uncultured, commoners who comprised the bulk of the House membership. Unlike most of his colleagues, he was unable to play politics as a game or to consider debate as an academic exercise. At the end of the day or the end of a session of Congress, he could not simply walk away from the antagonisms that had gone before, as most of his colleagues did. Instead, he carried grudges with him permanently and seemed to collect them as battle scars or trophies of war. On racial issues, he talked the rhetoric of a humanitarian, at least toward black southerners, yet he absolutely opposed allowing the flood of new immigrants arriving daily on the shores of Boston and New York to continue, calling everyone who did not descend from northwestern European stock "obnoxious." Not surprisingly, in the second session of the Fifty-first Congress, he would introduce the first of many bills for restricting this wave of new immigration. Lodge brought much grief upon himself by this complex combination of personal quirks and seemingly contradictory racial views.[25]

Continuing his introductory speech on the bill that would, for better or worse, come to bear his name, Lodge declared that "freedom was national and slavery sectional. So it may be said with equal truth that honest elections are national and dishonest elections are sectional." He compared Mississippi and New Jersey, both Democratic states with roughly 1,131,000 people, but contrasted the number of votes cast in each during the 1880s. The former had cast, on average, 116,000 votes per federal election; the latter 275,000. Their number of congressmen was the same, of course, meaning Mississippi had one representative for every sixteen thousand votes cast while New Jersey had one for every forty-three thousand. Furthermore, the representatives from Mississippi held more power in chairing and serving on committees than did those from New Jersey. He cited other similar discrepancies between northern and southern states to support his contention that southern politics was out of phase with the rest of the nation's politics.[26]

Next, Lodge turned his attention to the race problem, opining that the only solution lay in black southerners gaining freedom of the ballot. His argument can be summed up thus:

> The wrong of slavery was expiated by the North, which condoned it, as much as by the South, which upheld it. . . . The negroes in the United States did not come here by any will or action of their own. They did not seek to force themselves upon us as the Chinese, whom we excluded, tried to do. . . . It is idle to say that they [blacks] are better off than they would have been if they had staid [*sic*] in their native wilderness. Better an eternity of savage freedom than the civilization which came to them with the hammer of the auctioneer in one hand and the slave-driver's whip in the other.[27]

Lodge concluded his racial sermon with a series of curiosities and contradictions, which would only fuel the opposition's arguments against his bill. He proclaimed the praises of loyal and faithful "negro-Americans" who had helped save the Union in the late war, then noted that they should not be seen as objects of sentimentality by humanitarians. He added that the practice of using "qualifying adjectives" that "denote race distinctions" as prefixes to "American" should stop. He then questioned the wisdom of his progenitors passing the Fifteenth Amendment twenty years earlier, but decreed that "now that the deed has been done, it is federal responsibility to protect it." He ended his speech with the most important statement (and the one most often overlooked by historians) made during the course of the three debates on the race problem in the Fifty-first Congress: "If any State thinks that any class of citizens is unfit to vote through ignorance, it can disqualify them. . . . It has but to put an educational qualification into its constitution."[28]

Lodge's speech received great, prolonged applause on the Republican side and in the galleries. Little did the partisan admirers, or Lodge himself, realize, however, that the last point in the speech would help open the door for constitutional disfranchisement of blacks in the South for the next seventy-five years. That development, which came first in the form of the Mississippi Constitution, is of such paramount importance that it will be dealt with in-depth in a later chapter.

Meanwhile, as Lodge took his seat after his opening remarks, James C. Hemphill, a four-term representative of South Carolina, began delivering the rebuttal for the Democrats. Having the burden of framing an argument that would discredit a bill which was foreordained to pass, Hemphill first attacked Lodge's bill on constitutional grounds. He began with an exegesis of Article I, Section 4, of the U. S. Constitution, which says: "The Times, Places, and Manner of holding Elections for senators and representatives, shall be prescribed in each State by the Legislature thereof, but the Congress may at any time by Law make or alter such Regulations, except as to the places of chusing [sic] Senators." Written in the pithy language that characterizes all of the Constitution, this section seems, at least superficially, to give Congress power to regulate federal elections. Whereas Lodge had taken the broad interpretation of the Constitution, believing that such power was so clearly expressed that he hardly bothered to frame an argument about it, Hemphill took the opposite opinion and approach. He pointed out that seven of the original thirteen states "declared against the power of Congress to exercise this authority" mentioned in Section 4. These objectors would have struck that section from the Constitution altogether, said the South Carolinian, had they been given the choice. Since they did not have that choice, however, they could only ratify or reject the document as a whole. Early Congresses harbored no illusions about their own powers thereafter, said Hemphill, and did not try to invoke Section 4 of the Constitution to try to control federal elections until 1842, when a Whig-dominated Congress passed a law requiring that every congressman be elected from a separate district within each state. A curious assortment of southern, western, and northern states—Georgia, Mississippi, Missouri, and New Hampshire—blatantly disregarded the law, however, and, in effect, nullified it. Hemphill then read the New Hampshire nullification resolution, which said, "*Resolved,* That we can not sanction so unauthorized an interference in our domestic relations . . . and we can not regard the same as binding upon the States." Ohio and New York also sent resolutions to Congress protesting the new law. Hemphill emphasized the fact that three northern states had taken that position. He gleefully added, as a footnote to history, that the American people showed what they thought of the law in the midterm elections of 1842: Congress went Democrat by a two to one margin.[29]

Hemphill then tackled specific provisions within the Lodge bill that seemed to him to defy logic. First, at that time there were seventy federal circuit court districts in the United States and 335 congressional districts. Within those congressional districts were thousands of counties. Within some of those counties were dozens of cities with a population of twenty thousand or more. Surely there would be an overlap of citizens petitioning for supervision in many of these places, which would undoubtedly cause utter chaos, declared Hemphill. It would easily be possible that, in some districts, each ballot would be handled by seven different supervisors and canvassers and counted in as many as six separate circuit courts.[30]

Furthermore, noted Hemphill, the bill provided a chief supervisor for each federal judicial district, three canvassers for each congressional district, three local supervisors for each polling station, and as many deputy marshals as the chief supervisor of the district saw fit to appoint. Under the old supervisory law, six thousand supervisors and eleven thousand deputy marshals had been stationed in New York City alone for the election of 1876. One hundred fifty-five of these marshals protected a single polling station. Likewise, under the old law, one thousand armed guards patrolled a single precinct in South Carolina in 1876. The sheer number of supervisors, canvassers, and marshals that would be involved under the Lodge bill, if supervision resulted from petition, said Hemphill, would be staggering.[31]

To compound the problem, continued the South Carolinian, all supervisors and deputies would be residents of the districts they were appointed to oversee, meaning they would have a stake in the outcome of the elections. As paid officials, they would, in effect, need to find evidence of abuse in order to keep their jobs. In addition, for some, their jobs would not be complete until two months after election day, when all of the votes would have been counted, when the governor would have certified the returns, and when the documentation of a fair election would have reached the House of Representatives in Washington, D.C. At five dollars per day for each person so employed, complained Hemphill, the amount that the government might spend to ensure a free ballot and a fair count could be astronomical.[32]

If all such problems did not provide reason enough to kill this bill, said Hemphill, plenty more reasons could be listed. For one, the people of any given district would have no voice in who supervised their elections. Instead, federal district judges, most of whom were either Republicans or sympathetic to the GOP, would appoint the supervisors, whereupon those supervisors would serve for life. Which would be worse, asked Hemphill, to give such unbridled power to the Republicans for life or to let the several states manage their own elections as they had always done before? Answering his own question, he asserted that it would be better for a few congressional districts to get stuck for two years with representatives who won their elections through fraud than for the whole country to live perpetually under a system that could easily devolve into a national tyranny at any time. If even half the corruption of the ballot that Lodge alleged actually existed, Hemphill reasoned, then one could only conclude that the American people must be fundamentally corrupt. If that was the case, would not the supervisors be corrupt, too? How could Congress possibly trust these supervisors who would be appointed for life? As appointees of the judicial branch of the federal government, they would be all but beyond the reach of congressional oversight. As federal agents, they would be beyond the reach of the states. In essence, there would be no way to control the supervisors other than by blind faith in the judicial system. Hemphill spoke on behalf of all Democrats in saying that, while he respected the judiciary, he did not, and could not, have blind faith in it.[33]

The South Carolinian then turned the tables on the Republicans, complaining of their milder form of corruption—the gerrymander—and criticizing Speaker Reed at the same time. Consider Maine, he said, "the State so ably represented by the gentleman who has been elected dictator of this House," where seventy-three thousand Republican votes elected four congressmen in 1888, while fifty-four thousand Democratic votes elected none. Hemphill cited similar statistics for six other northern states, using them as evidence that the supposed Republican dominance of the North was really a "sham." He compared the GOP to a preacher who spoke beautiful words on Sunday but served the devil with all his might the other six days of the week. At that point, Representative Sereno Payne of New York stood to object, but Hemphill cut him off before he could interrupt, saying, "Just wait a moment; you can say it afterward. . . . it does not amount to anything anyhow," to which the Democrats gave a hearty laugh.[34] Such insulting language certainly did not help the Democrats' cause, but Hemphill, like most of his colleagues on both sides of the aisle, could not resist the opportunity to mock the opposition.

Continuing his counterattack, Hemphill noted:

A good deal has been said in this country of late about the New South. What this country really needs is a new North. It needs a North that will take a view of all the facts and not be guided by their own preconceived prejudices. It needs a North which will not waste all of its time and energy in reforming other people's abuses. It needs a North that will sometimes look at its own shortcomings and not always on those of people a thousand miles away; and it needs a North which will believe that when a man in the South of the Anglo-Saxon race happens by any untoward circumstance to come into serious collision with another man of the African race that it is not always because the other man is black.[35]

Hemphill ended the opening statement for his party by remembering the ills of Reconstruction in the Palmetto State. He read from a speech that former carpetbagger governor of South Carolina Daniel Chamberlain had recently made in Boston, saying, "I see men running to and fro . . . wringing their hands in despair . . . over our portentous race problem. I confess I share in no such excitement. . . . It is, in my judgment, at least nine parts out of ten the babble of professional or ill-informed philanthropists and the [self-]interested jargon of demagogic politicians." After Chamberlain left South Carolina in 1876, he did not return until 1889, noted Hemphill, whereupon he found a much better state of affairs in his erstwhile southern home. "I find that since 1876 both races in South Carolina have prospered . . . that the negro has never known such an era of advancement and prosperity." What more evidence could any rational person possibly need that Democratic control since the redemption has been good for the South, asked Hemphill? Therefore, he concluded that local white Democrats must rule, no matter the cost to the GOP or to African Americans. Besides, he explained, "It is the home of our fathers," who purchased it with their blood in the American Revolution. Hemphill's remarks drew great applause on the Democratic side, but these opponents of the elections bill had no time to savor the moment, for the Republicans stood ready to counter his arguments.[36]

In congressional debates, the opening statements generally set forth the main points that each side will argue for the remainder of the debate. Successive speakers, more often than not, merely expand upon the arguments made in the opening statements. The House debate of the Lodge bill was no exception. Although Democrats protested that, under the Reed Rules, they did not have adequate time to make their case against the bill to the American people, the fact is, in six days of debate, they added little of substance to what Hemphill said on the first day. Some, however, squeezed the maximum number of provocative thoughts into their limited time, and all added more substantive discussion to the debate than did the Republicans, who preferred to spend the remainder of their time throwing the Democrats off stride with bloody-shirt diversions. Indeed, the Lodge bill debate offered the perfect opportunity for Republicans to revisit the ill feelings engendered by the Civil War and, often, to gloat over the Union victory. The Democrats' felt compelled at every turn to digress from the issues of the Lodge bill in order to defend both the South and the defunct Confederacy against these bloody-shirt attacks.[37] Other diversions cropped up, as well. Both sides argued over, for instance, the superiority of their respective states and sections to the rest of the nation and world, the character and intellectual capacity of African Americans, interpretations of the Holy Bible and the U. S. Constitution, and the future course of national politics, among other topics.[38]

These digressions interested most congressmen participating in the Lodge bill debate much more than the topic of supervising federal elections, and they can likewise prove more entertaining to the historian. They can easily distract from the task of understanding the provisions of the Lodge bill and determining whether it represented good legislation based upon fundamentally sound principles that might have helped solve the southern race problem. In order to avoid that pitfall, these fascinating digressions, although duly noted, must otherwise be ignored in this study.

Some diversions in the debate cannot be ignored, however, because they illustrate the unusual divisiveness of the Federal Elections Bill. The most notable such cases involved individual congressmen who engaged in heated verbal exchanges that would have likely led to fisticuffs or some other form of physical assault had they occurred outside the halls of Congress. One case involved two young, first-term Virginians, a black man named Edmund Waddill Jr. and a white man named Henry St. George Tucker. The point of contention between them was nothing more than which man should be entitled to the floor. Tucker held the floor until his allotted time expired, upon which Waddill rose to speak. Tucker, however, insolently refused to yield to Waddill, as he would have customarily done had a white man interrupted him. Tucker instructed his black challenger to "sit down" and not speak until some white representative offered the floor to him. Needless to say, Waddill could not appreciate Tucker's angry, insulting outburst of racial prejudice, and the two men exchanged threats. To prevent a possible physical altercation on the floor of the U. S. House of Representatives, the Speaker called both men to order repeatedly, but they continued their mutual harangues for several minutes until both men wearied of the situation. Waddill subsequently got his chance to speak. Ironically, both men would go on later in life to distinguish themselves at the bar. Waddill became a U. S. Circuit Court Justice, and Tucker became the dean of two law schools—Washington and Lee University and George Washington University.[39]

A similar case involved Democrat Richard Bland of Missouri, the renowned cosponsor of the Bland-Allison Silver Purchase Act of 1878, and Louis E. McComas, a four-term Republican representative of Maryland, who would later become a U. S. senator and a professor of international law at Georgetown University. They almost came to blows over the question of which of the two of them evinced more hypocrisy in his record of legislation toward African Americans.[40] If such encounters between unhappy statesmen are any indication of the acrimony that a federal elections law would have unleashed upon American society between blacks and whites, northerners and southerners, or Democrats and Republicans, one might reasonably conclude that it was for the best that the Lodge bill never became law.

The few speeches made after the opening statements that actually addressed the issues under consideration in the Lodge bill can be summarized briefly. Those speeches were especially rare on the side that supported the bill, because the bill's sponsors did not need to strengthen their case in order to secure passage. Jonathan H. Rowell of Illinois, who had helped author the bill, argued that both a constitutional duty and an obligation to practice noblesse oblige toward the minority race dictated that the Fifteenth Amendment be enforced through a federal elections law.[41] Robert P. Kennedy of Ohio, a former brigadier general in the Union Army, pointed out that the democratic ideal of majority rule, regardless of who constituted the majority, demanded passage of the bill.[42] Frederick Greenhalge, an English-born first-term representative of Massachusetts, who would later go on to serve as governor of the Bay State, rationalized the need for the bill through an analogy. If all is well in one's own house, he asked, but a neighbor's home is being robbed, is it not morally imperative that one rush to that neighbor's aid? The happy homeowner in this parable represented white northerners, the victim of robbery represented black southerners, and the robbers were white southerners. How could white northerners possibly justify not rushing to the aid of black southerners by passing a federal elections law, Greenhalge asked?[43]

The Democrats delivered significantly more numerous and well-expounded (if not more historically accurate) arguments against the Lodge bill than did the Republicans for it. Three of the most notable indictments of the bill came from dissenting southern Republicans. Hamilton Ewart of North Carolina, a single-term representative who was purported to be the originator of the Lodge bill's sobriquet, the "force bill," declared that party icons such as Abraham Lincoln and Ulysses Grant would never have supported such a plan to federalize congressional elections. He also pointed out that the "Boston blue-blood" Henry Cabot Lodge had never stepped foot on southern soil in his life, except in Maryland and the District of Columbia, and consequently had no firsthand knowledge of either southern elections or the southern people. Had he spent time in the South as had Lincoln and Grant, said Ewart, he would never have proposed such a scheme, but would rather show mercy and leniency toward the South, as did these deceased Republican icons. He added that, if his party really wanted to do something to help black southerners, it would pass a national education bill along the lines of the then-defunct Blair Education Bill.[44]

A single-term southern Republican from Louisiana named Hamilton Coleman agreed. Coleman added that, besides passing an education bill, the Republican Congress should allocate more money for building levees in flood-prone regions of the South, pay off the balance due to depositors of the failed Freedmen's Bank, and pay off the southern people's Civil War damage claims. All of these ideas would, he claimed, benefit the southern people, black and white alike, make everyone happy, and thus destroy the solidarity of the Democratic Party in the South. A federal elections law would not, he contended. It would exacerbate the problem instead.[45] Yet another single-term southern Republican, Nathan Frank of Missouri, agreed that the Lodge bill, as it now stood, would have that effect. He made the objective and sensible observation that, until such time as Congress could draft a Federal Elections Bill with bipartisan support, the idea should be tabled.[46]

All thirty-six northern House Democrats joined their southern counterparts and the handful of Republican dissidents in denouncing the Lodge bill. James Covert, a seven-term representative of New York argued that Lodge's plan allowed "an irresponsible and insignificant minority," with absolutely no proof of wrongdoing, to call in supervisors on demand.[47]

Later, Benton McMillin, a six-term representative from Tennessee, asked Lodge directly about the veracity of that charge. Lodge answered that, if one hundred citizens of a given district called for supervision, surely they would only do so because they had a legitimate reason. Joseph E. Washington, in his second term from Tennessee, immediately chimed in that "one hundred of the worst citizens in my district would call for supervision at every election."[48]

Other northern Democrats added equally significant points to the discussion. Roswell P. Flower of New York, a future governor of the Empire State; Richard Vaux of Pennsylvania, a former mayor of Philadelphia, who, at seventy-four, was the oldest member to speak on the Lodge bill; and John L. Chipman, a former judge, now in his second term from Michigan, all attacked it on the grounds that it would "prostitute the judiciary." Giving judges power to control the outcome of elections by appointing federal supervisors would be a "constant temptation . . . set before them. Visions of political advancement will haunt their waking and sleeping hours."[49]

William McAdoo, a three-term Democratic representative of New Jersey who would soon become the assistant secretary of the navy in Grover Cleveland's second administration and later the police commissioner of New York City, proclaimed that the Lodge bill would also prostitute the clerk of the House of Representatives. The bill provided for a $5,500 fine and possible imprisonment for any clerk who received the certificates of election presented by the states rather than those presented by the federal supervisors. McAdoo, a native of Ireland who, as an immigrant, claimed to possess an above-average understanding of both contemporary and historical European politics, added that the bill was so "revolutionary, dangerous, and drastic" that not even the most centralized and despotic governments in Europe would think of passing such a law. How then could the democratic United States tolerate this bill?[50]

Amos J. Cummings, a two-term Democratic representative of New York, argued that the Lodge bill called for three supervisors per polling station, only two of whom could belong to the majority party in Congress at the time of the election. He noted that the language of the provision implied that the other supervisor must be a member of the other major party, but that was not necessarily true. He actually could be a "Greenbacker, Prohibitionist, Woman's Suffragist, Mugwump, Independent, Featherhead, or anything but" a member of the majority party.[51] William Mutchler, a three-term Democrat from Pennsylvania, and Samuel Yoder, in his second term from Ohio, spoke about the character of actual supervisors already employed for life under the existing supervisory law. Mutchler read a list of the criminal records of fifty of the worst supervisors in New York City and Philadelphia, which he took from newspapers and police reports in both cities. The list consisted of the names of people guilty of almost every type of illegal and immoral behavior imaginable, from running brothels to organizing gambling rings and from buying and selling votes to stealing money and horses. Yoder read House Report 2681 from the Forty-eighth Congress, in which the House impeached U. S. Marshal Lot Wright of the southern district of Ohio for violating his power as an election supervisor. The House Committee on Elections found Wright guilty of appointing and arming various felons to serve as his deputies and to oversee the polling in Cincinnati in the elections of 1882.[52]

Southern Democrats generally could not stick to the facts as well as their northern counterparts because of the sectional distractions already mentioned. Occasionally, however, one would make a salient point. Thomas R. Stockdale of Mississippi, for instance, in the longest speech delivered on the Lodge bill, explained that the core of the Republicans' case for passing the bill lay in the claim that "honest men who do not commit election frauds need have no fear of this bill. Why, Mr. Speaker," he remarked, "the gentleman from Massachusetts [Lodge]" is enough of a historian "to know that the Inquisition was established and maintained upon precisely that theory."[53] Just as the Inquisition represented a display of force by the Church against alleged heretics, added James B. McCreary of Kentucky, so did the Lodge bill represent a display of force by the GOP against the alleged political heresy of Democrats and racial heresy of white southerners. The term "force bill" described the measure perfectly, he said, because it would force black and Republican rule upon the South and because the GOP had determined to force it through Congress against the will of the majority of the people in the United States.[54]

The greatest contribution of the southern Democrats to the debate doubtless came from Hilary Herbert of Alabama. Herbert was perhaps the most important leader of the Democratic Party in fighting the Lodge bill because of the book he edited especially for the purpose entitled *Why the Solid South?* The book extensively documented the alleged evils of Reconstruction in the various southern states. Fourteen southerners from the House and Senate contributed chapters covering their respective states. This hastily prepared collection of essays did not convince Republicans to drop the Federal Elections Bill, but it did help persuade the vacillating segment of the northern public to join the Democrats in opposing a return to the sectional animosities of Reconstruction. More important, it turned out to be a masterpiece polemic against black suffrage and the extension of federal power, to which future historians, such as William A. Dunning and his doctoral students at Columbia University, would turn to help justify their negative interpretations of Reconstruction. The book contained fourteen chapters, one for each of the eleven Confederate states, plus chapters on Reconstruction in Missouri, West Virginia, and Washington, D.C. Although the book had no effect on the way any member of the House voted on the Lodge bill, under Herbert's able editing, these firsthand accounts certainly presented a formidable amount of ideological ammunition with which Democratic senators could bombard their Republican counterparts during the Senate filibuster later in the year.[55] The essential argument of the work merely reiterated the traditional Democratic Party line of local autonomy and state rights, which is well summarized in this excerpt: "Our ancestors believed that local self-government was the greatest of blessings. . . . The unwisdom [*sic*] of departing from this theory has never had a more convincing illustration than in the reconstruction laws of Congress and the results which followed. . . . there is always danger of mistake when voters in any one part of the Union undertake to pass upon questions peculiar to a far-distant section of the country."[56]

Despite waging a fierce battle, the Democrats had no power to forestall the vote on the Lodge bill beyond the time allowed under the Reed Rules. Thus, after six full days of debate, the Speaker called for the vote. When the clerk took the roll, 155 representatives voted "yea" and 149 voted "nay," with twenty-four members absent and not paired for voting. No Democrats voted for the bill, only one Independent voted for it, and only two Republicans (the two southerners named "Hamilton") voted against it. Thus, July 2, 1890, became the humanitarians' finest hour in the Fifty-first Congress. And to Democrats, it appeared to prove their suspicions that the GOP majority represented a juggernaut, an unstoppable force crushing all opposition, even the will of the American people. Yet, they saw the passage of the Lodge bill in the House not as a milestone but merely as an expected stepping stone toward absolute Republican control of the nation. They also realized that the House debate was only the opening scene in a much larger drama. They expected the real test to come in the Senate, which, as yet, had adopted no equivalent of the Reed Rules for limiting debate. The bill arrived in the upper chamber on July 7, ready for discussion and modification. Meanwhile, the white South cursed, stomped, and then settled down to grieve while it awaited the Senate debate that it believed would inevitably occur before the summer was over.[57]

House Democrats did not let the bill go to the upper chamber peacefully. They continued to make impromptu speeches and arguments against the Federal Elections Bill at every available opportunity, hoping to provide Senate colleagues with more ammunition for their own verbal fusillades against the hated measure. For instance, on August 6, the Republicans introduced an appropriation bill, which was a routine and daily custom in the House that usually garnered little notice. This particular bill, however, caught the attention of the Democrats because it called for back payment of special deputy marshals who had supervised congressional elections in 1888. After almost two full years, they had not been paid the $34,745 collectively owed them. William McAdoo used this bill as a launching pad for one last tirade against the Lodge bill, the substance of which showed how difficult it was to keep track of the amount of money owed to the supervisors already employed—imagine how much harder it would be, said McAdoo, under the Lodge bill.[58]

Such ex post facto arguments in the House had little impact on what senators thought of the bill. All Democrats and most Republicans had their minds made up already. The course of the bill in the Senate seemed sure to everyone. It was common knowledge that without a change in the Senate rules, Democrats would filibuster the Federal Elections Bill indefinitely, thus turning one of the most important debates in late nineteenth-century America into nothing more than a test of endurance. Such had occurred with a similar bill in 1875, and the Democrats had won. Republican floor manager of the Senate George Frisbie Hoar thus called for a limitation of debate immediately upon introduction of the controversial bill on August 7 and scheduled a vote for September 4.[59]

William P. Frye, a Republican senator from Maine, spoke up in agreement with Hoar's plan, saying that if debate was not limited, everyone knew the outcome of the bill from the beginning. Other Republican senators concurred, including Frank Hiscock of New York and George Edmunds of Vermont. Over the next two weeks, three other Republican senators, Henry Blair, Matthew Quay, and Rhode Island senator Nelson Aldrich, all followed suit in proposing to limit debate. While most Senate Republicans agreed on that much, they disagreed about the scheduling of the debate on the Federal Elections Bill because they also had to make time to hear the McKinley bill, which had already been on the docket awaiting action for a month. On August 12, Republican power broker Matthew Quay arranged a deal with Senator Arthur P. Gorman, whom the Democrats chose to be the floor manager on their side of the Federal Elections Bill debate. Gorman, a party boss from Maryland, like all of his fellow Democrats, considered raising the tariff to be by far the lesser of the two evils. He agreed to debate the McKinley bill immediately and postpone consideration of the Lodge bill until the second session. Hoar, in frustration and disappointment, drew up a document called "Senators Agreement as to the Election Bill and the proposed change of rule." It ensured that the Federal Elections Bill would be top priority in the second session and would be immediately considered upon the Senate's reconvening in December. Thirty-five colleagues signed it immediately, and six others signed it before the beginning of the second session.[60] Outside of Congress, astute observers suspected that something was amiss with the Quay-Gorman deal. One northern newspaper voiced that fear, saying Senate Republicans "have allowed themselves to be fooled" again by the Democrats.[61] Frederick Douglass held out hope, however, that the deal did not mean the end of the bill, only its delay, saying: "Shall we get mad and denounce and renounce the Republican party? Has that party sinned away its day of grace? Are there no remaining reasons for giving it our confidence? I entertain no such thought. The Federal election and educational bills are not dead, nor are their friends idle. Mr. Cabot Lodge and Mr. Blair and their friends in the Senate and in the House may permit delay but will not suffer defeat."[62]

While it was evident to onlookers that the Democrats intended to make the passage of the Federal Elections Bill as difficult as possible for the GOP, and while it was also clear that some Republican senators felt lukewarm about the bill, most observers agreed with Douglass. Few questioned that the bill would ultimately become law. Public opinion therefore immediately judged it as though its passage was a foregone conclusion, as the next chapter will reveal.

Chapter 5

JUDGING THE INSANITY

Public Reactions to the Inflammatory "Force Bill" and the Tyranny of the Majority

As a matter of force an election is just as decisive as the battle of Waterloo.

—*Kansas City Journal*

We need no great standing armies . . . our revolutions are bloodless.

—*New York Press*

During and after the tension-filled week of debate between Democrats and Republicans in the House, the press and the public likewise discussed the merits and demerits of the Federal Elections Bill. For a variety of reasons, far more opposition to the bill appeared than support for it. Albion Tourgee, who had pushed so vehemently for a new supervisory law, actually opposed Lodge's bill, considering it too lenient toward the South.[1] Murat Halstead also changed his opinion in 1890 to side with the money Republicans, who opposed the bill as an unnecessary stumbling block on the path to North-South reconciliation.[2] Carl Schurz opposed it because he believed it would destroy southern prosperity by driving out northern capital and would simultaneously cause a swift worsening of southern race relations. What would the GOP get in return for these calamities, asked Schurz? It

108

would get "assurance of future tariff bills by the hundred." He added, "Let the peace and prosperity of the South go to the bottom of the sea, if only the protectionists can gain some more congressmen in Negro districts to pass more tariffs in their interest! This is the milk in the election bill!"[3] The reputed leader of the GOP, James G. Blaine, urged party leaders "to drop the force bill and assiduously cultivate the Farmer's Alliance," which he correctly predicted would soon cause a "great political upheaval at the South."[4] Blaine meant only the white Alliance, of course, because it opposed the bill, while the black Alliance supported it.[5]

In the newspapers, the supporters' and the detractors' arguments were predictable. One paper stated the supporters' main point of contention succinctly—that if Congress did not pass the bill, it would be a "silent participator" in crimes committed against blacks in the South.[6] Another proclaimed that the motto of the GOP should be "Let justice be done, though the heavens fall."[7] One opposing paper commented that when the Lodge bill "is translated into cold-blooded Anglo-Saxon, it means that if the South doesn't vote the Republican ticket it must be made to," and that "Its passage would be the most ominous incident in the history of our times."[8] Another pegged the bill as "the most infamous measure which ever engaged the attention of Congress . . . it is too plain that sectional hatred is the germ from which [this] legislation has sprung," yet it stood merely as an example of what lay in store for the nation with "the autocracy which has assumed control of American legislation" in power.[9] Not all of the opposition came from newspapers focusing on the South's race problem. The Catholic press equally despised the bill simply for the fact that it seemed to threaten local autonomy, which wove the very fabric of American democracy. Reciting the same mantra used against the Blair bill, Catholics asked, if Congress would regulate race relations, might it not soon regulate religion, too? One Catholic paper opined that the Lodge bill "would govern this country on the same plan that Great Britain governs Ireland. Undoubtedly this is the worst bill of this generation."[10] The opposition press had more reasons to hate the bill than the supporting press had to commend it and was thus more outspoken and adamant in its opinion.

The most notable newspaper opposition came in the third week of July 1890, when the *Atlanta Constitution* attempted to foment support for a revolutionary action to show southern and Democratic disdain for the Lodge bill, which it labeled the "stillborn child of hate!"[11] On the advice of Governor John B. Gordon of Georgia, the paper called for a southern boycott of all northern products should the bill pass the Senate. Although this drastic measure caused alarm in certain manufacturing centers of the North, it received little support outside of Atlanta. Most Democratic papers mulled over the idea for a few days before calling for unity among themselves in repudiating the idea of the boycott. A general agreement surfaced that held such a move would be tantamount to the South's threat of secession in 1860 if Abraham Lincoln were to be elected president. Once such a threat is made, it must be carried out. And, just as secession led the South into a devastating military conflict, so would a boycott bring economic warfare that might prove just as disastrous for the South.[12] One paper thus called the boycott "the weapon of the weakling" and informed readers that the South should not think itself that weak.[13] Another warned that threatening the North with a boycott would only strengthen the GOP's resolve to pass the bill.[14] The *Constitution* soon dropped the idea.

The *Savannah Morning News* supported a much more practical approach in protesting the Lodge bill. It reported that the Savannah Board of Trade sent a resolution to "the mercantile houses of the North who enjoy a lucrative trade" with the southern port city, which definitely lassoed the attention of some influential New York City businessmen. If only other southern cities would follow this example, the Savannah paper believed, the "force bill" could still be defeated.[15]

The most significant reaction to the Lodge bill came in the form of Mississippi's constitutional convention, which lasted from August 12 to October 1. The purpose of the convention was to establish new qualifications for voters in order to limit, if not altogether eliminate, the black vote in the Magnolia State. Contemporaries and historians alike have well understood the paramount importance of Mississippi's fourth constitution to the course of American race relations. Immediately after it went into effect on November 1, 1890 (not by popular ratification but simply by decree of the state legislature), Albion Tourgee called it "the most important event" in American history since South Carolina's secession from the Union in 1860. Tourgee correctly predicted that, like South Carolina's action, the new Mississippi Constitution would serve as a catalyst prompting other southern states to follow a bad example and that the results would ultimately prove ruinous for the South.[16]

Wisconsin Senator John Coit Spooner basically agreed, although he modified Tourgee's argument slightly. He considered the new constitution to be the most important thing to happen to American race relations since the formulation of the "Mississippi plan" of 1875, which Mississippi Democrats used to overthrow the Republican administration of carpetbagger Governor Adelbert Ames. That plan had called for native white Democrats to "redeem" the state from black and Republican rule by any means necessary, including violence and intimidation toward black voters and impeachment of Republican officials. Like South Carolina's secession, it also served as a model for other southern states to emulate in overthrowing their Republican governments. Spooner thus dubbed the Mississippi Constitution of 1890 the "second Mississippi plan."[17] This term accurately described the document's intent, for over the next few years all former Confederate states and even several non-Confederate states followed its example, rewriting their constitutions to disqualify African American voters.[18]

Modern historians have almost unanimously agreed with the contemporary humanitarian assessment of the significance of the Mississippi Constitution to American race relations after 1890. Rayford Logan, for instance, argues that the document had a more detrimental effect on African Americans than anything else since slavery. He also points out that the constitution did not merely spring from the devious minds of white Democrats in Mississippi. Ironically, the Republican leadership of Massachusetts actually paved the way for the new constitution. Logan notes that the contemporary northern press called the qualifications to remove black voters from the rolls "the Massysip' idea," although the venerable historian never explains exactly what the term meant, precisely what the Massachusetts-Mississippi connection entailed, or how that nexus came about.[19] Nor has any other historian adequately explained "the Massysip' idea." An explanation is thus long overdue, and it adds a great deal of important information to our story.

To begin, the Mississippi legislature called the constitutional convention of 1890, with the approval of the state's Democratic machine, which consisted of newly elected Governor John M. Stone, Senator J. Z. George, and Supreme Court Justice Lucius Q. C. Lamar. Its sole purpose was to draft a constitution that would circumvent the federal supervision of elections by disfranchising blacks without violating the Fifteenth Amendment. The idea for the convention had been debated in the newspapers of the state and in the legislature without success for six years already, but Robert Lowry, the Bourbon governor from 1881 to 1889, refused to agree to the idea. Lowry opposed wholesale black disfranchisement, partly because of his Bourbon mentality of paternalism toward blacks and partly because he feared federal retaliation. After the election of the Republican president and Congress in 1888, however, the threat of the Federal Elections Bill suddenly and dramatically brought the issue of the constitutional convention to the fore. It became the main issue of the gubernatorial campaign in 1889, which Stone won easily by promising to approve a constitutional convention should the legislature call one.[20] In his inaugural address in January

Republican Leaders Past and Present. *The old leaders and the new.* (*Puck,*
1890.) The original leaders of the GOP (Charles Sumner, William
Seward, Salmon P. Chase, and Abraham Lincoln) are shown here representing monuments of good government who tower above and easily
overshadow their 1890 counterparts (George Frisbie Hoar, Thomas B.
Reed, Matthew Quay, and Benjamin Harrison).

1890, Stone made public the plans for the convention but, fearing federal interference, added that "Never was a look more important before a leap is made."[21]

Mississippi Democrats thus watched the developments on Capitol Hill in early 1890 carefully. Soon they realized that the GOP fully intended to go through with its plan to pass a Federal Elections Bill, whether Mississippi changed its state constitution or not. Thus, there was no need to postpone the convention any longer—they had nothing to lose. Moreover, the Mississippi machine, trying to find the silver lining inside the cloud of doom, reasoned that now might even be the most opportune time imaginable to rewrite the state constitution. Perhaps with national attention focused upon the Federal Elections Bill battle in Washington, the convention could do its work without too much northern Republican scrutiny. If not, at least all the congressional discussion of election laws would provide the Mississippians with the perfect opportunity to find out what type of voter qualifications, if any, northern Republicans might allow them to write into their new constitution. The two main options that the Mississippi press had been considering throughout the early months of 1890 before the convention were literacy tests and property qualifications. The question was, which, if either, would the GOP be more likely to let Mississippi get away with.[22]

How the literacy test option won out over property qualifications is the most interesting part of the story. It begins not in Jackson, Mississippi, but in the northern press and in Washington, D.C., fully a year before the constitutional convention. In adjoining articles published in the *North American Review* in 1889, Albion Tourgee and John Tyler Morgan precipitated a new strain of thought concerning potential solutions to the race problem by mutually advocating that southern states adopt literacy tests. Tourgee predicted that the constitutional limitation of suffrage based upon a literacy test would be the only solution to the race problem that would "command the approval of a majority of the people of the North."[23] Morgan was not sure about that, but he and fellow southern Democrats had always lamented the fact that the Republican-controlled federal government held the former Confederate states to a different standard than northern states with regard to voter qualifications. He explained that Massachusetts had enacted a literacy test in 1857 for the sole purpose of controlling the voting strength of its ethnic immigrant population. Why should not southern states be allowed to disqualify their undesirable voters as well, asked Morgan? How is one a violation of the Fifteenth Amendment, but not the other?[24]

Morgan later took his argument even further, making the ultimate racist case for disfranchising black voters. In 1890, in an introduction to a new edition of Alexis de Tocqueville's classic volume *Democracy in America* (1830), which he coauthored with John J. Ingalls, the Alabamian incorporated Tourgee's theory into his own philosophic musings. He noted that the famed young Frenchman Tocqueville had been fascinated with "the general equality of conditions" in America, despite the existence of the peculiar institution of slavery in the South at the time. Morgan explained that the foreign visitor meant only equality "among the white race, who are described as 'We, the people,' in the opening sentence of the Constitution." The Founding Fathers never included blacks in their definition of "the people," said Morgan. Adding blacks to "the people" was, he asserted, a political maneuver of the Republican Party, which, despite the Reconstruction amendments, public opinion never sanctioned. If the American public did not put its stamp of approval upon such a radical amendment to the Founding Fathers' Constitution, the amendment could never be enforced. "Public opinion," Morgan declared, "is the vital force in every law in a free government."[25]

Morgan went on to explain that the Founding Fathers and Tocqueville both considered it axiomatic that public opinion is always the driving force behind any democratic political system. Not even the Declaration of Independence or the Constitution, Morgan opined, could have survived without a majority of the American public supporting them. Thus, if the majority of the American people refused to support the Fifteenth Amendment, should it stand? Should it be law? And by contrast, if the American public decreed that only members of the male sex should vote—and it did—or if it approved an educational test for voters, as Albion Tourgee claimed, then why could it not also dictate that race or skin color be among the qualifications for voting? It should be able to, contended Morgan, because it would put the government back exclusively in the hands of "the people," as the Founding Fathers defined that term.[26]

Even if Tourgee was right in predicting that northern public opinion would support southern literacy tests, the question remained whether Republican congressmen would accept the same as the solution to the race problem or fight the spirit of the times as they had done during Reconstruction. Southern Democrats who seized upon the idea of adopting literacy tests, therefore, probed their northern colleagues across the aisles in the House and Senate to find out. In January 1890, Senator Samuel D. Pasco of Florida, in a long soliloquy that few senators were present to hear, took the lead in urging his southern brethren to look seriously at the Massachusetts example of adopting the literacy test as the best potential solution to the South's ballot problems. Fearing a backlash from Hoar and Massachusetts' senior senator Henry L. Dawes, Pasco sought to disarm them with an outwardly humble but cleverly sarcastic appeal for the Bay State "to be patient with her Southern sisters," for most, he said, were not as old and experienced in establishing sound principles of democratic government as was the state whose origins dated back to the *Mayflower*.[27]

All southern Democrats desired to know whether there was any real chance of northern Republicans granting the South leniency in establishing new voter qualifications, but that desire absolutely consumed Senator J. Z. George of Mississippi. He, like all other southerners, sincerely believed the Republicans had strictly prohibited such qualifications in the Reconstruction constitutions that the several Confederate states had been forced to adopt as a prerequisite to readmission to the Union. In addition, George was sure that if Mississippi disfranchised black voters based on a literacy test—even a fair one—the Republicans would strip the state of a proportionate amount of congressional representation, essentially cutting its representation in half. Facing the prospect of a dreaded Federal Elections Bill that threatened to bring back the onerous days of Reconstruction, however, even emasculated congressional representation looked good to George in 1890, if that was what it would take to prevent a return to black and Republican domination of the state. Congressional representation or not, at least native white Democrats would control the internal affairs of their state.[28]

As the only member of Mississippi's Democratic machine in Congress, George had the burden of probing the opinions of the northern Republican policy makers in Washington about voter qualifications. In March 1890, while speaking on behalf of the Blair Education Bill, the Mississippian lured George Frisbie Hoar into a conversation whereby he might ascertain directly whether the Republicans would allow the Magnolia State to follow the example of the Bay State in adopting a literacy test. He began his snare with a tirade against the northern Republican congressmen's neo-abolitionist habit of trying to settle the South's race problem from afar, or, as he put it, trying "to prescribe . . . the rules by which electors shall be made" in other states. He looked at Hoar, saying: "If you would keep your intermeddling from outside of the State of Mississippi; if you would allow these diverse races, locally intermingled, and yet in all attributes which distinguish men from one another as far apart as the poles—if you would allow us to work out our own salvation without your external and, I might add, infernal intermeddling, we might at last work out something."[29] Hoar responded by asking George what potential solution he proposed. George answered that he wished Mississippi could adopt a literacy test as Massachusetts had done long ago, but the state's Republican constitution of 1867 prohibited it. He then read the section of the 1867 constitution which forbade both education and property requirements. Hoar corrected George, saying that the Republicans' intention in making that rule was merely to ensure that if whites kept black southerners down intellectually and economically—and surely they would try—they would only be hurting themselves, because those poor, uneducated blacks would still get to vote, and they would still control the outcome of elections. It was a way of convincing white southerners that they would enjoy better government if those black voters were educated, property-owning taxpayers. George asked Hoar if he was sure about that interpretation. Hoar proudly responded that of course he was sure about it. He had been one of the Republicans who helped draft the readmission act and the Reconstruction amendments, and, therefore, his interpretation of the Mississippi Constitution of 1867 was absolutely correct. So, George in effect asked, if Mississippi wanted to have a literacy test now, it could do so? Hoar replied that, so long as it was fairly applied to both races, it would be fine. George then asked Hoar to repeat for the record that one of the founding fathers of Reconstruction approved of Mississippi having a literacy requirement. Hoar obliged. In this colloquy, George essentially made it appear that the literacy test about to be written into the new constitution was all Hoar's idea. Thus, if it later proved to be an instrument of racial discrimination, as George knew that it surely would, he and all other white Mississippians could point the finger of accusation toward the senator who represented the "cradle of liberty."[30]

Hoar's stance during this exchange made him appear to onlookers as either a traitor to the humanitarian cause or incredibly naive. The latter is the more plausible of the two theories, considering how the national press excoriated him for falling into the Mississippian's trap. One northern paper ridiculed him thusly: "Can Senator Hoar be of that class who learn not even from experience? Several times before has he returned to 'tackle' the Mississippian and each time . . . he has 'gone to grass,' but never before did his back strike the ground with such emphasis. . . . The republican senators confess with some amusement that Senator Hoar's 'walloping' as they call it, left him in such distressed condition mentally that he had to 'haul off for repairs.'"[31] By the time the Federal Elections Bill debate finally arrived in the House of Representatives in June, George and Hoar had already set the table for the Mississippi constitutional convention to adopt the literacy test to disqualify black voters. The coup de grâce, however, came in the House debate itself, as Henry Cabot Lodge made the opening statement for the

Republicans and, in effect, urged the southern states to adopt literacy tests as voting qualifications. At first glance, it seems a curiosity of the highest order that Lodge would encourage the southern states to disfranchise their illiterates—most of whom were black—in the same bill he hoped to use to enforce their voting rights. The fact is, he did not believe any southern state would adopt an education qualification to control its voting population, as his own state of Massachusetts had done, because of the South's desire to allow illiterate whites to continue voting. He later explained that "Nothing in this bill . . . prevents a state from excluding ignorance from the suffrage. Massachusetts has an educational test." Any southern state, he said, "can do the same, but will not because . . . [each] wishes to exclude black ignorance and let white ignorance vote."[32]

Lodge was foolishly convinced, as were many other northern Republicans (including Hoar), that this notion was true. He was, of course, wrong. He simply misread the southern Democrat mind-set. The Democratic leaders of some southern states, most notably Mississippi, would have eagerly adopted education qualifications long before 1890 had they thought they could get away with it. Like Hoar before him, Lodge did not realize that the statement he made in Washington about the literacy test would soon be used by some of his most fierce adversaries in Jackson, Mississippi. Other Republicans realized Lodge's error, however. As Jonathan P. Dolliver of Iowa put it, criticizing Lodge's skewed logic, "I had rather see the nation governed by men who obey the Constitution without being able to read it than by men who trample upon the Constitution, but can read it in ten languages."[33]

At the assembly in Jackson, Mississippi, which began, coincidentally, on the same day that the Quay-Gorman deal took place in Washington, the delegates discussed the two main ideas for circumventing the Fifteenth Amendment—the property qualification and the literacy test. With Hoar and Lodge having already pronounced their blessing upon the literacy test, most of the delegates in Jackson considered it the best choice. Moreover, educational qualifications for voters seemed to be the wave of the future, while property qualifications seemed to be a throwback to the pre-Jacksonian generation when aristocrats controlled state governments and excluded the common man from politics. The delegates quickly discarded the property requirement idea. Fearing, however, that there could come a time when some new national education bill might surface, become law, and reeducate (and thus re-enfranchise) Mississippi's black population, the convention added an "understanding clause" into the new constitution. Its purpose was simple. It would allow illiterate whites, upon giving a "reasonable" interpretation of some passage of the new constitution, to vote. Blacks would be disallowed based upon their rendering what white pollers would have predetermined to be an incorrect interpretation. Mississippi's government would thus be securely placed in the hands of whites for generations to come.[34]

For added protection, however, the Mississippi convention also incorporated into the constitution several other methods of ensuring white control. One was the two-dollar per voter poll tax, a device that had been forbidden in some states since colonial times. It was to be paid a year in advance of each election, and the receipt of payment had to be presented at the polling station on election day. As with the understanding clause, the poll tax could be strictly enforced for blacks and laxly enforced for whites. For another safeguard, a residency requirement of one year in the district in which a voter intended to vote was added. In addition, the convention gerrymandered Mississippi's legislative districts, carving thirteen additional white districts out of the state's black majority counties. Yet another feature of the new constitution was the adoption of the Australian ballot, which, like the literacy test, seemed to be a wave of the future. Massachusetts had already adopted this method of private voting, and other states throughout the nation were giving it serious consideration as well. This secret balloting was intended to prevent the buying and selling of votes because, even if some unscrupulous politico payed a voter to vote a certain way, he would have no assurance of the voter's compliance. The Australian ballot gave an air of legitimacy to the new Mississippi constitution because, in theory, voters of both races would be free to vote their consciences.[35]

In reality, however, Mississippi's political leaders had a more devious intention. As one contemporary constitutional expert explained, "If votes were taken *viva voce* [as was still done in two states in 1890], so that it could always be determined with absolute certainty how every person had voted," ascertaining the legitimacy of the returns would be easy. "But when secret balloting is the policy of the law, and no one is at liberty to inquire how any elector has voted . . . and when consequently the avenues to correct information concerning the votes cast are carefully guarded against judicial exploration," there is no way of proving fraud. It thus becomes one person's word against another's.[36] The Australian ballot, rather than ensuring pure elections, likely made it easier for the Democratic machine of Mississippi to control the outcome of elections.[37]

Despite the constitution's November 1 ratification, it was not designed to affect the vote cast in the election of 1890. The complicated registration procedure ensured that it could not be utilized until the election of 1892. In that first usage, it decreased the number of Democrat voters by more than half, but it cut the Republican vote by 96 percent.[38] Yet, the fact that it did actually disfranchise over half of all the white Democrats in the state partly gave it the legitimacy that J. Z. George so badly desired. The factors that seemed to add the greatest amount of legitimacy at the time, however, were black delegate Isaiah Montgomery's public support of the new constitution and the lack of overt criticism from Mississippi's other leading black public figures, former U. S. Senator Blanche K. Bruce and former U. S. Representative John R. Lynch.[39]

While the Mississippi constitutional convention lingered through the end of the summer, in Boston, Henry Cabot Lodge continued to try to influence both the Senate and public opinion with explanations of the purpose of the Federal Elections Bill and the necessity for passing it. In September, he coauthored an article in the *North American Review,* the periodical he once edited. The other author, who took an opposing point of view, was Terrence V. Powderly, president of the Knights of Labor, the largest labor union in the country. The main point of Lodge's half of the article was "nothing that is right and honest need fear the light." Of course, Thomas R. Stockdale of Mississippi had already responded to that point in the House debate over the Lodge bill with his reference to the Spanish Inquisition. Lodge found it "amusing" that a portion of the national press was "raving in mad excitement merely because it is proposed to make public everything which affects the election of the representatives of the people in Congress." Answering that portion of the press which repeatedly called his bill a "force bill," he declared that it was actually more of an "anti-force bill," for it was "intended to stop the exercise of illegal force by those who use it at the polls North or South; and it is exactly this which the opponents of the bill dread." Concerning the Democrats' argument that the bill was sectional, expensive, and bad for business, that was basically the old "doughface" argument of the 1850s repackaged, he said. In those days before the Civil War, noted Lodge, the South, with influence out of all proportion to its population, blustered and bullied the North and the West with threats of boycotts, secession, and war. Now, when the North wanted simply to enforce the Constitution, said Lodge, the South was again overreacting. But the North would not be unprepared this time, he cautioned. New York and Ohio had already armed and alerted their militias in case of another civil war, and other northern states were soon to follow.[40]

Powderly used his half of the article to declare himself neutral in party politics and to oppose the Lodge bill on the grounds that it was a hypocritical attempt by one section of the country to control another. "We do not hear of the brutal assaults, shootings, mobbings, and violent demonstrations in the North that we read of as happening on election day in the South," because the Republican Party "employs a more refined system of doing violence to the election laws of the nation." Powderly was particularly disturbed by the many instances in the North of industrial employers forcing their workers to vote the Republican ticket in order to keep their jobs and by the property requirements that kept so many urban workers disfranchised there. He believed the answer lay not in federal supervision of elections but simply in adopting the Australian ballot throughout the country.[41]

Lodge's half of the article drew a negative response from southern Republican A. W. Shaffer, chief federal supervisor of elections in North Carolina, who had perhaps the best perspective on the issue of any person on either side. He explained that the original 1871 Supervisors' Law worked at least somewhat in the North because of "faithful courts, honest juries, and a correct public opinion," but it had no such effect in the South because "Here public opinion tolerates, when it does not justify, all crimes for the maintenance of the supremacy of the Democratic party." Thus, the original bill was "a visible monument of the folly" of the Lodge bill, which was nothing more than a "miserable caricature of a long dead and forgotten statute." Moreover, said Shaffer, the Lodge bill was political "quackery and malpractice," a "sickly-sentimental and half-hearted" attempt to fix America's electoral system. The best evidence for this conclusion, he said, could be seen in the presidential election of 1888 in North Carolina. One "district was as well supervised . . . as it could have been if Mr. Lodge had been present in person at every poll," yet it still suffered great corruption. Finally, Shaffer complained that southern Republicans "who have borne the brunt of the political crimes for the last twenty-five years" have always been ignored by party bosses and policy makers of the North. "They have asked for bread, they have received a stone."[42]

In Congress, various House Democrats answered Lodge's article, and none of them yielded an inch. On September 26, "Fightin' Joe" Wheeler of Alabama, a former Confederate military leader, used a momentary lull in the daily business to launch an attack on the bill, which he believed would turn "back the wheels of civilization."[43] He read from one of the GOP's main organs, William E. Chandler's *National Republican* of Washington, dated July 3, the day immediately following passage of the Lodge bill. It predicted that, once the bill became law, six or seven southern states would go Republican, adding twelve or fourteen new senators and twenty new representatives to the GOP's majority. Following this new Republican hegemony in the South, separate schools for the races would then be abolished, and laws against intermarriage of the races would be repealed. Wheeler then blasted the North for what he considered hypocrisy, pointing out that interracial marriages were presently illegal in both Indiana and Pennsylvania. He read an excerpt from the Keystone State law that explained, "It is not prejudice, nor caste, nor injustice of any kind" to prohibit racial intermarriage "but simply to suffer men to follow the law of races established by the creator himself." He added that "balance," not "force," was the key to good and healthy government in the United States. Indeed, he explained, "the world marvels at this wonderful structure. . . . the wisest and most sagacious statesmen see the secret to our success in this one great safeguard within our constitutional system."[44]

As a result of the Lodge bill pending in Washington and the Mississippi Constitution being drafted in Jackson at the same time, national public attention became focused on the issue of black suffrage and the extension of federal power in the summer of 1890 more than any other time since the ratification of the Fifteenth Amendment in 1870. The debate over America's race problem even garnered considerable attention abroad. Many European intellectuals, who were collectively under the influence of Social Darwinism and racial imperialism at the time, agreed that African Americans should be disfranchised. As one contemporary English writer observed, the most humanitarian thing that Congress could do for black people under the circumstances would be to allow the race problem to work itself out naturally, without federal interference. This do-nothing policy would spare them the violence and retaliation that would surely result from enforcing the Fifteenth Amendment. Whether blacks "should" have the right to vote was a question best left for theologians to decide. Politicians in the here and now could only do what was pragmatic. In other words, the issue of right and wrong was not as important as the issue of cause and effect. If the Republicans insisted on doing right, the effect would be catastrophic for blacks.[45]

In the midst of this important public debate came the midterm election of 1890, and Democrats waited expectantly for voters to vindicate them. Indeed, many incumbent Republicans, especially those who had played a role in the Lodge bill debate, lost their bids for reelection. Several others had understood that their party's controversial record in the first session would make it difficult for them to be reelected and thus chose not to run. Even President Harrison, who engaged in a month-long national speaking tour in October, realized the tenor of public opinion on the Federal Elections Bill controversy and rarely mentioned it in his speeches, emphasizing more popular issues instead. Republican congressmen who ran on their record of legislation in the first session of the Fifty-first Congress found, however, that most voters could not appreciate their work.[46]

Thus, despite the GOP's best efforts, the result of the midterm election was the largest turnover in the history of Congress. The GOP lost 154 seats. Whereas the Republicans had come to power in 1888 with a seven-vote majority and then increased that majority to twenty-four after settling the seventeen contested elections, in November 1890, voters gave the Democrats a 130-vote majority. House Democrats who had prophesied a public backlash against the activism of the Reed House felt absolutely vindicated by the result and squandered no opportunity to say so. They listed the reasons for the backlash as the "force bill," the Reed Rules, the McKinley Tariff, and the exhausting of $461 million from the treasury surplus on pensions. They also proclaimed that voters had intentionally overthrown the "Jacobins" (Republican radicals), who suppressed the moderate voice of the "Girondins" (Democrats and money Republicans).[47] Allusions to Revolutionary and Napoleonic France appeared in the Democratic press as well. Several newspapers hailed the election as the "Waterloo" of the Republican Party, and some considered it a "death blow" to the GOP.[48] Although opinion was divided over which issue in particular caused the backlash, a contingent of newspapers of all stripes and from all sections of the country considered the election a "referendum" on the "force bill."[49]

Despite such contemporary interpretations of the election, there is a more historically accurate explanation for the turnover of 1890. The North always contained a large number of uncommitted voters who, more often than not, went Republican, but in this election they chose the Democrats merely as the lesser of two evils. Democratic propaganda was more sophisticated and thus more effective at convincing these doubtful voters of the improprieties of the GOP's legislative agenda than the Republican propaganda machine was at countering it. Further evidence suggests that, had the Republican-led Senate passed the Lodge bill instead of the McKinley bill in the first session, the outcome of the election could very well have been different. Some House Republicans held that opinion long before the midterm election, but the Quay machine silenced them.

The most notable case occurred in September, when Robert P. Kennedy of Ohio denounced the Senate, and Quay in particular, for choosing to table the Lodge bill until after the election. Kennedy said, "The other day when I went down the steps of this capitol, after I had spoken in this assembly, on the pavement below I met an old colored man, bowed with years, his hair gray, curly, and crisp; and with tears in his eyes and quivering lip he shook my hand and blessed me because I had spoken on behalf of his people." Why was Quay and his faction of the Republican Party afraid to do the same, he begged to know? Fellow House Republicans did not think

Kennedy's criticism was justified, however, and voted to expunge his whole speech from the *Record*, calling it "out of order." As a result, Kennedy chose not to seek reelection in 1890.[50]

Democrats hoped, of course, that the result of the election would convince Senate Republicans to drop the Federal Elections Bill, but they also feared that it would make the Senate humanitarians even more determined to pass it while they had the chance. When the upper chamber assembled on December 1, Democrats were disappointed but not surprised to learn that the Senate, which was relatively unaffected by the House shake-up, was determined to push ahead with its "utterly desperate . . . suicidal act."[51] Arkansas Senator James K. Jones expressed the Democrats' incredulity at the Republicans' determination: "The session of this Congress which has recently closed was distinguished by three things, the passage of the McKinley bill, the attempt to pass this [elections] bill, and the violent methods of forcing measures through the popular branch of Congress. Upon these issues we went to the people, and the result is the most astounding, crushing, overwhelming defeat of the party responsible for all this."[52]

John G. Carlisle of Kentucky, the former Speaker of the House, who had been elected to the Senate in early 1890 to serve out the remainder of deceased Senator James B. Beck's term, predicted that the Republicans' staunch refusal to change their current course would backfire, for it would only strengthen the white South's resolve to remain solid. "As long as political parties are divided upon the present issues [elections bill, protective tariff, and centralization]," he explained, "the South will be Democratic, no matter what repressive laws may be enacted or how arbitrarily they may be enacted. . . . But while the politics of the South cannot be changed by law, its business may be ruined by the agitations and disturbances" of the Federal Elections Bill. Carlisle also predicted that, despite all of the clamor surrounding the bill, the Senate would ultimately "allow it to die on the calendar and be buried with [the] other rubbish at the end of the session."[53]

The result of the midterm election put no damper on the House's ex post facto debate over the Lodge bill. As the second session began, House Democrats continued to blast it at every opportunity. Benjamin Enloe of Tennessee called it a "legislative bastard," because no one knew who its real father was. Was it Lodge, Rowell, Hoar, Spooner, or Chandler? Or was it really the longtime Republican supervisor of elections in New York City, John I. Davenport, a man who sat in the gallery every day during the House debate, and a man whom Democrats hated even more than Reed, Harrison, or any of the other reformers? Davenport, who had held his position perpetually since 1871, had developed an unsavory reputation as a manipulator of election results and soon became a focal point in the Senate debate on the Federal Elections Bill. One of the Democrats' first actions in the upper chamber was to demand that Davenport's and his many assistants' payroll records for the last twenty-nine years be sent from the U. S. Treasury to the Senate for investigation. Meanwhile, Enloe showed that someone had written a second version of the Lodge bill before November for distribution as election propaganda. Whereas the old version was seventy-five pages and fifty-seven sections long, the new one was nine pages and eight sections long. Whoever wrote it had cut out the parts containing the "force" in the "force bill," said Enloe, ostensibly to make it more palatable to voters.[54]

If that was the case, the strategy did not work. No doubtful voters went Republican because of an easier-to-swallow version of the Lodge bill. Nevertheless, the bill's sponsors in the Senate believed that making the bill shorter and milder was a prudent move. Hoar and Spooner realized that the original bill would not only be impossible to drive through the Senate, but that it might also make the opposition's protest, which had been peaceful to that point, turn violent. Indeed, Hoar had already received a great amount of "hate mail" for supporting the bill. More important, Hoar feared that the coming Fifty-second Congress, which would be controlled by Democrats in the House, would repeal a stringent bill, rendering all of the Republicans' efforts futile. Thus, the Senate Committee on Privileges and Elections, which included Democrats James L. Pugh of Alabama and George Gray of Delaware, diluted, reworded, and shortened the original bill considerably, taking out long sections that dealt with issues peripheral to elections, such as selection of juries for trying cases of alleged fraud. Moreover, the committee "mitigated the severity of the penalties" for crimes committed at the ballot box, changed the number of petitioners necessary for having supervision in a district from one hundred to five hundred, and cut the number of supervisors per district from three to two. Hoar reasoned that "it is better to have the second best law kept permanently on the statute book than to have the best law there half the time."[55]

The result was a bill that looked much like the one Hoar had introduced in April. According to Hoar, the replacement bill was merely a blend of the old Supervisors' Law of 1871 and "provisions of a law which has been in operation in England for twenty-two years with general public satisfaction." On August 7, Hoar expressed his obvious contentment with the new bill as he introduced it to the Senate, telling his southern colleagues that "this is not a question of the domination of a negro majority over you; it is a question of the domination of a white man's minority over us."[56]

Hoar and fellow sponsors of the Senate bill understood the necessity of diluting congressional bills in order to secure their passage, and they seemed well satisfied with their proposed legislation. The public, however, could not appreciate such compromises. Indeed, many African Americans and rabidly partisan Republican newspaper editors expressed either disappointment in the Senate bill or outright opposition to it. As John Mercer Langston of Virginia, who had given his undivided support to the Lodge bill, complained with obvious disgust, the Senate bill "isn't worth the paper on which it is written."[57] Hence, the changes in the bill ultimately had the opposite effect of what Hoar intended. The strategy converted no Democrats, money Republicans, or Independents into supporters, and, even worse, it created dissension in the humanitarian ranks. To partisan Republicans, the Senate bill was a poor substitute for the original, and to the rest of the nation, it was no improvement over the original because it was merely less severe. Senate Democrats especially could not appreciate the magnanimity of the new bill. It actually frustrated them that the new bill seemed so mild compared to the old. How could they fight a mild bill as zealously as their House counterparts had fought the harsh Lodge bill? They resolved to create the zeal by demanding, upon Hoar's introduction of the new Senate bill, that Lodge's bill, which partisan Republicans had rammed through the House in a mere seven days, be read in its entirety to the upper chamber.[58]

The American public was likewise not ready to embrace the new bill as an improvement over the old Lodge bill. As one independent newspaper put it, it was still a "force bill," and it was still "putrid . . . a stench in the nostrils of the nation, and it should at once be consigned to the grave that is beyond the reach of the resurrection trump . . . let the clods of oblivion rattle on its coffin without delay."[59] Making matters worse for the humanitarians, however, was the fact that losing the support of vocal African Americans such as John Mercer Langston fanned the flames of southern demagoguery, which were already blazing out of control. With a "see, I told you so" attitude, South Carolina governor-elect Ben Tillman commented that if Senate Republicans continued to swim against the tide of public opinion by passing the Federal Elections Bill, they would be sorely "disappointed in their calculations. The negroes in the South are no longer so wedded to the Republican party that they will do its bidding, and the attempt by Federal officials to drive them as heretofore is bound to produce most injurious results. . . . the negroes have become indifferent to politics. It would be a great misfortune to them and to the country if they should be stirred up again as they were in the Reconstruction era."[60]

The aged and experienced Hoar sincerely wanted to help black voters enjoy their constitutional rights, yet he might have listened to the appeals of such detractors had it not been for his younger and more cavalier cohort Spooner. The Wisconsin senator was just as sincere as Hoar in his desire to purify southern elections, but he was less convinced of the odds of failure than the elder statesman from Massachusetts. Spooner even assumed the mantle of his ill colleague from New Hampshire, William E. Chandler, in persuading a reluctant President Harrison to support the Federal Elections Bill publicly in his third State of the Union address. Indeed, Spooner's earnestness, zealousness, and vigilance in supporting the bill were practically all that kept interest in the controversial measure alive.[61]

As Chairman of the Committee on Privileges and Elections, it was Hoar, however, not Spooner, who had the daunting task of driving the unpopular bill through the Senate. He also had the dubious honor of matching wits with the Democratic manager of the debate, Arthur P. Gorman. This Maryland politico privately planned "one of the most spectacular filibusters in the history of the Senate," although he was careful not to admit it publicly. He claimed instead that the Democrats needed to debate the bill and its amendments thoroughly in order that both parties could work out a final, compromise version.

Gorman was an interesting character. He did not fit the description of a typical Gilded Age senator. In appearance, he was one of the few public men of his day who wore neither a beard nor a mustache. His clean-shaven, boyish-but-handsome face did not make him look the part of party boss. Nor did his age and experience. At fifty-one, he was not old by Senate standards, and he was only in his second term. Moreover, he was not a lawyer and had no legal training, yet his natural forensic abilities caused many of the best legal minds in the Senate to defer to him. He had been a page in the Senate from age eleven to twenty-seven and had helped guard the Capitol against possible Confederate attack during the Civil War. He called himself a Unionist War Democrat at the time and was a friend and confidant of Andrew Johnson, whom he faithfully supported throughout his tumultuous term, including the impeachment trial of 1868. Later in the same year, he became president of the "National Association of Base Ball Players," when the soon-to-be national pastime was still in its infancy. Gorman, in fact, helped raise the game to the level of respectability that it would enjoy throughout the twentieth century. He subsequently became a Maryland tax collector, a state legislator, and the president of a local canal company. In 1888, he became the leader of the pro-Cleveland bloc at the Democratic National Convention. As a Democrat who came of age during the Civil War and Reconstruction, Gorman understood what it meant to be in the minority and to stand on the unpopular side of great public issues. Such a lifetime of hardship in the political arena only served to bolster his determination to fight the Federal Elections Bill.[62]

An important part of Gorman's job as floor manager was to schedule the order in which his Democratic colleagues would speak. At the outset of the debate, the eight former Confederate generals in the Senate—William B. Bate, Matthew Butler, Alfred Colquitt, J. Z. George, Randall L. Gibson, John Tyler Morgan, Matthew Ransom, and Edmund Cary Walthall—resented Gorman's dictation to them about when they could speak, yet all eventually fell in line behind his leadership. To these seasoned veterans of war and politics, the battle would be about preserving white supremacy in the South and protecting their states from the interference of the neo-abolitionists, whereas to the Unionist Gorman, it would be more about protecting the rights of the minority party in the Senate. These divergent motivations for opposing the bill complemented one another nicely, however, so there was no notable dissension within the minority party once the battle began.[63]

Aside from the two party managers of the debate, the other key player in the upcoming Senate drama was Vice President Levi P. Morton, who had followed an interesting path to the second-highest office in the land. In 1881 and again in 1885, this extremely wealthy, Vermont-born, Dartmouth-educated businessman had failed in his only two runs for the Senate from his adopted state of New York. He had served as Minister to France under the Garfield-Arthur administrations, and by all accounts he was a good diplomat. Prior to that appointment, he had served two terms as a representative in Congress from New York City. His early career as an international banker and shipping tycoon had earned him such a fortune that he could have lived comfortably without ever working again. His sense of duty as a patriotic American citizen with a pedigree that extended back to the *Mayflower,* however, and his need to be in a position of power, compelled him to seek high office. His ancestors had helped build the Plymouth colony, and he had helped build Wall Street into the world's premier financial center. What was he to do with the rest of his life if not serve his country? Morton would do just that, sometimes to the consternation of the Democrats, and sometimes to his own party, for he was a money Republican, a neo-doughface, and a genuinely nonpartisan presiding officer of the nation's highest legislative body.[64]

As the relatively peaceful autumn of 1890 gave way to winter, the nation awaited with great anticipation the coming struggle in the Senate. Even though the American public had already passed judgment against the Federal Elections Bill, Hoar and the humanitarian Republicans were undeterred in their determination to force it upon the nation. Gorman and the Democrats thus felt they had no choice but to assemble their forces for the inevitable conflict and draw up their battle plans. In December, the nation, and indeed the world, would watch in amazement as the unstoppable force met the immovable object.

Chapter 6

THE STORMY AND TURBULENT SEA OF DEMOCRATIC FREEDOM

The Senate's Epic Struggle for Control of the Nation's Racial Destiny

There is force all through this bill. It is the prominent and salient feature, and the people, with instinct that rarely fails them, have dubbed it "the force bill," and so it is known throughout the length and breadth of this country, and will never have any other popular title than that.

—Senator George Gray of Delaware

There is no force in it but the force of law.... Still Senators on the other side call it a force bill.

— SenatorJoseph N. Dolph of Oregon

The Federal Elections Bill debate captivated the American public like few other congressional debates had ever done. Even the showdowns over similar measures on Capitol Hill during Reconstruction paled in comparison, for two reasons. First, during Reconstruction, the public expected and accepted partisan and sectional fights in Congress as a residue of the great and terrible war that had recently engulfed the nation. Since Reconstruction, however, a spirit of sectional reconciliation and, to a lesser extent,

129

bipartisanship had prevailed. The introduction of the Federal Elections Bill destroyed those congenial feelings. It thus seemed to be out of place and time, making it more fascinating to the public than any similar measure ever introduced before. The second reason was the sheer amount of time that the bill pended in Congress. Altogether, it lay before Congress for about eight months, more than seven of which were spent in the Senate. From the time the House took up the bill in July 1890 until the Senate finally tabled it in February 1891, the national press reported on its status almost every day. Adding even more drama to this already dramatic debate was the Democratic filibuster in the Senate, which lasted longer than any previous filibuster ever had—about two months. The filibuster itself might have bored the public rather than fascinated it had it not been for the fact that Republican leaders threatened to break the stalemate by changing the rules, as the House had already done, to limit debate. The contest in the Senate captured national attention, therefore, because it raised two separate questions: would the revolution that "Czar" Reed began in the House carry over to the Senate? And would the Republicans force federal supervision of elections on the nation?[1]

Historians have generally been more interested in the filibuster of the Federal Elections Bill in the Senate than with the actual measures that the bill contained. In fact, rarely have historians adequately analyzed the contents of the bill to determine if the bill was good legislation and if it was a sensible solution to suffrage abuses and the race problem. This oversight must be corrected. Historians have also, despite their preoccupation with this particular filibuster, often failed to recognize that all filibusters are not the same. The stereotype of the filibuster is that it is always purely a time-killing mechanism and that it cannot possibly bring any illumination to the bill under consideration. That misconception must also be corrected. While all filibusters are by nature obstructive, some can also be instructive. The first half of the Senate filibuster of 1890–1891 actually cast far more light on the contents of the Federal Elections Bill than the brief House debate ever did, and was thus instructive to the American people. The Democrats stayed on-message and hammered away at the provisions of the bill throughout December, a fact that some Republicans, in moments of frankness, acknowledged. When they did digress, they still tried to stick to subjects that were at least peripheral to the bill. Although a few notable verbal altercations occurred between hotspurs on opposite sides of the aisle who brought sectionalism into the discussion, the Democrats tried to continue the Senate tradition of congeniality toward their Republican adversaries, a hallmark that had long set the upper chamber apart from the lower.[2]

The Democrats' explanations for the necessity of a filibuster of the Federal Elections Bill were quite rational considering the upper chamber's tradition of unlimited debate, which was as old as the Senate itself. George Gray of Delaware justified his side's belief in thoroughly debating a bill before voting on it by reading from John Richard Green's *History of the Making of England.* He paraphrased Green as saying that the world has often "laughed at Parliaments as 'talking shops.' . . . But talk is persuasion and persuasion is force, the one force which can sway freemen to deeds such as those which have made England what she is." Matthew Butler noted that filibustering was "often the most effective way to bring a question sharply to the attention of the people and give them the opportunity to pass upon it." He anticipated correctly that the longer the Federal Elections Bill stayed in the public eye—no matter how it stayed there—the more the American people would have the opportunity to evaluate it; and the longer the people looked at it, the more they would protest it. Therefore, it was in the best interest of the nation, as William B. Bate of Tennessee put it, "to exhaust all parliamentary means" to keep the bill in the public eye as long as possible. John W. Daniel of Virginia pointed out that even the bill's Senate sponsor, George Frisbie Hoar, conceded that this bill was "more misunderstood than any measure" in American history. Was that fact not all the more reason to go through it line by line in careful consideration of every provision? John E. Kenna of West Virginia added that, considering how controversial this particular bill was, its "discussion may go on indefinitely."[3]

Republicans, when it was in their best interest, agreed that extended discussion of congressional bills promoted the general welfare of the nation by preventing passage of bad legislation. As Thomas B. Reed wrote just before his party gained the majority in Congress and, consequently, just before he was elevated to Speaker of the House: "What is a legislative body for? It is not merely to make laws. It is to decide on all questions of public grievance. . . . A negative decision by a legislative body is of as much value to the community as a law. Time is not lost when cases are investigated and action refused. Half the grievances of mankind turn out to be unfounded as soon as somebody is found to listen to them."[4] George Frisbie Hoar, in an article in the popular Boston periodical *The Youth's Companion,* wrote something very similar just before the Democratic filibuster began in the Senate: "In the United States the process of change is slow and is meant to be slow. . . . If any citizens be disposed to be impatient . . . let them remember that it was in this way that our fathers laid the foundation of their Government. . . . They meant that it should declare the will of the people. But the will so declared was to be mature, deliberate, well considered. . . . They were building for centuries, not for hours." Hoar added in conclusion that the plodding pace of Congress served as a "constitutional barrier against popular error or caprice."[5]

Historians thus should not automatically deem all filibusters as wastes of time, for if a filibuster resulted in the Senate jettisoning poorly framed legislation, it was time well spent. Filibusters can also have another desirable effect: they can force impatient sponsors of bills to compromise, and to perfect their otherwise imperfect legislation before passage. Either result is not only a victory for the minority party, but can also be a victory for the American people. In the case of the Federal Elections Bill filibuster, the Democrats hoped to kill it, but realistically expected to keep it under consideration at least long enough to force compromises in its provisions. In this study, therefore, the filibuster is treated not as time wasted, but as integral to understanding precisely why the Democrats hated the bill so vehemently.

On December 1, 1890, upon convening the second session of the Fifty-first Congress, the Senate quickly dispensed with the routine business of swearing in new senators, introducing resolutions for pensions and local pork, and listening to the Clerk read the president's annual address to Congress. As soon as practicable, Hoar moved to consider HR 11045, the Lodge bill. Gorman countered with a motion not to take up the bill, reminding the Republicans of the results of the midterm elections. He urged his opponents to drop the bill and move on to the more pressing economic issues that the voters wanted Congress to address. Banks all over the country were on the verge of collapsing, he noted, because the U. S. Treasury Department had no power under the law to help prop them up beyond the actions it had already taken. In addition, a serious flaw had been discovered in the McKinley Tariff, which threatened to wreck the tobacco industry if not addressed in this brief session. Hoar responded that such issues proved the need to vote on the Federal Elections Bill as soon as possible. When Hoar called for the yeas and nays on taking up the controversial measure, his motion carried forty-one to thirty, with fifteen absent and not paired for voting. Knowing that Hoar's next move would be to introduce his shorter, milder substitute bill, the Democrats began their stall tactics immediately, demanding that the longer, harsher House bill be read in its entirety, which, under existing Senate rules, was their privilege. After the Clerk had droned monotonously through half of the old Lodge bill to an almost empty chamber, Hoar interrupted to introduce his substitute bill, which the Clerk then began to read at length. In due time, William Boyd Allison of Iowa, whom one contemporary described as a man who always "looks wise and says nothing," made a motion to print the House and Senate bills side-by-side in parallel columns for easy comparison.[6]

Upon completion of the mundane reading of the bill, Hoar chose to forgo making an opening statement. Democrat David Turpie of Indiana, therefore, actually opened the Senate debate on the bill. It is interesting that, out of eighty-eight potential speakers in the Senate, Turpie should have been the first to speak on the Federal Elections Bill. He was in his first term in the Senate after having defeated Benjamin Harrison for the seat in a contested election in 1887. Harrison had been the incumbent, and his party had controlled the Indiana House. The Democrats controlled the Hoosier State's Senate, however. When the final tally resulted in Turpie having two votes more than Harrison, the Republicans levied a charge of fraud, but they could not substantiate it. The loss freed Harrison to become a willing and available presidential candidate the following year—one who knew all too well the need for electoral reform. Since Harrison went on to urge passage of a Federal Elections Bill, it seems somehow ironic, yet appropriate, that Turpie was the first senator to speak against it.[7]

Turpie's opening argument had little to do with the substantive issues of the bill, nor was it even remotely similar to anything previously said in the House debate. It was a strange history lesson about black-white race relations in America from colonial times to 1890, which showed that an important part of the Democrats' strategy was to use history and tradition to fight the Republican racial agenda. The benefit of this strategy was twofold: first, the Democrats could easily consume a great amount of time by providing what they considered necessary background information before launching into the actual attack on the provisions of the bill; and second, they strengthened their ideological position by contrasting the traditions of earlier generations on racial matters with those the GOP now proposed. The gist of Turpie's speech was that American race relations had passed through two stages. First, there was a "primitive era" when the nation either practiced or silently condoned black slavery and when it committed fratricide against Native Americans. After the Civil War, the nation had moved into the "medieval age" of race relations, which contained "the seed and promise of progressive betterment."[8] Yet, as much as some Republicans wished they could expedite the process of racial equality, said Turpie, only time, not force, could move the nation into its age of racial enlightenment. And, most important, if the Republicans hoped to improve the lot of black southerners, they would first need to grant full social and political equality to blacks in the North. As an Indianan, Turpie knew that blacks in the North were only marginally better off than their southern counterparts.

Since his northern Republican opponents could not refute that argument, Turpie's opening speech accomplished its purpose. It immediately reversed the roles of the parties in the debate, putting the Republicans on the defensive from the outset.[9]

Later, fellow Indiana Senator Daniel Voorhees reinforced Turpie's argument about Republican hypocrisy toward African Americans living in the northern states. "The tall sycamore of the Wabash," as Voorhees was known, had a largely undistinguished career in the Senate, but he enjoyed one great achievement in being the catalyst behind the building of the Jefferson Building of the Library of Congress, which is considered one of the great architectural marvels of modern history. Voorhees had a long history of supporting the southern viewpoint on state rights and racial issues, having once been a member of the infamous Knights of the Golden Circle, a northern Democratic organization that supported the Confederacy in the Civil War. He complained of what appeared to him to be Republican hypocrisy on the issue of voting rights, particularly in his home state of Indiana. He noted that "the present Administration of this Government had now been in power one year, nine months, and eighteen days. Its entire existence has been filled with sighs and groans and lamentations over the sins and shortcomings of other people in their alleged frauds on the ballot box." Yet, sixty days after fellow Hoosier Harrison took office, noted Voorhees, GOP leaders hatched a plot to "import" black voters to Indiana, West Virginia, and Connecticut to ensure Republican control of those states. The plan was to "colonize" from eight to ten thousand black men or families in each state to increase Republican numbers there. For proof, Voorhees read letters written by high-ranking Republican officials in the three states. He then astutely pointed out that never in any of the letters was the welfare of those blacks mentioned. He concluded his objurgation of the GOP by complaining that "the suppression of the colored vote" in the South continued to be "the perpetual theme of the Northern sectionalist who, in proportion to his ignorance, increases in zeal and malice. . . . As the maiden wants her lover every hour, so the Republican politician . . . wants the African, provided always that he is a voter and votes the Republican ticket."[10]

James L. Pugh of Alabama, who had already expressed his views on the subject eight months prior, was the first southern Democrat to speak in the Senate debate on the Federal Elections Bill. This haggard old ex-Confederate was a carryover from the "primitive era" of which Turpie had spoken. Far from embracing Turpie's idea of "progressive betterment" for the races, he favored a regressive approach, recasting the old slaveholders' argument of paternalism to imply that southern blacks had been disfranchised for their own good. He complained of the "fatal mixture of white and black suffrage" in which were "compounded natural elements that no chemist has ever yet discovered could be mingled together in the same laboratory so as to prevent fermentation and explosion." Pugh then questioned why the Republicans believed that suffrage was "the sole measure and only test of 'justice' to the negro." Clearly, it would be in the best interest of black southerners not to vote, said the Alabamian, because of the volatile nature of black-white race relations that currently prevailed.[11]

Hoar soon expressed his impatience with the Democrats' racial pontifications and moved for a vote on the bill immediately. George Gray of Delaware, a first-term Democrat who left no distinguishing mark on the Senate after 1890, answered the motion, saying that before he cast his vote on the bill he would like the opportunity to "trespass a little further on the time of the Senate." He did just that for the next two days. Gray, realizing that Hoar's impatience resulted partly from the fact that the first two Democratic speakers hardly mentioned the provisions of the Federal Elections Bill at all in their long speeches, thought it wise to pursue a different line of argument. Thus, he initiated another phase of the Democratic strategy, which he called "smoking out" the flaws in the bill, marking the first substantive discussion of the actual provisions of the bill.[12]

Gray began by making a comparison of the existing supervisory law of 1871 and the bill at hand, trying to show that both measures gave the federal government the most sweeping powers of centralization and intrusiveness in American history to that time. Both authorized the supervisors to make investigations of suffrage abuses by house-to-house canvasses in which they could demand that residents answer their questions on the spot, under penalty of law, without the presence of an attorney or any other safeguard to the liberties of private citizens. Gray continued by tediously picking apart the Federal Elections Bill's hiring provisions. He explained that not only were chief supervisors appointed for life, but they also had the power to appoint their own successors, which he equated to an absolute monarchy in disguise. "We do not want this chief supervisor. He is here for life, and you say we can not get rid of him. . . . I will tell you what I would do with him if I had my way. I would put him on board a ship . . . and I would make him a present to the Czar of Russia. Let him go there . . . and [populate] again the wastes of Siberia."[13]

Gray then explained how his own little state had conducted elections since 1776. Having only three counties, Delaware never took a statewide canvass. Each county presented its returns to the legislature separately. When a charge of fraud arose in any county, that county investigated the charge thoroughly before sending the returns to the legislature. In recent years, noted Gray, his state had been one of the "doubtful" or "swing" states and had experienced its share of suffrage abuses, none of which had anything to do with disfranchisement of black voters. The state's leading politicians from both parties had discussed possible ways to clean up the system, but they ultimately agreed that it would be best to leave it alone. Each side feared that any changes might give advantage to the other. The point was that Delaware's system represented the purest form of local sovereignty to be found in any state and, Gray believed, the most closely in line with the intention of the Founding Fathers. If his state did not even allow a canvass at the state level, how could it support national supervision of elections? Gray concluded his speech by stating with patriotic fervor, "I prefer, as all free American citizens, I think, must prefer, the stormy and turbulent sea of democratic freedom to the calm of a despotism."[14]

Northern Democrat and three-term Senator John McPherson of New Jersey later reinforced Gray's argument, saying of the chief supervisor under the Federal Elections Bill, "No Bonaparte who ever scaled the throne of France started with greater power towards a monarchy than that conferred upon this officer." Congress should discard this bill, he said, and allow the states to write their own laws reforming elections, just as New Jersey had done earlier in the year. The Garden State had provided for casting secret ballots and for establishing canvassing boards comprised of two members of each party. It was local, bipartisan, and was passed under the tutelage of a Democratic governor.[15]

First-term Senator James H. Berry of Arkansas continued the substantive attack on the provisions of the bill for the Democrats. This Confederate veteran had lost a leg in the Civil War before going on to enjoy a distinguished career in Arkansas politics. Elected governor in 1883, he served one two-year term, after which the legislature sent him to the U. S. Senate. Berry claimed to know with absolute certainty that federal supervision of elections would perpetuate one party's power over the other because the GOP had recently applied the old supervisory law of 1871 in Arkansas. In 1888, Arkansas played host to two highly controversial congressional elections, both of which involved alleged Democratic fraud, intimidation of voters, and even murder. The defeated Republicans, needless to say, contested and won both under the Reed Rules in early 1890. Then, in September 1890, President Harrison appointed a new Republican district court judge to serve the state's eastern congressional district. Under the terms of the 1871 law, the new judge in turn appointed a chief supervisor for his district for the November 1890 midterm elections. The

Harrison appointee chose John McClure, a highly partisan Republican who had been Chief Justice of the Arkansas Supreme Court during Reconstruction and who later worked as editor in chief of the main Republican newspaper in the state. McClure was currently serving as chairman of the state's Republican Executive Committee. Not surprisingly, complained Berry, the eastern district of Arkansas went Republican in 1890. When McClure did not find a legitimate case of Democratic wrongdoing he trumped up charges in order to hand the election to the Republicans. There had never been even the remotest chance, contended Berry, that a Democrat would win the eastern district under the watch of such a blatant, outspoken partisan.[16]

Continuing the criticism of the supervisory aspects of the Federal Elections Bill, John Tyler Morgan later commented on the expense of maintaining the elaborate supervision required by the measure. He noted that each deputy supervisor would be paid about $50 per election. Each precinct would have three of these well-compensated deputies, for a total of $150. Some highly populated districts contained as many as forty precincts, bringing the cost of supervision to $6,000 per district, per election. Said Morgan: "That is a large sum of money to go into the hands of the class of people who will apply for these positions of supervisors. There are many post offices in the United States that do not pay anything like that amount of money, and yet the mails of senators are burdened with petitions and applications for appointments to those places." Morgan added that many poor Alabamians would love to have a job that paid so well, even if it was only temporary employment.[17]

John W. Daniel of Virginia hammered away at the theme of corruption in the supervisory process, criticizing John I. Davenport, the chief supervisor of elections in New York City, who was a controversial character and an easy target for Democrats. Daniel explained that, in 1877, Charles Devens Jr., the U. S. Attorney General under the Hayes administration, censured Davenport for arresting and holding five thousand immigrants who had voted in the election of 1876. These immigrants had a right to vote, argued Daniel, because they had been naturalized in 1868. In the censure, Devens complained that Davenport should have been removed from his position but that there was no power vested in any agency or branch of the federal government to remove a corrupt supervisor from office under the 1871 statute. Who in their right mind, asked Daniel, would grant an individual such a powerful job for life knowing there would be no way to ensure his honesty? No one, he answered, not merchants, farmers, manufacturers, or even most black southerners. Who wanted this bill then, he begged to know? Again, he answered his own question: no one but "a few partisans and Negroes" who needed "a banner to carry in battle."[18]

Daniel relentlessly attacked the Federal Elections Bill, reading from the December 10, 1890, edition of the *New York Sun* to show the probable effects of the extension of Republican supervision under the measure. The paper reported that a U. S. Grand Jury had just "administered a stinging rebuke" to John I. Davenport for his supervisory activities in the recent midterm elections. Davenport had issued five thousand warrants of arrest for alleged perpetrators of voting fraud, but the jury indicted only three of them. Daniel asked his fellow legislators to pause and consider that statistic carefully. Three out of five thousand seemed an unbelievable number, yet a jury of carefully selected American citizens made that judgment. What would the Republicans do in light of such a fact, asked Daniel—arrest the jury itself for conspiracy to commit vote fraud? It seemed so, given the paranoia of GOP leaders, said the Virginian.[19]

Zebulon Vance of North Carolina pounded away at the same theme, reading excerpts from the 1879 House committee investigation into the conduct of John I. Davenport. The report showed conclusively that Davenport was guilty of highly questionable activities as chief supervisor of New York City elections. George Frisbie Hoar rose to the defense of the maligned supervisor by reading a letter that Davenport had recently written to him denying all allegations against him and welcoming the opportunity to appear before Congress again to testify and be cross-examined. John Tyler Morgan answered that it would change nothing. In his opinion, the supervisor-for-life idea, which was the heart of the Federal Elections Bill, simply created too many opportunities to make dishonest officials out of otherwise honest men. Party allegiance would take precedence over impartial judgment. Consider how the five Supreme Court justices voted in the presidential election dispute of 1876, argued Morgan: "Can any man deny in the United States Government to-day, after the eight-by-seven vote and after all the other things we have seen done in the Government . . . that every judge when he puts on the ermine still remains a Democrat or still remains a Republican and that whenever he has an opportunity without the violation of his oath he will throw all of his influence in favor of the party to which he belongs?"[20]

Second-term Senator William P. Frye of Maine rebutted the attack on John I. Davenport, saying "five times he has been brought before the court and five times he has been pronounced not guilty." Furthermore, he noted, in the first case, Tammany Hall naturalized between forty and sixty thousand resident aliens in a matter of days for the purpose of voting in the

1868 election. These new voters were given between fifty cents and two dollars each to vote the Democratic ticket, with "a glass of whisky thrown in." Then, adding his thoughts on the Federal Elections Bill for good measure, Frye asserted that it "is not one-tenth part stringent enough" and if he could, he "would put the bayonet behind it." He concluded with his opinion of why virtually all white southerners opposed the bill, wryly declaring that "the devil never was fond of holy water." He then sarcastically apologized for bringing up the sectional issue, because he did not want to start on the "Southern question at this [late] hour of the day. When I discuss that, I propose to start in the morning." He actually had no intention of prolonging the debate by such an abrasive and unnecessary digression, but he could not resist the immediate opportunity to throw one quick, venomous barb at his southern Democrat adversaries.[21]

John E. Kenna of West Virginia smugly reminded Frye that there were not enough Republicans in all the nation to put a bayonet behind the bill in order to enforce it because the Democrats now controlled far more votes than the GOP. Frye quickly responded that there would be more than enough Republicans if the disfranchised black southerners got to carry their fair share of bayonets. Matthew Butler later answered that charge by noting the contradiction in Frye's statement: "A 'free ballot and fair count' at the point of the bayonet is an impossibility. They are incongruous elements and will not assimilate."[22]

Near the midpoint of the December debate, J. Z. George of Mississippi took the floor and, in one of the longest speeches ever made in the history of Congress, explained why the Democrats believed that the Federal Elections Bill was unconstitutional. He delivered what was, according to most contemporary accounts, an extraordinary exegesis of the U. S.Constitution. George sought to prove that the Founding Fathers never intended the federal government to become so centralized that it abolished the sovereignty of states. He covered the ratification conventions of the original thirteen states one-by-one to illustrate how concerned the citizens of those states were about protecting their local sovereignty under the new Constitution. He recounted how, over the long course of early American history, both the Federalist and Whig Parties had tried numerous times to subvert the will of the vast majority of the American people by steering the federal government toward centralization. He read resolutions of the Illinois and Ohio legislatures against the 1842 law that the Whig Congress passed requiring uniform elections throughout the states and noted how the voters turned out the Whigs in record numbers in the next election. George also read an 1843 resolution of the Massachusetts legislature, which condemned the three-fifth's compromise and called for a constitutional amendment to change it. The Bay State took that action, however, not because it wanted blacks to have equal representation in Congress, explained George, but because it wanted to eliminate their representation altogether. If they had no representation at all, the northern states would gain even greater control over the House of Representatives. He concluded by inserting into the *Record* the documents of the states of Massachusetts, New Hampshire, and New York ratifying the Constitution and by muttering in exhaustion, "I feel like the weary traveler who is almost in sight of the promised land, and would like to make a landing."[23]

Fellow Democrats called George's argument "invincible and unanswerable," and some ranked it alongside the best speeches ever delivered in Congress, including those of the Great Triumvirate of Clay, Webster, and Calhoun.[24] The Democratic and Independent newspapers of the country agreed, calling George an "intellectual giant." Even the Republican press begrudgingly admitted that George, whether right or wrong in interpreting the Constitution, had made a brilliant case against the authority of the national government to pass a Federal Elections Bill. George's genius lay not in making some new and original argument, however, but merely in repackaging the old states' rights argument and presenting it with more clarity than any antebellum southerner ever did.[25] As an interesting sidebar, the *New York Herald* characterized George as "a very able man" with "a good store of learning," but a man who "takes his shoes off when he feels like it, props his feet on his desk, talks aloud to anyone whenever he wants to, stamps about the chamber, goes to sleep when he feels inclined, snorts at speeches he does not like, and does not care what anyone thinks about him." He acted, said the paper, quoting one observer, like an "educated hog." Upon reading this "educated hog" characterization, Senator Ingalls of Kansas exclaimed, "Great Scott! . . . Who in all this world has ventured to call that man 'educated'?" That witticism no doubt represented the feelings of many Republicans concerning George.[26]

Unlike the national press and public, the Republican advocates of the bill in the Senate could appreciate neither George's interpretation of the Constitution nor his extensive soliloquy, which they believed had little bearing on the substantive issues under consideration. Thus, they offered a resolution that the Senate go into all-night sessions in order to speed up the business at hand. It was the classic anti-filibustering ploy whereby the majority party hoped to outlast the minority party. Not surprisingly, the Democrats rose en masse to object. John Tyler Morgan rebuked the Republicans for not engaging them in debate, fuming, "You had better consider this bill.

You had better debate it with us . . . you had better convince the country that the bill is right and we are wrong," or, he was sure, the American people would soon revolt against the Senate the way they revolted against the House in the midterm elections. Later, Morgan accused George Frisbie Hoar of not even knowing what all of the provisions of his own bill said. He compared the bill to Sanskrit for its complexity. Surely, such a complex and controversial document required a point-by-point explanation, said Morgan.[27]

The seasoned veterans on the Republican side realized that the best strategy to combat the filibuster was to resist Democratic efforts to lure them into unnecessary defenses of their position, which would only prolong the debate. Some less-experienced Republicans either would not or could not resist, however. Morgan's tirade struck a nerve with several of them, who finally took the Alabamian's bait and made brief defenses of their bill during the next few days. James F. Wilson, Iowa's junior senator, took the floor in an attempt to refute George's interpretation of the Constitution. Wilson had a long history of supporting both Republican economic programs and humanitarian causes. In his first year in Congress, 1861, he had been a driving force behind the law giving African Americans the right to vote in Washington, D.C. He later strongly supported all three Reconstruction amendments and every subsequent Radical measure, while simultaneously milking federal tax dollars for his own benefit in the Credit Mobilier scandal of the Grant years. The scandal hardly damaged his reputation, however, and the Iowa legislature even promoted him to the Senate in 1882. In 1890, he was among the only Republicans left who still held on to the old abolitionist's adage that the U. S. Constitution was a "covenant with hell." Wilson summarily explained that the Constitution as originally written had been a "great mistake," for it undermined the enlightened doctrine of egalitarianism in the Declaration of Independence. The Thirteenth, Fourteenth, and Fifteenth Amendments, he argued, realigned America's two most famous documents ideologically.[28]

Another young Republican who entered the fray against George's interpretation of the Constitution was Joseph N. Dolph of Oregon. This second-term senator never enjoyed a distinguished career in national politics, as did many of his colleagues, yet his role in the Federal Elections Bill debate was among the most prominent for the Republicans. This Oregonian, who, although only in his forties, wore a long white beard, became the main antagonist of the Democrats, playing the role of gadfly or majority party whip. In defending the Republican philosophy of a strong central government, he waved the bloody shirt relentlessly, accusing the South of all manner of evils and mercilessly attacking both the new Mississippi Constitution and South Carolina's newly elected governor, "Pitchfork" Ben Tillman. Dolph's South-bashing, not surprisingly, incited a verbal riot that was totally counterproductive to helping illuminate the provisions of the bill under consideration. John Tyler Morgan answered Dolph's attack by reading an Oregon constitutional statute prohibiting interracial marriages of whites to either blacks, Chinese, or Indians. Citing Frederick Douglass, who was married to a white woman, as an example, Morgan pointed out that if the Douglasses were to leave Maryland and move to Oregon, they would be branded as criminals. According to state law, they would be sent to jail for not less than six months. Morgan relished his chance to lash out at what he perceived to be the hypocrisy of some northern Republicans by telling Dolph, "You took care, very good care, never to take any of your own medicine." When the testy young Oregonian asked Morgan to yield the floor in order that he may offer rebuttal, the experienced Alabamian refused, saying, "I want the Senator to have due time for reflection before he speaks." Dolph did not get the floor again that day. Later, Shelby Cullom of Illinois and even the normally tactful George Frisbie Hoar entered the fray with denunciations of the South's racially discriminatory social structure, which resulted in further verbal sparring between northern and southern senators.[29]

Although the debate was routinely sidetracked by someone injecting the venomous fangs of North-South sectionalism, reasoned arguments and valid points still managed to find their way into the exchanges now and then. John W. Daniel of Virginia noted, for instance, that the National Farmers' Alliance, a nascent political force controlling more than a million votes, had denounced the bill earlier in the week in its Ocala Platform. Did Republicans not care to compete for the votes of farmers? he asked. George Vest of Missouri added that the National Colored Farmers' Alliance, which had met at Ocala, Florida, at the same time but in their own segregated facility, did not even mention the bill in its platform. The black Alliance complained instead, said Vest, about the McKinley Tariff and the Conger Lard Bill, both of which were economic measures that directly affected farmers, black and white alike. Did this not prove, he asked, that most black southerners were more interested in economic betterment than in political equality? Did it not also show that Senate Republicans had their priorities out of order?[30] He continued, saying that he had recently read a statement opposing the Federal Elections Bill written by "the most intelligent negro whom I have met in years." He referred to Mississippi planter Isaiah Montgomery and his now infamous support of the Mississippi Constitution and simultaneous denunciation of the elections bill published in the *New York*

World in September. Henry Blair interrupted to ask Vest whether Montgomery was a full-blooded Negro. Before Vest could answer, Randall L. Gibson of Louisiana chimed in, "as black as the senator's coat." Blair replied sarcastically, "I wanted it settled, whether a pure negro knew anything or not." Blair intended his comment to tear down the common racist stereotype of the day that only mulattoes, not pure blacks, had the mental capacity necessary to make insightful political judgments.[31]

Edmund Cary Walthall, the junior senator from Mississippi, also employed the Democratic strategy of defending the South while simultaneously attacking the Federal Elections Bill. This highly regarded former Confederate general was not fond of public speaking and took the floor only when he felt absolutely compelled to do so. His defense of the South centered upon the new Mississippi Constitution. He wanted everyone to know that, despite the stereotype of his state as a backwater of illiterate farmers and racist demagogues, there had not been a single act of violence committed with regard to an election in the Magnolia State in the five years and nine months that he had been a senator. "Compare this record with that of any other State, large or small," he said, "and see if any Senator can produce a better one from his own state." George Edmunds of Vermont injected, "the Senator is more crazy than usual," because ever since the Democrats "redeemed" the state in 1875, "nobody needed to be killed any more." Walthall stopped to question his detractor, asking if he had any firsthand knowledge of affairs in Mississippi. Edmunds answered no, "I am not familiar with it at all, any more than I am with Poland, where there is peace." With smug satisfaction Walthall retorted, "I imagined that the Senator from Vermont, as he admits, was entirely ignorant of the matter . . . and I will proceed."[32]

"I venture the statement as a matter of opinion," continued Walthall, "that there are more negroes in office this day in Bolivar County [Mississippi] than in any other county in the United States and more than in the entire States in the North which have always been under Republican control. Out of forty-four officeholders in that county, thirty-one of them are negroes." He noted that the county was 90 percent black, but added that "the white population is intelligent and enterprising," implying that if the whites had wanted to, they could have easily thrown off the yoke of black rule. He also pointed out that Isaiah Montgomery was not the only African American in Mississippi to oppose the Federal Elections Bill and support the new state constitution. A "colored Representative from Adams County [George F. Bowles of the Mississippi legislature], whose Republicanism is as orthodox as any Senator here," also made a public speech to that effect.[33]

Racial Harmony in the South. "*Mean, but futile . . . President Harrison's Spite can not Disturb the Growing Harmony between the Whites and Negros [sic] of the South.*" (*Puck,* 1890.) In a double entendre that simultaneously lampooned Benjamin Harrison's physical stature and his political impotence, cartoonists often portrayed the president as a midget wearing his grandfather's giant-sized hat. Here he represents the Republican Party attempting to break up the happy union that black and white southerners supposedly enjoyed in the post-Reconstruction era.

Zebulon Vance continued the simultaneous defense of the South and attack on the Federal Elections Bill by accusing northern Republicans of hypocrisy once again. He pointed out that, while the Republicans complained about the Democrats having more than their fair share of representation in the southern states, they were guilty of the same thing in a different way in the northern states: "In voting to admit Idaho and Wyoming, whose united population does not equal that of one Congressional district in my State, [they] voted to make one man, Mormon, Chinaman, or Indian, in these States equal to three [men] in North Carolina in the House of Representatives. And this exertion does not seem to produce [in them] either weariness of muscle or the least shortness of breath." Vance added that, after the November midterm elections, which turned the majority party into the minority party, Republicans now controlled only twelve states with a combined population of nine million, while the Democrats controlled thirty states with a combined population of fifty-three million. Yet, the GOP would still exercise the majority power in both houses of Congress until the current session ended in April 1891, making one man in Republican states in the meantime equal in representation to approximately six in the Democratic states. Vance then attacked the supporters of the Federal Elections Bill as pseudoreformers, asking why they never called for changing the political system that allowed twelve million Americans to have more congressional representation than fifty-three million other Americans.[34]

Following the same line of reasoning, John R. Reagan of Texas read statistics designed to prove that black southerners were no more underrepresented in Congress than were white Democrats in the North. While there were approximately 397,000 Republican voters in the South who enjoyed no representation in Congress because of black disfranchisement, there were about 585,000 Democrats in the North who enjoyed no representation in Congress because of Republican gerrymandering.[35] Rufus Blodgett, a Democrat in his first and only term from New Jersey, agreed, arguing that peace in the South was more to be desired than voting rights for black southerners. After all, he reasoned, what are egalitarianism and democracy supposed to produce but a society of peace and prosperity? If, as experience had shown, they produced the exact opposite, then why insist upon them? Perhaps governments based upon those noble ideals are not always the best governments, said Blodgett; perhaps every situation is different and should be dealt with accordingly.[36] Later, Alfred Colquitt of Georgia—a second-term senator, former Confederate general, and member of the state's so-called Bourbon triumvirate that had "redeemed" Georgia from Radical Republicanism— echoed those remarks with his usual poetic flare: "Suffrage is no panacea. Has it prevented sectionalism, race prejudice, or class prejudice? Can it heal the grief of a wound, satisfy hunger, clothe the naked, educate the ignorant, reform the criminal? Is it not everywhere abused? Where do you not hear complaints of impurities in balloting?"[37]

William B. Bate of Tennessee continued upon that train of thought and delivered one of the most provocative speeches of the entire debate. Bate was a former Confederate general who had been severely wounded at Shiloh. He was also a two-term governor of the Volunteer State who was now in his first term in the Senate. He expounded on the theme that Reagan had introduced the day before, asking why, if there were so many underrepresented groups of American citizens, did blacks get all the attention? The answer, he asserted, was that a group of professional politicians called "convention negroes" incessantly agitated the issue. "Where is the evidence of the existence of incurable disease which demands the use of a quack medicine like this bill. . . . It is the whine of the 'convention negro' . . . which is the only real excuse for its enactment." Bate expressed his antipathy for the nation's black political leaders, declaring that "The convention negro, or professional colored politician . . . toils not, neither does he spin, yet Solomon, in all his glory, was not his equal in politics." He continued his racist pronouncement by noting that "We have in this country many thousands Irishmen, Germans, French, Spaniards, Scandinavians, [and] Welsh; but they amalgamate with the natives and disappear from our politics as members of a different race from the American people. It is only the 'convention negro,' who is an American citizen of the African race, who does not disappear," implying that some black leaders earned their livelihoods by agitating the race problem.[38]

Besides airing his racist views, Bate also offered the Senate a history lesson, comparing and contrasting the American and French experiments with democratic government in 1789. He thought it more than just a little coincidental that in the same year the National Assembly of France abolished the long-standing right of the king to order arbitrary arrests and imprisonments the United States ratified its Constitution. He asked whether any senator thought that the American people of that generation would have been willing to give arbitrary power to the central government of the United States, such as was contained in the Federal Elections Bill, at the same time that the French people were finally taking away arbitrary power from their central government. Bate then compared the present situation in the southern United States to that of Great Britain's rule of Ireland. In Ireland, as in the American South, the people were being subjected against their will to the force of obtrusive central government. "In one country its measures are known as coercion acts; in the other, as force bills; they are interchangeable terms. . . . In Ireland or America, it matters not how this bill may be disguised by terms, it means government by military power."[39]

Bate concluded with what he called a "Synopsis of Argument Against the Election Bill," which contained five reasons that the bill was bad legislation in his opinion: first, the public opposed the bill; second, it was unconstitutional; third, it would reignite the flames of sectional hatred left smoldering from the Civil War; fourth, previous supervisory laws proved that federal supervision of elections did not work; and fifth, it was inconsistent with America's governmental traditions. The fifth point contained nine subpoints: (1) it would establish supervisors with tenure for life; (2) it would mix the judiciary with partisan politics; (3) it would invite one form of corruption into the political process in an attempt to get rid of another; (4) it would increase rather than decrease contested elections; (5) it would require military force in order to be effective; (6) it would incite riots; (7) it would cost more than the nation could afford if implemented at every election in all districts where supervision was requested; (8) it would quickly prove to be an unworkable system; and (9) it was an attempt by one party to take advantage of its majority status and gain absolute, permanent hegemony over the nation.[40]

Following Bate on December 19 was the first western "Silverite" Republican to join the debate, William M. Stewart of Nevada. A sagacious-looking man with a long white beard, Stewart had been one of Nevada's original senators, elected upon the admission of that state to the Union in 1864. This venerable, complex statesman had been more instrumental in moderating the Radical Republicans' racial agenda during Reconstruction than any other member of Congress still serving in 1890. Before the Civil War, he had actually been a doughface—inclined to agree with, or at least be sympathetic to, the southern point of view on racial matters. In the 1850s, he had established a law firm in California with one of the South's most famous pre–Civil War statesmen, Henry Stuart Foote of Mississippi. He had also married Foote's daughter, Annie, and had developed a great respect for southern culture as a result. When the issue of black suffrage was first put to Congress in 1866, he opposed it unequivocally, saying "I believe the Anglo-Saxon race can govern this country. I believe it because he has governed it. I believe it because it is the only race that has ever founded such institutions as ours. . . . I believe the white man can govern it without the aid of the negro." In that same year, Stewart also voted to kill the Freedmen's Bureau. Afterward, like most other Republicans, he quickly grew to despise President Andrew Johnson, which caused him to convert to a Radical on subsequent racial issues, seemingly for no other reason than to spite the Tennessee tailor. The most important of these issues was the Fifteenth Amendment, the final draft of which Stewart authored.[41]

After Reconstruction, Stewart experienced another conversion, reverting to his initial disapproval of black political equality. His main reason for doing so was to please his Nevada constituents, the western silver lobby, and the railroad tycoons of the West Coast, all of whom seemed interested in humanitarianism only so far as it did not impede the nation's, or their own personal, economic progress. He also placated his southern family members and his own conscience with his change of position, rationalizing that economic growth and technological advancement would help African Americans more than would the right to vote.[42] Stewart thus opposed the Federal Elections Bill and became the first Republican to dissent publicly on the issue. In speaking against it in the Senate, he cited five reasons for his disapprobation: first, if a supervisory law was needed, the existing supervisory law was sufficient; second, the Fourteenth Amendment to the U. S. Constitution provided that persons charged with violating the civil rights of blacks could have their right of habeas corpus suspended, which, if carried out, would be the only punishment necessary for individual violators; third, the Fourteenth Amendment also provided for reducing the representation of states found guilty of violating the civil rights of blacks; fourth, the Democratic interpretation of Article I, Section 4, of the Constitution was correct—the states alone, not Congress, had the right to decide voter qualifications; and fifth, the Federal Elections Bill would have the opposite effect of what its authors intended, for it would only consolidate the white vote of the South even further, increase the misery of blacks, and revive the sectional antagonism that was otherwise dying out.[43]

Stewart indicted colleagues who professed humanitarianism for what he deemed hypocrisy, especially those who had served in the Senate during Reconstruction. He asked why they had voted against giving President Grant arbitrary power to enforce the Fifteenth Amendment in the "force bill of 1875" but now wanted to give the same type of power to President Harrison. George Frisbie Hoar, although experienced enough as a senator to know better, was unable to sit silently before his accuser. He responded that the 1875 bill was designed to circumvent the U. S. Supreme Court ruling that only states, not individuals, could be guilty of violating the Fifteenth Amendment. It said that if two or more individuals acted in concert to deprive a black man of his right to vote, the state where the guilty parties resided could be held liable for their actions, and the president could then enforce martial law in that state. Hoar believed that such an interpretation of the Supreme Court ruling was incorrect and dangerous because it would punish too many people for the crimes of a few and would give the president an unwarranted amount of arbitrary power. The current bill under consideration, by contrast, applied only to specific congressional districts, not to entire states. Stewart disagreed with Hoar's recollection of the design and intent of the 1875 bill, saying that if Congress were ever to do something about the southern race problem, Reconstruction had been the time to do it, not now. If it was not done then, the failure to do it proved that wise men saw the folly of continuing the course and abandoned it. Why resurrect it now?[44]

What the historian can glean from this discussion between these two Republican ideologues is that those senators who lined up on the money Republican side of the party did not always favor the "let alone" policy merely for avaricious economic reasons. Sometimes they had genuine convictions on interpretations of the Constitution and Supreme Court rulings that differed from the reformers' view. Other times, a senator's personal recollections of Reconstruction and his role in making the laws of that turbulent era contributed to his reluctance to lead the nation into another period of racial and sectional turbulence in the 1890s.

Stewart's entry into the debate as the first Republican dissenter marked the turning point in the battle over the Federal Elections Bill. It showed for the first time that the Democrats' hope of a Republican split might come to fruition. It also caused the bill's sponsors to begin to exhibit desperation along with their exasperation. It forced them to abandon their initial strategy of saving precious time by not engaging the Democrats in debate. They realized that, while there had never been any hope of persuading Democrats to change their minds through a long-winded defense of their bill, they would now be forced to contend with the disenchanted money Republican faction of the party in order to succeed in passing the bill. Their decision to engage in the debate initiated the second stage of this Senate showdown. Whereas legitimate Democratic complaints that actually helped illuminate the provisions of the bill consumed the first half of the debate, Republican attempts to vilify southern Democrats and to achieve cloture by any means necessary would largely consume the second half.

The Democrats had accomplished four major goals in the first half of the debate: (1) they had staved off a quick Republican victory in the Senate and forced the sponsors of the Federal Elections Bill to engage them in a battle of attrition; (2) they had defended their position skillfully, seized the offensive in the battle, and now forced the supporters of the bill to explain to the nation precisely why this legislation was necessary and how it would solve the race problem; (3) they had divided the Republicans into rival factions; and (4) they had swung the tide of public opinion even further against the bill through their clever arguments. The Democrats, whether right or wrong in their position, had certainly demonstrated through the first half of the debate that they were excellent politicians, orators, and propagandists. The only question was, could they finish what they had started? The next chapter provides the answer.

Chapter 7

SHOWDOWN ON CAPITOL HILL

The Filibuster, the Cloture Rule, and the Defeat of the Federal Elections Bill

We are about to witness the final act in the great political drama in which the Republican party has been playing the role of star for a quarter of a century. . . . Whether the performance shall end in comedy or tragedy . . . remains to be seen.

—*Senator John E. Kenna of West Virginia*

The majority and the minority each stand responsible to their several constituencies for their course, their conduct, and their speeches. There may be a difference, as there is upon the election bill, as wide as the poles between those who favor it and those who oppose it. Each must stand upon his own judgment, his convictions, and his conscience as to what his duty is and how he shall perform it.

—*Senator John R. Reagan of Texas*

As the year 1890 came to a close, the annual yuletide mood of joyful celebration and goodwill toward men enveloped the nation as usual. Unfortunately, good cheer did not make an appearance at Capitol Hill, for the Senate was engaged in one of the most heated ideological battles it would

151

ever see. Senate sponsors of the Federal Elections Bill found themselves in a
quandary after fellow Republican William M. Stewart of Nevada made
known his emphatic opposition to the bill. They already knew that several
of their Republican colleagues were not strong supporters of the idea of
passing a new federal elections law, but they had hoped these senators would
not express such strong opposition as Stewart had voiced. The sponsors
realized that they did not possess the votes necessary to pass the bill without the support of at least some of the Silverites and eastern money Republicans. The historian can only speculate whether they wrangled with these
unsupportive colleagues in the cloakroom or in some other place outside
the Senate chamber to try to persuade them to remain faithful to the reformers' cause. What is certain, however, is that after Stewart's speech the
sponsors changed their initial strategy of not defending and explaining their
bill to one of at least seizing the initiative, answering their critics, and trying to put them on the defensive.

The result of this change of strategy was a much livelier and more
interesting debate. The American public and the national press, which had
previously followed the debate with plentiful interest, now became more
fixated than ever on the issue. The senators themselves recognized their
moment in the spotlight, and some of the key performers in the drama
enjoyed every moment of their starring roles, playing to their national audience like actors on a stage.[1] Leading national newspapers poked fun at
these prima donnas who held both the nation's attention and its racial destiny in their hands. The *New York Herald,* for example, cleverly wrote with
tongue-in-cheek: "Look down from the gallery of the Senate, you patriotic
Americans, and contemplate a most impressive spectacle.... Notice as you
enter the chamber the atmosphere of eminent respectability, profound,
sombre, palpable, almost thick enough to be cut with a knife.... That is the
air of Senatorial dignity which envelops each member like a cloud. It ex-
udes from his personality as the odor of sanctity from the saints."[2] Beneath
such hyperbolic humor lay a serious problem that the newspapers were
addressing: senators, because of their exalted position, seemed to be removed from the mainstream of American society and thus out of touch
with the common people. Indeed, no man, no matter how underprivileged
he had previously been in life, could remain a commoner at heart after his
selection to the U. S. Senate. The prestige of the office changed even the
humblest public servant. Those who spent the majority of their long and
celebrated careers in the Senate tended to undergo the most stark transfor-
mations. They, as a class, possessed a degree of arrogance rarely seen in
democratic government. They considered the House of Representatives,

the president, the Supreme Court, and all state governments subservient to the Senate, and they put on airs accordingly.[3]

Throughout the late nineteenth century, both parties' designated leaders always had their hands full trying to keep this collection of massive egos in the Senate in line with party leadership. The personal ambition of senators certainly clouded their judgment at times and made them unruly at other times. Many senators hoped to inherent the mantles of Daniel Webster, Henry Clay, and John C. Calhoun as the recognized leaders of their country (or at least their respective sections of it). As one historian has noted, "The public now and again picks out here and there a Senator who seems to act and speak with true instinct of statesmanship and who unmistakably merits the confidence of colleagues and of people," and several senators in the Fifty-first Congress—the leaders on both sides of the aisle—hoped to be the one picked in the present generation.[4] Their leadership on the Federal Elections Bill would be their moment to prove their mettle. George Frisbie Hoar, the somber, highly cultured junior Republican senator of Massachusetts who now led the fight to solve the southern race problem through electoral reform, was not among those seeking celebrity. He debated or argued when necessity dictated, but he always preferred action to rhetoric. He sometimes criticized overly loquacious colleagues, even when he agreed with them, no matter how renowned they were as orators, or how esteemed they were as pillars of American government.[5] He once said of Republican icon Charles Sumner that "Mr. Sumner thought the rebellion [Civil War] was put down by a few speeches which he made in the Senate, and he looked upon the battles fought as the noise of a fire engine going by while he was talking."[6] Now Hoar had the difficult task of scheduling the sequence of Republican speakers and trying to keep order among those who did seek celebrity.

The first speaker for the reformers in the second phase of the debate was John Coit Spooner, who helped write the bill under consideration but had not yet spoken on its behalf. In the longest Republican speech of the debate (he held the floor for more than three hours), he opened discussion on December 20, blasting the Democrats for their frequent "rudeness" toward the reformers, saying an "epithet never convinces any intelligent mind." He launched into a bloody-shirt tirade, in which he fired a volley at the Mississippi Constitution, complaining that, for some inexplicable reason, a majority of the American public seemed to think it was a "unique, beautiful" solution to the South's race problem. He asked whether public opinion or the Constitution should rule the country. He explained that "Senators on the other side belong to a different school of constitutional construction from that in which we have been brought up. They belong to the strict constructionists . . . to a school of constitutional lawyers who readily found in that instrument power to tear the Union to pieces, to scatter the Constitution to the winds, but never were able to find in it power to maintain the Government or enforce the Constitution or the laws enacted under it." Finally, Spooner engaged in a shouting match with George Gray of Delaware, who wanted to know whether Wisconsin was without spot or blemish in regard to election purity. Spooner responded that his state was more pure than most and that it was working to achieve perfection, which was more than any southern state could say. He favored taking the southerners who disfranchised African Americans "to the whipping post" where they should be "given a generous castigation."[7]

Judging from newspaper reports, Spooner's speech, although lacking in a substantive discussion of the provisions of the Federal Elections Bill, proved quite effective at convincing the large portion of the northern public that had previously become disillusioned with the reformers' cause to rally around the banner of racial justice once again. As one paper put it, Spooner's impassioned appeal "breathed life into the dying bill."[8] Unfortunately for Spooner, his speech changed no Silverite or eastern money Republican's mind and only aggravated the Democrats. It particularly stirred the ire of the ex-Confederates in the Senate, including the former adjutant general of the Confederacy, Wilkinson Call of Florida, who threatened that, should the Republicans pass the Federal Elections Bill, every state in the South would resurrect and apply the old southern doctrine of nullification to it. Call's threat provoked an unproductive and very time-consuming exchange between northern and southern senators, much to the satisfaction of the Democrats. Spooner's speech irritated J. Z. George to an unusually high degree. George vowed to make a long, elaborate defense of the Mississippi Constitution before the filibuster was over, which he soon did, consuming more than four-and-a-half hours on the last day of 1890.[9]

Despite the fact that time was precious in the brief second session, the proponents of the Federal Elections Bill continued, day after day, chipping away at the veneer of legitimacy that made the Mississippi Constitution possible. They argued that, even though the constitution did not blatantly violate the letter of the Fifteenth Amendment, everyone knew that the only real purpose of the document was to ensure white supremacy in Mississippi. Even Mississippi newspapers admitted as much. But since the election provisions in the constitution were not to be implemented until 1892, there was not yet any actual, concrete evidence of wrongdoing on the part of the state. The proponents of the Federal Elections Bill could only hope that, by repeatedly putting J. Z. George and supporters of the constitution on the defensive, they could wear down the filibusterers while simultaneously convincing the eastern money Republicans and western Silverites of the necessity of passing their bill. Their strategy backfired, however, for George consistently proved up to the task of defending the Mississippi Constitution with rational arguments against all who challenged it. He reminded the Senate, for instance, that his state's new constitution contained the very prescription for ending violations of the Fifteenth Amendment that both George Frisbie Hoar and Henry Cabot Lodge had advocated in the first session of Congress—the literacy test. Throughout his defense, George kept a cool demeanor, showing himself able to withstand the constant public scrutiny that naturally accompanied his elevation to the status of a political celebrity without cracking under the pressure.[10]

The strategy also produced exactly the opposite result among the eastern money Republicans and western Silverites than the sponsors of the bill had intended. In the midst of one of George Frisbie Hoar's harangues against the Mississippi Constitution, fellow Republican Henry M. Teller of Colorado interrupted to ask whether there was "anything in this bill which touches the wrong of which he [Hoar] complains?" Teller seemed an unlikely detractor of the Federal Elections Bill and an even more unlikely supporter of the Mississippi Constitution. He had established a reputation as a humanitarian during and after Reconstruction. In 1878, he had headed a congressional committee to investigate electoral frauds and violence in the South, in which he found Louisiana and South Carolina culpable. Yet, now he desired to know whether any provision in the Federal Elections Bill would address the problem of circumventing the Fifteenth Amendment through use of literacy tests and understanding clauses, which provoked one of the most important exchanges of the entire debate. Hoar realized the poignancy of the question, and, in a moment of complete candor, meekly answered, "No, I do not suppose there is." Teller responded, then "it is not worth while for us now to raise the question whether Mississippi has violated morals and ethics or not. She has kept herself within the Constitution and the law, offensive as her action may be." He also reminded Hoar that Massachusetts had "what is called there the intelligence restriction" in its constitution, the purpose of which was to prevent illiterates and other undesirables from voting.[11]

Teller's interjection effectively silenced Hoar and the reformers long enough for the Silverites to take control of the business of the Senate. They tabled the Federal Elections Bill temporarily in order to consider other bills waiting on the docket. Edward O. Wolcott, Colorado's junior senator, took the floor to explain the abrupt change of business. He proclaimed matter-of-factly that the authors of the elections bill needed time to rethink some of its provisions before forcing it upon the country. A man who was noted not for the power of his intellect but for the passion of his oratory, Wolcott declared that "there are many things more important and vital to the welfare of this nation than that the colored citizens of the South shall vote." Several other important bills needed consideration before the end of the session, he said, adding that "were none of those vital measures before us for consideration, I should still be against" the Federal Elections Bill. He noted that the bill made no distinction between state elections and congressional elections, both of which were held on the same day in most states. Such a system would allow the supervisors conceivably to intervene in local elections as well as federal. Wolcott declared that "any meddling with state elections is, to my mind, intolerable." He urged the bill's framers to insert a provision changing congressional elections to a separate day, a proposal that fellow Silverite William M. Stewart seconded. Both men agreed that only after making this change would they even consider voting for the bill. In the meantime, they would move on to other business.[12]

When John Coit Spooner rose to express his disdain for the westerners' action, Henry M. Teller explained that there were presently 150 resolutions pending to amend the Federal Elections Bill. He accused the bill's proponents of trying to force their will on everyone else by refusing to give those amendments due consideration. Besides, he notified Spooner, the people of the West did not support the bill; they supported "financial legislation" instead, because "the best minds in this country assert to-day that we are on the very verge of a financial panic."[13] As a result of the Silverite motion, the Senate spent nine days considering modifications to the Sherman Silver-Purchase Act, much to the pleasure of the Silverites, eastern money Republicans, and Democrats and much to the consternation of the reformers. One observer wryly commented about the traitorous act of the Silverite-money Republican faction: "Silver is a base metal, and it has always had a base effect on weak characters like Judas."[14]

At the end of the nine-day delay, the sponsors of the Federal Elections Bill were able to regain control of the business of the Senate, whereupon they immediately resumed consideration of the bill. Realizing that time was now more precious than ever, the sponsors of the bill finally resorted to the all-night sessions that Senator Preston B. Plumb of Kansas had long advocated. This action initiated the third phase of the debate, when the Democrats began to filibuster not for instruction but mainly for obstruction. Even then, they occasionally made an illuminating point. The Democrats knew that the Republicans' patience had reached its end, and that the remainder of the debate would be little more than a test of endurance. They anticipated that they could survive all-night sessions as well as the Republicans, but they also knew that it would not take many nights of making such a sacrifice before the proponents of the bill would begin to call for a cloture rule. The Democratic press tried to prepare the American public for the defeat that seemed inevitable should the Senate adopt a cloture rule: "The most important and valued right of a minority in all deliberative bodies is that of a full and free discussion, and whenever the day comes that it is denied, that will be the dawn of a day which will see the downfall of the liberties of the people.... The election or force bill may, before the close of the present congress, become the law of the land, and our people must prepare themselves to meet the contingencies that may arise, bravely and in the same spirit of patient endurance that distinguished them in the dark days of reconstruction."[15]

During the first all-night session on Friday, January 16, 1891, grieving Democratic Senator Charles Faulkner of West Virginia, who had just returned from attending his wife's funeral in Martinsburg, began the slow and deliberate mechanism of obstruction. In a speech that had little direct relevance to the Federal Elections Bill, Faulkner made it to 2:30 A.M. on Saturday morning before the bill's sponsors issued the first quorum call to "compel" attendance of senators, a process that was repeated frequently over the coming week. For the next two hours, the sergeant at arms, E. K. Valentine, tried to locate senators and notify them of their duty to attend. Since the Senate traditionally requested rather than compelled the attendance of senators during filibusters, Valentine knew that his action would be highly unpopular among the gentlemen with whom he would have to work for the rest of the session, and he accordingly made only a halfhearted effort to honor the chair's order. He reported to the Senate at 4:30 A.M. that he had been unable to locate several senators and that others could not attend due to illness. Interestingly, almost as many Republican reformers had vacated the Senate during the filibuster as had Democrats and their allies. Thus, at times, it was they rather than their filibustering opponents who dragged out the quorum call. The roll call lasted about five hours. Finally, at 9:30 A.M., a quorum arrived, and the most spectacular filibuster in American history to that time resumed. Faulkner then concluded his speech some eleven hours after having begun it.[16]

As the filibuster dragged on through Saturday, January 19, frustration increased among the sponsors of the Federal Elections Bill, and the determination of the opposition grew proportionately. Both sides began

The Republican 'Chariot' Runs into Resistance. Blocked! (*New York Herald*, 1891.)
In December, the Republican Reformers in the U. S. Senate ran into the most
notorious filibuster in American history to that time, as Democrats sought to thwart
their efforts to pass the Federal Elections Bill. Here, the cartoonist shows Speaker
of the House Thomas B. Reed trying to help pull the legislation from one side
while Senate floor manager George Frisbie Hoar tries to push it from the other.
Vice President Levi P. Morton is shown trying to drive the bill through (which is a
marginally accurate portrayal at best), while President Benjamin Harrison (inside
the coach), Secretary of State James G. Blaine, and nearly blind Senator William
M. Evarts of New York are merely along for the ride. John J. Ingalls of Kansas, who
was voted out of office because of the rise of Populism in November, is shown as
having fallen off the political wagon and his career sinking fast.

attacking each other mercilessly, with little mention of the provisions of the bill under consideration. The sponsors of the bill cited case after case of southern ballot box abuses that were documented in southern newspapers and in the testimonies of victims and witnesses at congressional hearings between Reconstruction and 1890. Democrats matched them case for case with examples of alleged Republican duplicity that were documented in northern newspapers, periodicals, and in letters that northerners wrote to Democratic congressmen. Senator Samuel D. Pasco of Florida read, for example, a statement from Terrence V. Powderly of the Knights of Labor:

> There can be no worse intimidation practiced anywhere in the country than is practiced in Pennsylvania, the cradle of protection and the headquarters of the great party of so-called morality. I have seen the mine bosses stand around the polls with cigar boxes on their arms, in which were tickets, and as an employee came along the cover was raised and a ticket handed to him. The poor workman was not told in so many words to vote the ticket, [but] if he failed to do so he would lose his job in about a week's time, without being told why he was discharged.[17]

George Vest of Missouri followed with yet more condemnation of the GOP, citing a specific case of corruption that occurred in Indiana under the old supervisory law of 1871 involving William Dudley, who, at the time, was the U. S. Marshal for Indianapolis and the treasurer of the Republican National Committee. Vest related the story of how Dudley appointed six hundred Republican deputies to supervise the city election of 1880. Democratic Senator Joseph McDonald of Indiana petitioned the federal court to appoint some Democratic supervisors to work alongside the Republicans. Over the course of the election day, only four repeaters were arrested, but the Democratic supervisors, not the Republicans, had caught all four. The repeaters went to trial and to jail, but the Republican machine immediately bailed them out and sent them out of town. Democrats later secured a letter allegedly written by Dudley to GOP leaders in Indiana discussing how much money the party's treasury had allotted to pay "floaters" to vote the Republican ticket in 1888. Dudley went to trial for this allegation, but appealed to the federal judge in private to release him, because he claimed to have enough "dirt" on high-ranking Republicans in both Indiana and Washington, D.C., to cause an "explosion" that would destroy the Harrison administration, wreck the Republican National Committee, and end the political career of Senator Matthew Quay of Pennsylvania. Through a series of unexplained circumstances, the judge resigned his post, presumably because of intimidation from the Quay-Harrison machine, and the Hoosier president appointed his replacement. To no one's surprise, said Vest, the new judge pronounced a mistrial, and Dudley escaped scot-free.[18]

Quay, who was the leader of the money Republicans and thus not a supporter of the bill, immediately interrupted Vest, hoping to deflect attention away from his shady dealings as a party boss and to show the Democrats that he was firmly on their side. He thus introduced his own sarcastic version of the Federal Elections Bill, which he intended as an illustration of the absurdity of the idea of the national government supervising elections. His bill took the idea to its logical extreme, giving full power of enforcement to both the army and the navy, such that the military could blockade the southern coastline and treat the southern states as belligerent nations if they did not allow blacks to vote. Nothing came of his bill, of course, and whether it had any effect on the thinking of any of his colleagues is doubtful. It certainly did not hurt the opposition's case, however, and the Democrats never again mentioned Quay's questionable character in the debate.[19]

Thirty hours into the all-day and all-night filibuster, Nelson Aldrich of Rhode Island finally called for a recess. Before leaving, however, he served notice that he would call for a vote on limiting debate, and then schedule a vote on the Federal Elections Bill on Tuesday, January 20. When Tuesday arrived, Aldrich indeed tried to call for a vote on cloture, but Isham G. Harris of Tennessee, a former Confederate governor, managed to draw the Rhode Islander into an argument over Senate rules that consumed a great deal of time and steered the issue far away from what Aldrich intended. The Senate never got the chance to vote on the cloture resolution that day. The Democrats subsequently regained control of the floor.[20]

As the Democrats casually yielded the floor back and forth to one another, the proponents of the Federal Elections Bill and the cloture resolution finally rose in protest, complaining that one party should not be allowed to hold the floor exclusively and indefinitely, as the Democrats seemed intent upon doing. They entreated Vice President Morton to stop the obstructive tactic. Morton, however, initially did not agree that he should use his authority as president pro tem of the Senate in a way that the public might construe to be in imitation of "Czar" Reed in the House. Yet, when John Sherman of Ohio, one of the longest-serving, most powerful, and most respected members of the Senate demanded the same from Morton, the vice president finally consented. He instructed the Democrats to choose one man to hold the floor, or else to yield it to a Republican. But he also notified the Republicans that his decision applied only for one day. He wanted time to consider the propriety of establishing such a rule permanently. He instructed J. Z. George, who held the floor at the time the Republicans interrupted, to continue speaking or yield to a Republican, but not to yield to a Democrat. George thus continued with yet another extended defense of the Mississippi Constitution. When, after four hours, he appeared near the point of physical exhaustion, Nelson Aldrich asked him to yield the floor. George had no choice but to agree. He had to abide by Morton's ruling. Aldrich, of course, brought up his cloture resolution again, but, ironically, there was no Republican majority present at the moment. He thus left it pending for the next day, when he hoped to force a vote on it. When the next day—Wednesday, January 21—arrived, however, the Democrats and their money Republican allies engaged in the disappearing quorum act, thus preventing a vote on the cloture rule.[21]

On Thursday, January 22, Morton, after two days of reflection, informed the Senate that he had reached a decision concerning Democrats yielding the floor to Democrats indefinitely. Before Morton could finish his sentence, however, the Democratic floor manager, Arthur P. Gorman, sprang to his feet in a panic and angrily cut him off. Knowing full well what the decision would be, Gorman began damning the Republicans, fuming that "In August last we had two measures before this body. One was the tariff bill . . . the other was the elections bill." If the latter was a great humanitarian effort to bring purity to the democratic processes of the nation, he argued, the other was merely a "measure which was intended to rob four-fifths of the people of the United States for the benefit of the other one-fifth." Yet, the Republicans took their precious time considering the tariff bill and were now trying to force the Federal Elections Bill upon the Democrats without the normal due process of unlimited debate. Morton tried to call Gorman to order, but the impassioned Marylander refused to stop speaking. Morton, a nonpartisan and a gentleman-statesman who believed the vice president's job was to preside with fairness toward both sides rather than to show partiality toward his own party, did not force the issue for the moment, but waited for Gorman to finish venting his frustrations.[22]

When Gorman finally ran out of epithets to hurl and curses to pronounce upon the Republicans, he yielded the floor to fellow Democrat John G. Carlisle of Kentucky, the former three-term Speaker of the House. At that point, Morton finally stepped in, asserted his authority, stopped the debate, and ruled in favor of Aldrich's point of order: Democrats could not yield the floor to Democrats indefinitely, and this rule would apply for the remainder of the Federal Elections Bill debate. Isham G. Harris appealed the decision, but the majority voted down the appeal and sustained Morton's decision. Thus, Aldrich took the floor, read his resolution to limit debate, and Morton authorized the Senate to vote upon it. Gorman begged that it be tabled, Morton flatly refused, and the Senate voted. In the midst of the roll call, Matthew Ransom, the seldom-heard senator from North Carolina, rose to a point of order. He claimed that he had attempted to get the chair to recognize him before the roll call began, but Morton had refused to stop the vote already in progress. Then, strangely, George Frisbie Hoar (of all people) came to Ransom's defense, corroborating that the senator from North Carolina had indeed tried to get Morton's attention before the roll call began. Morton capitulated, the voting stopped, and a new vote was taken on whether Ransom should be heard before the voting commenced on the Aldrich resolution. The majority voted down the question of hearing Ransom, and the roll call on limiting debate resumed. As it proceeded, Gorman rose to stop it again, asking that the resolution be put into writing. Joseph N. Dolph rose to object, but Morton sustained Gorman's request, noting that under Senate Rule XXI, Gorman had the prerogative of asking for the resolution in writing. After a brief delay to put it in writing, the Aldrich resolution limiting debate finally carried, thirty-six to thirty-two.[23]

Although it seemed that the Republicans would easily proceed with the vote on the Federal Elections Bill at that point, the Democrats had not completely run out of ways to obstruct its passage. Isham G. Harris rose to argue that Aldrich had not given the required twenty-four hour notice before submitting his cloture resolution for a vote, and it was, therefore, null and void. Technically, Harris was correct. Aldrich had informed the Senate on Saturday of his intention to hold a vote on Tuesday, and it was now Thursday. In practicality, of course, every senator knew the vote would inevitably come, but Harris objected that the vote upon the Aldrich resolution should not have been taken without a new twenty-four hour notice. Morton sustained Harris's objection and ruled in favor of the minority, saying that debate was in order for another twenty-four hours. The Republican vice president, based upon a seemingly insignificant technicality, actually annulled the vote on cloture, and the Democrats continued to monopolize the floor.[24]

The opponents of the Federal Elections Bill had thus staved off defeat for at least one more day, and this small victory gave them their second wind. Francis "Frank" M. Cockrell of Missouri, a former Confederate general who had been wounded in the futile defense of Atlanta in 1864, then initiated a new phase of Democratic filibustering, aimed primarily at destroying the credibility of the Aldrich resolution rather than dissecting the provisions of the Federal Elections Bill. Cockrell, whom political opponents accused of continuing subversive activities against the United States long after the Civil War was over, stated that he and his five sons faithfully read every issue of the popular periodical *Youth's Companion.* In one recent issue, George Frisbie Hoar had written an article entitled "The Senate," in which he explained that the business of the upper chamber was meant to be slow and deliberate because thoroughly examining each bill before passage produced the best possible legislation. After reading Hoar's article, Cockrell said he could not believe that the senator from Massachusetts would support a resolution to limit debate in the Senate. He read aloud the whole article, which he called a "mighty beacon of light, a cloud by day and a pillar of fire by night to guide the footsteps of American youth," then shouted, "Where is the Senator from Rhode Island [Aldrich]? I do not see him in his seat. He ought to be in here to hear this. How has he dared to come in here with this device for cutting off debate?" Aldrich soon arrived and interrupted Cockrell to notify the Senate of his intention to call for another vote on his resolution in exactly twenty-four hours. Hoar also rose to defend himself against Cockrell's cutting satire, saying, "The American people are not fools" who do not understand the difference between legitimate debate and obstruction. This filibuster, he declared, was just as much a "conspiracy" against "national authority" as was the "rebel congress that met at Richmond." George Gray of Delaware chimed in, asking rhetorically whether it was also a "conspiracy" against "national authority" when Republicans filibustered.[25]

Cockrell resumed his tirade against alleged Republican hypocrisy, noting that in his article Hoar had denigrated the House for passing bills "not only without discussion and amendment, but even in ignorance of what they contain." The Missourian then endeavored to document the whole history of attempts to limit debate in the Senate. Attempts had been made in 1841, 1850, 1862, 1873, and 1883, but they failed each time no matter whether Democrats, Republicans, or Whigs controlled the Senate. Cockrell concluded his remonstrance by turning his attention to the Federal Elections Bill. Evidently, said Cockrell, the proponents of the bill believed that America's federal system of government did not work and that they must therefore replace it with a centralized system. "Oh humiliating confession! What a spectacle to present to the republics of the world who are imitating our example."[26]

George Gray of Delaware took up the fight after the Missourian had grown weary. He decried the Aldrich resolution for its ambiguity. The resolution allowed only a "reasonable time" for debate, after which cloture would be forced upon the Senate. George Edmunds of Vermont retorted that the vice president or acting pro tem would have the authority to determine what was "reasonable." No one, he said, could question the fairness of Levi P. Morton in the chair. He also reminded Gray and the Democrats that, no matter how partisan a senator tended to be when occupying his regular seat in the Senate, he invariably ceased to be partisan when he took the pro tem's chair. He named, for example, Isham G. Harris, who was normally as rabidly partisan as any Democrat, but he suddenly transformed into a fair-minded statesman when he served as pro tem. Edmunds could have named himself with equal accuracy and effect. Gray, impervious to the argument, continued, recounting what was likely an anecdotal story from his youth in Delaware. "A poor drunken negro," he said, had allegedly stolen two chickens. His trial was accorded all the seriousness of a much graver crime, complete with a superior court judge, a state prosecutor, twelve petit jurors, and twenty-four grand jurors. The young Gray asked an older, wiser gentleman in the audience why the state should waste such time and money on a petty criminal like this, thinking that a lowly Justice of the Peace should have simply sent the man to the "whipping post" and let him go. The old man clutched his arm and replied, "My young friend . . . it is the price we pay for our liberties." Gray explained that hearing endless debate upon issues that one party thinks trivial was analogous to holding a jury trial for petty larceny. It was simply the price to be paid to ensure the liberties of the American people. He reasoned that the Aldrich resolution should also be given careful consideration, but only after the conclusion of the Federal Elections Bill debate. He believed that it should, in fact, be postponed until the beginning of the Fifty-second Congress.[27]

Nelson Aldrich himself disagreed, of course, and on Saturday, January 24, just as he promised, he again called for a vote on his cloture resolution. He amended it, however, to say that debate should be limited to thirty minutes per senator. When the Democrats and Silverites scorned that notion, a heretofore unheard senator, Wilbur F. Sanders, who would have the honor of representing the newly admitted state of Montana for only three years, took the floor. In a speech that lasted much longer than the proposed thirty-minute time limit, he rejected the ideology of his western Silverite colleagues on humanitarian issues. "The time to do right is here and now. . . . It is never inopportune to do justice," he stated. Blacks had been preparing themselves for twenty-five years for the duties of American citizenship, he boldly declared, and "It is twenty-five years more than we require for the most ignorant immigrant that comes to our land to instruct himself in the mysteries of democratic government, wholly new to him, and, in some instances, petrified in a language of which he is entirely ignorant." The Federal Elections Bill, he asserted, was not some exotic Republican experiment, but merely a commitment to enforce the law of the land as already written into the Constitution. "If we are going to abandon law, if every man is to be a law unto himself, anarchy is already here."[28]

John Tyler Morgan, in what turned out to be the last speech ever made on the Federal Elections Bill, provided the Democratic response to Sanders's humanitarian appeal. He remarked that the Montanan's speech was like dumping "a bucket of cold water" on the Aldrich resolution because it lasted about two-and-a-half hours. He then berated Aldrich, a representative of the smallest state in the Union, for trying to silence the representatives of so many large, populous states. Morgan held the floor for the remainder of the day and into Monday, January 26, adding nothing substantive to the debate.[29]

As the senator from Alabama droned on tediously, Edmund O. Wolcott of Colorado noticed that the Democrats and Silverites possessed a majority at that instant. Hoping to capitalize on this rare opportunity to drop the Federal Elections Bill, he abruptly interrupted Morgan with a motion to consider an apportionment bill. The supporters of the Federal Elections Bill objected, of course, but they were outnumbered. When the vote was taken, the Democrats and Silverites carried the motion 35 to 34. With only four weeks remaining in the second session of the Fifty-first Congress and with other legislation awaiting consideration, the sponsors of the Federal Elections Bill never again got the opportunity to resume debate on the bill. Nor did Nelson Aldrich attempt to force his cloture resolution again. The reformers simply gave up and (apparently) accepted their defeat. Just that quickly, the months of work that had gone into finding a solution to the race problem had come to nought. Henry Blair, alone among the reformers, tried to be optimistic about the gloomy situation, saying, "Let the Republican party pass the education bill and all will be well."[30] That, of course, was not to be. Thus ended, anticlimactically, one of the most bitter struggles in the history of Congress.

The defeat of the Federal Elections Bill marked a turning point in American history. It represented the Republican Party's final abandonment of the humanitarian ideals of Reconstruction. That meant, in effect, that it also marked the exact point in time that the federal government abandoned the cause of finding a solution to the South's race problem and of providing some means to uplift the African American race. Not until the advent of the civil rights movement more than a half-century later would African Americans be able to count on the federal government to protect their rights. Although the plan of supervising congressional elections had never proven to be an effective solution to the problem of ballot box fraud or voter intimidation, it was arguably better than doing nothing. History shows conclusively the sad results of the do-nothing policy. Therefore, it seems sensible to conclude that the reformers' idea was worthy of all the attention it received both at the time and since then in the history books. Yet, the historian must give due consideration to the opposition's arguments against the Federal Elections Bill—some of which were valid, most of which were compelling, and all of which were at least provocative—before reaching any conclusions about the likely efficacy of the reformers' plan. By far the most important criticism of the bill was that it would have made life even more difficult for blacks in the South than it already was, because it would have renewed the violence and bloodshed of the closing days of Reconstruction, when blacks paid dearly for their attempts to exercise the franchise. It is difficult for the historian to argue with that point. The only deterrent to such a backlash would have been for the federal government to authorize another military occupation of the South. The historian must ask, would any Republican administration, even with a majority in both chambers of Congress, realistically be prepared to enforce the law if necessary through another military occupation of the South? Considering the fact that neither Ulysses S. Grant nor Rutherford B. Hayes had been prepared to do so before, and keeping in mind that the American public in general would have recoiled in horror at such an action, the answer is, obviously not. Whether they *should have* been prepared to do so is another question altogether, and one for posterity to debate, but one that lies beyond the pale of this study.

If the outcome of the Federal Elections Bill debate seems a tragedy, the Republican Party's performance in the great drama was nothing short of a comedy of errors. Levi P. Morton's even-handedness as the moderator of the debate could be construed as either a lack of leadership or a traitorous act. The contemporary Republican press characterized his action in both ways. Either way, Morton never found a warm spot in the hearts of Republican Party leaders thereafter, and, in fact, his betrayal/dereliction of duty became the death knell of his career in politics.[31] More important than Morton's neutrality, however, was the internecine squabbling between the money faction of the party and the reformers. The historian must ask, why did the western Silverites divorce themselves from the reformers and side with the Democrats in opposing the Federal Elections Bill? This question has been answered wrongly in some previous historical studies, and it has been completely ignored in others. It, therefore, deserves serious consideration and analysis, which the following chapter provides.

Chapter 8

SILVER, SECTIONALISM, SIOUX INDIANS, AND SINOPHOBIA

Why Many Westerners Opposed the Federal Elections Bill

It had been the settled policy of this Government and this country before the war never to embrace in manhood suffrage the Indian, the Chinaman, nor the negro. And the first two are still excluded from the ballot.

—Senator Alfred Colquitt of Georgia

It is well enough for our friends on the Pacific coast to stand here and appeal to us to help them to protect American civilization, American homes, and American firesides from the Chinese. Do they think there is no civilization, that there are no homes, and no firesides in the South?

—Senator George Vest of Missouri

The Senate debated the Federal Elections Bill for fifty-six days, thirty-three of which the filibuster consumed. Never had the nation witnessed a filibuster of this magnitude, and only rarely would it see such again. While the nation marveled at the spectacle, Americans breathed a collective sigh of relief when the battle finally ended. Some partisan Republican newspapers admitted defeat graciously and called for Congress to move on. As one put

167

it, "Give us the shipping bills, the appropriations bills, the apportionment bill, the copyright bill—give us business, not partisanship. That is what the people want." Other partisan Republican papers expressed bitterness, and most that did so ignored the consequences of the defeat as touching black America, focusing instead on the effects of the failure for the GOP. Many believed that the bill had served as a litmus test of true republicanism and that the Silverites had proved themselves traitors. The influential *New York Tribune* went further than any other Republican organ in denouncing the western senators' defection. It harped upon allegations of a quid pro quo between Democrats and Silverites, whereby the former would support legislation increasing the coinage of silver if the latter would help defeat the Federal Elections Bill.[1] *Tribune* readers, including other newspaper editors, picked up on that conspiracy theory and helped perpetuate it. One Ohioan, for instance, lamented to John Sherman that the West had sold the black man to his enemies "for thirty pieces of silver, or maybe they got more."[2]

The western senators clearly betrayed the trust of African Americans, but to assume that a silver conspiracy lay behind this betrayal is neither scholarly nor judicious. There is no evidence to support the allegations of any corrupt bargain between Democrats and Silverites involving silver. The bill's sponsors gave no indication that they believed in a conspiracy between the Silverites and the Democrats, although they certainly blamed both groups individually for their action. But while the Democratic resistance was to be expected, the Silverite defection came as a stunning blow. "Think of it—," said John Coit Spooner, "Nevada . . . barely a respectable county—furnishes two senators to betray the Republican Party and the rights of citizenship" for African Americans. This betrayal so damaged Spooner's faith in the American political system that he stepped down at the end of his term and took a six-year hiatus.[3]

Despite the lack of supporting evidence, the quid pro quo silver theory continues to find its way into history books that mention the Federal Elections Bill. Perhaps historians have been prone to accept that explanation because it is easier than probing for other possible causes of the westerners' actions. This would be especially true of those scholars who do not consider the issue central to their studies, which comprises most of those who have written about it. Certainly, historians who focus on the South's race problem are often inadvertently myopic, missing the panoramic view that shows the issues affecting the West.[4]

It is easy to see the mining interests of the western states as a motivation for Colorado's and Nevada's four senators to push for silver legislation. Nevada had long been the major producer of silver in the nation, and, in 1889, miners struck a huge new vein in Colorado. It is also easy to overlook the fact that most southern Democratic senators were always strongly in favor of the increased coinage of silver. Indeed, most southern Democrats were lifelong bimetallists who had always hated the "Crime of '73" which did away with silver coinage. They strongly supported the Bland Silver Coinage Bill of 1876 that brought silver back into usage, and they vehemently opposed the Allison Amendment to that bill, which severely limited the amount of silver to be coined. They considered the Bland-Allison Act better than nothing, but, throughout the 1880s, they continued to push for the unlimited coinage of silver. In the summer of 1890, they voted for the Sherman Silver Purchase Act, which increased the amount of silver the federal government would coin. The increase, however, was not nearly enough to satisfy most southern Democrats. Included among these outspoken proponents of silver were J. Z. George of Mississippi, who wrote an extensive treatise on free silver in 1893, and John Tyler Morgan of Alabama, who would have waged a campaign against the Sherman Act were it not for saving his energy to fight the battles over the Butler bill and the Federal Elections Bill.[5]

The South and the West alike had been suffering from economic deflation in the late 1880s, and both called for inflation to stimulate the economy and relieve the suffering farmers. Although some proponents of inflation advocated printing greenbacks, the method of choice for most was restoring the coinage of silver at the pre-1873 ratio of sixteen-to-one. Interestingly, despite the mining interests of the West, southerners called for this measure just as vociferously as did westerners.[6] It is clear, therefore, that western Republicans could not hope to gain the southern Democrats' support for their pet silver legislation, because they already had it and, in fact, had always had it. This fact alone takes all of the credibility out of the quid pro quo silver theory.[7] But it still leaves unanswered the question of why the westerners opposed the Federal Elections Bill. It certainly was not because they wanted to get the bill out of the way as soon as possible, whether by passing it or defeating it, in order to push their economic agenda forward. If such had been the case, they would not have consistently opposed the Aldrich resolution for cloture.[8] Why would they oppose cloture unless they were honestly following the dictates of their consciences or constituencies in believing, like the eastern money Republicans, that the bill was bad legislation or the wrong policy for the federal government to pursue at that time? At least five Senate Republicans, including three westerners, went on record as opposing the Federal Elections Bill between the time party leaders first conceived the idea in the campaign of 1888 and the time the

Free Silver and the Force Bill. *"You beat my dog, and I'll beat yours!"* (*Puck*, 1890.)
It was popularly believed at the time that some western senators, such as William
M. Stewart (R-Nevada) shown here, opposed the Federal Elections Bill simply to
spite the GOP leadership (represented here by Benjamin Harrison) who opposed
the coinage of silver.

Fifty-first Congress convened, which proves that there were reasons to dislike the measure that had nothing to do with silver.[9]

    Henry M. Teller of Colorado, whom nobody previously questioned
as being a humanitarian, claimed to have opposed the Federal Elections
Bill because he truly believed it would not have solved the South's race problem but would have instead exacerbated it, an opinion that reflected the
views of his constituency. He emphatically denied that his objection was
based upon any deal with southerners. Moreover, despite the Sherman Silver Purchase Act, which he voted for in the first session, he still wanted the
Senate to reconsider passing a free silver bill before the second session expired. According to a Colorado newspaper, Teller would have opposed *any*
bill the Senate chose to debate near the end of the session that prevented
consideration of a free silver bill. He was clearly disappointed with his party

in 1890–1891 for not supporting free silver, and his disillusionment with the GOP only increased thereafter. He subsequently became an independent Silver Republican in 1896 (which was tantamount to being a Populist) and a Democrat in 1903.[10]

William M. Stewart of Nevada said the same but gave different reasons for his opposition. He still considered himself "a friend of the colored man" in 1891, just as he proved to be when he drafted the Fifteenth Amendment in 1869. But he claimed that he now knew from experience that such a bill would cause the white men of the South to make "war upon the defenseless race." It was in the best interest of African Americans, therefore, not to pass the measure. He also believed the bill "would subvert the Government of the United States and substitute military dictation for civil authority in the elections in the several States." Finally, he objected to the fact that so many of his colleagues supported the bill—undoubtedly the most important legislation of its kind since Reconstruction—without having read it. As he explained, it was "a long bill, sweeping in its provisions, and sufficiently ambiguous to puzzle ordinary readers. I found by my conversations with Republican Senators that very few of them possessed any real knowledge of the provisions of the bill."[11]

The explanation that each western senator voted his conscience appears more than a little plausible when one considers that even among the senators representing the Great Plains states—which typically supported radical, partisan Republican legislation—there was barely lukewarm support for the Federal Elections Bill. William Boyd Allison of Iowa, who had been a staunch Radical during Reconstruction, uncharacteristically gave no verbal or moral support to the bill or its sponsors, although he voted quietly for the Aldrich resolution. His silence was deafening to the reformers who sponsored the bill. Likewise, Preston B. Plumb, who represented Kansas, a state that was about to become the hotbed of Populism, never favored the bill but felt torn between following the party leadership and his conscience. Even though he voted with the humanitarians on the Aldrich resolution, he and Hoar had a behind-the-scenes argument over his lack of vocal support, which led to the permanent termination of their long friendship. Plumb's main concern in 1890 was the suffering farmers of his state, who could not appreciate the attention being given to the South's race problem at the time, despite the fact that many of them were Jayhawkers or sons of Jayhawkers. In the midst of the Federal Elections Bill debate, he, apparently working independent of Stewart and the Silverites, proposed a free silver bill of his own. Plumb's fear of publicly supporting the elections bill turned out to be well-founded, for his colleague, John J. Ingalls, who was the lone vocal supporter of the bill among Great Plains senators, incurred the wrath of his constituents for his preoccupation with the issue while Kansas farmers were starving. Indeed, the Kansas legislature turned Ingalls out of office before the year was out. (Upon Ingalls's ouster, one newspaper, alluding to Ingalls's penchant for waving the bloody shirt, reported that the "people of Kansas decided to fill up the bloody chasm" by throwing "John J. Ingalls into it.") Republican William D. Washburn of Minnesota, who faced challenges from soon-to-be Populist leader Ignatius Donnelly in 1890, was quite aware of his agrarian constituency's concerns, and he knew that the black voting rights issue was not one of them at the time. He thus voted with the Democrats to table the Federal Elections Bill in January 1891 so that the Senate could consider pressing economic business before the session expired in March.[12] The advent of Populism was therefore a major reason for the western Republican defection from the party line on the issue of electoral reform in and after 1890.

The Populist movement arose precisely because of the mutual interests of the South and West—interests that transcended party lines. The two regions made strange bedfellows in that, until the end of the 1880s, the West had been almost as solidly Republican as the South was Democratic. By 1890, however, many westerners had come to feel that the GOP leaders served the interests of the northeastern financial establishment to the neglect of the common man in America. It thus appeared to be in the best interest of some westerners to cross party lines and form an alliance with the other region of the country also suffering from economic hard times. This "new sectionalism," as one contemporary writer called it, pitted the South and West against the Northeast (which was defined as New England, the Middle Atlantic states, and the Great Lakes states, with its hub being at Wall Street in New York City). The Northeast contained sixteen states with a population of some thirty million, whose primary source of revenue sprang from industry and commerce, while the South and West contained twenty-eight states with a population of about thirty-two million, whose main economic base lay in agriculture.[13]

The "new" sectionalism that caused such friction in the last decade of the nineteenth century was not really all that new. It represented the continuation of a long-running ideological feud between rural agrarianism and urban industrialism that had begun fully a century before under the aegis of Thomas Jefferson and Alexander Hamilton. This dichotomy had always loosely followed geographic lines, pitting the Northeast against the South and the ever-shifting West. The rift had only widened over time because of the achievement of Manifest Destiny in 1848 and the explosive settlement of the Trans-Mississippi frontier resulting from the Homestead Act of 1862 and the railroad boom thereafter. By 1890, in the Populists' estimation, the settled and developed areas of the West combined with the South to produce 80 percent of the nation's natural resources, while 90 percent of the corporations that developed those resources were headquartered in the Northeast. As the Populists saw it, the tremendous growth of northeastern corporations, banks, insurance companies, and railroads caused a steady stream of capital to flow out of the South and West to the Northeast.[14] Many early historians of Populism agreed with this assessment, saying the Northeast held the South and West in a state of vassalage like that of the old European feudal system. Some even described the Northeast's control of the rest of the nation as a type of domestic economic imperialism. Although recent scholarship has found such assertions suspect, whether true or not, that perception among Populists at the time certainly muddied the political waters in and after 1890.[15]

Exacerbating this sectional tension was the tariff issue, which had long been one of the main points of contention between the opposing ideologies of the Northeast and the South and West. By 1890, the tariff had become a particularly sore subject because northeastern congressmen pushed the McKinley Tariff—the highest tariff in American history—through Congress over the objections of most southerners and many westerners. Moreover, opponents of the high tariff feared that northeastern manufacturing interests were intent on passing even higher tariffs in the future. While some southerners and westerners advocated a free-trade policy, others did not oppose the tariff altogether. They merely called for it to be set reasonably low. But all agreed that the Republican Party, following the lead of the old Federalist and Whig Parties, had taken ridiculous liberties in raising the tariff higher and higher since the Civil War. The highest rate in the original tariff law of 1789 was a mere 8.5 percent on certain enumerated items. Now, in 1891, the highest rate stood at 50 percent, which translated (in the minds of antiprotectionists) into a back-breaking cost-of-living increase on two-thirds of the American people to benefit the other one-third. Congressmen representing many agrarian districts—even districts within the Northeast—understandably wanted no part in levying such a high and divisive tax as the McKinley Tariff on the nation.[16]

Further intensifying the sectional tension was the disparity in population between the three sections, which assured that the Northeast would always hold a larger share of seats in the House of Representatives than the South or the West held. Only by combining their voting strength, therefore, could southerners and westerners hope to achieve a controlling interest in

Congress. The very threat of such a combination caused some northeasterners to complain that both regions were overrepresented in Congress. After the Thirteenth and Fourteenth Amendments abolished the three-fifths compromise, the South, which had recently been in arms against the United States, actually gained representation in Congress. By 1890, the former Confederate states boasted thirty more seats than they had held in 1860, while New England lost one, despite a massive increase in immigration to the Northeast during that same period of time. Northeastern Republican leaders held over from Reconstruction resented this apportionment because they had designed the Fourteenth Amendment especially to benefit African Americans, but white southern Democrats disfranchised black voters and used the Amendment to bolster their own numbers.[17] To many northeasterners, this seemed to nullify their victory in the Civil War because it meant, in effect, that the votes of Confederate veterans were worth more than those of Union veterans. Likewise, northeastern critics resented the sparsely populated West's fast-increasing and disproportionate representation in the Senate. Indeed, they decried the fact that the six New England states, with a population of nearly five million, had only twelve senators in 1891, while the nine Pacific and Rocky Mountain states had a combined population of less than three million but had eighteen senators.[18]

Yet, even with their disparate representation in the upper chamber during the Fifty-first Congress, western senators were unable to pass legislation that would relieve the suffering of their farmers because the Northeast still controlled the House. Those westerners in the process of becoming Populists thus began to see themselves as victims and to feel compelled to assume a posture of self-defense in dealing with the Northeast, just as southerners had done for decades.[19] Westerners in general began to understand the long-standing southern complaint that northeastern Republicans were arrogant, autocratic, overbearing, and guilty of selective compassion toward less fortunate peoples. Indeed, while northeastern Republicans often expressed compassion for black southerners, they rarely did so for white western farmers. For instance, when one agrarian congressman opposed the McKinley Tariff in the House on the basis that the yeoman farmer, not the factory owner, needed relief, Congressman Henry Cabot Lodge of Boston responded callously that there were "other people in this country besides farmers." Such an attitude sounded much the same to American farmers as Marie Antoinette saying (allegedly) "let them eat cake" on the eve of the French Revolution. It is not surprising, therefore, that the so-called Populist revolt followed on the heels of the very Congress that passed the McKinley Tariff, mainly to benefit northeastern corporations, while passing almost no legislation for the relief of suffering farmers.[20]

Ironically, the reinvigorated West-South alliance of the Populist era did not emerge because the old North-South sectional strife that created the post–Civil War bloody-shirt mentality had waned. In fact, it arose precisely at the same time as the most intense manifestation of the old North-South sectionalism since Reconstruction—during the Federal Elections Bill debate. Consequently, the old sectionalism and the new competed for the hearts and minds of westerners in 1890–1891. Westerners who embraced the new sectionalism were likely to become Populists, while those who clung to the old were likely to remain in the Republican fold. But, either way, the Populist revolt had such a tremendous impact upon not only the West but the whole nation that it helped bring the long-overdue "farewell to the bloody shirt." The defection of western Republicans from the party line on the Federal Elections Bill marked the beginning of the end of the old Civil War–era sectionalism.[21]

Besides the economic interests that united the South and West, other equally important common ground could be found between the two regions. Racial issues helped solidify the burgeoning alliance of white southerners and westerners around 1890. Like the South, the West was also burdened with racial problems. Many white westerners saw Native Americans, Chinese immigrants, and black migrants as threats to their desired way of life. Whereas the first two racial groups constituted long-standing problems for the West, black migrants represented a relatively new challenge. The migration of black southerners to the West that had begun soon after Reconstruction showed no signs of ending anytime soon. It seemed, in fact, that black migration would almost surely increase in the 1890s, especially in the absence of some new legislation such as the Butler Emigration Bill to help discontented black southerners leave the United States altogether. The idea of setting aside territory in the West for African Americans was highly unfavorable to the average white westerner. At a time when most white westerners wanted to rid their region of the presence of the Indian "savages" and the Chinese (not to mention the thousands of Mormons who had settled the Rocky Mountain West), adding a third minority race to the western milieu seemed out of the question.[22] A few blacks in the West seemed no cause for alarm, but as Colorado Governor John Evans put it, a "hoard" of them would be an unwelcome addition to his state.[23]

The West clearly had its own racial problems to consider at the very time that the Northeast was again becoming absorbed with the South's race problem. The idea of northeastern Republicans forcing their racial views on other sections of the country struck fear in the hearts of white southerners, but it also seemed abhorrent to the average white westerner.[24] If the northeasterners would pass a bill enforcing the civil rights of black southerners, which would effectively end the white man's hegemony in several states, might they not someday launch a crusade to extend the rights of citizenship with all its privileges to the Indians and Chinese of the West? Such a scenario was not outside the realm of possibility. Southern congressmen recognized this western fear and aversion and used it to their advantage. By voting with the West on issues that would keep white civilization there safe from the threat of Indians and Chinese, they could anticipate that western congressmen would do the same for them on matters of importance to white southerners. Here, then, was an ulterior motive for western Republican senators to vote against the Federal Elections Bill. Although it certainly was not their primary motivation in opposing the controversial measure, it was the closest thing to a quid pro quo deal that the South and the West ever made.[25]

It is quite interesting that the western Indian problem came to the fore in a major, tragic way in December 1890—the very time that the U.S. Senate began debating the Federal Elections Bill. The problem had deep roots, of course, in early American history, but the policies of the Republican administration of President Benjamin Harrison beginning in 1889 intensified it. Working with both the Fiftieth and Fifty-first Congresses, the Harrison administration reclaimed most of the Indian Territory of Oklahoma and forged a policy of intolerance toward Native Americans not seen since Andrew Jackson's presidency (1828–1836), when the removal of the eastern tribes was completed with the infamous "Trail of Tears." Harrison's Indian policy, shaped largely by Massachusetts Senator Henry L. Dawes who headed the Committee on Indian Affairs, drew sharp criticism from a vocal minority of Americans, including, ironically, some Democrats and southerners.[26]

The most intense opposition, however, came, not surprisingly, from Native Americans themselves. Tribes situated on Great Plains reservations—mainly the Sioux under the leadership of Sitting Bull—beseeched federal lawmakers to provide relief for their suffering. They, like their white neighbors, were experiencing one of the worst droughts in the nation's history, were not being helped much by the Bureau of Indian Affairs, were literally starving to death, and were not allowed to live nomadically or hunt wild game as was their custom. When the Native Americans' appeals went unanswered, they turned to the only means of help left to them. They called on the Great Spirit in the Ghost Dance, a religious ritual that had recently started in Nevada and that had spread throughout the West in 1890. Although the Sioux harmed no one with their appeals to the Great Spirit, federal policy makers feared that the Ghost Dance would incite an Indian uprising. As a result, in a senseless act of aggression, an agent of the U.S. Army killed Sitting Bull, who had recently starred in Buffalo Bill's Wild West Show but whom government officials considered an ever-recalcitrant tribal leader. Sitting Bull's death prompted one western newspaper to report gleefully that now Sitting Bull had finally been transformed into a "good Indian—[because] dead Indians are always good."[27] Two weeks later, a misunderstanding of the nature of the Ghost Dance and of Indian mannerisms ultimately led the Army to massacre a whole village of Sioux at Wounded Knee, South Dakota. At least 150 Indians died there, and probably closer to three hundred.[28]

This tragic episode occurred on December 29, 1890, precisely the same time that the battle over the Federal Elections Bill was reaching the height of its intensity more than a thousand miles away in the U.S. Senate in Washington, D.C. Newspapers all over the country carried stories of the unstable western Indian situation throughout the month of December, leading up to the atrocity at Wounded Knee. Thereafter, the papers blared headlines of the massacre right beside the latest updates on the ongoing Federal Elections Bill filibuster. It is clear, therefore, that the western race problem was fresh on every senator's mind as the upper chamber debated a potential solution to the southern race problem. Democrats, particularly southern ones, relished every chance to point out the Republican Party's less-than-sterling record on Indian affairs and to note inexplicable differences in how the party chose to deal with Indians and blacks. The federal government under GOP control had made blacks citizens of the United States collectively with no strings attached, but Indians were only allowed to become citizens individually after dissolving their tribal relations and taking land in severalty. Meanwhile, the Bureau of Indian Affairs had also spent an average of $6 million annually training the nation's 250,000 Indians (who were not citizens) in the ways of the white man's civilization, but, with the defeat of the Blair Education Bill in 1890, it now refused to educate the nation's eight million blacks (who *were* citizens). Likewise, it had spent an untold sum of money moving Indians from place to place against their will, but it refused to appropriate funds for blacks to emigrate voluntarily to locations of their own choosing. Finally, while it had liberated blacks from slavery and allowed them to roam the country freely, it had corralled Indians onto reservations and severely restricted their freedoms.[29]

Such contrasting racial policies baffled many southern congressmen,

Uncle Sam's Double Standard. Consistency? (*Puck*, 1891.) The convergence of the Wounded Knee Massacre with the U.S. Senate's deliberation upon the Federal Elections Bill in December 1890 suddenly and dramatically thrust the issue of the federal government's traditional double standard on racial issues into the national media spotlight.

or so they claimed. Senator Matthew Butler of South Carolina called them "a curious commentary on common sense, to say nothing of humanity."[30] Congressman Thomas Hooker of Mississippi, who had a reputation as a racist in regard to black southerners, asked rhetorically of the Republican Indian policy, "is it not most unjust?" Senators Wilkinson Call of Florida, J. Z. George of Mississippi, Arthur P. Gorman of Maryland, James K. Jones of Arkansas, and George Vest of Missouri all agreed. Other prominent southerners, including educator and writer J. L. M. Curry of Virginia and Georgia's former U.S. Senator Joseph E. Brown, also spoke out against the Republican Indian policy. Although many such southerners seemed superficially to be concerned for the welfare of the Indians, they undoubtedly hoped that by pointing out the errors of the Republicans in handling Indian affairs, they would give the GOP leaders second thoughts about their renewed activist policy toward southern blacks. Thus, they favored not a reversal of the Republican Indian policy, which would have given Indians the same civil rights that blacks had been granted in the Reconstruction amendments, but a reversal of the Republican policy toward blacks, which would have reduced them to the level of the Indians.[31]

Westerners, realizing that southern concern for the welfare of the Indians was largely a political ploy, did not feel threatened by the tactic. Humanitarian appeals to help Native Americans did not faze most western congressmen, no matter who made the appeals. Indeed, they felt no remorse about the removal of Indians from regions that the white man wanted for his own settlement to reservations in remote, undesirable areas. They believed that anyone who felt ashamed of the U. S. government's treatment of the Indians, either currently or historically, was deluded with false notions of that primitive race's true character. As California Representative William Vandever remarked, "no matter what ideas may have taken possession of the public mind by reason of this fancy sketch of Helen Hunt Jackson [author of *A Century of Dishonor*, 1881] a few years ago . . . a man who goes . . . and sees the Mission Indians as they are will lose his sympathy for them."[32]

The personal experiences of various western members of Congress in dealing with Indians illustrate Vandever's assertion. Henry M. Teller, for instance, a humanitarian from New York who moved to Colorado in the 1860s, had felt very sympathetic toward Indians before going west. Once he actually encountered Indians who had not been acculturated into white society, however, his views changed immediately, radically, and irreversibly. "We who have seen live Indians," he said, "know that, as a whole, they are a filthy, lazy, treacherous, [and] revengeful race of vagabonds."[33] Accordingly, he did not believe the federal policy toward the Indians was or ever had been too severe, observing that "in the history of the treatment of aborigines anywhere in the world there has been no such lavish expenditure of money by any nation as we have expended for the Indians. . . . it is not true that we have treated them improperly." Even if they had been mistreated, said Teller, "it is in harmony with Divine purpose . . . the world was made not for savages but for civilized men." Joseph N. Dolph, the firebrand from Oregon who expressed such concern for the welfare of black southerners during the Federal Elections Bill debate, concurred.[34]

Despite the fact that Indian problems in the West crested in 1890 and that the Billion Dollar Congress spent a great deal of time debating Indian affairs, Chinese immigration represented the great racial issue of the future in the West. Whereas the number of Indians was declining, the Chinese population in America was growing, and it seemed destined to overtake the fast-dwindling Indian population in the near future. Westerners thus saw the Indian problem as a passing concern that would soon be alleviated, while they believed that Chinese immigration would be their region's next big race problem. Astute southerners realized that sinophobia gripped some parts of the West with a tenacity comparable to that with which negrophobia gripped the South, and they capitalized on that fact, forging an alliance with westerners to ensure white rule in both sections of the country.[35]

The Chinese had become a notably large immigrant group after the California Gold Rush of 1849. Overpopulation, drought, famine, and floods contributed to their desire to emigrate from China. Anti-Chinese sentiment appeared on the Pacific coast of the United States with the arrival of the first large wave of Chinese immigrants in the 1850s. As the railroad and mining industries grew in the West, the number of Chinese "Coolies" increased to the extent that some westerners wanted to stop their immigration as early as the 1860s. By the 1880s, calls for their exclusion had reached a fever pitch, and in 1882, the Chinese Exclusion Bill passed Congress, and Republican president Chester A. Arthur signed it into law. The bill disallowed Chinese immigration only temporarily, not permanently, which many westerners thought inadequate. Some wanted not merely a permanent exclusion policy but also a forced removal policy.[36]

By the time the Fifty-first Congress convened, anti-Chinese sentiment in the West had reached its zenith. California Representative Thomas Jefferson Clunie introduced a bill for the permanent exclusion of the "Mongolian invaders," arguing that "There is no room in this country for any race we cannot mix with and dwell with in harmony." Fellow Californian William R. Morrow, who demonstrated his humanitarianism by helping to establish the American Red Cross, nonetheless found no place for the Chinese in America. He noted that in the legislation Congress passed in the 1880s restricting Chinese immigration, there was only "one purpose in view . . . to execute the will of the people of the United States." By 1890, however, the will of the people had changed, he explained, such that only the "permanent and absolute exclusion of all classes of Chinese" would now suffice.[37] The national zeitgeist of race relations was thus transforming rapidly.

Some white westerners objected to the Chinese presence in America because it provided a labor supply that undercut the standard rates paid to white workers. Others resented the Chinese for refusing to assimilate into American society or to adopt white American culture. The Chinese did not want to become citizens of the United States, detractors argued; they merely wanted to exploit the American job market and then send their earnings back home to China. Although such claims were in many cases accurate, at the bottom of the western sinophobia was, of course, racial stereotyping.

Unlike the stereotyping of America's other large minority groups, however, there was no consensus on what the characteristics of the Chinese were supposed to be. Some observers considered them dumb, cowardly, dirty, and dishonest, as the following story told by California Congressman Clunie, a San Francisco resident, indicates:

> I once in the course of my profession as a lawyer had a Chinaman call on me, and, as I understood him, ask how much I would charge to defend a Chinaman accused of murder. I told him $1,000 was my fee. He went away, returning after several days with a sack of silver. He said, "I killee my man; here is your money." I was shocked. I said, "You killed him? Then you should hang." He said, "I kill him. How many men you likee me get say I no killee him?" This but illustrates their regard for truth.[38]

Conversely, others were equally convinced that the Chinese were superior to whites in intelligence, thrift, enterprise, and industry, which threatened white civilization in the West in a different way. One newspaper claimed exuberantly that a "Chinaman has yet to be found who can not learn his English alphabet in one day and be ready . . . to read [English] words" the next day![39] William Stewart of Nevada agreed, claiming that the Chinese propensity for hard work and fast learning would "ruin our civilization."[40] He concluded that "competition with them is impossible. . . . It is impossible for our race to labor as incessantly as they do . . . their industry so far surpasses ours that wherever they come, we must [leave]."[41]

Although sinophobia was almost exclusively a western phenomenon, until 1890 it had been the responsibility of eastern politicians to pass legislation restricting Chinese immigration, because so few western states existed before then. Northeastern Republicans had a mixed record on the issue, and many seemed unable to make up their minds, changing their views over time. Benjamin Harrison, before becoming president, incurred the wrath of western congressmen by twice voting in the Senate against Chinese exclusion. On the campaign trail in 1888, however, he changed his position and endorsed exclusion. Interestingly, in the same breath that he used to advocate a hard-line policy toward the unwanted Asian immigrants, he proclaimed his support for black voting rights in the South.[42] John Sherman likewise changed his position on Chinese exclusion, voting in 1864 to allow Chinese immigration and voting against it thereafter. In 1890, in an apologetic explanation, he said that the year 1864 had been the apex of the Civil War, a time when the "whole country was denuded of labor." As a war measure only, therefore, had he welcomed the Asian workers, whom he since found repulsive as a class of laborers: "Any class of people who were so low and so lacking in manhood as to barter away their freedom should not be permitted to be brought into this country, to compete with our laborers who were struggling to elevate themselves in the arts of manhood." He referred to the fact that many Chinese immigrants signed contracts with Chinese bosses, in which they became indentured servants in America—a servile working class that Sherman likened to "mere serfs."[43]

Many other prominent northeastern Republicans who had reputations as humanitarians never changed their views on Chinese exclusion, but they also never managed a consensus with one another on the issue. William M. Evarts of New York made his position known in 1890, saying, "I have always been from the beginning, and am now, for the exclusion of Chinese immigration." Both George Frisbie Hoar and Henry L. Dawes of Massachusetts strongly opposed exclusion, while Justin Morrill of Vermont and Nelson Aldrich of Rhode Island (not to mention William Boyd Allison of Iowa, who was not a northeasterner geographically, but typically voted with the northeastern party leaders on most issues) opposed it somewhat less vocally.[44] With northeastern senators divided over the issue, a West-South alliance stood a fair chance of getting anti-Chinese legislation passed. In return for helping westerners, southern senators surely hoped for, if not expected, western support in preventing passage of the Federal Elections Bill.[45]

Southern senators excoriated those Republicans who took a racist stance toward the Chinese while simultaneously showing humanitarian concern for black southerners. Their typical argument went: "they make rigid laws against the Chinese and treat them as an inferior race and entitled to no rights, and at the same time claim that the African is the equal in all respects with the white man and should be protected in every privilege."[46] Senator James B. Eustis of Louisiana made a particularly compelling case against the inconsistent Republicans, saying, "You have a race prejudice against the Chinese. So have I. I avow it. I proclaim it. I say there is such a thing as antagonism of the races. You deny it when it comes to the question of the negro and the white man." Why could the Republicans not simply be honest and admit that the races were not and could never be equal, asked Eustis?[47]

Foremost on the list of Republicans whom southerners enjoyed tormenting for their inconsistency on racial issues was Joseph N. Dolph of Oregon, who struggled to find a plausible explanation for his conflicting views on the black and yellow races. His most common argument was that, since the Chinese were not citizens, the United States owed them nothing, whereas it "owed something to the Negro," who was by moral and legal right a citizen.[48] Southern Democrats found such an explanation lacking, to say the least. In their minds blacks should not be citizens any more than the Chinese or Indians, and the only reason they were was because of the vengeful social engineering of the Radical Republicans of Reconstruction. During the Federal Elections Bill debate, therefore, James B. Eustis asked Dolph to answer the following hypothetical question:

> The population of Oregon amounts to 312,000 people. Suppose Congress had never passed a law prohibiting the immigration of Chinese into this country. Suppose that about a million and a half of Chinamen had immigrated into the State of Oregon. Suppose that Congress passed a law giving the right of citizenship and naturalization to those Chinamen. . . . Suppose that those million and a half Chinamen had banded themselves together and . . . established in Oregon a Chinese State government, as they would have had a perfect right to do. . . . Suppose that the white people of Oregon, not believing that a Chinese government is exactly the kind of government that they ought to live under, had overthrown that Chinese government. . . . Who would you support, the Chinese or the whites?[49]

Dolph initially avoided answering the question, calling it a waste of time to engage in such meaningless speculations. Yet, when pressed, he admitted that he agreed with the vast majority of white people on the Pacific Coast who "do not believe that the Chinese laborers are a desirable population." When pressed further, he unfurled the bloody shirt, blurting out that Oregonians "are made of different stuff" than southerners. Oregonians, he said, would never defy a law of the United States, reject a constitutional amendment, or commit treason against their country, as the former Confederate states had done. John Tyler Morgan replied to Dolph's statements by reading the Oregon state constitution, which, until 1887, said that "No negro, Chinaman, or mulatto shall have the right of suffrage" and which forbade whites to intermarry with blacks, Chinese, or Indians of one-fourth or more blood. Considering such laws, were Oregonians really that much different than Alabamians, he asked?[50]

Later in the Federal Elections Bill debate, Edward O. Wolcott of Colorado took up the hypothetical question that Eustis had asked Dolph. He chided his fellow western Republican for an "evasive" answer and declared with absolute starkness that, if such a scenario occurred in Colorado, "in some way and by some method, I know not how, the white vote would govern."[51] Wolcott, whose "total lack of senatorial dignity," as one observer commented, gave "his associates in the Senate pain," made no pretenses of being a humanitarian. In that regard, he was more genuine than many of his fellow Republicans, who professed great compassion for the less fortunate but did not always demonstrate it.[52] Wolcott truthfully expressed what he believed was the will of the majority of his constituency[53] and in so doing embodied a new Republican mentality for the 1890s. He stood, in fact, among the vanguard of a new generation in his views of American race relations because he admitted, with neither pride nor shame, what he believed was the matter-of-fact need for white supremacy in the United States.

This new frame of mind that Wolcott presaged transcended all sectional and socioeconomic divisions, connecting the three major parties, bidding farewell to the bloody shirt, New Nationalism, and paving the way for the ages of Progressivism, Imperialism, and Jim Crowism.[54] It showed that the Civil War and Reconstruction years had merely been an unwelcome interlude in the traditional, natural alliance between the South and the West, and that the time for the nation's new "manifest destiny" had arrived. The old manifest destiny had entailed the overspreading and subduing of the continent by the white man in order to take physical control of the vast expanses of howling wilderness in the West. The new would require inundating the continent with the idea of white supremacy in order to take psychological control of all other races who inhabited the land, whether red, yellow, brown, or black.[55]

This new age that began around 1890 would be one of realism rather than idealism in race relations. It would replace the old dogma of enlightened egalitarianism embodied in the Declaration of Independence, the Emancipation Proclamation, and the Reconstruction Amendments, with pseudoscientific Social Darwinism, segregation laws, and state constitutions that contained all kinds of racially motivated suffrage restrictions. While the South would lead this racist charge, the West would support it, and, consequently, the Northeast would ultimately be forced to accept white supremacy as the new American way—the zeitgeist of the coming age. By 1891, therefore, the southern Democrats, with the help of some influential western Republicans, had succeeded in destroying the Republican reformers' civil rights agenda for African Americans by portraying them as hypocrites on other racial matters. They asked, with great effect, a question that still today must give pause to the impartial historian: how could these professing humanitarians support a federal policy of virtual genocide against Native Americans and support a law barring the golden door to the Chinese in the West, while simultaneously fighting one of the fiercest congressional battles in American history to make life better for black southerners? There is no satisfactory answer to this question, for the reformers' argument that one group are citizens while the others are not fails to pass the test of true humanitarianism. That argument represented instead a type of Nationalism, which fit both then and now much more easily into the larger ideology of the racists than into the ideology of egalitarians, humanitarians, or racial reformers.

The showdown on Capitol Hill in 1890–1891 was a clear victory for the racists. It forced many of the reformers to reconsider their positions on racial issues. Either they would have to begin treating all racial and ethnic groups with the same humanitarian concern or stop professing to be humanitarians. Unfortunately, they ultimately chose the latter, as the next chapter will reveal.

Chapter 9

THE "PECULIAR SITUATION" OF AFRICAN AMERICANS AND ETHNIC MINORITIES IN THE UNITED STATES

How Racism Became Fashionable in the 1890s

The southern man apparently denied to the negro social recognition, not primarily because he was a negro, but because he was a slave. The northern man seems to hate the negro primarily on account of his color.

—*John Snyder, physician and archaeologist from Illinois*

The proud Anglo-Saxon will not and can not be ruled by Ethiopian blood.

—*John H. O'Neall, Democratic representative of Indiana*

The white westerners' aversion to Native Americans and the Chinese was not extraordinary in 1890. Nor was it comparable only to the white South's negrophobia. It was rather symptomatic of a larger problem afflicting white America. Put succinctly, white America suffered from the blight of racism. Each section had its own unique race problems, and none was more racist than the other. If it seemed that the South was more racist, it was only because its racial minority was by far the largest, the by-product of earlier generations of slaveholders. The Northeast, however, despite the presence of its humanitarian and reformer element, exhibited racism as well. Its two most prevalent manifestations of racism were xenophobia (ethnophobia) and black segregation. The former is a strain of racism that is often downplayed in histories of American race relations as less severe and, therefore, less important than racism based on skin color. Discussion of the latter is more prominent in historical studies, but it has usually, and inaccurately, been considered a southern, rather than a national, phenomenon.

Northeasterners had generally been more apologetic about racism in the United States than people in other sections of the country before the 1890s, but many were also in denial about the racism they harbored in their own hearts and minds. Reverend Henry Field, a New York missionary to southern blacks, for instance, felt afraid to say what he really thought about the South's race problem because of the negative reception he would receive from his northern contemporaries, most of whom had never stepped foot in the South. "No young author could afford to risk his reputation by writing a book to apologize" for southern race relations, said Field, for "it would be howled down as soon as it was born. No man is strong enough to fight against the sympathies of the age." Yet his conscience compelled him to do so. As he explained, "I have been so oppressed by [the southern race problem] that I could not keep from speaking, even if it were only to ask questions. That is the way to get light, by groping after it. Confession of ignorance is the first step towards knowledge." His groping ultimately led him to conclude that, given the realities of the times in which he lived, white southerners (racist Democrats) had the most sensible opinions on the subject, not northern Republicans.[1] His groping also helped to bring to light the disingenuousness of many of his professing humanitarian colleagues. Dr. Edward H. McGill, president of Swarthmore College in Pennsylvania, agreed with Field. He applauded the southern states' recent efforts to elevate black southerners and indicted the northern states for lack of the same, saying, "in that part of this country where the Negro has suffered most, where he has been enslaved, his condition to-day is more favorable than in the so-called free states. . . ."[2] Because of the dual criticism of social leaders such as Field and the Democratic and Silverite political leaders of the Billion Dollar Congress, a decrease is visible after 1890 in the number of outspoken egalitarians and humanitarians of the Northeast who were willing and able to guide the national racial destiny as they had done during the abolitionist and Reconstruction generations. Northeasterners as a whole began to accept racism and, in many cases, embrace it as a natural state of affairs in race relations worldwide.[3]

Dr. James Buckley of New York urged his fellow northern humanitarians at the First Mohonk Conference on the Negro Question to "keep this prejudice of the North constantly in view, and endeavor to remove it," otherwise there would be no hope of curing the South of its racism. Former Union general and head of the Freedmen's Bureau O. O. Howard blamed northern racism on the lack of true religion in America, saying "I think we ought to labor to get some genuine Christianity inside of our church edifices and into society." Only then could white Americans—no matter which section of the country they lived in—learn to love blacks, Chinese, Indians, and anyone else who was different in color or culture.[4]

Why did this evolution toward the Northeast accepting racism as normal and natural occur, and how was it manifested? By 1890, the ethnic composition of the American people had changed dramatically from what it had been in the antebellum era. Immigrants from various European countries, which once had little or no notable presence in the United States, actually outnumbered the nation's eight million African Americans, making new immigrants collectively the largest minority group in the nation. These ethnic groups included Austrians, Greeks, Hungarians, Italians, Lithuanians, Norwegians, Poles, Russians, and Turks, among many others. From the Mediterranean Sea to the North Sea and from the Balkans to the Baltic, by the thousands they came to fulfill their American dreams. The vast majority of these new immigrants arrived in the United States in northeastern ports, and in the Northeast they largely stayed, overspreading all of the states north of the Ohio and east of the Mississippi Rivers and trickling across the northern Great Plains states. Comparatively few immigrants moved to the agriculturally depressed South, much to the chagrin of white southerners. In 1888, southern political leaders established the Southern Inter-States Immigration Commission for the purpose of inducing a larger proportion of the immigrants to move South.[5] The effort, however, proved futile, mainly because the southerners were selective in their recruiting, aiming for the literate and already-acculturated immigrants. As one Georgia newspaper explained it: "The South would welcome millions [of immigrants], and be safer and richer because of their presence. But the South does not need or desire an influx of hundreds of thousands of . . . peasants, poverty struck and grossly ignorant. She wants immigrants from the North, who are Americans already . . . this is not a section where we can afford to . . . add indefinitely to the mass of ignorance."[6] Indeed, the South already possessed what many white southerners believed was the world's superior and irreplaceable labor class: African Americans. Thus, the South did not need more poor, uneducated laborers. It needed only immigrants with, as former Mississippi Governor Robert Lowry put it, "potential" for establishing businesses and industries.[7]

Why most immigrants shunned the South was a topic of debate in Congress and the press. Four-term Republican Congressman Louis E. McComas of Maryland believed the "white man's government of the South" repelled "the vigorous youth of the North." He added, "I am sorrowfully convinced that it is a love of a broader freedom that induces the American farmer to carry his sons to trench and irrigate the parched desert, to face cyclones, [and to] brave arctic weather" on the Great Plains rather than to settle in the South.[8] One South Carolina newspaper disagreed, arguing that most European immigrants simply preferred the frigid temperature of the North to the sweltering heat of the South. The northern climate more closely replicated the climate of their European homelands. Moreover, those few Europeans who were willing to move to a hot climate, said the paper, were choosing the newly opened expanses of Africa as their destination, instead of the American South.[9]

Both theories about why most immigrants spurned the South were, of course, absolutely wrong. Most immigrants stayed in the North simply because they had more and better economic opportunities there and, as time went on, increasingly because they had family and friends there. Some no doubt avoided the South because they did not wish to compete with African Americans for the few jobs available, but many certainly avoided the deep South cotton states because they were not immune to racism. They preferred not to be surrounded by blacks. It was not uncommon for members of one racial or ethnic minority group to despise another just as old-stock white Americans despised both. The feeling was mutual. Blacks reciprocated the aversion to new immigrants moving south. Black southerners who were fortunate enough to hold industrial jobs certainly did not wish to see a flood of white immigrants moving south to compete for those jobs. Thus, if there was any racial antipathy between immigrants and black southerners, both groups caused it. The two groups were not always in competition for jobs, though. Sometimes they worked side by side in southern coal mines and factories. On rare occasions, their shared economic interests made them natural allies, as histories of Populism and unionization in the late-nineteenth-century South reveal. Yet, more often than not, immigrants avoided allying with blacks because blacks occupied the lowest station in American society. Most immigrants realized that, in order to attain social mobility in their new nation, they must not make permanent alliances or friendships with those at the bottom of the social hierarchy.[10] Thus, for any number of reasons, the new immigrants by and large remained in the northern states and increasingly posed a new social problem there in the 1890s.

These poor masses of ethnic immigrants had come to America for many of the same reasons that drove the Chinese to the California coast, with economic opportunity being foremost on the list. Just as the Chinese largely huddled in San Francisco, the new European immigrants typically huddled in New York City, Boston, and Philadelphia, although many made their way west to Cleveland, Cincinnati, Chicago, Milwaukee, and Minneapolis, among numerous other destinations. The eastern seaboard cities, which had traditionally been controlled politically, socially, and economically by the old-stock whites—particularly those of English ancestry—suddenly found themselves swamped with foreign-born populations speaking multiple languages, practicing sundry versions of Christianity and Judaism, and having no experience with democratic government. The descendants of the Puritans especially tended to resent these first-generation immigrants for their peculiar social customs and religious practices, which threatened to disrupt the traditional, monolithic culture of New England.[11]

The old ruling elite of the Northeast justified its ethnophobia using the same type of conservative arguments that the white South and the white West used to justify their brands of racism. They said that the new immigrants jeopardized the welfare of the American polity and the nation's traditional values because most were uneducated and unaccustomed to democracy. Moreover, they complained that some were unwilling and others were incapable of assimilating into the mainstream of American society, which was built predominantly upon the Protestant faith, the English language, and the democratic political process. Therefore, immigration should be limited to those who could and would assimilate and who seemed likely to contribute to the general welfare of the nation, to the exclusion of those who seemed likely to become a drain on the nation's resources because of their illiteracy and incapacity for self-improvement.[12]

Despite expressing concern about protecting the nation as a whole from such undesirables, old-stock northeasterners were really more interested in protecting their own social and political hegemony in their section of the country. John Sherman, who was of New England Puritan ancestry, championed the cause of poor illiterate blacks—as long as they remained in the South—yet he argued for the exclusion of the poorest and neediest white immigrants, saying, "Neither a pauper . . . nor any man unable to make his living, nor an imbecile, nor one who has a defect or imperfection of body or mind . . . should be allowed to immigrate to this country."[13] His idea of excluding the mentally, physically, educationally, and economically challenged carried the day and, in 1891, became the law of the land. President Harrison approved Sherman's immigration restriction plan, which

Sound Advice to the Fifty-second Congress. Uncle Sam. "Stop Wranglin' 'bout yer tariff an' yer silver, gents, an' tackle this fust." (Harper's Weekly, 1891.) Upon the failure of the Republican Reformers in the Billion Dollar Congress to make the United States a more inclusive society, American politicians and the public as a whole began to show openly a very pronounced regression in racial and ethnic attitudes. Notice that the petition to restrict immigration is held underneath an American flag by a grizzled-looking Uncle Sam.

barred the golden door to "All idiots, insane persons, paupers or persons likely to become a public charge, [and] persons suffering from a loathsome or a dangerous contagious disease. . . ."[14] Consequently, immigrants who could meet the standards of admission to the United States were occasionally forced to leave loved ones who could not meet them, behind. In fact, this law denied more than twenty thousand immigrants entry into the United States in the decade of the 1890s. How many of these denials resulted in broken families is unascertainable, but it must have been a considerable number. Whatever amount of suffering Sherman's law caused immigrant families, old-stock Americans remained coldly indifferent to it.[15]

More often than not, the ethnophobes of the Northeast were, like Sherman and Harrison, Republicans, which baffled many Americans of foreign birth. John P. Altgeld, a German-born American who was a federal judge in Chicago in 1890 and later became the governor of Illinois, expressed dismay at the treatment of the new immigrants flooding into the Northeast. He noted that some of the most ardent Republicans currently, as well as some of the most devoted Unionists in the Civil War, were first-generation immigrants. He thought it incomprehensible that the GOP would shun such a large class of Union-loving, potential Republican voters merely because of their ethnic backgrounds.[16] Yet, that was precisely the case, and the ethnophobes seemed to be justified in their position after Altgeld pardoned the German immigrant anarchists who were arrested for Chicago's Haymarket Square riot of 1886. From their point of view, was such a pardon not proof that ethnic minorities colluded for their own self-interest rather than promoting the welfare of the nation at large?[17]

Ethnophobia did not just suddenly arise among northeasterners around 1890. The old-stock Protestants of New England had always despised the Irish, who first became a large presence in the Northeast in the 1840s. They loathed the Irish's Catholicism and their stereotyped proclivity for drinking, rowdiness, and ignorance. The new wave of European immigration during the Gilded Age did not diminish the ill feelings toward the Irish, either. It merely gave the old-stock Protestants more ethnic minorities to look down upon. To southern and western observers, the new wave of anti-immigration sentiment represented just one of several ways that the Northeast displayed hypocrisy on racial matters. One Missouri newspaper called it merely the latest manifestation of "Puritan Know-Nothingism," meaning that it showed a continuation of the traditional Anglo-Protestant mentality of cultural arrogance and ethnocentrism that the Northeast had exhibited throughout U. S. history. Indeed, most of the northeastern reformers who sought to dictate the solution to the South's race problem in 1890–1891 were descendants of the Puritans and Pilgrims, whose religious intolerance is well-documented in countless histories of New England. During the years of the Early Republic, these colonial Anglo-Protestant groups manifested their self-righteousness politically through the Federalist Party. In the Jacksonian era, these sons of the Puritans shifted their political voice to the Whig Party, while they found a new moral consciousness in the abolition movement. Over the next three decades thereafter, some members of this elite group evolved into Free-Soilers, some into Know-Nothings, and some into Radical Republicans. By the 1890s, they were searching for a new identity, which many found in the Immigration Restriction League that Henry Cabot Lodge organized in 1894.[18]

Despite being one of the best-educated men in Congress, Henry Cabot Lodge was also among the most vocal anti-immigrationists in the Northeast. His xenophobia rested upon either stereotypes and generalities or utterly false assumptions that the hordes of "non-Teutonic" immigrants arriving daily on the shores of Boston and New York were more prone to criminal and deviant behavior than old-stock Americans. The majority of them, he asserted, were willing to work for lower wages than the traditional laboring classes, which eroded "the quality of American citizenship," a theory that sounded much like a typical western argument for Chinese exclusion. To combat this problem, Lodge favored a national literacy test for immigrants.[19]

Lodge's racial views were complex, sometimes inexplicable, often contradictory, and always controversial. He used the term "race" to mean "nationality" or "ethnic group." He believed the existing "races" were evolutions from the three original, pure racial strains: Indo-European, Hamitic, and Semitic. As evolutions, they were "artificial" races, yet they were races all the same. Italians, for instance, were just as different from Englishmen as were the Sioux Indians or African Americans (he used the word "nigger" in an off-handed comment embedded within one of his congressional speeches in 1890). Lodge once remarked that "You can take a Hindoo [*sic*] and give him the highest education the world can afford," but he would still be a "Hindoo." A single generation of education would not convert him into an Englishman, said Lodge, much less would it make him qualified for American citizenship.[20]

Lodge's views on what constituted a "race" were not unusual at the time. They resulted from a lack of scientific understanding of the topic. Despite the best efforts of the most intellectual thinkers in the world, no scientific definition for the term "race" had yet been formulated. Consequently, there was no test that could be applied to determine a person's race officially. Opinions about how many distinct races existed varied widely, from as few as four or five to as many as several hundred.[21] For the purpose of determining citizenship and voting rights under the Fourteenth and Fifteenth Amendments, the various states arrived near a consensus, delineating four races: Caucasian, African, Chinese, and American Indian. The first two were generally considered citizens eligible to vote, while the latter two were not. Groups whose race seemed less defined, such as southeastern Europeans with swarthy complexions, posed a serious problem, however, and many old-stock Americans did not believe they should be entitled to citizenship or suffrage.[22]

Lodge's racial views typified those of most old-stock Americans in that he believed in the inherent superiority of the "Anglo-Saxon race," by which he meant the white English-speaking peoples. The term, although not new in 1890, did not become ingrained in the American lexicon until about that time. Once ingrained, few people stopped to ponder the meaning of "Anglo-Saxon," and thus few recognized, or were willing to admit, its inaccuracy. Those who paused to consider semantics, however, understood that "The Anglo-Saxons are as extinct as the mastodon, and the English people might as well be called Normans or Britons as Saxons" and that "Americans are not only *not* Anglo-Saxons; they are not even Englishmen." Sometimes Lodge and others substituted "Teutonic" for "Anglo-Saxon," as if the terms were interchangeable. Technically, the Teutonic peoples included all those ethnic groups descended from the original, ancient Germanic tribes, not just English-speaking groups. As applied to Americans, it simply meant old-stock whites, and that is exactly what Lodge intended: people like himself were superior to all others. People like himself should, therefore, control the United States and should, in fact, rule the world.[23]

In the late 1880s and early 1890s, the notion that Anglo-Saxons were destined to rule the world began to dominate the thought processes of both the American public and the nation's political leaders when considering racial issues. One need only survey widely circulated periodicals of the day, such as *North American Review, Forum,* and *Arena,* to notice this sudden upsurge in interest and virtual consensus in that belief. This shift in perception was a major factor that helped usher in the age of American Imperialism. Another factor was that the most militarily powerful European nations had already begun their own programs of imperialist expansion, and the United States could not afford to lag behind. American naval captain Alfred Thayer Mahan's book, *The Influence of Sea Power On History*

(1890), argued that a strong navy was essential to national defense and that the United States had better keep pace with the Europeans by engaging in a massive naval buildup. Under the leadership of Secretary of Navy Benjamin F. Tracy and key Republican congressmen such as Senator William E. Chandler of New Hampshire, the Harrison administration began modernizing the U. S. Navy in preparation for the eventuality of major naval wars abroad.[24]

Most southern politicians, needless to say, adhered to this racist/imperialist philosophy, but many northern Republicans did as well, including some of the leading supporters of the Federal Elections Bill. Frank Hiscock of New York conceded it as though it were a foregone conclusion and common knowledge, saying, "I grant the superiority of the Anglo-Saxon race."[25] Likewise, John J. Ingalls, who championed the cause of the black southerner's right to vote, nonetheless believed in a sort of international manifest destiny whereby the Teutonic peoples should rule the world. John Hay, a northern Republican whose public life began as Abraham Lincoln's personal secretary and ended as William McKinley's and Theodore Roosevelt's secretary of state, agreed. Hay almost single-handedly brought Ingalls's ideology to life. He underwent a life-changing transformation around 1890 in which he abandoned his early egalitarian ideals. Once he became secretary of state in 1898, he presided over the most pronounced period of overseas imperialistic expansion in the nation's history. He rationalized the takeover of underdeveloped regions of the world on the dual notions that only Anglo-Saxons were capable of establishing efficient governments and that there was no chance that the "backward" races would be able to catch up in his lifetime. The English-speaking peoples would, Hay believed, only be doing the backward races a favor by ruling over them and schooling them in the art of good government.[26]

What is evident and striking is that there existed what may appear to some students of history an inexplicable contradiction in the northern Republican imperialist mind-set. Lodge, Ingalls, Hay, Hiscock, McKinley, and Roosevelt, among many others, believed in the inherent superiority of Anglo-Saxons and, therefore, the inferiority of dark-skinned peoples. They relished the idea of establishing Anglo-Saxon supremacy around the world. Yet, they paradoxically favored allowing the supposed inferior race of the American South to help rule the southern states based upon the democratic ideal of majority rule. Since there was not yet a great emphasis on proving Anglo-Saxon supremacy overseas in 1890–1891, this contradiction did not surface in any of the congressional debates of the Fifty-first Congress. Had it surfaced, Democratic and western Republican opponents certainly would have added it to their formidable arsenal of reasons why they believed that northeastern Republicans were guilty of applying a double-standard, or what they would have labeled "hypocrisy," on racial issues.

The professing humanitarians of the Northeast demonstrated other seeming contradictions between their idealistic beliefs and their actual words and deeds as well. For example, Henry Blair, during the debate on his education bill in the Fifty-first Congress, read aloud a letter written by an unnamed, highly educated black man and, with a choice of words that some modern observers would judge to be racist, pronounced emphatically that "His letter is written about as well as though it came from a white man." This statement seems to indicate that he believed in an inherent difference in the mental capacity of blacks and whites (or perhaps he just used a poor choice of words in trying to say that blacks were generally not educated as well as whites).[27] John Coit Spooner, who defended the Federal Elections Bill so eloquently, once lumped "colored" people together with "idiots," "lunatics," and "Injuns," and jokingly expressed gratitude to the Almighty that no member of his family belonged in any of those categories.[28] Even George Frisbie Hoar, who came as close to being a genuine egalitarian as any man in Congress and who would emerge in time as one of the leading critics of American Imperialism, sometimes made statements that seemed to contradict his professed beliefs in racial equality. For instance, he opposed the Harrison administration's nomination of Frederick Douglass as the ambassador to Haiti on the grounds that Haitians did not respect black ambassadors as much as they did white ones, and, therefore, the tradition of appointing African Americans to that post should be terminated. Viewed in the context of the fact that Hoar had not yet formulated a definite position on imperialism in 1890, as he later would, it seems evident that his objection resulted from a desire to establish Anglo-American control over the troubled little island-nation and thereby imbue it with stable government for the first time in its existence because the black Haitian people had demonstrated no ability to do it themselves.[29]

Such examples of seemingly racist attitudes and statements on the part of professing humanitarians reflect the philosophy of quasi-scientific realism that arose around 1890 to replace the social/racial idealism of the Reconstruction era. This realism that began to pervade the thought processes of Americans originated mainly in the ivory tower, where the ideology of Social Darwinism was fast becoming the orthodox explanation for racial and ethnic differences and the quasi-scientific justification for white supremacy. Beginning in 1889, various well-respected professors and intellectuals in America and Europe, who had previously published occasional treatises on Social Darwinism, began to write and publish extensively on the subject. The topic fascinated the American public and no doubt helped sell magazines and periodicals. The idea that the fittest races survived, evolved, and developed through ever-advancing stages of civilization was a simple, plausible explanation for a complex set of questions. Some of the most educated people in the world applied this ideology to the American race problem.[30]

British intellectual James Bryce, who toured the United States in 1890, was one of these well-educated ideologues. To him, Social Darwinism decreed that races evolved from a state of barbarism to civilization over periods of centuries. To take savages from the wilds of Africa, therefore, and infuse them into the most advanced national civilization the world had ever seen, as the United States had done, went against every law of nature. Enfranchising black Americans was especially a perversion of the natural development of civilization, argued Bryce, considering that England's white agricultural laborers, who were roughly their English equivalent in terms of social status, did not attain the privilege of suffrage until 1885.[31]

Nathaniel Southgate Shaler, a professor at Harvard who had lived in the South as well as the North, developed a sophisticated Social Darwinist argument concerning the races. He believed that northern Europeans had developed superior brains because of centuries of coping with winter weather, which peoples who inhabited regions close to the equator did not have to confront. He incorrectly considered Africa, compared to northern Europe, to be a land of "enduring ease" where food was plentiful and could be acquired with minimal effort and forethought. Consequently, he believed that millions of people had survived and reproduced there over time who would not have survived had they lived in a region where harsh winters created the need for more-developed brains. Northern Europeans thus survived by rationing provisions for months at a time, which indicated that they had a highly developed understanding of cause and effect. Hence, their descendants had earned the right through centuries of development to "rule the world."[32] Even so, said Shaler, only a few men among the white race in any given generation were really qualified to possess such control over domestic political affairs, much less international affairs. "The combination of political interest, foresight, and valor in the use of the electoral franchise is so rare among those of our own race," he proclaimed, "that we can barely maintain the institutions which depend upon it for their support." How could inferior races, therefore, possibly hope to compete in the white man's political arena? Indeed, if this combination of characteristics, which was so rare even among the white race, alone produced good government, how could blacks make a positive contribution to the American polity?[33]

Social Darwinists often cited the lack of forethought, or foresight, as a particularly pronounced deficiency of the black race. William Chauncy Langdon echoed Shaler's thoughts on the topic, saying blacks as a whole lacked the understanding of action and consequence that had become a hallmark of the white race's scientific and political ingenuity. Thus, blacks were unable to learn from their mistakes or to heed the lessons of history, he said, and would make the same blunders time and again. They would live only for the day, taking no thought of the future, he contended, which prevented them from escaping the cycle of dependency upon more advanced races. This dependency then perpetuated itself in each succeeding generation. Langdon justified his belief based partly on an interview with an unnamed seventy-year-old former slave. The elderly gentleman lamented the indiscretions of America's black youth who had never experienced slavery, telling Langdon: "The trouble is that most of the young negroes think that emancipation and the franchise gave them a right to a living without working for it; to social equality without manners or decency; to place without the slightest training or experience; and to the respect of the white people without any character." Langdon agreed, saying, only those few young African Americans who were wiser than their peers would diligently strive to learn from the past and to improve their condition through hard work, saving, and investment.[34]

English biologist T. H. Huxley, who was among the foremost purveyors of Darwin's theory of evolution in 1890, not to mention a strong proponent of Social Darwinism as well, agreed with Langdon's assessment. He added that not only must every race earn its place in society by hard work and common sense, but even every individual within each race must succeed or fail based on his own initiative or lack thereof. Contrary to the American political creed expressed in the Declaration of Independence, he argued, people were not born equal. For evidence, he cited the fact that no two siblings in any given family, although born and raised in the same home, having the same parents, and having the same cultural and economic circumstances, will grow to have the same abilities or desires. Those who desired the right things and had natural ability would succeed, while their brothers and sisters without those virtues would fail. By nature, it just so happened, said Huxley, that more individuals possessed those virtues among the white race than among the black.[35]

Social Darwinists frequently attributed any success that a black man had in business, industry, or academia not to his natural inclinations or abilities, but to the fact that he had a "habit of imitation" of the white man.[36] Some pointed to the fact that the natives of Africa had not achieved the level of evolution of the white race as proof that African Americans were inherently inferior. Reverend A.W. Pitzer of Washington, D.C., for example, asked rhetorically at the First Mohonk Conference:

> Has the Negro race at any period of time or in any country of the globe been a factor in the history-making of the world? If so, when and where? He has no history, and has never been a history maker. . . . The Negro of to-day is the product of his sad and dismal past. The wild, naked, man-eating savages of equatorial Africa are the same blood and race as the Negro of this republic. We must deal with him as he is. We cannot shut our eyes to facts. They may be hard and painful things, but they are also stubborn and immovable things. It is not fair to judge him with the same standard of measure that we apply to the Anglo-Saxon.[37]

Dr. Merrill E. Gates, president of Rutgers College, agreed, remarking concerning the limitations of educating blacks, "If we expected to bring out a type of Negro manhood after the model of the Plymouth Rock Pilgrim, we should probably be disappointed."[38] Other participants at the Mohonk Conference disagreed, however. Albion Tourgee praised the accomplishments of African Americans, noting that "the colored people of the South have accomplished more in twenty-five years, from an industrial point of view, than any people on the face of the earth ever before achieved under anything like such unfavorable circumstances."[39] Massachusetts educator Reverend A. D. Mayo sided with Tourgee. He believed that the propensity of blacks for imitating the white race showed great promise for their future. Once the process of imitation had reached completion, he said, black society would replicate the white man's civilization, and the cycle of dependency would be broken. He cited Native Americans as an example of a race who could not, or would not, imitate the white race, to their own peril. Those races that imitated Anglo-Saxons, believed Mayo, would survive and prosper; those that did not would die out.[40]

People who took such an optimistic view of the condition of the black race were in the decided minority. The majority of the intellectuals of the day simply painted all blacks with the broad brush of negative stereotyping. For example, Reverend Dr. A. F. Beard, the corresponding secretary of the American Missionary Association (AMA), claimed to know precisely what factors were keeping African Americans down and out. He said they

Black Stereotype. (*Boulder* [Colorado] *News,* 1892.) African Americans were typically portrayed as being happy, albeit ignorant, and, in many cases (such as this one), conniving and dishonest. Here an unkempt dandy is shown plotting the theft of a plump Thanksgiving turkey, for which he soon lands in jail. Such portrayals could be seen in periodicals from coast to coast, not merely in the South, by the early 1890s. White Americans by and large, whether northern, southern, or western, felt no compunction about negatively stereotyping blacks in this way.

lacked "right character," a "proper home life," a "sense of values," "orderliness and method," and "accuracy." Concerning the latter, Beard explained that the terms "'Almost' and 'altogether' mean the same thing to the Negro. His 'pretty near' is the same as absolute right." Blacks also lacked a sense of "time," he claimed. "He is in time when he is in church before the benediction."[41] Not all stereotyping was so negative, however. Miss D. E. Emerson of the AMA countered concerning African Americans that "We all know their great love of music" and how they "are a very sympathetic people, very kind," as well as "very forgiving and loving in their natures."[42] Even the most genuine humanitarians, who viewed blacks in the most positive light they could see in that day, almost universally acknowledged the superiority of the white race over the black.[43]

Corroborating the ideas of Social Darwinists and other intellectuals were the discoveries and theories of explorers, adventurers, missionaries, and diplomats in Africa, especially Henry M. Stanley, George Washington Williams, and Bishop Henry McNeal Turner. Beginning in 1872, Stanley's autobiographical accounts of his explorations of Africa first aroused the American public's curiosity in the dark continent. Stanley's work sparked American and European interest in Africa throughout the 1880s. Interest reached its peak in 1890, with the publication of Stanley's *Through the Dark Continent,* which was particularly popular. It contained detailed documentation of barbaristic tribal practices committed routinely in the African interior, which bolstered the argument for the inherent inferiority of the black race. Most political and scientific journals and periodicals of the day cashed in on the public fascination with Africa, carrying stories in every edition, which supposedly reliable eye witnesses recorded, about the barbarism and cannibalism of various tribes of inner Africa. The racists in the Fifty-first Congress cited such fanciful sketches with great effect.[44]

Williams, a mulatto from Pennsylvania who was on assignment by the U. S. government in the Congo, reported that Stanley and the other adventurers were telling the truth about the backwardness and barbarism of inner Africa. "Cruelties of the most astounding character are practiced by the natives," wrote Williams, "such as burying slaves alive in the grave of a dead chief, cutting off the heads of captured warriors in native combats," selling boys as slaves and girls as concubines, and other equally gruesome and savage practices.[45]

Turner, who visited Africa for the joint purposes of evangelization and to assess the problems and potential of black American emigration there, unwittingly advanced the racist mentality of his generation by his espousal of Social Darwinism and a prominent scientific field of the day, phrenology, which was the study of human heads, skulls, and facial features for the purpose of determining cranial capacity and intelligence. Phrenology gave a great degree of legitimacy to racial stereotyping, and Turner, like many educated people of his day, conveniently categorized members of his race as intelligent or mentally challenged based on their physical appearance. Turner observed several striking physical differences between native Africans and African Americans. Upon visiting Liberia, he wrote: "I have found out that we poor American negroes were the tail end of the African races. We were slaves over here [in Africa], and had been for a thousand years or more before we were sold to America. Those who think the receding forehead, the flat nose, the probiscated mouth and the big flat bottom foot are natural to the African are mistaken." Turner believed that the "big blood" or "first class" Africans with "straight heads" had not been sold to America as slaves unless they experienced the misfortune of being captured in battle. Even if the Africans who ended up as slaves in America were generally less intelligent than their native African counterparts, opined Turner, they and their descendants could still "beat the world" in grasping foreign languages quickly, in learning to play musical instruments skillfully, and in practicing honesty and forthrightness.[46]

Not everyone who visited Africa agreed with Turner's assessment of the physical characteristics and personality traits of native Africans vis-à-vis African Americans. There was, in fact, much disagreement among those who had actually made personal observations. One German colonist in Africa, for instance, considered the Americanized Africans living in Liberia to be superior to the natives in physical appearance. He added that natives tended to resemble monkeys and gorillas, whereas the Americans did not. "More than once," he claimed, "in the dark forest I have just escaped killing a negro for a baboon."[47] One white Presbyterian missionary in the Congo wrote about native Africans with much greater esteem, however, saying, "I find the wild African a very agreeable fellow. He has a good deal of self-respect, and unbounded instinctive respect for the white man. . . . He is charmingly unsophisticated, fresh, and natural and is genial, eager to please and be pleased."[48]

Black intellectual and religious leader Alexander Crummell, who was, like Turner, a Pan-Africanist, never claimed to believe in Social Darwinism. Yet he defined "race" much the same as did Henry Cabot Lodge, with no mention of skin color, calling it a "compact, homogenous population of one blood, one ancestry, and lineage. . . . Indeed, a race is a family."[49] Like Turner, Crummell stereotyped races, admitting that his own race was less advanced than most other races. It was not, however, because of incapacity, he argued. Instead, African Americans suffered from a seemingly permanent victim complex, said Crummell, such that they could not overcome a "morbid concentration upon an intense and frenzied sense of political wrong." He likened African Americans to the Irish, whom he considered a separate race. They also seemed incapable of escaping centuries of victimization. The result of the Irish's victim complex was that "commerce, industry, and manufactures, letters and culture, have died away from them." Crummell, who was first and foremost a preacher, hoped to elevate the African American race above the mentality of victimization, which prevented the growth of intellectualism and the entrepreneurial spirit within the black community. In that sense, he had an interesting and unusually enlightened position on the question of the development of races.[50]

Although some people could, like Crummell, draw parallels between the black experience and the experiences of other racial and ethnic groups, most Americans could not see the black-white race problem of the American South as comparable to any other race problem in the United States or the world. While public opinion favored the exclusion of the Chinese, the final subjugation of the Indians, and a restriction of white immigration for the public good, there was no consensus about how to deal with African Americans. One white southerner expressed his frustration over the issue by commenting, "If we were dealing with a few tribes of red men or a few sporadic Chinese, the question would be easily disposed of."[51] But because there were some eight million blacks concentrated in the South, all living with the stigma of slavery and the resulting mentality of victimization, the issue remained in 1890 what it had long been, a "running sore," as black professor W. S. Scarborough put it, in the body politic that could not be cured easily.[52] Scarborough mused that, between 1865 and 1890, African Americans had graduated from the "peculiar institution" and entered the "peculiar situation." They were now suspended between a "selfish, arrogant, and supersensitive South, and a vacillating, over-sympathetic North," and both groups prevented the black man from fulfilling his potential.[53]

Indeed, while blacks and other minority groups shared a common dispossession from the mainstream of American society, no group was ever quite as victimized as blacks. In the North, Irish and German servants, whom old-stock whites looked down upon as dirty and inferior, in turn looked down upon blacks, refusing to eat at the same table with them or work alongside them, no matter how clean, educated, or polite the African Americans were. Moreover, northern labor unions, which were comprised overwhelmingly of first-generation, non-Teutonic European immigrants, began to exclude blacks and, in fact, to act violently toward them. Such ethnic minorities were not the main perpetrators of the policy of exclusion toward African Americans in the North, however. The sons of the New England Puritans actually pioneered the practice of segregating the races in the United States while the South was still practicing slavery. Gradually, after the Civil War and Reconstruction, white southerners began to consider segregation as the wave of the future in American race relations because, like the literacy qualification for voting, segregation had already been tested and approved in the North. As late as 1884, Henry Woodfin Grady pleaded with the South's political leaders to adopt the same type of racial segregation as the North had long promulgated. Indeed, before the Jim Crow laws of southern infamy were instituted, old-stock white northerners commonly refused to share railroad cars with free blacks, to sit with them in theaters and restaurants, or to use other public accommodations in common with them. Although the first segregation law appeared in a southern state in 1873, many southern states had no such laws as late as 1887. Even in 1889, the southern states still lagged behind the North in segregating the races, and the *New York Times* urged them to catch up.[54] As the *Cincinnati Gazette* observed regarding the state of Ohio in 1889, "The color-line is everywhere. It is in every church. It is in society. It is in politics." Why should it not be drawn in the South, too?[55]

During the House debate on the Federal Elections Bill, three-term Democrat James Richardson of Tennessee used the northern color line with dramatic effect to bolster his party and section's cause. He documented with a massive amount of evidence instances of racial discrimination in nine northern states that had occurred since the Fifty-first Congress convened. After a lengthy reading of forty-two separate accounts reported in more than twenty northern newspapers, he finally stopped, saying that he had not come close to exhausting his supply of such cases, but he had proven his point. He concluded: "I most sincerely trust that henceforth no man, here or elsewhere, will have the audacity, the temerity, the reckless disregard for the truth to such a degree as to assert that discriminations are made against the negro alone in the Southern States of the Union. They are made in the North, South, East, and West, and will continue to be so made so long as the white man is a white man and the negro is a negro."[56]

The main argument for racial segregation was that it was natural and instinctive for races to associate with their own kind. Hence, mixing the races broke the rules of nature. Southerners and northerners alike argued that not only did the supposed superior race recognize this natural order, but the inferior races recognized it as well. Senator John Tyler Morgan of Alabama explained that "It is as instinctive with the negro to admit" this natural order "as it is with the white race to demand and assert it. . . . Race separation is the only cure for race aversion."[57] Senator Edward Cary Walthall of Mississippi concurred, saying segregation "is a reciprocal arrangement, is absolutely just, is supported by public sentiment and enforced by the courts." For proof that blacks not only accepted but actually preferred segregation, he quoted L. W. Moore, a black representative in the Mississippi legislature from Bolivar County, who said publicly that it would keep "the average negro in Mississippi . . . reasonably content with his condition." It was just this propensity of blacks to commune among themselves by choice, declared Walthall, that caused white southerners to need a "solid South," because whenever "whites would divide upon reason . . . blacks would unite upon race."[58]

White Virginian Philip A. Bruce believed that blacks had an "independent tendency," just like whites. That is, given the choice, they would congregate together and "live apart" from whites. Doing so ostensibly gave blacks freedom to develop and practice their own unique culture. He cited black churches as the prime example. They had developed their own form of worship, a form not contrary to white religion but unique nonetheless. When left alone to worship as they pleased, without fear of mockery or persecution from whites, black Christians, concluded Bruce, were happy.[59]

Many other white southerners likewise truly believed that blacks preferred segregation to conflict. Before he died, Henry Woodfin Grady convinced the whole staff of the *Atlanta Constitution* that segregation was the most sensible solution to the race problem. Once Grady was gone, the paper reported every instance thereafter when blacks did anything separate from whites. It reported, for example, about a black veterans' parade in Georgia held on January 1, 1890, to celebrate the Emancipation Proclamation and a black state fair held in South Carolina, to which whites were not invited. Were not such actions proof that blacks preferred to be separate from whites, asked the *Constitution*?[60]

Missing from such reports of wishful-thinking whites were examples of other black meetings refuting the argument that blacks preferred segregation. The National Convention of Colored Americans, for instance, which met in Washington, D.C., in January 1890, protested to the federal government for the Interstate Commerce Commission laws to be strengthened to prevent segregation on trains.[61] John Edward Bruce, a black journalist, speaking at the Inaugural Afro-American League Convention in Chicago resented the white arrogance that created racial segregation. He considered white Americans in general "modern barbarians" who flattered themselves with false notions of their automatic superiority based upon their whiteness.[62]

Yet, the argument that blacks preferred segregation gained popularity through repeated usage by whites and by the fact that most whites misconstrued the statements of black leaders on the subject. Black North Carolinian J. C. Price, for instance, stated unequivocally that blacks did not aspire to social equality with whites—they merely asked for their constitutionally protected political rights. "One is a question of law," said Price, "and the other is a matter of choice." To put his argument in perspective, he contrasted the situations of "poor white trash" and black Americans, saying: "Prior to the war a poor white man was as much a social pariah as a free colored man. The aristocracy took no notice of him as a social equal. . . . Since the war there has been little diminution of this feeling. . . . [yet] This class of white men have all their civil and political rights, but no one asserts that they are trying to force themselves into social equality."[63] A. J. Reed of the League of Colored Republicans in Baltimore tried to explain the difference between political rights and social equality by declaring, "We don't want . . . to marry your daughters, but we want every right to which we are entitled under the constitution, and for that we mean to fight. They tell us that if this movement succeeds, that one may walk up the street and see standing in front of some big establishment a big, buck nigger in a policeman's uniform. I tell you the colored man aims higher in life than that . . . [but] any man who says that the colored race is for social equality is either densely ignorant or a rascal."[64] Such explanations notwithstanding, most white Americans could not make the distinction in 1890 between political rights and social equality. Consequently, when they heard black leaders renounce any claims to social equality, they construed that African Americans wanted separation and that they were content with the racial status quo.

Other black leaders, such as T. Thomas Fortune, W. S. Scarborough, and Frederick Douglass, refused to sacrifice social equality in order that blacks might keep or gain their political rights. Douglass advocated integration in all walks of life as the only solution to the race problem. Scarborough, professor of Greek and Latin at Wilberforce University, agreed, although without the idealism of Douglass. He called for "fair play" and "tolerance" of racial differences not only in politics but also in society. However, he also accepted the idea of black emigration as a last resort, while simultaneously declaring that he believed race "prejudice . . . will gradually fade away."[65] Fortune, a mulatto who was nearly white in appearance, was perhaps the most adamant of all black leaders of his day in demanding that African Americans were entitled to every right and privilege afforded Anglo-Saxon Americans. As a result, his newspaper, the *New York Age*, became one of the most successful and influential black papers in the country during and after the 1890s.[66]

Complicating the issue of segregation was the fact that interspersed throughout the nation were people of color who, like Fortune, could not easily be classified as either black or white based on their physical appearance alone. Even in 1890, years before the charge became popular, some whites were convinced that there was a conspiracy among black leaders to instigate worldwide racial amalgamation. Frederick Douglass, who was himself racially mixed, lent credence to this belief by marrying a white woman. T. Thomas Fortune countered this charge by asking, if blacks hatched this conspiracy, why was there so much miscegenation caused by whites during the slave era? He berated the white supremacists who feared amalgamation by explaining that the "best white blood has for two hundred years gone into the black race; and if it now and in the future returns to plague those who sowed to the wind," they should not now begin to "whine like babies over their supposed misfortune, and appeal to the rest of mankind for sympathy."[67] Although Fortune certainly won the battle of words on the subject, segregationists won the war. They solved the complex problem of classifying racially mixed Americans in a simple way: they conveniently considered everyone who was not lily white to be black, thus depriving them of both civil rights and social equality.

The issue of segregation was more complex than the racists of the day made it out to be. Some forward-thinking individuals looked not at the likely results of segregation in their own day and time but to the probable effect of segregation on the black race in the future. As the United States' commissioner of education, W. T. Harris of St. Louis theorized that the continuation of racial segregation over a period of time would lead to black Americans reverting to African savagery, barbarism, belief in outrageous superstitions, and the practice of "voudooism." Thus, if some degree of racial integration could be achieved without causing racial amalgamation, that would be a positive change.[68]

The fear of racial amalgamation that gripped the thoughts of so many southerners at this time seems, like many other aspects of race relations discussed in this study, irrational by modern standards. It seemed quite rational in its day, however, owing again to the widespread dissemination of the primitive scientific knowledge available. Reverend John Thomas Gulick, a noted Darwinian scholar, published a series of reports between 1887 and 1891 explaining that interbreeding of the human races might appear harmless in the first generation, but continued interbreeding resulted in partial sterility in the second generation, and in "the third or fourth generation the family dies out." Moreover, the children produced after the first generation appeared "generally weakly" and suffered from a variety of characteristics that diverged from either of the original races, such as baldness and lack of body hair. Although he based his findings primarily upon a study of two Japanese ethnic groups that had begun amalgamating, his work implied that similar results must necessarily follow for other instances of racial mixing. He also discussed many types of "segregation" among various animal populations around the world, using the word "races" in place of "species," again showing that unnatural interbreeding often produced unhealthy or otherwise undesirable offspring. Gulick's scientific data and consequent interpretations received, arguably, the ultimate stamp of approval when the U.S. government published his work in the *Annual Report of the Smithsonian Institution* for the year 1891. President Harrison, as well as various members of his administration and of Congress, signed this report.[69]

The Billion Dollar Congress became the point of confluence for all of the multifarious streams of racism that ran through America around the year 1890. Democrats and southerners used the pro-segregationist, pro-Social Darwinist, pro-Anglo-Saxon, and anti-immigrational stances of the North to great effect and advantage in all three debates over the southern race problem. With one breath they lamented the condition of "The poor negro!" against whom "God, nature, and man all seemed to conspire" because he was under the "curse of Ham." With the next breath they lampooned him as "undisciplined, full of unbounded expectations, imaginative [superstitious], without judgment, lacking the faculty of using the proper means for certain ends, fond of dress and pleasure, living only for the present," and requiring "a century of civilization to . . . make him a fitting factor in our enlightened system of government."[70]

Democrats and southerners also made jokes at the expense of blacks, telling stories using the common black dialect of the day and justifying the mockery upon the notion that no one was more willing and able to laugh at himself than the black man.[71] Above all, they stereotyped and judged the whole race collectively as objects of pity, eulogizing the poor unfortunate creatures who seemed destined to remain perpetually at the bottom of American society, if they did not die out altogether. As John Tyler Morgan put it, "The negro is a grateful man. He is a good man. [but] He is *not* a wise man." And because of that indisputable fact, predicted Morgan, black Americans would still hold relatively the same position in society seventy-five years later.[72] How prophetic Morgan proved to be. It was precisely seventy-five years after he spoke those words in 1890 before black southerners would again be found worthy by a presidential administration and a majority in Congress to have their constitutional civil rights protected. Morgan was, of course, wrong about why blacks would still occupy the bottom rung of the social hierarchy in 1965. The real reason was that succeeding generations of racists would cause it to be so until then.[73]

After the Federal Elections Bill's final hurrah in the Senate in early 1891, rarely would northerners or Republicans resurrect the race issue in national politics again for more than a generation. So the Billion Dollar Congress came to a close, having failed to find an acceptable solution to the southern race problem. The white South had defended its ideology with every ounce of fortitude it could muster. White northern Democrats, as neo-doughfaces, had echoed the southern point of view. Western Republicans had jettisoned their traditional views on the issue and joined with the Democrats, leaving northeastern Republicans alone to bear the flickering torch of humanitarianism. President Harrison had inexplicably become virtually unheard and invisible on the issue, failing to rally the Republican forces at a time when his leadership was most sorely needed. A few black voices rose in protest, but the day when neo-abolitionist oratory could inspire the northern public was over. The black voices that the northern public chose to hear affirmed the arguments of the former slaveholders in saying that, indeed, African Americans were not yet prepared for equal citizenship. The majority of African Americans, of course, either remained silent or lacked the ways and means of making their voices heard, which seemed to indicate to the northern public that they were, just as southern Democrats claimed, reasonably content with their condition. A wearied northern public was thus ready to move on and leave the race problem in the hands of another generation. In the end, the racial and ethnic melting pot that was the United States had achieved the closest thing to a consensus that a nation of sixty-two million people was capable of: it had collectively chosen the path of least resistance. Ubiquitous racism, rationalized by Social Darwinism, Imperialism, and xenophobia would become the orthodoxy— the socially acceptable mentality of the coming Jim Crow era, the new national zeitgeist.

CONCLUSION

Assessing the Billion Dollar Congress and Its Effects on American History and Race Relations

The Fifty-first Congress ended yesterday, and if it had a soul may the Lord have mercy upon that soul.

—*The Nashville American*

The Fifty-first Congress . . . will stand in history as a shame to its members and a warning to their successors.

—*The Providence Journal*

The Nation must naturally experience a feeling of relief at the death of this Congress, as it did when the civil war ended.

—*The Albany Argus*

Throughout the time that the Fifty-first Congress wrestled with the southern race problem, Democrats charged that Republican claims of concern for the welfare of African Americans were disingenuous. As one put it, in 1865 the Republican Party was the "savior of the negroes," but since Reconstruction black voters had become the savior of the GOP. Such charges contained more than a grain of truth. The black vote had made the difference in Republicans winning the White House in 1872, 1876, and 1888. The majority of white voters in these elections went Democratic. Despite owing such victories to black support, after the close of the Billion Dollar

210

Congress in April 1891, the Republican reformers abandoned all hope of achieving federal civil rights legislation for African Americans. They certainly had their opportunities to try again. In 1896, after four economically disastrous years of Democratic rule, they regained hegemony over the national government with the election of William McKinley as president and a Republican majority in Congress. The GOP owed this victory not to the black vote, however, but to the German and Irish vote, which went predominantly Republican for the first time in American history. Thus, there no longer appeared to be a need to secure the black vote to ensure Republican victories, and, consequently, neither was there a need to continue trying to find a solution to the southern race problem. The GOP, not surprisingly, never resurrected the issue.[1]

Even in 1890–1891, the majority of rank-and-file Republicans among the northern public showed only a perfunctory interest in rewarding African Americans for their loyalty to the party of Lincoln. The humanitarian-minded minority in the North talked a great deal about alleviating the suffering of African Americans, but they did very little, considering the potential for reform that existed under Republican control in the Fifty-first Congress. The favorite plan of their political leaders—the Federal Elections Bill—appeared partisan, sectional, and highly inflammatory to a majority of Americans. Moreover, it seemed to be a facade hiding an ulterior motive: a need to shore up lagging numbers in the Republican vote. The bill's sponsors certainly hoped to enforce black voters' constitutional rights as well, but only if that goal could be accomplished without sacrificing any other aspect of the GOP's Billion Dollar agenda, and only if they did not have to apply the same racial standard to the Northeast and the West as they applied to the South. Republican intentions behind the Federal Elections Bill, while noble, were arguably a misguided use of humanitarian sympathy, because what African Americans really needed at the time as much as, if not more than, the right to vote was federal economic relief. The year was 1890, after all—the eve of the Populist revolt—and most black southerners, like their white neighbors, earned their meager livelihoods in the fields. Unfortunately, no federal relief came. Although the nation's first "billion dollar" Congress could have easily afforded to help suffering farmers, it did nothing for them. Black Representative Henry P. Cheat, of North Carolina believed that the GOP had its priorities out of order. He did not oppose the Federal Elections Bill, but he complained that, if his party was really sincere about alleviating the suffering and deprivation among his race, it would first pass the bill that he had introduced to reimburse depositors of the failed Freedmen's Bank and then pass either the Blair Education

Bill or some similar federal education bill. But alas, he lamented, "Both of these bills are quietly sleeping—'under the new rules'—notwithstanding the fact that this Administration with its Republican majorities in the House and Senate and [its] Republican President could have enacted both bills into law several months ago. Gentlemen, why do you not show your sympathy for the colored people in a practical manner when you have such a favorable opportunity?"[2] The Freedmen's Bank bill died the death of the vast majority of bills that are introduced in any session of Congress: it went to committee, where it garnered little support and thus received no serious consideration. The Blair bill, which Cheathem so strongly advocated, received, by contrast, a great amount of consideration, but it ultimately failed. Contrary to popular misconception, it did not fail because of opposition from the twelve new western senators who were sworn into office in 1890, for ten of the twelve actually supported the bill. Instead, nine Republican senators from the older northeastern and midwestern states switched their votes to oppose it. Who then was responsible for the defeat of the Blair bill? The answer is, ironically, many of the same people who pushed the Federal Elections Bill. They were, of course, not solely responsible. Nine former Democratic supporters likewise changed their minds on the issue of federalizing education.[3] Why these Democrats changed positions on the Blair bill cannot be ascertained. From reading their speeches in the debate, however, one can reasonably speculate that their fear of the Federal Elections Bill—which they knew was about to be introduced—forced their overreaction to all other bills designed to empower African Americans, whether politically, economically, or intellectually. In other words, the Federal Elections Bill in a roundabout way killed the Blair Education Bill.

While the Blair bill ceased to garner the nation's attention after 1890, the Federal Elections Bill, although dead, was not allowed to rest in peace. The Democrats used it as their main rallying point in the presidential campaign of 1892. Their *Campaign Textbook of the Democratic Party for the Presidential Election, 1892*, contained a full forty pages of discussion of the "force bill." Most Republican congressmen, meanwhile, steered as far away from the race issue in their campaign as possible.[4] GOP managers even jettisoned Vice President Levi P. Morton, who would forever be linked to the failure of the bill, and replaced him with the editor of the *New York Tribune*, Whitelaw Reid, who had supported the bill in his newspaper to the bitter end. Ironically, once nominated, Reid spoke not a word on the issue as a candidate. The incumbent Harrison likewise remained silent on the issue, focusing instead on the more positive aspects of his first term. The GOP strategy essentially called for distancing Harrison from the bill.

Nonetheless, some supporters felt compelled to defend their candidate on the issue. Frederick Douglass, for example, tried to spin the question, saying: "The position taken by President Harrison upon the election bill, called by our enemies in the South the 'force bill,' should endear him to the colored people as long as he lives, and they should revere his memory when he is dead. To the President the credit is due for creating the bill in the first place, and then pushing it through the House and almost through the Senate. His moral influence, as well as his official endorsement and assistance, were behind the measure. . . . That bill meant protection to the lives of every colored voter in the South."[5] And on another occasion, Douglass proclaimed that "The President of the United States is true to his trust. No man since Gen. Grant has stood by us more firmly than has Gen. Harrison."[6]

Despite the Republicans' efforts to get their ticket punched in 1892—which included spending the unheard-of sum of six million dollars on the campaign—Harrison and Reid lost in 1892. Many congressional races followed the same pattern. Democratic candidates from doubtful districts and states enjoyed much success by harping upon the Federal Elections Bill, while Republican candidates could benefit only by remaining silent on the issue and distancing themselves from the actions of the unpopular Billion Dollar Congress.[7]

The GOP suffered a permanent black eye on the issue of racial reform from its espousal of the doomed Federal Elections Bill. This defeat caused a tremendous shake-up in the leadership of the party and left lasting political scars on several of the bill's sponsors. Henry Cabot Lodge, for instance, lost decisively in his bid for reelection as overseer of Harvard College, ostensibly because Harvard wanted to bridge the North-South divide and thus could not endorse a known sectionalist as its leader. He lived out the remainder of his political career labeled as a sectional antagonist who was from then on always on the unpopular side of the "Negro question." This stigma prevented him from ever being seriously considered as a presidential contender, although it did not damage his reputation within Massachusetts state politics: the legislature sent him to the U.S. Senate in 1893. John J. Ingalls of Kansas, the Jayhawker crusader for the manipulation of the black vote, lost his bid for reelection to the Senate to Farmers' Alliance candidate William A. Pfeffer, whose only crusade was to relieve the suffering of farmers in the Sunflower State. John Coit Spooner, out of disgust with the filibustering and obstinance of his opponents, chose not to seek reelection in 1891, which left a great vacuum in the ranks of the Republican reformers. He would later return to the Senate, but he remained essentially silent about the race problem for the rest of his career. In addition to these, William M. Evarts, who had served the state of New York in public office since the Civil War and who had sided with the reformers on the Federal Elections Bill debate, retired from the Senate because of old age and ill health, opening the door for a Democrat who vehemently opposed any bill for civil rights reform to take his seat.[8]

Prominent Republican senators who strongly supported the bill but did not face reelection any time soon included William E. Chandler, George Frisbie Hoar, and John Sherman. Although they retained their seats, none of them ever brought up the issue of enforcing the Fifteenth Amendment again. William McKinley alone among prominent Republicans seemed to get a second chance at remaking his political career after the Billion Dollar debacle. After being defeated for reelection to his House seat in 1890, he won the governorship of Ohio in 1891 and the presidency of the United States in 1896, but he never again championed the cause of African American civil rights.[9]

The Federal Elections Bill imbroglio also left a lasting impression upon Democrats and African Americans. It caused a backlash of retaliatory Democratic legislation and of black defections from the party. The Democratic majority in the Fifty-second Congress repealed forty-two of the forty-nine sections of the old supervisory law of 1871. It is worth noting that the Republican minority, still reeling from the tumultuous turnaround, simply allowed this incredible reversal to happen without making any serious effort at resistance. They did not filibuster, and they hardly uttered a word publicly in opposition. Frederick Douglass, shocked at his party's backsliding on the issue of enforcing the Fifteenth Amendment, spoke aloud what he believed many white Republicans must have been thinking regarding black voters at the time: "We cannot protect you, we therefore propose to join your oppressors. Your suffrage has been rendered a failure by violence, and we now propose to make it a failure by law."[10] The GOP's abandonment of the voting rights issue also drove many black leaders out of the Republican Party, at least temporarily. Among the party's defectors were Henry McNeal Turner, T. Thomas Fortune, and J. C. Price. These and many others subsequently supported Grover Cleveland for president in 1892. After Cleveland's victory, they firmly believed that the black vote had handed the election to the Democrats. The black editor of the *Kansas City World*, C. H. J. Taylor, verbally expressed the disdain that many African Americans obviously felt for the party of Lincoln after 1890–1891, calling Republican leaders the "white political scum" who had always deceived his people. Most of those who remained loyal to the party, such as Frederick Douglass, Blanche K. Bruce, Henry P. Cheathem, John R. Lynch, and John Mercer Langston, were beholden to the GOP for either past or current job appointments or their seats in Congress.[11]

Other results of the Federal Elections Bill fiasco included permanent changes in parliamentary procedures in Congress. The use of filibustering, which proved so effective for Senate Democrats in the Fifty-first Congress, increased dramatically thereafter, a change that eventually led to the adoption of a cloture rule similar to the one that Nelson Aldrich tried so desperately and unsuccessfully to obtain in 1891. The increase of filibustering in the upper house of Congress also contributed to the demand of Progressives for direct election of senators, making these elite representatives more accountable to the people, a demand that was realized with the adoption of the Seventeenth Amendment in 1913. Another result was the immediate adoption of the new Reed Rules in the House by the Democratic majority of the Fifty-second Congress. Democrats winced as they implemented the very rules that they had condemned two years earlier, but the payback made the repulsive action worth it. Republicans, despite having brought the disempowerment of the minority upon themselves, tried to spin the issue in their own favor by claiming vindication for their policy of limiting debate in the House. A final result of the defeat of the Federal Elections Bill was that fraudulent elections actually increased in the United States in the 1890s. Although most of this increase resulted from the southern states no longer fearing federal intervention and thus embarking on a wholesale campaign to disfranchise black voters, some of the increase resulted from the intense competition between the two major parties for the swing vote in the northern states. Both parties began to apply with equal effect what might accurately be called (to coin a term) "Quayism." Matthew Quay's machine that helped put Benjamin Harrison into the White House and a Republican majority in Congress in 1888 had arguably set a new standard for election fraud, or at least for partisan manipulation of the electoral system.[12]

So, in the final analysis, what is history to make of the Billion Dollar Congress? This extraordinary legislative body amassed the staggering sum of more than seventeen thousand bills and resolutions—1,085 of which passed. It was an astounding record of achievement in an era noted for congressional gridlock and the "politics of dead center." Moreover, this Fifty-first Congress became the only Congress in American history to be immortalized by a moniker (a Democratic term of derision, actually), and it came by the name honestly. The "Billion Dollar Congress" really was a "billion dollar" Congress, for it actually did spend more than a billion dollars, and it was the first to do so. It spent $1,038,447,826.27 to be precise. This total showed an increase of almost $250 million more than any previous Congress had ever spent, which was an almost unfathomable amount in an era noted for its conservative, laissez-faire approach to national economics. Added to the small government growth that occurred under Democratic control from 1880 to 1888, the Billion Dollar Congress helped grow the budget of the federal government by a whopping 300 percent from 1880 to 1890, while the American population grew at the brisk clip of 22 percent.[13] In 1889, the federal treasury held the largest surplus in the nation's history to that time, but by 1891 the Billion Dollar Congress had proudly exhausted it on pensions, naval appropriations, public buildings, river and harbor improvements, and a host of other local and federal projects. So adept was this Republican Congress at spending taxpayer money that its own members popularized the term "pork" (which had been infrequently used before this time) to describe their fiscal extravagance.[14]

Speaker of the House Thomas B. Reed accepted the opprobrious sobriquet the "Billion Dollar Congress" without protest, although he did not appreciate being called "Czar." He and the Republican majority proudly defended their legislative record. Such astronomical spending, however, led Democratic newspapers to pronounce with certainty against this growth of government that "in the history of the nation, the Fifty-first Congress has accomplished less good and perpetuated greater injury than any other [Congress] that ever assembled to legislate for the people";[15] this "Congress made the worst record of any Congress in American history";[16] and "The Fifty-first Congress was reckless in many things. . . . No spendthrift come suddenly into a fortune was ever more riotous."[17] One Democratic organ enumerated its criticisms by proclaiming that "The leaders of the late Congress . . . shocked the country by substituting the despotism of the Speaker for the temperate rule of the majority. They set the example of unscrupulous disregard of public opinion. . . . They decided contested election cases according to partisan exigencies, regardless of evidence or decency. [And] They blew the embers of sectional hatred. . . ."[18] Senator Alfred Colquitt of Georgia put it more succinctly—no doubt referring to General William Tecumseh Sherman's march through his state in 1864—"A Billion Dollar Congress! Why, an invading army would not have destroyed more property in a ruthless march of destruction through the country."[19]

Republican newspapers' defenses of the GOP's legislative record cleverly avoided mentioning the fact that a huge majority of the bills and resolutions that the Billion Dollar Congress passed concerned nothing more than pensions or local pork-barrel projects. It did not matter, anyway. Their defenses were overshadowed by their need to place the blame for failure on someone. They tended to blame the Silverites for all the failure of the Fed-

Public Indictment of the Fifty-first Congress. *"Look at the leaders of the disgraceful Fifty-first Congress!"* (*Puck*, 1891.) Neither the Democratic press nor the majority of the American public showed much kindness to the outgoing Fifty-first Congress. Historians, however, have found it remarkable, albeit not for the reasons that the Republican humanitarians had hoped.

eral Elections Bill, but they had no answer for why the voters overwhelmingly repudiated the Republican majority in the House. Generally, in this name-calling, the papers condemned their party's leaders for allowing their agenda to be defeated, rather than praising them for at least trying to solve the southern race problem. As one put it: "The Congress now awaiting burial deserves severe condemnation. It could have redeemed the pledge made by the Republican convention of 1888 to protect the ballot from being trampled upon and made an instrument of fraud, and failed. That was the loss of an opportunity which may not come again for years. Everything was ripe for it. It can not be explained away."[20]

The fairest assessments of the work of the Billion Dollar Congress came, not surprisingly, from the independent press, which tended to line up with the Democrats on the overall record of the Congress, if not on every item. As one independent paper explained, "The record of the late Congress has, in a word, been a shameful record of partisan selfishness and political scheming.... But the country has avenged itself."[21] Another paper summed up the independents' attitude aptly, saying, "If the people believed one set of partisan papers, the late Congress would be canonized. If they believed the other set [it would be] condemned without measure. The truth is between the extremes. A [great] deal of effective work was done by the two houses. It is work which will tell upon the history of the country for a long time to come."[22]

Indeed. But the one striking and ironic feature of the legislative record of the Billion Dollar Congress is the absence of any legislation to relieve the oppression of African Americans. And why? Because, as Senator John Tyler Morgan of Alabama correctly observed, "Public opinion . . . will ultimately neutralize statutes that violate the instincts of the white race."[23] In other words, it was not merely the resistance of Democratic politicians and a few Republican defectors that neutralized the humanitarian agenda of this Congress but the fact that public opinion favored the minority party's position on racial issues in 1890–1891. Of course, public opinion can be swayed on even the most important social issues, and the politicians and propagandists that make the best case for their point of view often prevail with the people. On the issue of the South's race problem, southern Democrats definitely proved better at purveying their beliefs to the American people than did the Republicans.

This remarkable group of southern politicians led mainly by Senator Morgan, but also partially by J. Z. George of Mississippi, Zebulon Vance of North Carolina, and George Vest of Missouri, has been inexplicably all but forgotten to history. Yet, arguably, their impact upon the course of American history, and particularly African American history, was just as great as that of their more celebrated antebellum predecessors John C. Calhoun, Henry Clay, and Jefferson Davis. In fact, these Gilded Age sages merely carried on the long tradition of southern politicians dominating national politics on racial issues despite representing a section with a minority of the American population. The ability of southern Democrats such as Morgan and his cohorts to prevail against the odds and guide the ship of state was thus nothing new. Frederick Douglass perhaps said it best when he derisively declared, "As a matter of fact, the South has always been able to outwit the North in politics."[24]

And what happened to African Americans as a result of the victory of these ex-Confederates and their neo-doughface sympathizers in the Billion Dollar Congress? Injustices against them increased at a phenomenal rate, particularly in the South, with the 1890s becoming the decade when constitutional disfranchisement, Jim Crow segregation, and lynch law all fell like a biblical plague upon the already downtrodden race. Southern states, one after another, followed Mississippi's lead in rewriting their constitutions to remove the majority of black voters from their voting rolls. State laws converted segregation from a mere social custom into a strictly enforced legal institution. National courts, northern public opinion, and international imperialist sentiment all upheld this conversion. Finally, as southern whites ceased to fear the intervention of outsiders in local affairs, they committed more lynchings in the 1890s than in any other decade in American history.[25]

In the wake of all such negative changes in the nation's collective racial attitude, even the most outspoken humanitarians and egalitarians abandoned their earlier advocacy of civil rights and fair treatment of blacks. George Washington Cable and Albion Tourgee, for instance, became conspicuously silent on the issue. Lewis Harvey Blair, once a champion of equal opportunity for blacks, changed his mind, saying, "experience and observation have convinced me of the fallacy of my premises." Tom Watson underwent perhaps the most notable transformation of any national figure of the day, shifting from a friend of blacks to one of the most virulent racist demagogues in American history.[26]

African American responses to this nadir in which they found themselves varied greatly, but there were essentially only three courses of action they could take. One was that some black leaders continued to protest for civil rights, but white America in and after the 1890s increasingly ignored them. The death of the Federal Elections Bill marked the end of the line for those expecting the federal government to rescue African Americans by protecting their civil rights. Although many black leaders continued to appeal to both the government and white society throughout the nadir, they reaped comparatively little reward from their labor. One white southern Democrat summed up what must have been the collective mind-set of such disappointed hopefuls, saying of the Republican Party: "Might not the southern negro, when you ask him for his vote, respond by asking you, 'Where is that forty acres of ground and where is that mule'?"[27]

Many of the common black folk of the South turned to the remaining choices, which were less attractive than securing the right to vote but which would yield more immediate results. Some opted for migration out of the South. Most who did so realized that white northerners and westerners would not embrace them or give them social equality, but they could at least hope to find better economic opportunities outside the South. More than 130,000 ended up in Oklahoma, where their hopes of betterment were largely dashed on the rocks of the ubiquitous racism of the day. A few hundred managed to escape the South through emigration abroad. Most went to Liberia, where they lived out the remainder of their days in the harsh and challenging situation they had chosen for themselves, rather than staying in America and living under the difficult circumstances that white America had thrust upon them. In 1890–1891, for the only time in American history, both obstacles that had killed all previous colonization plans—lack of interest and lack of money—could have arguably been overcome. A reasonable claim can be made that the Billion Dollar Congress, in control of the largest government surplus in the nation's history, had both the money to fund a massive emigration project and a majority of representatives and senators who showed no fear of spending down the surplus.

The final option, which most African Americans took, was the path of least resistance, otherwise known as accommodationism, although critics considered it (to coin another term) "neo-Uncle Tomism." Isaiah Montgomery proved that this approach pleased white America when he defended his white colleagues' rationale for the literacy test and poll tax in the Mississippi constitutional convention of 1890. Other notable black leaders soon began to echo this defense of second-class citizenship for their race, particularly during the presidential campaign of 1892, on the grounds that Democrats at least spoke their feelings about the black race truthfully rather than acting hypocritically like the Republicans. Many blacks thus chose to align with honest racists rather than with those who seemed to be quasi-humanitarians, pseudo-egalitarians, and failed reformers. After Booker T. Washington made his famous Atlanta Compromise speech in 1895, and after the U. S. Supreme Court handed down its decision in the case of *Plessy v. Ferguson* in 1896, accommodationism ultimately became the most common and acceptable strategy for coping with the nadir.[28] And so it remained for more than a generation, as white supremacy became the national zeitgeist. Blacks could only wait. For as New York missionary Reverend Henry Field once said, "No man is strong enough to fight against the sympathies of the age."[29]

NOTES

Abbreviations

AC	*Atlanta Constitution*
ACS	American Colonization Society Papers
ACS	*The Annual Reports of the American Society for Colonizing the Free People of Colour of the United States, Vols. 64–91, 1881–1890*
AU	Ralph Brown Draughon Library, Auburn University
BD	*Biographical Directory of the United States Congress, 1789–1989*
BH	*Biloxi Herald*
CR	*Congressional Record*
DU	Manuscripts Department, Perkins Library, Duke University
JCL	*Jackson Clarion–Ledger*
LA	*Leavenworth Advocate*
LC	Manuscripts Division, Library of Congress
LD	*Literary Digest*
MAA	*Memphis Appeal–Avalanche*
MDAH	Mississippi Department of Archives and History
MHS	Missouri Historical Society
MSU	Special Collections, Mitchell Memorial Library, Mississippi State University
PO	*Public Opinion*
RMN	*Rocky Mountain News*
SMN	*Savannah Morning News*
UC	Archives, Norlin Library, University of Colorado
UNC	Wilson Library, Southern Historical Collection, University of North Carolina at Chapel Hill
USC	Manuscripts Department, South Caroliniana Library, University of South Carolina
WBD	*Webster's Biographical Dictionary*

Introduction

Epigraphs. The *Philadelphia Press* quoted in *PO* 10 (1891): 390. The word "negro" in this quote was not capitalized in the original text, nor was the term capitalized in most other publications in the late nineteenth century. See the comments of renowned contemporary writer Albion Tourgee in Barrows, ed., *Mohonk Conference on the Negro Question,* 103. The word will be quoted throughout this study as it appeared in the original text. Sometimes it will appear as a proper noun and other times it will not.

Mansur quoted in *CR* 21: 7, 6899 (all *CR* notes cited in the format of volume: part, page).

1. James C. Hemphill Scrapbook, 1889–1890, Hemphill Family Papers, DU; Garraty, *The New Commonwealth,* ix, 33, 335. The zeitgeist, or "spirit of the times," describes a phenomenon that some philosophers, social scientists, and historians have termed "cultural hegemony," meaning a general acceptance of certain cultural mores within a society during a specified time period. For this usage, see Takiki, *Iron Cages,* vi–viii. Other historians have called this same phenomenon "The New American Spirit," which fostered the age of racial imperialism abroad and discrimination domestically. For discussion of what constitutes a national, or international, "new spirit," see James A. Field Jr.'s untitled article in Grob and Billias, eds., *Interpretations of American History,* vol. II, 175–77. For other perspectives on the racial zeitgeist, see Fierce, *The Pan-African Idea in the United States, 1900–1919,* 222, and Hale, *Making Whiteness,* 23. Another German term that can be used interchangeably with zeitgeist is *volkgeist,* which refers to a singular mentality among a large group of people. See Kantrowitz, *Ben Tillman and the Reconstruction of White Supremacy,* 3.

2. Hofstadter, *The Age of Reform,* 164; Rutland, *The Republicans,* 108; Hirshson, *Farewell to the Bloody Shirt,* passim.

3. It should be noted that the Republican majority at the convening of Congress in December 1889 was only nine in the House and six in the Senate. It increased during the first session through settling contested elections in the House and by adding two new western states' senators (Idaho's and Wyoming's) in the upper chamber. Oberholtzer, *A History of the United States Since the Civil War,* vol. V, 103–4; Morgan, ed., *The Gilded Age,* 4; Barnes, *John G. Carlisle,* 163; Stubbs, *Congressional Committees,* passim; *Members of Congress Since 1789,* 178–79.

4. Quoted in George W. Cable, "The Freedmen's Case in Equity," *Century Magazine* 29 (1885): 409–18, cited in Wynes, *Forgotten Voices,* 21. See also Ellison, *The Black Experience,* 36.

5. Quote, *Ohio State Journal,* cited in *PO* 10 (1891): 391. See also *SMN,* 6 February 1890; Dinnerstein, *Natives and Strangers,* 229–31; Takiki, *Iron Cages,* vi.

6. Harrison's First Annual Message to Congress, cited in *CR* 21: 1, 91.

7. Perman, *Struggle for Mastery,* passim; Daniel, *Standing at the Crossroads,*

26. The issue of black emigration is covered in chapter 2 of this study, while the issue of black disfranchisement is covered in chapter 5.

8. *RMN,* 7 January 1890.

9. Palmer, *"Man Over Money,"* passim.

10. Hoar, "Are the Republicans in to Stay?," 616–24. More than twenty-five years later, after the Democratic Party had converted to Progressivism under the leadership of Woodrow Wilson, a leading Democrat would finally admit that "The Republican party was for half a century a constructive party and the Democratic party was the party of negation and complaint." Franklin K. Lane to Woodrow Wilson, 8 June 1916, quoted in Gould, *Reform and Regulation,* 169.

11. Carlisle, "The Republican Program," 585–96.

12. Vest, "The Hopes of the Democratic Party," 539–49. See also *Indianapolis Sentinel,* cited in *PO* 10 (1891): 540.

13. *New York Star,* cited in *PO* 10 (1891): 391.

14. "The Weak Point of the Democratic Party," *Belford's Magazine,* cited in *LD* 1 (1890): 338. In hindsight, it is easy to see that the differences in the two parties' positions were, in fact, not as great as contemporary pundits believed.

15. *Members of Congress Since 1789,* 178–79; DeSantis, *The Shaping of Modern America,* 39.

16. For a concise synopsis of the evolution of Republican factionalism before 1890, see Dobson, *Politics in the Gilded Age,* passim.

17. Kovel, *White Racism,* 29; Schriftgeisser, *The Gentleman from Massachusetts,* 106; DeSantis, *Republicans Face the Southern Question,* 213; Parker, *Justin Smith Morrill,* 287; Hirshson, *Farewell to the Bloody Shirt,* 235. The GOP began in 1854 as a single-issue third party. Its issue was "free soil, free labor, free men," to quote historian Eric Foner. The word "free" as used in this context by northerners in the 1850s meant only that they opposed the expansion of slavery into the territories and that the forces of free market capitalism should control the nation's economic destiny. It did not mean that they were necessarily concerned with the welfare of African Americans. See Foner, *Free Soil, Free Labor, Free Men,* passim; and McPherson, *Ordeal By Fire,* 99–101.

18. Sproat, *"The Best Men,"* 17–19, 36–37, 42, 199, 206–7; idem, Introduction to Ross, *The Liberal Republican Movement,* xv; Moos, *The Republicans,* 147, 161, 179, 180–84; Myers, *The Republican Party,* 111.

19. Unsigned letter to Matthew Ransom, 22 November 1888, Folder 230, Matthew W. Ransom Papers, UNC. Some senators, such as Orville Platt of Connecticut, intensely resented the notion that the Senate was a "millionaire's club." See Coolidge, *An Old-Fashioned Senator,* 411–14.

20. Sage, *William Boyd Allison,* 47, 123, 125, 135, 246–47, quotes on 47, 123.

21. It should be noted that, while there were more Republican millionaire-types in the Senate, Democratic senators were not exactly living in poverty either. John G. Carlisle of Kentucky, for instance, also built a mansion in Washington, D.C., in 1890. Yet, he was not personally wealthy. His new mansion represented

the ultimate extent of his opulence in his old age, not a new or sudden accumula-
tion of money. See Current, *Pine Logs and Politics,* 234–35; DeSantis, *The Shaping
of Modern America,* 41, 44; Barnes, *John G. Carlisle,*158.

22. Kehl, *Boss Rule in the Gilded Age,* xiv–xvi, 104–7, 126–27, 148.

23. Sievers, *Benjamin Harrison,* 144–45; DeSantis, *The Shaping of Modern
America,* 99.

24. Hedges, ed., *Speeches of Benjamin Harrison,* 9–16; Sievers, *Benjamin
Harrison,* 28–29, 149; Kehl, *Boss Rule in the Gilded Age,* 133.

25. White, in *The Republican Era,* shows just how central economic issues
were to the GOP of this era by writing an administrative history of the party in the
Gilded Age without mentioning racial issues at all.

26. Pension claim form, Francis M. Cockrell Papers, DU; Disability Pension
claim form, Folder 6, Box 1, David H. Nichols Papers, UC; *Philadelphia Press,* 7
March 1891, cited in *PO* 10 (1891): 538; Ainsworth, "Electoral Strength and the
Emergence of Group Influence in the Late 1800s," 319; Filler, ed., *Democrats and
Republicans,* 114; Rhodes, *History of the United States,* vol. VIII, 346.

27. Clarkson, "The Politician and the Pharisee," 613–23; Frederickson, *The
Black Image in the White Mind,* 208. Frederickson's book is one of the most important treatises ever written in the field of American race relations. Readers are urged
to consult the two chapters from pages 198–255 of his book for a thorough treatment of how white northerners perceived both African Americans and the race
problem in general during the late nineteenth and early twentieth centuries. Further discussion of the reasons for the transformation of the national zeitgeist on
racial issues from the humanitarian to the racist points of view are provided herein
in chapter 3 of this study.

28. Barrows, ed., *Mohonk Conference on the Negro Question,* quotes 84, 94,
and 82.

29. Ibid., 9.

30. Woodward, *The Strange Career of Jim Crow,* passim; McPherson, *The
Abolitionist Legacy,* 137–38, 299–301; Trefousse, *Reconstruction,* 64–65, 77; Hale,
Making Whiteness, xi–xii.

31. Dinnerstein, *Natives and Strangers,* 229–31; Takiki, *Iron Cages,* vi.

32. It should be noted that the Progressives who emerged to reform so
many aspects of American society around the turn of the twentieth century did
address most of the corruption associated with the immigrant vote in northern
cities. For a more thorough treatment of these issues, see Daniels, *Not Like Us,*
passim.

33. Blanton Duncan to William C. P. Breckinridge, 8 January 1889, Box 783,
Breckinridge Family Papers, LC; Socolofsky and Spetter, *The Presidency of Benjamin Harrison,* ix–x.

34. Quoted in "The News at the Capital," vol. 12, Gorman Scrapbooks, UNC, 44.

35. Quoted in Turpie, *Sketches of My Own Times,* 302–3.

36. Muzzey, *James G. Blaine,* 368, 379.

37. Dobson, *Politics in the Gilded Age,* 170.

38. Dunn, *From Harrison to Harding,* vol. I, 3–6, 17; Sievers, *Benjamin Harrison,* 3, 61.

39. *CR* 21: 1, 5; Dewey, *National Problems, 1885–1897,* 127; Faulkner, *Politics, Reform, and Expansion,* ix, 1; *Presidential Elections Since 1789,* 38–39; Kehl, *Boss Rule in the Gilded Age,* 104–7, 112; Sievers, *Benjamin Harrison,* 149.

40. "Private" John Allen, Democratic representative of Mississippi, quoted in *CR* 21: 11, 10779.

41. It should be noted that this view of Blaine as the strongest leader of the GOP in 1888 and 1889 quickly diminished afterward as the old statesman's health and vitality steadily worsened. "Blaine Was There," vol. 12, Gorman Scrapbooks, UNC, 85; ibid., vol. 17, page 63.

42. *Houston Post,* 3 July 1890, quoted in *LD* 1 (1890), 328.

43. Quoted in Summers, *The Gilded Age,* 213.

44. Mayer, *The Republican Party,* 221.

45. Foraker, *I Would Live It Again,* 132–33.

46. Quoted in unidentified newspaper clipping, vol. 17, Gorman Scrapbooks, UNC, 8.

47. Louis T. Michener to E. W. Halford, 1 and 5 October 1889, Harrison Manuscripts, Series I, LC, cited in Crofts, "The Blair Bill and the Election Bill," 236–37.

48. Harrison Inaugural Address, 4 March 1889, in *CR* 21: 1, 3–4; *RMN,* 23 May 1889; Cullom, *Fifty Years of Public Service,* 248–49; Sievers, *Benjamin Harrison,* 29, 37, 43.

49. Miscellaneous clippings, Hemphill Scrapbook, 1889–1890, DU, 1; Sinkler, "Benjamin Harrison and the Matter of Race," 197–214; idem, *The Racial Attitudes of American Presidents,* 242–88; Williamson, *The Crucible of Race,* 113.

50. *The* (Topeka) *American Citizen,* 26 April 1889, 3 May 1889, cited in Dann, ed., *The Black Press, 1827–1890,* 181–82.

51. Quote from Fortune's Afro-American League Inaugural Convention, January 1890, cited in Foner and Branham, eds., *Lift Every Voice,* 721–22.

52. Turner quoted in *Christian Recorder,* 1 April 1886, cited in Foner and Branham, eds., *Lift Every Voice,* 640.

53. *CR* 21: 7, 6715–20; ibid.: Appendix, 442–44; Miscellaneous clippings, vol. 12, Gorman Scrapbooks, UNC, 54; *Brooklyn Eagle,* 27 January 1890, and *Washington Pilot,* 20 December 1890, cited in *PO* 10 (1890): 270, 391; *The Advocate,* 20 April 1889, and *The American Citizen,* 3 May 1889, cited in Dann, *Black Press,* 181–82; Bancroft, ed., *Papers of Carl Schurz,* vol. V, 73; Fishel, "The Negro in Northern Politics, 1870–1900," 474, 478, 480; Brotz, ed. *African-American Social and Political Thought, 1850–1920,* 353; Dewey, *National Problems 1885–1897,* 162–63.

54. *CR* 22: 1, 410. Similar statements can be found throughout the pages of the *Congressional Record* and southern newspapers alike. See, for example, *SMN,* 4 February 1890.

Chapter 1. To Empty a Running Stream

Epigraphs. SMN, 3 January 1890; *CR* 22: 2, 1622–23.

1. Many historians have chronicled the various pre-1890 colonization and back-to-Africa movements. Among the standard works covering the antebellum era are: Staudenraus, *The African Colonization Movement, 1816–1865;* and Miller, *The Search for a Black Nationality.* The standard treatment of the African American migration of 1879 is Painter, *Exodusters.*

2. Blyden, *The African Problem and Other Discourses, Delivered in America in 1890,* 30; Franklin and Moss Jr., *From Slavery to Freedom,* 98, 168–70; Meier, *Negro Thought in America, 1880–1915,* 288.

3. Crogman spoke these words at the National Educational Association Meeting in Madison, Wisconsin, in 1884. Quoted in Foner and Branham, eds., *Lift Every Voice,* 628.

4. "Seventy-third and Seventy-fourth Annual Reports," *ACS Reports;* Cornelius Smith to William E. Chandler, 26 May 1889, cited in Crofts, "The Blair Bill and the Election Bill," 235; R. S. Flagg to William Coppinger, 4 May 1891; H. E. Ellis and R. L. Davis to Coppinger, 31 August and November 1890, cited in Redkey, *Black Exodus,* 5–10; Fortune, "The Afro-American League," 2–6; McMath Jr., *American Populism,* 9–10; Daniel, *Standing at the Crossroads,* 11, 56.

5. Brill, "Notes of a Reisebilder aus Liberia," Reel 315, ACS Papers, LC; Lynch, *Edward Wilmot Blyden,* 131–32; Redkey, *Black Exodus,* 47–57, 73–87. For a succinct history of the ACS and Liberia, see Brooks, *Integration or Separation?,* 156–63.

6. Hemphill Scrapbook, 1889–1890, DU, 9; "Seventy-third and Seventy-fourth Annual Reports," *ACS Reports; AC,* 1 January 1890; *LA,* 5 February 1890; *Literary World* 21 (1890): 291; McKinley, *An Appeal to Pharoah* [*sic*],128–42, 152–57, 180; Blyden, *The African Problem,* 1–36; Brotz, ed., *African-American Social and Political Thought,* 112; Lynch, *Edward Wilmot Blyden,* vii–viii.

7. "The Stanley Controversy—A German-American View," *New York Belletristiches Journal,* cited in *PO* 10 (1890): 175; Ray, "Notes and Comments: Stanley's Pygmies," 253–54; George Washington Williams, "An Open Letter to His Supreme Majesty Leopold II, King of the Belgians and Sovereign of the Independent State of Congo by Colonel, The Honorable Geo. W. Williams, of the United States of America," cited in Hill and Kilson, eds., *Apropos of Africa,* 113–24.

8. Quoted in McKinley, *An Appeal to Pharoah* [*sic*], xviii.

9. Miscellaneous documents, Matthew C. Butler Papers, DU; Hemphill Scrapbook, 1889–1890, DU, 23, 102; *BD,* 718.

10. Fry, *John Tyler Morgan and the Search for Southern Autonomy,* xi, 1, quotes 10, 39–40; Anders, "The Senatorial Career of John Tyler Morgan," 1, 29.

11. *CR* 21: 1, 419.

12. Ibid., 420.

13. Ibid., 420–27. For further explanation of the need for black Christians from the United States to populate Africa, see Blyden, *The African Problem,* 83–84, 90.

14. *CR* 21: 1, 420, 428.

15. Ibid., 428–29.

16. Ibid., 622–29. See also *SMN*, 4 February 1890.

17. "Decline of the Negro in America," *Philadelphia Record*, quoted in *PO* 10 (1891): 418.

18. *CR* 21: 1, 629.

19. Ibid., 630.

20. Ibid., 802; Ingalls had been an original pre–Civil War Jayhawker, having migrated to his adopted state of Kansas from Massachusetts in 1858. He embodied the duality of the Republicans as humanitarians and moneygrubbers, as well as any member of the Billion Dollar Congress. He constantly expressed concern for the welfare of southern blacks, even urging President Harrison to make civil rights the great issue of his administration, but he also used the race issue for political advantage at every opportunity. He desired to increase Republican voting strength in the South, according to his biographer, more than he wanted to make life better for African Americans. He showed little regard for the black Exodusters in his own state, whose votes the Kansas GOP did not need in order to win elections. He believed strongly in the superiority of the Caucasian race, but, because of his Scandinavian background, he carefully avoided using the most common term of the day, "Anglo-Saxon." His true love lay in making money off of land speculation and railroads, and he seemed to enjoy wielding power almost as much as making money. He especially took pride in the fact that he had been on the winning side in the Civil War and squandered no opportunity to remind his ex-Confederate colleagues that his side had won and theirs had lost the war. See Williams, *Senator John James Ingalls*, vii, 12–13, 76–77, 115–19.

21. Ingalls seems to have held the Machiavellian, or *realpolitik*, political philosophy that the end justifies the means. By his logic, Republicans had the right to use every weapon at their disposal to win elections, including manipulating voters, gerrymandering districts, and tampering with ballot boxes. Democrats did the same things, of course, and won elections as a result. Why should these criminals be allowed to win, reasoned Ingalls? Why not fight fire with fire? In actuality, the Kansan owed his first election to the Senate in 1873 to similar underhanded methods, and it seems clear that he would have been an unscrupulous politician no matter what the opposition did. He once publicly called the idea of cleaning up American politics a naive, "iridescent dream," adding that "The Decalogue and the Golden Rule have no place in a political campaign" (quoted in Williams, *Senator John James Ingalls*, 119–20). His occasional unethical behavior, coupled with his tactless and cynical proclamations about the American political system, made him unpopular outside of Kansas. Although he kept a strong base of Republican supporters in Kansas, the newly elected Populist legislature of the Jayhawk state turned him out of the Senate in 1892. The Populists of Kansas did not necessarily single out Ingalls. They would have likely turned any other Republican out of office in 1892 for agitating the southern race issue rather than focusing on the

needs of suffering white farmers at home. *LA,* 18 October 1890; Williams, *Senator John James Ingalls,* 119–23, 154.

22. Quoted in Blassingame and McKivigan, eds., *The Frederick Douglass Papers—Series One, Vol. 5,* 451.

23. *CR* 21: 1, 802–7.

24. Biographer Glenn Tucker believes that Vance must be considered the undisputed chieftain of his party and his section in the Senate and contends that he was the only Democrat in the late 1800s capable of matching wits with such Republican intellects as John Sherman of Ohio, William B. Allison of Iowa, and George Frisbie Hoar of Massachusetts. That claim is an exaggeration, however, for several Democrats in the Fifty-first Congress could more than hold their own against the best Republicans of the day, as this study will show. But certainly Vance must be counted among the elite members of his party at the time, being in his fourth and final term as senator in 1890. He had also served as governor of North Carolina three times, including a term during the Civil War. Just as important, he was a true southern aristocrat by birth and association, looking the part of a pre-war nabob and carrying himself with sophistication and dignity. Yet, he did not at all act condescending but instead charmed everyone he met with his easy-going manner and his disarming wit. He could certainly be far more charismatic in oratory than most of his stuffy colleagues. See Tucker, *Zeb Vance,* 1, 4. One of Vance's admirers once mused "Phrase-making is said to be an attribute of genius," and "Vance gave expression and currency to more puns, witticisms, anecdotes and epigrams" than any man since Abraham Lincoln. After all, could not every American "repeat something good" that Vance said? His attributes served him well in the Senate, for when he spoke he tended to attract much attention from both sides of the aisle, not so much because his colleagues wanted to hear his ideas on whatever issue hung in the balance as they hoped to be entertained and amused. Quoted in Dowd, *Life of Zebulon B. Vance,* 2, 39, 69, quote 123. See also Weinstein, ed., *Zebulon B. Vance and "The Scattered Nation,"* passim.

25. *CR* 21: 1, 966–68; *AC,* 2 January 1890; *SMN,* 22 February 1890; Hemphill Scrapbook, 1889–1890, DU, 20. For a brief account of the out-migration of North Carolina blacks at this time, see Logan, "The Movement of Negroes from North Carolina, 1876–1894," 54–63. On causes of North Carolina out-migration, see the excerpts from the First, Third, Fourth, and Fifth Annual Reports of the Bureau of Labor Statistics of the State of North Carolina in Escott, et al., eds., *Major Problems in the History of the American South, Vol. II,* 69–70, 128–29.

26. *CR* 21: 1, 969–70.

27. *CR* 21: 1, 971–73. Hampton differed from all of his southern colleagues in the Senate in that he had been a prewar slaveholder and planter but became a staunch Unionist during the time of secession and war. After the war, he continued to epitomize the paternalistic planter class with his outward kindness toward blacks, and he gave the appearance that he desired to see them get decent treatment after emancipation. Although he certainly did not embrace the idea of full

political equality for blacks, he did not altogether oppose their participation in politics, as did many of his contemporaries, and many South Carolina blacks respected him for it. He did not make a habit of exploding in angry outbursts, as did his senior cohort Butler, but rather discussed the race issue calmly (and nearly dispassionately) and urged others to do the same. Few men on either side of the aisle could match him in that regard, however, and few could stay as close to the middle-of-the-road as he did on questions of race. This appraisal of Hampton's moderation on racial issues must be seen from the perspective of his generation, not our own. It should be remembered that the middle-of-the-road view on race in Hampton's generation was not the same as the middle-of-the-road view today. See Hemphill Scrapbook, 1889–1890, DU, 32; Jarrell, *Wade Hampton and the Negro,* ix, xi, 29–30, 51, 58, 61; Simkins, *Pitchfork Ben Tillman,* 156. During Reconstruction, Hampton had run headlong into opposition from northern Republican Radicals such as Charles Sumner and Thaddeus Stevens, whose vision for racial equality in the South ran far ahead of its time. In 1890, he found himself defending his state from a different sort of radical, openly racist Democrats such as Ben Tillman and Martin W. Gary, whose views on white supremacy would soon epitomize the whole era of Jim Crow racism and discrimination. These in-state rivals could not appreciate Hampton's tolerance of the limited participation of blacks in politics, and they set out to assert absolute white supremacy in South Carolina, a state that suffered from an unusual degree of racial tension at the time. See A. M. Salley to Alexander S. Salley Jr., 13 October 1888, 6 November 1888, 26 January 1889, 7 March 1890, 27 March 1890, 13 December 1890, Alexander S. Salley Jr., Papers, USC; Robert E. Mellichamp letter, James Island Papers, USC. Yet, despite his being one of the few voices of reason among southerners on racial questions in 1890, partisan Republicans considered him just as much their enemy as any neo-fire-eating Confederate among the southerners in Congress. To them, he had been South Carolina's leading Redeemer, the man who almost single-handedly overturned Radical Republican rule in 1876. Although Hampton claimed that he had led the so-called redemption of South Carolina only to rid the state of high taxes and corrupt leadership, his actions garnered him the reputation of a racist who simply wanted to get blacks out of positions of power in state politics. See Jarrell, *Wade Hampton and the Negro,* 124, 127.

28. *Woodville Republican,* 17 January 1891.

29. *CR* 22: 1, 629.

30. Ibid., 1360.

31. Ibid.: 1, 457.

32. Ibid.: 2, 1622–23; Miscellaneous documents, vol. 17, Gorman Scrapbooks, UNC, 8; Vest speech, Warrensburg, Missouri, 1870, George G. Vest Papers, MHS. According to a Savannah newspaper, the number of emigrants arriving at the port awaiting passage was one thousand, and they were not from Texas or Mississippi but from the Chattanooga area. See *SMN,* 9 September 1890.

33. *CR* 22: 2, 1623. Some Republicans and African Americans believed Vest

to be, as one newspaper put it, "a regular liar." *LA,* 1 November 1890. On efforts to encourage black migration to Kansas, see Painter, *Exodusters,* 153–58.

34. *CR* 21: 7, 6543.

35. Ibid., 6686; Redkey, *Black Exodus,* 57–72. Some black leaders of the day, such as R. R. Wright, truly believed that, in time, all whites would eventually evacuate the South, leaving it exclusively as a haven for blacks. See *SMN,* 3 September 1889.

36. Fortune, "The Afro-American League," 2–6.

37. *CR* 21: 4, 3786; *Jackson New Mississippian,* 19 December 1988; Redkey, *Black Exodus,* 23.

38. Angell, *Bishop Henry McNeal Turner and African-American Religion in the South,* 7; Ponton, *Life and Times of Henry M. Turner,* 33–36; Redkey, *Black Exodus,* 45, 57–71.

39. Harlan, ed., *The Booker T. Washington Papers,* vol. III, 134.

40. H. M. Turner to M. C. Butler, 10 April 1890, Matthew C. Butler Papers, USC. In 1890, southern Democrats were fiscal conservatives amid a tax-and-spend Republican administration and Congress. They could not really envision a federal emigration program requiring the millions that Turner advocated. It is interesting to compare the modest appropriation in the Butler bill to that of the next great attempt to secure federal aid for an emigration plan, Theodore G. Bilbo's repatriation bill of 1939, which called for spending $1 billion annually. Bilbo, a New Deal Democrat, justified this enormous (even by New Deal standards) proposal based on the dubious claim of having the support of eight of the nation's twelve million blacks. Although Bilbo's bill garnered a great amount of attention, the Roosevelt administration never gave it serious consideration. See Fitzgerald, "'We Have Found a Moses,'" 293–320.

41. Crummell, *Africa and America,* i, 184–85; Moses, *Alexander Crummell,* 4–5; Oldfield, ed., *Civilization and Black Progress,* passim.

42. Blyden, *The African Problem,* 90; Lynch, *Edward Wilmot Blyden,* 124.

43. Hubbard, "An Opportunity for the Negro," 116–18.

44. Berry, *A Century of Missions of the African Methodist Episcopal Church, 1840–1940,* 70–71.

45. The state of North Carolina did pass a law proscribing emigration "agents," who profited, often at the expense of their poor victims, from inducing black tenant farmers to leave their current labor arrangement for greener pastures elsewhere. This law was only nominally related to the back-to-Africa movement, which produced a mixed and mild reaction from white employers. See Ayers, *The Promise of the New South,* 22–23, 149–51; Gaither, *Blacks and the Populist Revolt,* 24, 43; and Logan, "The Movement of Negroes from North Carolina," 54–63.

46. For an example of how white leaders in the hill and Piedmont South reacted to the black out-migration of the late 1880s, see the comments of Stephen D. Lee, president of Mississippi A & M College, in Bond, *Political Culture in the Nineteenth-Century South,* 260. On the shift in white reaction from 1879 to 1890,

see Mandle, *Not Slave, Not Free*, 26; Going, *Bourbon Democracy in Alabama, 1874–1890*, 95–97; Wharton, *The Negro in Mississippi*, 70; and Logan, *The Betrayal of the Negro*, 142, 193–94.

47. For an example of how white planters typically reacted to blacks jettisoning southern fields for better economic opportunities elsewhere during the World War I years, see Lewis, "From Peasant to Proletarian," 77–102; and McMillen, *Dark Journey*, 272–81.

48. *LA*, 5 February 1890; *JCL*, 26 December 1889; *LD* 1 (1890): 724–25; Logan, *The Betrayal of the Negro*, 192–94.

49. "The Negro Problem," *Nation*, 23 January 1890.

50. Sanford, "American Interests in Africa," 409–29.

51. Hale, "Emigration and Immigration," 254–56.

52. Scomp, "Can the Race Problem Be Solved?" 365–76; Field, *Bright Skies*, 158–63; *SMN*, 9 February 1888.

53. A. Thompson of New York to Stephen D. Lee, 24 January 1890, Butler Papers, USC.

54. *JCL*, 5 December 1889; *Detroit Plaindealer*, 11 and 18 October 1889, cited in Dann, ed., *The Black Press*, 289–90.

55. *JCL*, 21 November 1889.

56. *CR* 21: 1, 966–68; *AC*, 2 January 1890; Hemphill Scrapbook, 1889–1890, DU, 20.

57. Bryce, *The American Commonwealth*, vol. II, 516.

58. *BH*, 8 February 1890; *AC*, 2 January 1890; *SMN*, 18 January 1890; Washington, *Historical Development of the Negro in Oklahoma*, 37; Williamson, *A Rage for Order*, 163–65; Katz, *The Black West*, 245–64; Redkey, *Black Exodus*, 99–104.

59. The record low for completed applications was eight in 1873, while the high was 180 in 1885. See the Addenda to Report on Emigration in "Seventieth Annual Report," *ACS Reports*. During the same period, the record low number of emigrants that the ACS actually sent in a given year was twenty-three in 1875, while the high was 143 in 1880. The record low for money donated during the same years was $6,930.13 in 1885, while the record high was $33,335.71 in 1873. See the Table of Emigrants and the Cost of African Colonization in "Sixty-ninth Annual Report," *ACS Reports*. It must be stressed here that there was a great difference in the number of letters of inquiry and the number of actual completed applications mailed to the ACS.

60. The ACS apologized for refusing applicants who were both "illiterate and impecunious," but it judged that they would be unable to "improve the condition of either themselves or Liberia." See "Seventy-seventh Annual Report," *ACS Reports*.

61. The exact number of people interested in emigrating cannot be ascertained, but speculation can be made based upon a comparison of the amount of money that hopeful emigrants forwarded to the ACS in each year since Reconstruction. The yearly receipts ranged from a low of $65.00 in 1886 to a high of $2,697.75 in 1891. The previous high was $1,218.75 in 1880, when the ACS esti-

mated that a half-million people were interested. It stands to reason that, since receipts in 1891 were more than double that of 1880, the figure one million could be an accurate estimate of those seriously entertaining the idea of emigration in 1890–1891. It should be emphasized that through this speculation the author is not arguing that there *were* a million hopeful emigrants. He is merely trying to point out that, based upon ACS receipts and estimates, there *might have been* that many. See *ACS Reports,* passim.

62. "Seventy-fourth Annual Report, 1891," *ACS Reports;* Bishop Henry M. Turner cited in Hill and Kilson, eds., *Apropos of Africa,* 276; Meier, *Negro Thought in America,* 61; Redkey, *Black Exodus,* 104.

63. Kenneth C. Barnes, *Who Killed John Clayton?,* 94, 107–12, quote 109; *Arkansas Democrat,* 7 October 1890, cited in *LD* 1 (1890): 724–25; "Seventy-fifth Annual Report," *ACS Reports.*

64. Seventh, Eighth, and Twelfth Letters of Bishop Henry M. Turner, 16 and 18 November 1891, and 5 December 1891, quoted in Hill and Kilson, eds., *Apropos of Africa,* 268–70, 276.

65. Quoted in Meier, *Negro Thought in America, 1880–1915,* 67.

66. Clarence A. Bacote, "Negro Proscriptions, Protests, and Proposed Solutions in Georgia, 1880–1908," in Wynes, ed., *The Negro in the South Since 1865,* 169.

67. Langston speech, John Mercer Langston Papers, LC, 114–15; *SMN,* 19 November 1889; Franklin and Moss Jr., *From Slavery to Freedom,* 307.

68. Smalls, "Election Methods in the South," 593–600, quote 600.

69. Brotz, ed., *African-American Social and Political Thought,* 323.

70. Rudwick, *W. E. B. DuBois,* 25–27. DuBois, in fact, gave Senator John Tyler Morgan, the main proponent of the Butler bill, a "no holds barred . . . long and blazing" rebuke. See DuBois, "A Negro Student at Harvard at the End of the Nineteenth Century," in Lewis, ed., *W. E. B. DuBois: A Reader,* 279.

71. John Dittmer, "The Education of Henry McNeal Turner," in Litwack and Meier, eds., *Black Leaders of the Nineteenth Century,* 266–67; Brotz, ed., *African-American Social and Political Thought,* 398.

72. Bracy Jr., et al., eds., *Black Nationalism in America,* 219, 222.

73. H. L. Duncan to Senator William E. Chandler of New Hampshire, 1 April 1891, Book 82, William E. Chandler Papers, LC.

74. Turner to Butler, 10 April 1890, Butler Papers, USC. The failure of the Butler bill did not deter strong proponents of emigration. In 1894, for instance, white Mississippian Charles H. Otken wrote a book arguing the emigration cause so energetically that it seems as though he thought he had discovered a new idea. See Otken, *The Ills of the South,* passim.

75. Contemporary skeptics of the plan and skeptical historians alike contend, of course, that the Butler bill was indeed a quixotic pipe dream. One of the latter has cited the lack of ships available for such a purpose as a factor that automatically made the Butler bill unworkable. It should be noted, however, that the Harrison administration was engaged in the biggest naval buildup in American

history to that time, and it is not at all unreasonable to suppose that naval ships could have been employed for that purpose. Hence, the letters of citizens to Senator Chandler, chair of the naval appropriations committee. See *Philadelphia Press*, cited in *PO* 10 (1891): 538. Regardless of what ships and what manpower was used to effect the project, the United States of America, as much or more than any nation in history, has always been willing and able to tackle challenges successfully that other nations would not or could not: the moon landing, the Manhattan Project, the Panama Canal, the Erie Canal, the first transcontinental railroad, and the revolution and subsequent founding of the nation as the first democratic-republic in modern history, just to name a few, are all examples of projects that might have been considered impossible until American ingenuity turned them into realities.

76. Senator Edmund C. Walthall of Mississippi, quoted in *CR* 21: 1, 860.

77. Senator Joseph N. Dolph of Oregon, quoting Blaine in *CR* 22: 1, 573–74.

78. Although *de jure* segregation had begun in some southern states as early as 1873, its growth was slow and uncertain, with the U.S. Supreme Court ruling upon its constitutionality in several cases throughout the 1870s and 1880s. By 1890, the issue was all but resolved, and the infamous decision in the 1896 *Plessy v. Ferguson* case represented the final word on the subject for more than a half-century. See Wilhelm, *Who Needs the Negro?*, 213; and Ellison, *The Black Experience*, 39. For another interesting perspective on how the failure of the emigration movement led to segregation, see Joel Williamson, "The Separation of the Races," in Williamson, ed., *The Origins of Segregation*, 33. More discussion of the rise of segregation is also provided in chapter 9 of this study.

79. *Independent* 42 (1890): 12–13.

Chapter 2. To Drain the Infinite Oceans

Epigraphs. CR 21: 2, 1687; idem, 1681.

1. *CR* 21: 2, 1088.

2. Quoted in "How Shall We Help the Negro?" *Century Magazine* 30 (1885): 273–80, cited in Wynes, *Forgotten Voices*, 40.

3. Lee, *The Struggle for Federal Aid*, 147–48; Evans, "Catholics and the Blair Education Bill," 273–98; Robison, "Governor Robert L. Taylor and the Blair Education Bill in Tennessee," 29. Tourgee's pre–Blair bill novels, *A Fool's Errand* and *Bricks Without Straw*, both advocated that the federal government take responsibility for educating black southerners. See Barrows, ed., *Mohonk Conference on the Negro Question*, 114.

4. Going, "The South and the Blair Education Bill," 271, 288; Brock, *The United States, 1789–1890*, 300; Barnes, *John G. Carlisle*, 112, 137, 152–53; Lee, *The Struggle for Federal Aid*, 149–55.

5. *JCL*, 14 and 21 November 1889; Hemphill Scrapbook, 1889–1890, DU, 11, 40, 64; Gatewood Jr., "North Carolina and Federal Aid to Education: Public Reaction

to the Blair Bill, 1881–1890," 465–88; McWilliams, *Hannis Taylor,* 19; Dyer, *"Fightin'*
Joe" Wheeler, 275, 283; Going, "The South and the Blair Education Bill," 276–87; Dowd,
Life of Zebulon Vance, 205–7, 210; Tucker, *Zeb Vance,* 461; Fry, *John Tyler Morgan,* 53.

6. Miscellaneous clippings, Scrapbooks One and Two, James L. Pugh Papers, AU.

7. J. Z. George quoted in *CR* 21: 3, 2153; Dyer, *The Public Career of William*
M. Evarts, 473–74; Burton, *John Sherman,* 322–23; Fry, *John Tyler Morgan,* 53;
McWilliams, *Hannis Taylor,* 19; Going, "The South and the Blair Education Bill,"
284–85, 87.

8. Harrison's First Annual Address to Congress, cited in *JCL,* 12 December
1889; Richardson, *William E. Chandler,* 242–43; *BD,* 629.

9. Crofts, "The Blair Bill and the Election Bill," 176; Socolofsky and Spetter,
The Presidency of Benjamin Harrison, 67–69.

10. Barrows, ed., *Mohonk Conference on the Negro Question,* passim; Wynes,
ed., *The Negro in the South Since 1865,* 188, 92.

11. "Promoting Mendicancy," *Nation* 50 (1890): 25; "The Negro Problem,"
Nation 50 (1890): 64; McPherson, *Abolitionist Legacy,* 129–30; Logan, *The Negro*
in American Life and Thought, 192.

12. *Nation,* 9 January 1890; "The Negro Learning Self-Help," undated, *New*
York Evening Post, cited in *PO* 10 (1890); Hemphill Scrapbook, 1889–1890, DU,
11, 40, 64; Crofts, "The Black Response to the Blair Education Bill," 60; Painter,
Standing at Armageddon, 78–79; Brotz, ed., *African-American Social and Political*
Thought, 332–33, 349; Going, "The South and the Blair Education Bill," 283;
McWilliams, *Hannis Taylor,* 19.

13. Quoted in Foner, ed., *Life and Writings of Frederick Douglass, Vol. IV,* 459.

14. Mayo, "The Progress of the Negro," 338; Stetson, "The New Basis of
National Education," *Andover Review,* cited in *LD* 1 (1890): 595–96; Crummell,
Africa and America, vii; Barrows, ed., *Mohonk Conference on the Negro Question,*
13, 15; Walls, *Joseph Charles Price,* xv; Crunden, *Ministers of Reform,* 52–63; Crofts,
"The Black Response to the Blair Education Bill," 59.

15. *CR* 21: 1, 630.

16. Ibid., 1085–86.

17. Ibid., 1085–97, quotes 1085, 1088, 1097, 1440.

18. Ibid., 1386–88.

19. Ibid., 1164–66.

20. Ibid., 1161–63, 1200–4, 1388, quote 1163.

21. Ibid., 1395.

22. Ibid., 1493–94, 1540–41; J. L. M. Curry to Manly Curry, 31 October 1889,
cited in Crofts, "The Blair Bill and the Election Bill," 186.

23. *CR* 21: 2, 1539, quotes 1491, 1546.

24. Keller, *Affairs of State,* 480, 483, 485; Lowry and McCardle, *A History of*
Mississippi, introduction; Evans, "Catholics and the Blair Education Bill," 277; for
further treatment of the disagreement over the purpose of education in this era,

see the series of eight articles, each by a different author but collectively entitled "What Shall the Public Schools Teach?" interspersed throughout *Forum*, Vols. 4, 5, and 6 (1888). These articles are listed individually in the bibliography.

25. Evans, "Catholics and the Blair Education Bill," 298.

26. Going, "The South and the Blair Education Bill," 287.

27. *CR* 21: 3, 2153.

28. Considering George's obstreperous personality, it is a wonder he did not change his opinion of the bill just to spite Blair. For an assessment of George's character, see *New York Herald*, 8 February 1891, cited in vol. 17, Gorman Scrapbooks, UNC, 8; *CR* 21: 3, 2146, 2152–53.

29. *CR* 21: 2, 1647–49; Miscellaneous documents, Charles James Faulkner Jr., Papers, DU; Hopkins, et al., eds., *Concise Dictionary of American Biography*, 285.

30. *CR* 21: 2, 1650–54, quote 1654.

31. *CR* 21: 2, 1656, quote; Cullom, *Fifty Years of Public Service*, 217.

32. *CR* 21: 2, 1678–82, quotes 1682; *New York Herald*, 8 February 1891, cited in vol. 17, Gorman Scrapbooks, UNC; Hilary A. Herbert, "Grandfather Talks about His Life under Two Flags," unpublished manuscript, Hilary A. Herbert Papers, UNC, 313–14; Carl C. Moneyhon, "Coke, Richard," in Garraty and Carnes, eds., *American National Biography*, vol. V, 186–87.

33. Hubert H. Bancroft, quoted in Lewis, *The Big Four*, 156–58.

34. *CR* 21: 2, 1687–88.

35. Reagan ranked among the most forceful of the Democratic orators of the late nineteenth century, standing alongside John Tyler Morgan for verbal dexterity on the Senate floor. Like Morgan, he belonged to the old school of antebellum secessionists. He was, in fact, a first-generation Texan, who had helped drive the Mexicans and Native Americans out of the Lone Star Republic. He later served as postmaster of the Confederate States of America, which made him the highest ranking Texan in the Confederate government. He then became the leading Redeemer of the Lone Star State and the principal author of the Texas Constitution of 1875. Since becoming a senator, Reagan's great contribution to national legislation was his coauthorship of the Interstate Commerce Act of 1887. See Proctor, *Not Without Honor*, 17–19, 54–55, 63, 269–73.

36. *CR* 21: 2, 1724–25. Democrat James K. Jones of Arkansas, a flamboyant first-term senator whose sobriquet was "the Plumed Knight of Arkansas," later reiterated Reagan's argument that a group of very independent-minded people, who had believed that self-reliance was the best deterrent of tyranny, had founded the United States, and that the nation needed to stay the course they had chartered. See *CR* 21: 3, 2078–79; Hopkins, et al., eds., *Concise Dictionary of American Biography*, 508.

37. *CR* 21: 2, 1724–25. Three-term Republican Senator Preston B. Plumb of Kansas, whom visitors to the Senate gallery often mistook for a doorman because of his poor wardrobe and unkempt appearance, later reiterated Reagan's argument that taxpayers of one state should not have to pay for the education of chil-

dren in another state. He strongly opposed Kansas, which was about to be in the midst of the Populist revolt because of its poor agricultural circumstances at the time (discussed in chapter 8), paying for black southerners to receive educations. See *CR* 21: 2, 1938; miscellaneous clippings, vol. 17, Gorman Scrapbooks, UNC, 8–11; Connelly, *The Life of Preston B. Plumb, 1837–1891*, vii, 227.

38. *CR* 21: 2, 1725; Wilson and Fiske, eds., *Appleton's Annual Cyclopedia of American Biography* (1889), 547–48.

39. *CR* 21: 2, 1865–71; Fowler, *John Coit Spooner*, 13, 28, 63, 134.

40. *CR* 21: 2, 1866; Hemphill Scrapbook, 1889–1890, DU, 11, 40, 64.

41. *CR* 21: 2, 1935–36. Although a lawyer by training, Barbour had spent most of his adult life as a railroad magnate, serving as president of the Orange and Alexandria Railroad from 1852 to 1885. In the mid-1880s, he had been instrumental in breaking William Mahone's Republican Readjuster control over Virginia politics. The Democratic Party rewarded him by sending him to the U. S. Senate. Despite being seventy years old, Barbour was in his first term as a senator in 1890. See Hopkins, et al., eds., *Concise Dictionary of American Biography*, 47. During the First Mohonk Conference, which was held only three months after the Blair bill debate ended, John Jay of New York remarked that Barbour's words "are especially deserving of consideration by those who have been deluded by the shallow and sophisticated arguments in defiance of reason and of history, but put forth with a pretense of high philosophy." By that, he meant that constitutional arguments did not provide a sound basis for opposing aid to education for African Americans. See Barrows, ed., *Mohonk Conference on the Negro Question*, 73.

42. *CR* 21: 2, 1937.

43. *CR* 21: 2, 1938–43. One-term Republican Senator Anthony Higgins of Delaware, who had quite an impressive educational pedigree himself—a bachelor's degree from Yale University and a law degree from Harvard University—was among these supporters of the Blair bill, and he perhaps should have had something thoughtful to add but did not. See *BD*, 1184.

44. *CR* 21: 7, 6227–28; quote, *CR* 21: 8, 7656.

45. Barrows, ed., *Mohonk Conference on the Negro Question*, 15.

46. *CR* 21: 7, 6083–89, 6332–51, 6369–72; Croft, "The Black Response to the Blair Education Bill," 59; Lee, *The Struggle for Federal Aid*, 2; Walls, *Joseph Charles Price*, 277; Parker, *Justin Smith Morrill*, 335–41; Daniels, *Not Like Us*, 34.

47. Gatewood, "North Carolina and Federal Aid to Education," 488.

48. Anderson, *The Education of Blacks in the South, 1860–1935*, 279.

49. Quoted in Foner and Branham, eds. *Lift Every Voice*, 739, 744.

Chapter 3. Charting New Waters

Epigraphs. Lodge, "The Coming Congress," 294–95; Mills, "Republican Tactics in the House," 666.

1. The rule changes brought by Speaker Thomas B. Reed revolutionized

the way House business has been conducted ever since. See Currie, *The United States House of Representatives*, 54–57.

2. *New York Independent*, 12 March 1890, quoted in *PO* 10 (1890): 537.

3. Judex, "The Speaker and His Critics," 237–50; Miscellaneous clippings, *LD* 1 (1890): 17–18; Robinson, *Thomas B. Reed*, 205–6; Dunn, *From Harrison to Harding*, vol. I, 23–25; Barnes, *John G. Carlisle*, 80.

4. Reed, "Obstruction in the National House," 421–28; idem, "A Reply to X. M. C.," 228–36; Robinson, *Thomas B. Reed*, 1, 3, 19, 35, 195.

5. Eaton, *A History of the Old South*, 376; Follette, *The Speaker of the House of Representatives*, 115–16; Alexander, *History and Procedure of the House of Representatives*, 237; Currie, *The United States House of Representatives*, 22–24, 54.

6. Reed, "Obstruction in the National House," 427–28; Barnes, *John G. Carlisle*, 109, 146.

7. William C. P. Breckinridge, Speech File, 4 August 1890, Box 801, Breckinridge Family Papers, LC

8. Reed, "Obstruction in the National House," quotes 421, 425; idem, "Contested Elections," 118–20; Mills, "Republican Tactics in the House," 666.

9. Palgrave, "The Recent Crisis in Congress," 367–75, quotes 368, 375; Reed, "A Deliberative Body," 148–56.

10. Bryce, "A Word as to the Speakership," 386, 392.

11. *CR* 22: 2, 1211–12; Chamberlain, "Counting a Quorum," 510–25; Taylor, "The National House of Representatives: Its Growing Inefficiency as a Legislative Body," 766–73; Towne, *Senator William J. Stone and the Politics of Compromise*, 13–14.

12. Benjamin F. Butler, "Should There Be a Union of the English Speaking Peoples of the Earth?," Speech to the Colby University Alumni, 2 July 1889, Folder 4, Box 8, Henry M. Teller Papers, UC.

13. *CR* 21: 11, 10781, quote; Gentry, *Private John Allen*, xiii–xiv; Schriftgeisser, *The Gentleman from Massachusetts*, 105.

14. Filler, ed., *Democrats and Republicans*, 183.

15. *Providence Journal*, cited in *LD* 1 (1890): 272.

16. Sievers, *Benjamin Harrison*, 172.

17. *CR* 21: 2, 1025–43; *BH*, 25 January 1890; Langston, *From the Virginia Plantation to the National Capitol*, 504; Dunn, *From Harrison to Harding*, 25–26, 59.

18. Reed, "Contested Elections," 112–20.

19. *CR* 21: 2, 1844–53, 1888–97, 1907–25, 1943–55.

20. Ibid.: 3, 2097; ibid.: 10, 9559, 9616, 9751; ibid.: 1, 239; William C. P. Breckinridge, Speech File, 4 August 1890, Box 801, Breckinridge Family Papers, LC; *New York Times*, 4 August 1890, and *Springfield Republican*, 20 September 1890, cited in *LD* 1 (1890): 443–44; Crofts, "The Blair Bill and the Election Bill," 244–46. As a result of the rampant violence and fraud in the 1888 Arkansas elections, Congress authorized federal supervision in the 1890 elections in "The Land of Opportunity" under the old 1871 supervisory law. See Barnes, *Who Killed John Clayton?*, passim.

21. *CR* 21: 10, 10154–69; "The Situation and Demands of the Colored American," Langston Papers, LC; Miscellaneous clippings, Scrapbook One, Pugh Papers, AU; Langston, *From the Virginia Plantation to the National Capitol,* 498.

22. Pingrey, "The Right of the Federal Courts to Punish Offenders Against the Ballot Box," *American Law Register,* cited in *LD* 1 (1890): 426; Byars, ed., *"An American Commoner,"* 94–96, 99; Matthews, *Legislative and Judicial History of the Fifteenth Amendment,* 97–109; Fishel, "The Negro in Northern Politics," 472–73.

23. Public notice of the "Executive Committee of True Democracy" in South Carolina to poll workers in the 1890 state elections, William H. Lyles Papers, USC; Smalls, "Election Methods in the South," 593–600; Pryor, "The Sufficiency of the New Amendments," 266–76; Seiders, "The Race Problem: A Criticism of Senator Hampton's Paper," 633–35; Cooley, *A Treatise on the Constitutional Limitations Which Rest upon the Legislative Power of the States of the American Union,* 753–58, 767–70, 786.

24. *CR* 21: 7, 6594; *BH,* 25 January 1890; Hampton, "The Race Problem," 132–33; Albion Tourgee to W. P. Nixon, 29 August 1889, cited in Crofts, "The Blair Bill and the Election Bill," 235; Filler, ed., *Democrats and Republicans,* 171; Brotz, ed., *African-American Social and Political Thought,* 352.

25. Representative Thomas R. Stockdale of Mississippi, quoted in *CR* 21: Appendix, 570.

26. DeSantis, *Republicans Face the Southern Question,* 216–17. For a good synopsis of this subject, see the historiographical essays in Grob and Billias, eds., *Interpretations of American History,* vol. I, 415–31, and vol. II, 116–42.

27. James Callaway to Morgan, 6 January 1890, Reel 2, John Tyler Morgan Papers, LC.

28. *CR* 22: 2, 1837.

29. Hart, "Do the People Wish Reform?" 47–56; Godkin, "The Republican Party and the Negro," 246–57; Edmunds, "Corrupt Political Methods," 349–60; Carlisle, "The Republican Program," 585–96; Hoadly, "Methods of Ballot Reform," 623–33; Bayard, "The Degredation of Our Politics," 117–32; "The Next Electoral Vote," *Harper's Weekly,* cited in *PO* 10 (1890), 4; Filler, ed., *Democrats and Republicans,* iii–iv. The issue of Social Darwinism as it touched American race relations in and around 1890 is discussed at length in chapter 9 of this study.

30. Miscellaneous clippings, Container 191, Thomas F. Bayard Papers, LC; *MAA,* 23, 24, and 26 November 1890; Sherman, *Recollections of Forty Years in the House, Senate, and Cabinet,* 1051–60; Foraker, *I Would Live it Again,* 82–83, 106; Garraty, *The New Commonwealth,* 294, 303–4.

31. Hamm, "The Art of Gerrymandering," 538–51. In 1872, the Mississippi legislature, under the leadership of black Republican John R. Lynch, gerrymandered the state to the advantage of the GOP, which contributed a small part to the antagonism of the races and parties in the state during Reconstruction. See Seip, *The South Returns to Congress,* 103.

32. Representative Asher G. Carruth of Kentucky quoted in *CR* 21: 7, 6859.

It should be pointed out that gerrymandering of state legislative districts sometimes occurred, and since state legislatures still chose U.S. senators in 1890, such redistricting could indirectly affect the composition of the nation's highest-ranking legislative body.

33. Hamm, " The Art of Gerrymandering," quote 550; *Nation* 49 (1889): 487; Rhodes, *History of the United States,* 359; Sievers, *Benjamin Harrison,* 175.

34. Hampton, "The Race Problem," 132–38; Matthews, *Legislative and Judicial History of the Fifteenth Amendment,* 17, 51, 57–74.

35. *CR* 22: 2, 1509.

36. Blackburn, "The Republican Platform," 10–18.

37. Carlisle, "Republican Promise and Performance," 243–54; Platt, *Autobiography of Thomas Collier Platt,* 210–11; Lynch, *Grover Cleveland,* 278–79; Faulkner, *Politics, Reform, and Expansion,* 94.

38. *CR* 21: 1, 450–58; Miscellaneous documents, Folder 132, Box 17, Henderson Papers, UNC; *Charleston News and Courier,* 9 May 1890; Filler, ed., *Democrats and Republicans,* 144–45, 165, 180.

39. *CR* 21: 11, 10781. Indiana, New York, and Mississippi were not the only states where Republicans were caught tampering with the electoral process. In 1889, a Republican named H. J. Hjelm was convicted of registering Republican voters illegally in Colorado. See *RMN,* 3 December 1889.

40. Bancroft, ed., *Papers of Carl Schurz,* vol. V, 79. Schurz is known also for being the first German American elected to the U. S. Senate and to serve in a presidential cabinet. See Kraus, *Immigration,* 61.

41. *New York World* and *Philadelphia Inquirer,* 17 February 1891, and *New York Herald,* undated, all quoted in *PO* 10 (1891): 416.

42. Quote, *Cleveland Plain Dealer,* 29 June 1890, cited in *PO* 10 (1891): 416; Kehl, *Boss Rule in the Gilded Age,* xiv–xvi, 104–7, 126–27, 148. It should be pointed out that contemporary critics gave Quay far too much credit for being a mastermind of manipulation of party leaders. He actually owned neither Harrison nor Reed, because neither man deferred to anyone else in the party except on rare, isolated occasions. It may have appeared to be as critics charged because the interests of all three men neatly coincided on several important issues.

43. Shurter, ed., *The Complete Orations and Speeches of Henry W. Grady,* v, 2; Nixon, *Henry W. Grady,* 6, 242–43; Gaston, *The New South Creed,* 17–18.

44. *Independent* 42 (1890): 7; Nixon, *Henry W. Grady,* 242–43, 250–51.

45. Harris, *Life of Henry W. Grady,* 623; Nixon, *Henry W. Grady,* 194–95, 231–34, 277, 323–30.

46. *Independent* 42 (1890): 7; Davis, *Henry Grady's New South,* 4; Nixon, *Henry W. Grady,* 290–98, 314–15, 337.

47. Keatley, "A New Race Problem," 207–11; Bancroft, ed., *Papers of Carl Schurz,* vol. V, 71–72; Keller, *Affairs of State,* 523; Nolen, *The Negro's Image,* 76; DeSantis, *Republicans Face the Southern Question,* 191.

48. Harrison's First Annual Message to Congress, 3 December 1889, cited in

CR 21: 1, 84–91; DeSantis, *Republicans Face the Southern Question*, 190; Robinson, *Thomas B. Reed*, 236–37.

Chapter 4. The Very Insanity of Democracy

Epigraphs. CR 21: Appendix, 429; Ibid., 401; *BD*, 1626–27.

1. *CR* 21: 1, 699–702; Chandler, "Our Southern Masters," 508–20; idem, "National Control of Elections," 715–18; Richardson, *William E. Chandler*, 390–91, 395–96, 412; DeSantis, *Republicans Face the Southern Question*, 205–6; Crofts, "The Blair Bill and the Election Bill," 230–36. For the Democratic point of view of this new Republican agitation, see Colquitt, "Is the Negro Vote Supressed?," 268–78.

2. J. E. Bruce to Chandler, 1 December 1890, Book 82, Chandler Papers, LC, quote. Other letters concerning the race problem in 1890 are scattered throughout the Chandler papers.

3. Tourgee, "Shall White Minorities Rule?" 143–55; idem, "The Right to Vote," 78–92; *Nation* 40 (1890): 1; Olsen, *Carpetbagger's Crusade*, 271–301, 305–6; Gross, *Albion W. Tourgee*, 13–15; Crofts, "The Blair Bill and the Election Bill," 250–59.

4. Albion Tourgee to W. P. Nixon, 29 August 1889, quoted in Crofts, "The Blair Bill and the Election Bill, 235.

5. Halstead, "The Torrid Zone of Our Politics," 634–43; Cable, "A Simpler Southern Question," 392–403; Morgan, "Shall Negro Majorities Rule?" 586–99; Takiki, *Iron Cages*, 206; Brotz, ed., *African-American Social and Political Thought*, 312.

6. In his second annual address, which came in the midst of the Federal Elections Bill fight in Congress, Harrison made no mention at all of the southern race problem. Sinkler, *The Racial Attitudes of American Presidents*, 242–88.

7. John Coit Spooner: to F. D. Jordan, 20 April 1890, to Richard B. Goss, 20 April 1890, to H. W. Morley, 23 April 1890, to Henry Tarrant, 18 June 1890, and to Albion Tourgee, 25 June 1890, container 109, John Coit Spooner Papers, LC; "The Southern Question," pamphlet by Theo Kaiandri, 1890 Correspondence, Box 783, Breckinridge Family Papers, LC, 13; Fowler, *John Coit Spooner*, 135–38; Hoar, *Autobiography of Seventy Years, Vol. II*, 150–65.

8. *Louisville Courier–Journal*, 11 December 1890, quoted in *LD* 2 (1890–1891): 217.

9. *CR* 21: 4, 3760; Miscellaneous clippings, Scrapbooks One and Two, Pugh Papers, AU.

10. Chandler, "National Control of Elections," 714.

11. Morgan, "Federal Control of Elections," 24–25.

12. *CR* 21: 1, 697–98; *Boston Post*, 26 April 1890, cited in *LD* 1 (1890): 16.

13. Watterson, "The South and Its Colored Citizens," 113–16.

14. Godkin, "The Republican Party and the Negro," 255.

15. *Nation* 49 (1889): 185; B. J. Sage, "Congressional Power on Education

and Elections," *Belford's Magazine* (May 1890), cited in *LD* 1 (1890): 3–4; DeSantis, *Republicans Face the Southern Question,* 200; Socolofsky and Spetter, *The Presidency of Benjamin Harrison,* 62–63.

16. Field, *Bright Skies,* 120–125. For the views of other religious leaders who agreed, see Hearne, "The Race Problem—The Situation," 690–705.

17. Levermore, "Impressions of a Yankee Visitor in the South," 311–19.

18. Storey, *Politics as a Duty and as a Career,* 5.

19. Chamberlain, "The Race Problem at the South," 607–27.

20. George Washington Campbell to Booker T. Washington, 16 July 1890, cited in Harlan, ed., *The Booker T. Washington Papers,* vol. III, 67.

21. *CR* 21: Appendix, 681–701.

22. Ibid.: 7, 6505–7, 6763–68; *BD,* 695, 1636.

23. Ibid: 7, 6537–40.

24. Lodge and Redmond, eds., *Selections from the Correspondence of Theodore Roosevelt and Henry Cabot Lodge, 1884–1918,* vol. I, passim; Groves, *Henry Cabot Lodge,* 3, 29; Garraty, *Henry Cabot Lodge,* 3, 4, 124; Viorst, *Fall from Grace,* 134; Schriftgeisser, *The Gentleman from Massachusetts,* 105; Barnes, *John G. Carlisle,* 188.

25. *CR* 21: 7, 6540–44; *MAA,* 1 December 1890; *LA,* 6 December 1890; Garraty, *Henry Cabot Lodge,* vii, 124; Schriftgeisser, *The Gentleman from Massachusetts,* 114–15, 170; Viorst, *Fall from Grace,* 134, Towne, *Senator William J. Stone,* 13–14.

26. *CR* 21: 7, 6540–43, quote 6540.

27. Ibid., 6543.

28. Ibid., 6543–44.

29. Ibid., 6548; U. S. Constitution, Article 1, Section 4, Paragraph 1; *BD,* 1169.

30. *CR* 21: 7, 6548–52.

31. Ibid., 6548–49.

32. Ibid., 6548–52.

33. Ibid., 6548–49.

34. Ibid., 6553.

35. Ibid., 6552.

36. Ibid., 6553–54.

37. For a sampling of some of the bloody-shirt speeches, see *CR* 21: 7, 6591–92, 6601–3, 6684–86. Many others are scattered throughout the Lodge bill debate.

38. For a sampling of some of the most engaging of these speeches, see *CR* 21: 7, 6671–72, 6674–77, 6693–95, 6703–5, 6728–29, 6763–68, 6811, 6853, 6881, 6895, 6933–34; *CR* 21: Appendix, 567–70.

39. *CR* 21: 7, 6560–66; *BD,* 1958, 1988.

40. *CR* 21: 7, 6679; *BD,* 856.

41. *CR* 21: 7, 6554–60.

42. Ibid., 6607–15; *BD,* 1301.

43. *CR* 21: 7, 6693–95; *BD*, 1092.

44. *CR* 21: 7, 6689–91; Powell, ed., *Dictionary of North Carolina Biography*, vol. II, 173; *BD*, 978.

45. *CR* 21: 7, 6773; *BD*, 808.

46. *CR* 21: 7, 6814–15; *BD*, 1024.

47. *CR* 21: 7, 6597–98; *BD*, 833.

48. *CR* 21: 7, 6795; *BD*, 1481, 2013.

49. *CR* 21: 7, 6603–7, 6773, quotes 6603, 6773; *BD*, 773, 1981.

50. *CR* 21: 7, 6674–75; *BD*, 1443.

51. *CR* 21: 7, 6682; *BD*, 856.

52. *CR* 21: Appendix, 440–42, 710–14; *BD*, 1556, 2097.

53. *CR* 21: Appendix, 570.

54. Ibid.: 7, 6728–29.

55. Tindall, *The Disruption of the Solid South*, 15.

56. Herbert, *Why the Solid South?*, 442.

57. *CR* 21: 7, 6935–41, 6982.

58. Ibid.: 9, 8232–35.

59. Ibid., 8842–47, 8355, 8383–84.

60. *The Miscellaneous Documents of the Senate of the United States for the First Session of the Fifty-first Congress*, nos. 184, 192, 204, 207, 214, 218, 219, and 221; *CR* 21: 9, 8848–49; Lambert, *Arthur Pue Gorman*, 150–51; Hirshson, *Farewell to the Bloody Shirt*, 226; Barrows, *William M. Evarts*, 459; Socolofsky and Spetter, *The Presidency of Benjamin Harrison*, 63.

61. *New York Independent*, 21 August 1890, quoted in *LD* 1 (1890): 524–25.

62. Quoted in the *Washington Post*, 21 October 1890, cited in Blassingame and McKivigan, eds., *The Frederick Douglass Papers, Series One, Vol. 5*, 455.

Chapter 5. Judging the Insanity

Epigraphs. "Force versus the Ballot," *Kansas City Journal*, quoted in *PO* 10 (1890): 153; "Ballots versus the Bayonet," *New York Press*, quoted in *PO* 10: 129–30.

1. Olsen, *Carpetbagger's Crusade*, 305–6.

2. Hirshson, *Farewell to the Bloody Shirt*, 224–25.

3. Bancroft, ed., *Papers of Carl Schurz*, vol. V, 71, 75; Benjamin Harrison admitted as much in an 1888 campaign speech, when he said, "The tariff question would be settled already if the six million black laborers in the South had their due representation. . . ." See Wallace and Townsend, *Lives of Harrison and Morton*, 307.

4. Quoted in Oldham, "The Great Political Upheaval at the South," 632.

5. Miscellaneous documents, Farmers' State Alliance (of South Carolina) Papers, USC; Miscellaneous clippings, Mrs. W. W. Ball Scrapbooks, Vols. I–III, USC; Crofts, "The Blair Bill and the Election Bill," 277.

6. *Baltimore American*, 30 June 1890, quoted in *LD* 1 (1890): 16.

7. *Cincinnati Western Christian Advocate*, 30 July 1890, quoted in *LD* 1 (1890): 442.

8. *New York Herald*, 27 and 30 June 1890, quoted in *LD* 1 (1890): 16.

9. *Natchez Daily Democrat*, 1 and 5 July 1890.

10. *Boston Pilot*, 19 July 1890, quoted in *LD* 1 (1890): 384.

11. *AC*, 20 July 1890; quote, 27 July 1890, quoted in *LD* 1 (1890): 384.

12. *Detroit Tribune*, 24 July 1890, and *Boston Pilot*, 26 July 1890, cited in *LD* 1 (1890): 384–85.

13. *MAA*, 26 July 1890.

14. *Detroit Journal*, 24 July 1890, quoted in *LD* 1 (1890): 385.

15. *SMN*, 13, 22, 24, and 29 July 1890.

16. Quoted in Crofts, "The Blair Bill and the Election Bill," 320.

17. *CR* 22: 1, 728. The most thorough treatment of the last days of Reconstruction in Mississippi is Harris's, *The Day of the Carpetbagger*; see particularly pages 602–643. For more information on the Revolution of 1875 in Mississippi, see Wharton, *The Negro in Mississippi*, 170–208. See also the following articles: Brough, "The Clinton Riot," 53–63; McNeilly, "Climax and Collapse of Reconstruction in Mississippi, 1874–1896," 283–474; Rowland, "The Rise and Fall of Negro Rule in Mississippi," 189–99; Edwards, "'Reconstructing' Reconstruction: Changing Historical Paradigms in Mississippi," 165–80; and Ellam, "The Overthrow of Reconstruction in Mississippi," 175–202.

18. Woodward, *The Strange Career of Jim Crow*, 82–83.

19. Logan, *The Negro in American Life and Thought*, 198.

20. *Jackson New Mississippian*, 12 February and 25 June 1890; McNeilly, "War and Reconstruction in Mississippi, 1863–1890," 531–32; Coleman, "The Origin of the Constitution of 1890," 76; Key, *Southern Politics in State and Nation*, 537; Nolen, *The Negro's Image*, 85.

21. Quoted in *Inaugural Addresses of the Governors of Mississippi, 1890–1980*, 5.

22. *JCL*, 24 January 1889; ibid., 6, 14, and 21 November 1889; ibid., 9 January 1890; Miscellaneous documents, Hemphill Scrapbook, 1889–1890, DU; McNeilly, "History of the Measures Submitted to the Committee on the Elective Franchise, Apportionment, and Election in the Constitutional Convention of 1890," 129–40; Calhoon, "Causes and Events That Led to the Calling of the Constitutional Convention of 1890," 105–110.

23. Tourgee, "Shall White Minorities Rule?" 149. Andrew White, former president of Cornell University, claimed that Methodist Bishop Atticus G. Haygood, president of Emory College in Atlanta, was actually the first to advocate literacy tests to solve the southern race problem, an opinion with which White agreed. He believed it would only disfranchise a majority of blacks temporarily because of the rapid advances being made in their educational opportunities. See Barrows, ed., *Mohonk Conference on the Negro Question*, 120.

24. Morgan, "Shall Negro Majorities Rule?" 596–97; see also *Constitution of the Commonwealth of Massachusetts*, 20th Amendment.

244 Notes to Pages 114–119

25. Morgan and Ingalls, Introduction to Tocqueville, *Democracy in America*.

26. Ibid. In his rambling pontification on who should be allowed to vote, the Alabama sage essentially set forth the theory behind the zeitgeist: that great political and social leaders do not create and sustain national moods or the spirit of an age, the masses do. In speaking of axiomatic knowledge about American race relations, Morgan formed another unlikely alliance, this time with southern egalitarian writer George Washington Cable. Despite his unquestionable humanitarianism toward blacks, Cable considered the Founding Fathers to have understood "an axiom" and to have possessed "a positive, intuitive knowledge" and "a God-given instinct, nobler than reason" about the place of African Americans in the national polity. They were enslaved and kept as slaves, he said, because they were inferior. (See Wynes, *Forgotten Voices*, 18.) Now, said Morgan, they were stuck in something like second-class citizenship for the same reason.

27. *CR* 21: 1, 697–98.

28. *Jackson New Mississippian*, 6 December 1887; *JCL*, 9 January 1890; Hampton, "What Negro Supremacy Means," 384; Kousser, *The Shaping of Southern Politics*, 140; James P. Coleman, "The Mississippi Constitution of 1890 and the Final Decade of the Nineteenth Century," in McLemore and Pitts, eds., *A History of Mississippi*, vol. II, 6.

29. *CR* 21: 3, 2154, quote; Johnston, "The Public Services of Senator James Z. George," 212.

30. *CR* 21: 3, 2155–57.

31. *Kansas City Tribune*, 23 March 1890, Scrapbook, Box 3, J. Z. George Papers, MDAH.

32. Garraty, *Henry Cabot Lodge*, 119.

33. Quoted in *CR* 21: 7, 6861; *BD*, 919.

34. *Natchez Daily Democrat*, 10 and 15 July 1890; *Vicksburg Herald*, 3 October 1890, cited in *PO* 10 (1890): 5. See also comments from the *Cleveland Leader*, cited in ibid.

35. John Steele Henderson to Mrs. John Steele Henderson, 15 December 1890, Folder 131, Box 17, Henderson Papers, UNC; Thompson, "Suffrage in Mississippi," 25–49; McNeilly, "History of the Measures Submitted to the Committee on the Elective Franchise," 134–36; Callcott, *The Negro in Maryland Politics, 1870–1912*, 160–61.

36. Quote, Cooley, *A Treatise on the Constitutional Limitations Which Rest upon the Legislative Power of the States of the American Union*, 789–90; see also Macy, *Our Government*, 86.

37. For more information on the Mississippi constitution of 1890, the best and most recent assessment is Cresswell, *Multi-Party Politics in Mississippi, 1877–1902*.

38. Burnham, *Presidential Ballots, 1836–1892*, 140–56.

39. Cromwell, "The Challenge of the Disfranchised: A Plea for the Enforce-

ment of the 15th Amendment," in *The American Negro Academy Occasional Papers, 1–22*, 5–6. See also Lynch, *The Facts of Reconstruction*, 100–103.

40. Lodge and Powderly, "The Federal Election Bill," 256–73, quotes 259–60. The governor of Ohio had, in fact, threatened to resist the enforcement of the elections bill in the Buckeye State, according to the *Chicago Herald*, 30 July 1890, cited in *LD* 1 (1890): 443.

41. Lodge and Powderly, "The Federal Election Bill," 271–72.

42. Shaffer, "A Southern Republican on the Lodge Bill," 601–9, quotes passim.

43. Dyer, *"Fightin' Joe" Wheeler*, 309.

44. *CR* 21: 11, 10548–51, quotes 10550, 10551.

45. Alice Bodington, "The Importance of the Race Question and Its Bearing on 'The Negro Question,'" *Westminister Review* (London), October 1890, quoted in *LD* 2 (1890): 34.

46. Hedges, ed., *Speeches of Benjamin Harrison*, 285; Hoar, *Autobiography of Seventy Years*, vol. II, 150–65.

47. McKinley Jr., et al., "What Congress Has Done," 513–32, quotes 530. This article contained both Republican and Democratic appraisals of the first session of the Reed House; pages 524–32 give the Democratic point of view. See also John S. Henderson to Mrs. John S. Henderson, 7 September 1890, Folder 130, Box 17, Henderson Papers, UNC; and Carlisle, "The Recent Election," 641–49.

48. First quote, *MAA*, 14 November 1890; second quote, J. Mazyk to William Mazyk, 16 November 1890, Mazyk Family Papers, USC.

49. See as examples *SMN*, 3 October 1890; *New Orleans Times–Democrat, New York World, Providence Journal*, and *Baltimore Sun*, all cited in *PO* 10 (1891): 539.

50. *CR* 21: 10, 10381–82. Evidently, the House later decided to reverse its decision, because Kennedy's speech does appear in the *Record* today. See also "To Republican Managers Everywhere," Book 82, Chandler Papers, LC; *BD*, 1301; and Kehl, *Boss Rule in the Gilded Age*, 147–48.

51. John S. Henderson to Mrs. John S. Henderson, 3 December 1890, Folder 130, Box 17, Henderson Papers, UNC; *MAA*, 13, 24, and 29 November 1890; Eckert, *John Brown Gordon*, 294–96, 303.

52. *CR* 22: 1, 413.

53. Carlisle, "The Recent Election," 646–47, quote; Nevins, ed., *Letters of Grover Cleveland*, 222.

54. *CR* 22: 1, 201, quotes 1331–32; Wang, *The Trial of Democracy*, 236.

55. Hoar, *Autobiography of Seventy Years*, vol. II, 152, 156, 157, quotes; Fowler, *John Coit Spooner*, 135–38.

56. *CR* 21: 9, 8842, 8846, quotes; Hoar, *Autobiography of Seventy Years*, vol. II, 150–65; Barrows, *William M. Evarts*, 459.

57. *Cleveland Gazette*, 22 November 1890, quoted in Crofts, "The Blair Bill and the Election Bill," 294. See also "The Situation and Demands of the Colored American," Langston Papers, LC; *Burlington* (Iowa) *Hawk Eye*, 9 August 1890, cited in *LD* 1 (1890): 470; and Wang, *The Trial of Democracy*, 236, 245.

58. *MAA,* 3 December 1890.

59. *Philadelphia Times,* 15 December 1890, quoted in *LD* 1 (1890): 470.

60. Quoted in *MAA,* 24 November 1890.

61. *New York Mail and Express,* 22 December 1890, and *Louisville Courier-Journal,* 11 December 1890, cited in *LD* 2 (1890–1891): 217; Fowler, *John Coit Spooner,* 154–57.

62. *MAA,* 4 December 1890; Lambert, *Arthur Pue Gorman,* 4, 10–11, 13, 77, 81, 153.

63. Kent, *The Democratic Party,* 306; Lambert, *Arthur Pue Gorman,* 145–48.

64. McElroy, *Levi Parsons Morton,* vii, 4, 28, 46, 130, 165; Hatch, *History of the Vice-Presidency,* 316–22.

Chapter 6. The Stormy and Turbulent Sea of Democratic Freedom

Epigraphs. CR 22: 1, 214; Ibid., 365.

1. Alton, *Among the Law-Makers,* 171–73, 225–34; Burdette, *Filibustering,* 52–57, 113; Haynes, *The Senate of the United States,* 397–99.

2. Matthews, *U.S. Senators and Their Words,* 92, 97–99; Alton, *Among the Law-Makers,* 279–83; Baker, *The Senate of the United States,* 3–4, 17, 43; 72–73, 102–3; Lambert, *Arthur Pue Gorman,* 155–67; Crofts, "The Blair Bill and the Election Bill," 31. In *CR* 22: 1, 883–85, see the comments of Republican Senator Eugene Hale of Maine on how "instructive" the early Democratic speeches on the bill were to him.

3. *CR* 22: 1, 205, 519, 584, 586, 633; John W. Daniel to Richard Krunes, 30 November 1891, John W. Daniel Papers, DU.

4. Reed, "Obstruction in the National House," 424.

5. Hoar, "The Senate," 620.

6. *New York Herald,* 8 February 1891, quoted in vol. 17, Gorman Scrapbooks, UNC; *CR* 22: 1, 1–26, 202–3, 297–98; *MAA,* 3 December 1890; Lambert, *Arthur Pue Gorman,* 153–54.

7. *CR* 22: 1, 50; Turpie, *Sketches of My Own Times,* 282–86.

8. *CR* 22: 1, 50.

9. Ibid., 50–54.

10. Ibid., 774–80, quotes 774, 778, 780; Miscellaneous clippings, Daniel W. Voorhees Scrapbook, LC; Kenworthy, *The Tall Sycamore of the Wabash,* 67, 102.

11. *CR* 22: 1, 76–77, quotes passim; Boyd, *Men and Issues of '92,* 301; Marks, *Alabama Past Leaders,* 239.

12. *CR* 22: 1, 114–28, quotes 114, 124; Thomas, ed. *Universal Pronouncing Dictionary of Biography and Mythology,* 1162.

13. *CR* 22: 1, 171–73, quotes 205, 208. Gray's actual quote used the word "people" as a verb meaning to populate.

14. Ibid., 209–17, quote 217; *BD,* 1299.

15. *CR* 22: 1, 820–24, 835–40, quote 824; *BD*, 1483.

16. *CR* 22: 1, 241–42; Joe Seagrave, "James Henderson Berry," in Donovan and Gatewood Jr., eds., *The Governors of Arkansas*, 73–78.

17. *CR* 22: 2, 1459. This argument, of course, contradicted the *Nation*'s earlier assertion that supervising elections was a thankless job that few upstanding citizens would want. See *Nation* 49 (1889): 185.

18. *CR* 22: 1, 245–55, quote 255; Thomas E. Gay Jr., "Daniel, John Warner," in Garraty and Carnes, eds., *American National Biography*, 499. For more on the Ocala Platform, see McMath, *American Populism*, 139–42, 147.

19. *CR* 22: 1, 359.

20. Ibid., 510.

21. Ibid., 330–34, quotes passim.

22. Ibid., 512–14, 586, quotes, 512, 514; Louis L. Gould, "Frye, William P.," in Garraty and Carnes, eds., *American National Biography*, 531–32.

23. *CR* 22: 1, 279–295, quote 293. For more insight on the question of constitutional interpretations in 1890, see Jameson, "National Sovereignty," 193–213.

24. *CR* 22: 1, 586, 805, quote 586.

25. Miscellaneous clippings, Box 3, George Scrapbooks, MDAH.

26. *New York Herald*, 8 February 1891, cited in vol. 17, Gorman Scrapbooks, UNC, 8.

27. *CR* 22: 1, 320–21; ibid.: 2, 1419–31.

28. Ibid.: 1, 325–29, quotes 325, 329; Leonard Schlup, "Wilson, James Falconer," in Garraty and Carnes, eds., *American National Biography*, 590–91. On the Credit Mobilier scandal, see White, *The Republican Era*, 367–68, and Summers, *The Gilded Age*, 77; on the Garrisonian view of the Constitution, see Thomas, ed., *Slavery Attacked*, 115–19.

29. *CR* 22: 1, 360–65, 470, 520–29, 558–75, 635–36, 676; *BD*, 919; Boyd, *Men and Issues of '92*, 135.

30. *CR* 22: 1, 245–55; 321–24; McMath, *American Populism*, 139–47.

31. *CR* 22: 1, 324. The Montgomery article, "The Remarkable Address," appears in the 23 September 1890 edition of the *New York World*. Montgomery's views reflected the accommodationist mentality that Booker T. Washington would later make famous. The rationale for this view was simply that southern blacks stood a better chance of living in peace if they did not agitate for their civil rights but rather focused on economic advancement through self-help. On the argument that mulattoes had greater intelligence than pure blacks, see Bruce, *The Plantation Negro as a Free Man*, 244; and McKinley, *An Appeal to Pharoah* [sic], 100.

32. *CR* 22: 1, 367–69, quotes 367, 369; Edmund Cary Walthall Papers, DU; Garner, "The Public Services of E. C. Walthall," 239–53.

33. *CR* 22: 1, 371–72. Bowles, like Montgomery, held the accommodationist point of view. See Mosley, Sr., *The Negro in Mississippi History*, 65.

34. *CR* 22: 1, 470.

35. Ibid., 583.

36. Ibid., 365–66, *BD*, 634.

37. *CR* 22: 1, 456; Miscellaneous documents, Alfred H. Colquitt Papers, DU; Miscellaneous clippings, Box one, Alfred H. Colquitt Scrapbooks, Hargrett Rare Book and Manuscript Library, University of Georgia; Hesseltine and Gara, "Georgia's Confederate Leaders after Appomattox," 10–11.

38. *CR* 22: 1, 635, 636, 676; Marshall, *A Life of William B. Bate*, 53–54; Phillips, *The Governors of Tennessee*, 101–4. This charge of certain civil rights activists earning their livelihoods by agitating the race problem can, of course, still be heard today coming from social conservatives. For more discussion of "convention Negroes," see Meier, *Negro Thought in America, 1880–1915*, 71.

39. *CR* 22: 1, 635, 675.

40. Ibid., 676.

41. Elliott, *Servant of Power*, ix, 8, 46, 55–60, quote 56; Boyd, *Men and Issues of '92*, 345. It should be noted that Stewart's version of the Fifteenth Amendment toned down the language of the Radicals, leaving the wording brief and vague, which eventually helped contribute to the southern states getting away with the disfranchisement of black voters.

42. Elliott, *Servant of Power*, 129–30.

43. *CR* 22:1, 678.

44. Ibid., 678–84.

Chapter 7. Showdown on Capitol Hill

Epigraphs. CR 22: 1, 511; Ibid., 880.

1. Cullom, *Fifty Years of Public* Service, 210–11, 217.

2. *New York Herald*, 8 February 1891, cited in vol. 17, Gorman Scrapbooks, UNC. The public disdain for the Senate's pomposity and aloofness during the Gilded Age led in 1913 to a Progressive Era reform of how senators are chosen. The Seventeenth Amendment to the Constitution replaced the tradition of state legislatures choosing senators with the direct election of senators by the people. For insight on how this change affected the nation's premier lawmaking body, see Baker, *The Senate of the United States*, 214–15.

3. Stern, *Republican Heyday*, 14; Rothman, *Politics and Power*, 2–3, 7–8; Haynes, *The Senate of the United States*, vii; Current, *Pine Logs and Politics*, 195–96.

4. Baker, *The Senate of the United States*, 203. Henry Blair, senior Republican senator of New Hampshire, epitomized this class of statesmen. He favored having the *Congressional Record*, which he called "our glorious little paper that we publish ourselves"—and which was filled with his speeches—distributed to every home in America, where it should occupy a place at the hearth beside the family Bible. See *CR* 21: 2, 1489. Blair's protracted soliloquies routinely emptied the Senate chamber, but he felt no compunction about it. Blair cared as much about his speeches affecting the future course of American history as he did about their affecting the fate of any bill under consideration. He also, like many of his Senate

colleagues, cared a great deal about his place in history. See John S. Henderson to Mrs. John S. Henderson, 2 September 1890, Folder 130, Box 17, Henderson Papers, UNC; *CR* 22: 1, 320, 818. Not all senators were so self-absorbed, however, and not all possessed the gift of gab. Some believed their speeches in the Senate to be mainly wastes of time. Justin Morrill, senior Republican senator of Vermont, for instance, took the self-deprecating approach, saying, "I never speak in the Senate without feeling afterward that I ought to have done better and am only comforted by the reflection that such contributions there all have an unmortal [*sic*] oblivion in the Congressional Record, read by nobody, but, stored away voluminously, will there abide until the crack of doom." See Parker, *Justin Smith Morrill,* 329. Juxtapose Morrill's philosophy with that of his southern Democratic colleague, John Tyler Morgan of Alabama, who believed that "Senators will find themselves mistaken if they think that what we say will not be read. . . . We are making history here, and I want it to be correct, true, and honest." See *CR* 22: 1, 320, 818. Some, such as Philetus Sawyer of Wisconsin preferred not to speak at all in the Senate, but to work quietly behind the scenes to accomplish his goals. His biographer notes that, "On the pages of the *Congressional Record* he left no impassioned oratory—in fact, he left no oratory at all—but he introduced and got passed more bills than any other senator of his time, and probably more than any other senator or congressman of any time." See Current, *Pine Logs and Politics,* 4, 199.

5. Cullom, *Fifty Years of Public Service,* 211.

6. Quoted in Parker, *Justin Smith Morrill,* 235.

7. *CR* 22: 1, 713–30, quotes 713, 716, 722, 728.

8. *New York Mail and Express,* 22 December 1890, cited in *LD* 2 (1890–1891): 244.

9. *CR* 22: 1, 730–34, 805–20, 891–94; ibid.: Appendix, 49–96; Garner, "Senatorial Career of J. Z. George," 256; *BD,* 730; Boyd, *Men and Issues of '92,* 74.

10. *CR* 22: 1, 820–24, 835–40, 867–72, 894–98.

11. Ibid., 867, 894–95; *Report of the United States Senate Committee to Inquire into Alleged Frauds and Violence in the Elections of 1878,* passim; Ellis, *Henry Moore Teller,* 117–18.

12. *CR* 22: 1, 873; *CR* 22: 2, 1447, 1463; Ellis, *Henry Moore Teller,* 188.

13. *CR* 22: 1, 874–83, quote 883. See also John J. Davenport to William E. Chandler, 8 January 1891, Book 82, Chandler Papers, LC.

14. William A. Giles to William E. Chandler, 29 January 1891, Book 82, Chandler Papers, LC.

15. *BH,* 17 and 18 January 1891.

16. *CR* 22: 2, 1432–44; Miscellaneous documents, Faulkner Papers, DU; Burdette, *Filibustering,* 54–57.

17. *CR* 22: 2, 1403–12, quote 1412.

18. Ibid., 1452. The Senate heard the case of "the Dudley Affair" early in the first session of the Fifty-first Congress. See ibid.: 1, 450–57.

19. *CR* 22: 2, 1464–68.

20. Ibid., 1564; Miscellaneous documents, Isham G. Harris Papers, DU; *Woodville Republican,* 17 January 1891.

21. *CR* 22: 2, 1564–68; Burton, *John Sherman,* 1, 45, 304, 310.

22. *CR* 22: 2, 1651–61, quotes interspersed throughout.

23. Ibid., 1661–66.

24. Ibid., 1666–73.

25. Ibid., 1673–82, quotes interspersed throughout; Thomas C. Reynolds to Montgomery Blair, 29 December 1874, Thomas C. Reynolds Papers, MHS; James A. Kennerly to Sister, 8 August 1864, Kennerly College Papers, MHS; Hoar, "The Senate," 620.

26. *CR* 22: 2, 1682–96, quotes 1683, 1696.

27. Ibid., 1696–1704, quotes 1702–4.

28. Ibid., 1706–18, quotes 1715, 1717, 1718; *BD,* 1764.

29. *CR* 22: 2, 1725–31, quote 1725.

30. Ibid., 1734–38, quote 1734.

31. McElroy, *Levi Parsons Morton,* 204; Hatch, *History of the Vice-Presidency,* 325–26; Hirshon, *Farewell to the Bloody Shirt,* 235; Olsen, *Carpetbagger's Crusade,* 303.

Chapter 8. Silver, Sectionalism, Sioux Indians, and Sinophobia

Epigraphs. CR 22: 1, 455; Ibid.: 2, 1613.

1. *Philadelphia Inquirer,* 27 January 1891, quoted in *PO* 10 (1891): 390; *Philadelphia Press,* 27 January 1891, and *New York Tribune,* 28 January 1891, cited in *PO* 10 (1891): 389–90; Burdette, *Filibustering,* 6.

2. H. Bartlett, quoted in DeSantis, *Republicans Face the Southern Question,* 213.

3. Fowler, *John Coit Spooner,* 157–59, quote 157–58.

4. For opposing points of view, compare Wellborn, "The Influence of the Silver-Republican Senators, 1889–1891," 462–80, to Merrill, *Bourbon Leader,* 151; DeSantis, *Republicans Face the Southern Question,* 209–13; Fowler, *John Coit Spooner,* 157–58; Logan, *The Negro in American Life and Thought,* 64; and Summers, *The Gilded Age,* 39. It should be noted that conspiracy theories can make the reconstruction of history more engaging than it would otherwise be, which may also partly account for some historians' acceptance of the quid pro quo silver explanation.

5. *Coinage Laws of the United States, 1792–1894,* 436, 499; Frank Burkitt, "Wool Hat Defended," and "The State's Finances," Frank Burkitt Papers, MSU; George, "Demonetization of Silver," 3–65; Watson, *History of American Coinage,* 182, 190; Dorset, *The New Eldorado,* 319–20; Seip, *The South Returns to Congress,* 206–15; Fry, *John Tyler Morgan,* 60–61.

6. Southern Alliance and Knights of Labor, "St. Louis Demands, December

1889," in Tindall, ed., *A Populist Reader*, 76; Weinstein, *Prelude to Populism*, 331–34; Goodwyn, *Democratic Promise*, 27, 119.

7. Historian H. Wayne Morgan has posited a more plausible quid pro quo theory involving the Silverites, which has nothing to do with Democrats, southerners, or the Federal Elections Bill. He has shown that the Silverites were interested in cutting a deal with the eastern Republicans whereby they would agree to support the McKinley Tariff only in exchange for a free coinage bill. They got the Sherman Silver Purchase Bill, which was not a free coinage bill but rather a reasonable compromise, and the easterners got their tariff. See Morgan, "Western Silver and the Tariff of 1890," 118–28.

8. Binder, *Minority Rights, Majority Rule*, 186–88; Wellborn, "The Influence of the Silver-Republican Senators," 476; Elliott, *Servant of Power*, 126. Ironically, Aldrich actually opposed the Federal Elections Bill, despite his efforts to force it upon the Senate. It was he, not the Silverites, who hoped to get the bill out of the way as soon as possible and move on to economic issues. See Stephenson, *Nelson W. Aldrich*, 437–38.

9. The senators named were Stewart and Jones of Nevada, Quay and Cameron of Pennsylvania, and Stanford of California. See *RMN*, 7 January 1890.

10. Senate speeches, 14 May 1890 and 6 January 1892, Folder 33, Box 7, Teller Papers, UC; *RMN*, 4 December 1889, 7 January 1890, and 19 December 1890; Ellis, *Henry Moore Teller*, 197–201.

11. Elliott, *Servant of Power*, 126–27, 297. Although congressmen routinely take positions on many bills without having read those bills thoroughly, the importance of the Federal Elections Bill compared to many others should have demanded that it be read more carefully than usual.

12. Quote, *Baltimore* Sun, cited in *PO* 10 (1891): 539; *LA*, 6 December 1890; Clanton, *Populism*, 33–35; Blegen, *Minnesota*, 388–89; Connelly, *The Life of Preston B. Plumb*, 322–23; Williams, *Senator John James Ingalls*, 118–19; Sage, *William Boyd Allison*, 245; Dinnerstein, *Natives and Strangers*, 215.

13. Haynes, "The New Sectionalism," *Quarterly Journal of Economics* 10 (1896): 269–95, cited in Tindall, ed., *Populist Reader*, 171–73; Davidson, *The Attack on Leviathan*, 113; McMath, *American Populism*, 10; Connelly, *The Life of Preston B. Plumb*, 325. Although Populists generally referred to this section of the country that they believed antagonized agrarians as "the East," that section is called the Northeast throughout this study because southeastern states were not included in the Populist definition of "the East." In the us-and-them views of Populists, all states north of the Ohio and east of the Mississippi Rivers were "the East." The lines separating what constitutes agriculture and what constitutes industry are quite nebulous, as are the lines between what should and should not constitute "the Northeast." The working definitions in this study follow as closely as possible the contemporary Populist definitions, even though they appear dubious with historical hindsight.

14. Anonymous Speech to the South Carolina Farmers' Alliance, circa 1890,

Patrick Henry Adams Papers, USC; Bensel, *Sectionalism and American Political Development, 1880–1980*, 73–88; Palmer, *"Man Over Money,"* passim; Seip, *The South Returns to Congress*, 291; Woodward, *Origins of the New South*, 48.

15. E. M. G. to George H. McMaster, 1 March 1892, McMaster Papers, USC; Webb, *Divided We Stand*, 20–24, 33–58; Davidson, *The Attack on Leviathan*, 27. The sectional interpretation of western history has fallen into historiographical dubiety in modern times. The "new western history" de-emphasizes it, essentially considering it an archaic carryover from the Progressive age of historical writing, caused by veneration of the memory of the pioneer of western history, Frederick Jackson Turner, who first propounded the idea. See the collection of essays in Limerick, Milner, and Rankin, eds., *Trails: Toward a New Western History*, passim; and Jacobs, *On Turner's Trail*, passim.

16. Reese C. Gregg to George H. McMaster, 14 December 1891, McMaster Papers, USC; Representative Edward Lane of Illinois, cited in *CR* 21: Appendix, 18; "Imperiled by Plutocracy," Scrapbook, Container 236, Bayard Papers, LC; Destler, ed., *American Radicalism, 1865–1901*, passim; Bancroft, ed., *Papers of Carl Schurz*, vol. V, 40–45; Mezerik, *The Revolt of the South and West*, 61–75; Ellis, *Henry Moore Teller*, 196.

17. The only "people" to notice benefits under the amendment were not people at all, but corporations, which the U. S. Supreme Court held had the same rights as human beings. Northeasterners had one of their own to blame for this, New York's Reconstruction–Gilded Age Republican leader, Roscoe Conkling, who lobbied the Court incessantly for eighteen years to rule that corporations were "persons" under the Fourteenth amendment. In 1886 and again in 1889, the Court obliged. Thus, although the humanitarian element of the Republican Party had passed the amendment to help the freedmen gain equality under the law, the party's money men succeeded in convincing the highest court of law in the nation that corporations deserved the same rights as human beings under the law. The net result was that the Northeast gained enormous wealth through combinations, trusts, and high tariffs, at the expense of the other sections, which included the South's black population. A measure that was designed to help the black man thus actually ended up taking from him, at least indirectly. See Schwartz, *A Basic History of the U.S. Supreme Court*, 44–45. It should be noted, however, that corporate investment has, over the long course of time, made possible the host of inventions and economic developments that have raised the standard of living for all Americans. As with so many issues, contemporaries could not foresee how their progeny could benefit from the investments of businessmen whom they saw as robber barons. It is, of course, quite apparent with historical hindsight.

18. Under the leadership of the Harrison administration and the Billion Dollar Congress, six new western states entered the Union (Washington, Idaho, Wyoming, Montana, North Dakota, and South Dakota), all of which were expected to vote Republican. Two western territories had populations larger than Idaho but were not added at this time (Arizona and New Mexico), ostensibly be-

cause they would have voted Democrat. *SMN,* 6 July 1890; David Brady, et al., "Heterogeneous Parties and Political Organization: The U.S. Senate, 1880–1920," in Silbey, *The United States Congress in a Nation Transformed, 1896–1963,* 117–23; Gossett, *Race: The History of an Idea in America,* 267; Sherman, *Recollections of Forty Years in the House, Senate, and Cabinet,* 1085; Crofts, "The Blair Bill and the Election Bill," vii, 229.

19. *RMN,* 3 October and 1 December 1889.

20. Quote, *CR* 21: 5, 5025. See also *SMN,* 11 April 1890. The Sherman Silver-Purchase Act, also passed by this Congress, represented an attempt by northeastern congressmen to appease the future Populists, but most farmers considered it an inadequate consolation. See Hicks, *The Populist Revolt,* 80, 306–7.

21. For one perspective on how Populism helped bury the bloody shirt by its opposition to federal supervision of elections, see "The Negro Question" (1892), authored by Georgia's Populist leader Tom Watson, cited in Tindall, ed., *Populist Reader,* 125. The term "farewell to the bloody shirt" is, of course, borrowed from Stanley Hirshson's book by that name.

22. There was talk of removing the Indians of the Great Plains to reservations in New England, and there had even been discussion of forcing the removal of Native Americans from the mainland altogether and placing them on islands off the coast of California. See *RMN,* 17 December 1890; Frederic Cople Jaher, Introduction to *New Nation* [Boston Magazine] (31 January 1891), passim; Stiff, "Nash Walker's Answer to Jim Crow," 37; Mothershead, "Negro Rights in Colorado Territory (1859–1867)," 212–13, 223; Bodington, "The Importance of the Race Question and Its Bearing on 'The Negro Question,'" *Westminster Review* cited in *LD* 2 (1890): 34; Dinnerstein, et al., *Natives and Strangers,* 209–11; Keller, *Affairs of State,* 441, 448, 457; DeSantis, *The Shaping of Modern America,* 128; Dippie, *The Vanishing American,* 149, 377.

23. Wayne, "Negro Migration and Colonization in Colorado—1870–1930," 104–8, quote 108.

24. The issue of black suffrage and civil rights divided the people of California, Colorado, Kansas, Montana, Nevada, and Oregon from the beginning, and, even after passage of the Fourteenth and Fifteenth Amendments, unanimity of opinion never existed on the issue in the West. See Taylor, *In Search of the Racial Frontier,* 105–29; and Hill, "The Negro in the Early History of the West," 142.

25. No evidence suggests that southern and western senators ever actually hammered out an official deal making them allies on racial issues, but there is much reason to believe that they instinctively understood their mutual interests and tacitly followed those instincts in their congressional voting. *CR* 21: 3, 2980; Berkhofer Jr., *White Man's Indian,* 148–49; Gyory, *Closing the Gate,* 225–27; Dippie, *The Vanishing American,* 162; Elliott, *Servant of Power,* 64.

26. *CR* 21: 3, 2171, 2177, 2218; ibid.: 8, 7546, 7665. Henry L. Dawes was one of the most interesting, and often enigmatic, senators of his day. His name will forever be linked to the General Allotment Act of 1887 (also known as the Dawes

Severalty Act), which created the most sweeping set of reforms in federal policy toward the American Indians in more than a half-century. Yet, Dawes's priorities during the Harrison administration were not with Indian affairs or any other humanitarian concern but with tariff revision. See Dawes, "A Year of Republican Control," 24–35.

27. *RMN,* 18 December 1890.

28. See also *CR* 21: 2, 1877–88; ibid. 8, 7545–47; ibid. 22: 1, 45–47, 69; *LA,* 1 November 1890; Burnette, "The Indian Question and Its Solution," *Washington Star,* undated, cited in *PO* 10 (1890): 228–29. See also miscellaneous clippings in the same edition of *PO,* 341–44, 368–69, and 513; Brown, *Bury My Heart at Wounded Knee,* 415–45; Spicer, *A Short History of the Indians of the United States,* 91–92; Sinkler, *Racial Attitudes of the Presidents,* 280; Dinnerstein, et al., *Natives and Strangers,* 206–7; Dippie, *The Vanishing American,* 201–2; and Berkhofer, *White Man's Indian,* 166, 174–75.

29. *CR* 21: 8, 7659–68; ibid. 22: Appendix, 17–18; *Report of the Commissioner of Indian Affairs to the Secretary of the Interior, 1890,* iii–vi; Miscellaneous documents, Randall Lee Gibson Papers, DU; Dippie, *The Vanishing American,* 201–2. See also the original documents "The General Allotment Act of 1887," and "A Creek Observer on the Effects of Allotment," in Spicer, *A Short History of the Indians of the United States,* 200–204, 284.

30. *CR* 21: 11, 622–23.

31. Quote, *CR* 21: 3, 2171; ibid., 2218; ibid. 22: 3, 202–3; Dippie, *The Vanishing American,* 173–74; Curry, *The Southern States of the American Union,* 221.

32. Quote, *CR* 22: 1, 310–11. See also *RMN,* 3 October 1889, and 5 January 1890; and *BD,* 1974–75. Jackson's critically acclaimed book detailed the cruelties that the Indians had suffered under the U. S. government's policies for the first century of the nation's existence. See Rolle, ed., *Helen Hunt Jackson, A Century of Dishonor,* vii–xxii. Brown, *Bury My Heart at Wounded Knee,* is still considered one of the best modern treatments of the tragic history of Native Americans in the West from the 1850s to 1890.

33. Ellis, *Henry Moore Teller,* 19, 35, 44, quote 48.

34. *CR* 21: 3, 2331.

35. Farwell, "Why the Chinese Must Be Excluded," 196–203; Miles, "The Future of the Indian Question," 1–10; Kercheval, "Fair Play for the Indian," 250–53.

36. *CR* 21: 1, 522, 583; Farwell, "New Phases in the Chinese Problem," 181–91; Lyman, *Chinese Americans,* 55–56, 62, 66; Elliott, *Servant of Power,* 64–65, 138.

37. *CR* 21: 3, 2310, 2311; *BD,* 796, 1539–40.

38. Ibid.

39. "The Chinese on the Pacific Coast," *Kate Field's Washington,* cited in *PO* 10 (1890): 177–78.

40. Quoted in Elliott, *Servant of Power,* 137.

41. *CR* 21: 3, 3429. For a white southerner's interesting views on the duality

of character in the Chinese, see the diary of Mrs. Robert M. Wallace of Charleston, 17 July to 3 September 1883, Mrs. Robert M. Wallace Papers, USC.

42. "Harrison's Chinese Record," "Squarely on the Issue," and "Harrison's Letter of Acceptance," vol. 12, Gorman Scrapbooks, UNC, 44, 74.

43. *CR* 21: 11, 10472, 10555; Burton, *John Sherman*, 330.

44. *CR* 21: 3, 2979, quote; ibid.: 10, 9520; Dawes, "The Chinese Exclusion Bill," 526–39; Gyory, *Closing the Gate*, 225–27.

45. *CR* 21: 3, 2980.

46. James H. Berry, senator of Arkansas, *CR* 21: 3, 2981. See also speeches of Senators Edward Cary Walthall of Mississippi and George Vest of Missouri, *CR* 21: 1, 857–58; ibid. 22: 1, 362, 370.

47. Ibid. 21: 3, 2980.

48. Ibid. 22: 1, 573–74. Interestingly, to Dolph's argument that "The Chinaman is not a citizen," Matthew Butler of South Carolina, an unlikely humanitarian, retorted, "He is a human being, though." See ibid., 363. Likewise, to Dolph's claim that the federal government owed something to blacks, Richard Coke of Texas replied that blacks were already receiving it, for "While the Chinaman and the Indian . . . are being driven out and exterminated, the negro of the South is being civilized, educated, and Christianized." See ibid., 627.

49. Ibid., 572.

50. Ibid., 573, 574, quotes passim.

51. Ibid., 873.

52. Quoted in "Types and Traits of National Senators," vol. 17, Gorman Scrapbooks, UNC.

53. Miscellaneous Clippings, Scrapbook no. 2, John C. Bell Papers, UC. See also "The Day Lynch Law Prevailed," *Empire Magazine*, 28–33.

54. For just a few examples of the common racist mentality of the day, which were acceptable to most white Coloradans, note the stereotypes of blacks in: *Boulder County Herald Weekly*, 11 August 1886, 26 December 1888, and 14 August 1889; *Boulder County Herald*, 14 May 1890, and 20 September 1893; *Boulder News*, 24 November 1892; *Denver Daily News* 18 August 1893; and *RMN*, 3 September 1893.

55. On the old manifest destiny, see Hietala, *Manifest Design*, passim.

Chapter 9. The "Peculiar Situation"of African Americans and Ethnic Minorities in the United States

Epigraphs. Quoted in Snyder, "Prejudice Against the Negro," 221; *WBD*, 1380; *CR* 21: Appendix, 411.

1. Field, *Bright Skies*, 113.

2. Quoted in Barrows, ed., *Mohonk Conference on the Negro Question*, 53.

3. The acceptance of racism was, in fact, not merely a national phenomenon in the 1890s, but an international one. European intellectuals and academics placed their stamp of approval upon the idea of white supremacy, just as many

Americans did. The European nations that engaged in imperialist expansion in the late nineteenth century actually preceded the United States in accepting and propounding the ideology of the inherent inequality of the races. This European approval of racism helped establish racism as the zeitgeist of America's imperialist age, and it helped the former humanitarians of the Republican Party justify abandoning blacks in America, as this chapter shows. The topic of international racism lies mainly beyond the scope of this study, but for more information, see Betts, *The False Dawn,* passim.

4. Buckley and Howard quoted in Barrows, ed., *Mohonk Conference on the Negro Question,* 97 and 56.

5. Miscellaneous documents, Folder 259, Ransom Papers, UNC; Kraus, *Immigration,* 63–85; Summers, *The Gilded Age,* 105–6.

6. "Immigration," *Macon Telegraph,* quoted in *PO* 10 (1890): 325.

7. Lowry, "The Needs of the South," cited in *LD* 1 (1890): 5–6.

8. *CR* 21: 7, 6678; *BD,* 1451.

9. "Immigration and the Negro," *Charleston World,* cited in *PO* 10 (1890): 34.

10. *CR* 21: 9, 8364–65; Langdon, "The Case of the Negro," 32; Daniel Letwin, "Interracial Unionism and Gender in the Alabama Coalfields, 1878–1908," in Escott, et al., eds., *Major Problems in the History of the American South, Vol. II,* 113–22; Daniels, *Not Like Us,* 41–42.

11. Faulkner, *Politics, Reform, and Expansion,* 6; Gossett, *Race,* 307; Sproat, "*The Best Men,*" 227. In 1890, 62 percent of the population of Cincinnati was of foreign birth, 63 percent of Boston, 83 percent of Cleveland, 88 percent of New York City, and 90 percent of Chicago. See *CR* 22: Appendix, 164–65.

12. *LD* 2 (1890–1891): 4–5; Kraut, *The Huddled Masses,* 149; Viorst, *Fall from Grace,* 116–18.

13. Sherman, *Recollections of Forty Years in the House, Senate, and Cabinet,* 1083.

14. Quoted in Daniels, *Not Like Us,* 44–45.

15. *Brooklyn Citizen,* cited in *PO* 10 (1890): 368; Daniels, *Not Like Us,* 45.

16. Altgeld, *Live Questions,* 109–12.

17. Wiebe, *The Search for Order, 1877–1920,* 51.

18. *St. Louis Republic,* quoted in *PO* 10 (1890): 226; Gossett, *Race,* 289–90; Daniels, *Not Like Us,* 43. It is not surprising that this Missouri paper would take such a dim view of northeastern republicanism, for Henry Cabot Lodge once remarked that Missouri represented "a lower civilization" than Massachusetts. See *CR* 22: 2, 1211–12; and Cook, "Race Riots in the South," *Boston Our Day,* cited in *LD* 1 (1890): 198–99.

19. Lodge, "The Restriction of Immigration," 27–36, quote 33. See also idem, "Lynch Law and Unrestricted Immigration," 602–12.

20. *CR* 21: 3, 2320; Garraty, *Henry Cabot Lodge,* 142–43.

21. Bay, *The White Image in the Black Mind,* 104. For a learned discussion of both the current and historical confusion over definitions and applications of this

term, see James A. Field Jr.'s untitled article in Grob and Billias, eds., *Interpretations of American History*, vol. II, 179.

22. *CR* 22: 1, 503; Richman, "Citizenship of the United States," 104–23; Matthews, *Legislative and Judicial History of the Fifteenth Amendment*, 16, 41. Race alone was not the only issue in determining who was entitled to these constitutional rights. Mental capacity and social worthiness also became a topic of debate. Should "idiots," "lunatics," and "tramps" be allowed the same rights as others? As with race and ethnicity, there was no consensus among even the best educated and most humanitarian of thinkers. See Bonaparte, "The Strength and Weakness of Popular Government in the United States," 284–92.

23. *Syracuse Standard*, quoted in *LD* 1 (1890): 21; Super, "The Mission of the Anglo-Saxon," 853–67; Garraty, *Henry Cabot Lodge*, 143.

24. For a set of analyses of the causes of the sudden surge toward American Imperialism in the 1890s, see "American Imperialism: Altruism or Aggression," in Grob and Billias, eds., *Interpretations of American History*, vol. II, 163–215.

25. *CR* 22: 1, 857, quote. For southern views, see ibid. 21: Appendix, 569; Matthew C. Butler Speech, Butler Papers, USC, 10; and McKinley, *Appeal to Pharoah* [*sic*], 33.

26. *CR* 21: 1, 858; ibid.: 7, 6858; Morgan and Ingalls, Introduction to Tocqueville, *Democracy in America;* Clymer, *John Hay*, vii, 67, 69, 84–84, 91.

27. *CR* 21: 2, 1397.

28. Spooner to M. Herrick, 25 June 1890, container 109, Spooner Papers, LC.

29. Sinkler, *Racial Attitudes of the Presidents*, 266; Franklin and Moss Jr., *From Slavery to Freedom*, 307; DeSantis, *The Shaping of Modern America*, 237–40. Interestingly, Douglass got the job and was transported to Haiti on the U.S.S. *Kearsarge* piloted by Commander Kellogg. Although Douglass was an official representative of the U. S. government, Kellogg refused to associate with him socially on the voyage. See *CR* 22: 2, 1820.

30. Historians have often called the racist science of this generation "pseudoscience." This term is misleading, however, because the scientific knowledge of the day was not so much *false* as it was merely primitive. Such a term also implies some type of diabolical intention inherent in the science of the day, when no such intention existed. The scientists of the late nineteenth century worked within the intellectual confines of the times. They must be credited for at least proffering theories and ideas that later generations could prove, disprove, or improve upon. See Hofstadter, *Social Darwinism in American Thought*, 172; Kraut, *The Huddled Masses*, 152; Viorst, *Fall from Grace*, 79; Gossett, *Race*, 281–83; Meier, *Negro Thought in America, 1880–1915*, 22–24; and Ellison, *The Black Experience*, 58–59.

31. Bryce, *The American Commonwealth*, vol. II, 494–95.

32. Shaler, "The African Element in America," 660–73, quote 665; idem, "The Peculiarities of the South," 477–88. Massachusetts Congressman Benjamin F. Butler, the former Union Civil War general, proffered the same argument a year

before Shaler's published articles appeared, arguing that warm weather "does not produce the men and women who make the energetic life-blood of the nation." He believed that cold weather forced people of North European descent to become industrious, whereas people whose ancestry developed closer to the equator became naturally lazy. Hence, all dark-skinned races were inherently inferior to Teutonic races, and southerners in the United States were naturally less industrious than (inferior to?) northerners. See Butler, "Should There Be a Union of the English Speaking Peoples of the Earth," Speech to the Colby University Alumni, 2 July 1889, Folder 4, Box 8, Teller Papers, UC.

33. Shaler, "The Nature of the Negro," 23–35, quote 35.

34. Langdon, "The Case of the Negro," 29–42, quote 37.

35. Huxley, "On the Natural Inequality of Men," 1–23; *WBD*, 751.

36. Mayo, "Progress of the Negro," 341.

37. Quoted in Barrows, ed., *Mohonk Conference on the Negro Question*, 70.

38. Ibid., 59.

39. Ibid., 25.

40. Mayo, "Progress of the Negro," 341; *CR* 21: 1, 969; ibid. 22: 1, 78.

41. Quoted in Barrows, ed., *Mohonk Conference on the Negro Question*, 19–20.

42. Ibid., 61–62.

43. Thomas U. Dudley and George Washington Cable are prime examples of genuine humanitarians who granted the superiority of the white race. Cable, however, did not believe in Social Darwinism, which he called "pure twaddle" because "it is not proved." See his quotes in Wynes, *Forgotten Voices*, 34, 43.

44. *CR* 21: 3, 2391. For examples, see Stanley, "Stanley's Explorations," 2–4; Ward, "Life Among the Congo Savages," 135–56; Thomson, "The Results of European Intercourse with the African," 80–88; and Howe, "The Last Slave-Ship," 113–28. A notable modern treatment of Stanley's adventures in Africa is Hochschild, *King Leopold's Ghost*.

45. Quoted in Hill and Kilson, eds., *Apropos of Africa*, 118. For more treatment of Williams's work in Africa, see Hochschild, *King Leopold's Ghost*, particularly pages 102–13.

46. Ibid., 270–73.

47. Brill, "Notes of a Reisebilder," Reel 314, ACS Papers, LC, 22, 58.

48. Sam N. Lapsley to John Tyler Morgan, 9 November 1891, Reel 2, Morgan Papers, LC, 3.

49. Quoted in Brotz, ed., *African-American Social and Political Thought*, 184; Rigby, *Alexander Crummell*, 175.

50. Quoted in Crummell, *Africa and America*, 16–17; Moses, ed., *Destiny and Race*, passim.

51. Watson, "The Negro Question in the South," 540–50.

52. Eustis, "Race Antagonism in the South," 144.

53. Scarborough, "The Future of the Negro," 81.

54. Hemphill Scrapbook, 1889–1890, DU, 2; *CR* 21: 9, 8365; ibid.: 22: 2,

1575; Snyder, "Prejudice Against the Negro," 222; Eustis, "Race Antagonism in the South," 147–54; Field, *Bright Skies,* 150–51; Davis, *Spearheads for Reform,* 95; Woodward, *The Strange Career of Jim Crow,* 3–10, 34–43, 65; Viorst, *Fall from Grace,* 39; Sproat, *"The Best Men,"* 235; Nixon, *Henry W. Grady,* 213–14; Meier, *Negro Thought in America, 1880–1915,* 21; Wynes, *Forgotten Voices,* 9; Ellison, *The Black Experience,* 39. For a study of the origins of segregation in the North, see Litwack, *North of Slavery,* passim.

55. Quoted in Quillen, *The Color Line in Ohio,* 3. See also Gerber, *Black Ohio and the Color Line, 1860–1915,* 57–58.

56. *CR* 22: Appendix, 96–103, quote 103.

57. Morgan, "The Race Question," Reel 11, Morgan Papers, LC, 3–5; *CR* 21: 8, 7734–36.

58. *CR* 21: 1, 861; ibid. 22: 1, 372–73.

59. Bruce, *The Plantation Negro as a Freeman,* 44–47.

60. *AC,* 5 January 1890; Nixon, *Henry W. Grady,* 214.

61. *CR* 21: 2, 1204.

62. Quoted in Bay, *The White Image in the Black Mind,* 103.

63. Price, "Does the Negro Seek Social Equality?" 558–64, quotes 561–62.

64. "Demands of the Colored Race," *Baltimore Sun,* 29 October 1889, in vol. 14, Gorman Scrapbooks, UNC, 82.

65. Scarborough, "The Race Problem," 560, quote 567; Lowery and Marszalek, eds., *Encyclopedia of African-American Civil Rights,* 465; Brotz, ed., *African-American Social and Political Thought,* 318–19.

66. Fortune, "The Afro-American," 115–18; Thornbrough, *T. Thomas Fortune,* 2–3; Lowery and Marszalek, eds., *Encyclopedia of African-American Civil Rights,* 197–98.

67. Fortune, "The Afro-American," 115–18, quote 117; Thornbrough, *T. Thomas Fortune,* 132.

68. Barrows, ed., *Mohonk Conference on the Negro Question,* 79.

69. Gulick, "Divergent Evolution Through Cumulative Segregation," *Annual Report of the Smithsonian Institution, 1891,* 269–336, quotes 332.

70. Senator Alfred Colquitt of Georgia, quoted in *CR* 22: 1, 453, 456.

71. See examples by Representatives Richard H. Clarke of Alabama and Samuel W. Peel of Arkansas in *CR* 21: Appendix, 403 and 445, respectively.

72. Ibid.: 8, 7734–36; ibid.: 22: 1, 503.

73. Black southerners regained federal protection of their civil rights with passage of the Civil Rights Act of 1964. See Donaldson, *The Second Reconstruction,* 37–38.

Conclusion

Epigraphs. Quoted in *LD* 1(1890): 695; Quoted in *PO* 10 (1891): 539; Quoted in ibid., 540.

1. Charles H. Mansur, quoted in *PO* 10 (1891): 690; DeSantis, "The Repub-

lican Party and the Southern Negro, 1877–1897," 73; Kraut, *The Huddled Masses*, 163.

2. *CR* 21: 7, 6772.

3. Lee, *The Struggle for Federal Aid*, 149–55.

4. Grover Cleveland to Richard Watson Gilder, 25 September 1892, cited in Nevins, ed., *Letters of Grover Cleveland;* Knox, *The Republican Party and Its Leaders*, passim; Nevins, *Grover Cleveland: A Study in Courage*, 441, 460; Knoles, *The Presidential Campaign and Election of 1892*, 144, 168–69; Welch, *The Presidencies of Grover Cleveland*, 12; Lynch, *Grover Cleveland*, 404.

5. Quoted in *Indianapolis Journal*, 1 June 1892, cited in Blassingame and McKivigan, eds., *The Frederick Douglass Papers, Series One, Vol. 5*, 487.

6. Quoted in the *Washington Post*, 21 October 1890, cited in ibid., 455.

7. Turpie, *Sketches of My Times*, 289; Dozer, "Benjamin Harrison and the Presidential Campaign of 1892," 49–77; Bass, "*I Am a Democrat*," 180–81; Olsen, *Carpetbagger's Crusade*, 303; Hatch, *History of the Vice-Presidency*, 325.

8. Groves, *Henry Cabot Lodge*, 24; Williams, *Senator John James Ingalls*, 118–19; Bass, "*I Am a Democrat*," 180–81; Fowler, *John Coit Spooner*, 157–59.

9. "The Senate in the Fifty-Second Congress," *St. Louis Globe-Democrat*, cited in *PO* 10 (1891): 565; Barnes, *John G. Carlisle* 188; Boyd, *Men and Issues of '92*, 100.

10. Frederick Douglass, "The Lesson of the Hour," quoted in Foner, ed., *Life and Writings of Frederick Douglass, Vol. IV*, 510; See also Buck, *The Road to Reunion, 1865–1900*, 281; Marshall, *William B. Bate*, 240–41; and Oberholtzer, *History of the United States Since the Civil War*, vol. V, 137–38, 233, 235.

11. Meier, *Negro Thought in America, 1880–1915*, 28–34, quote 32; Elsie M. Lewis, "The Political Mind of the Negro, 1865–1900," in Wynes, ed., *The Negro in the South Since 1865*, 36–37; Walls, *Joseph Charles Price*, 391–92. The change of party among black voters lasted only through Cleveland's second term. By 1896, most defectors had returned to the Republican Party as the lesser of two evils. See Franklin and Moss Jr., *From Slavery to Freedom*, 341; Morgan, *From Hayes to McKinley*, 480–81; and Summers, *The Gilded Age*, 226, 257–61.

12. Benjamin Harrison, *This Country of Ours*, 30–31; Lodge and Redmond, eds., *Selections from the Correspondence of Theodore Roosevelt and Henry Cabot Lodge, 1884–1918*, vol. I, 212; McElroy, *Levi Parsons Morton*, 185; Haynes, *The Senate of the United States*, 397–98, 407; Rothman, *Politics and Power*, 86, 244–45, 259–60; Keller, *Affairs of State*, 456; Dewey, *National Problems, 1885–1897*, 170. Both sections of the country—North and South—polarized after 1894. The North was almost as solidly Republican into the early twentieth century as the South was Democrat.

13. Joseph D. Sayers to William C. P. Breckinridge, 4 April 1891, 1891 Correspondence, Box 783, Breckinridge Family Papers, LC; *Pittsburgh Post*, cited in *PO* 10 (1891): 539; McKinley, et al., "What Congress Has Done," 513–18; Sievers, *Benjamin Harrison*, 172; Socolofsky and Spetter, *The Presidency of Benjamin Harrison*, 47, 55.

14. *Philadelphia Press,* 7 March 1891, cited in *PO* 10 (1891): 538; Wyeth, *Republican Principles and Policies,* 151; Dunn, *From Harrison to Harding,* 70.

15. *Natchez Daily Democrat,* 8 July 1890.

16. *St. Louis Republic,* quoted in *PO* 10 (1891): 539.

17. *Louisville Courier–Journal,* quoted in ibid.

18. *San Francisco Examiner,* quoted in ibid.

19. Quoted in "In Democracy's Citadel," vol. 17, Gorman Scrapbooks, UNC, 57.

20. *Chicago Inter-Ocean,* quoted in *PO* 10 (1891): 539.

21. *Providence Journal,* quoted in ibid.

22. *Brooklyn Eagle,* quoted in ibid.

23. Quoted in Fry, *John Tyler Morgan,* 56.

24. Quoted in Brotz, ed., *African-American Social and Political Thought,* 322; see also Chandler, *The Natural Superiority of Southern Politicians,* passim.

25. Derek A. Bell, "The Racial Imperative in American Law," in Haws, ed., *Age of Segregation,* 10–15.

26. Quoted in Wynes, *Forgotten Voices,* 8.

27. Asher D. Caruth, Democratic representative of Kentucky, quoted in *CR* 21: 11, 6860.

28. Rudwick, *W. E. B. DuBois,* 60–61; Washington, *Historical Development of the Negro in Oklahoma,* 37.

29. Field, *Bright Skies,* 113.

BIBLIOGRAPHY

Primary Sources

Manuscripts

Athens, Georgia. University of Georgia, Hargrett Rare Book and Manuscript Library.

Alfred H. Colquitt Scrapbooks.

Auburn, Alabama. Auburn University, Ralph Brown Draughon Library.

James L. Pugh Papers.

Boulder, Colorado. University of Colorado, Norlin Library, Archives.

John C. Bell Scrapbooks.
Dearfield Collection.
David H. Nichols Papers.
Henry M. Teller Papers.

Chapel Hill, North Carolina. University of North Carolina, Wilson Library, Southern Historical Collection.

Arthur P. Gorman Scrapbooks.
John S. Henderson Papers.
Hilary A. Herbert Papers.
Matthew W. Ransom Papers.

Columbia, South Carolina. University of South Carolina, South Caroliniana Library.

Patrick Henry Adams Papers.
Mrs. W. W. Ball Scrapbooks.
Matthew C. Butler Papers.

Farmer's State Alliance Papers.
James Island Papers.
William H. Lyles Papers.
Mazyk Family Papers.
George H. McMaster Papers.
Alexander S. Salley Jr. Papers.
Mrs. Robert M. Wallace Papers.

Durham, North Carolina. Duke University, Perkins Library, Manuscript Division.

Matthew C. Butler Papers.
Francis M. Cockrell Papers.
Alfred H. Colquitt Papers.
John W. Daniel Papers.
Charles J. Faulkner Jr., Papers.
Randall L. Gibson Papers.
Isham G. Harris Papers.
James C. Hemphill Scrapbooks.
Edmund Cary Walthall Papers.

Jackson, Mississippi. Mississippi Department of Archives and History.

J. Z. George Scrapbooks.

St. Louis, Missouri. Missouri Historical Society.

Kennerly College Papers.
Thomas C. Reynolds Papers.
George G. Vest Papers.

Starkville, Mississippi. Mississippi State University, Special Collections Department.

Frank Burkitt Papers.

Washington, D.C., Library of Congress, Manuscript Division.

American Colonization Society Papers.
Thomas F. Bayard Papers.
Breckinridge Family Papers.
William E. Chandler Papers.
John Mercer Langston Papers.
John Tyler Morgan Papers.

John Coit Spooner Papers.
Daniel W. Voorhees Scrapbook.

Government Publications

University of Mississippi Bureau of Governmental Research. *Inaugural Addresses of the Governors of Mississippi, 1890–1980.* Oxford, Mississippi,1980.
Congressional Quarterly. *Members of Congress Since 1789.* Washington, D.C.: Congressional Quarterly, 1977.
————. *Presidential Elections Since 1789.* 3rd ed. Washington, D.C.: Congressional Quarterly, 1983.
Constitution of the Commonwealth of Massachusetts. Boston: Wright & Potter Printing, 1902.
United States Government. *Biographical Directory of the United States Congress, 1789–1989.* Washington, D.C.: Government Printing Office, 1989.
————. *Checklist of United States Public Documents, 1789–1909.* 3rd ed. Vol. I. Washington, D.C.: Government Printing Office, 1911.
————. House. *Report No. 3823: Investigation of Certain Alleged Illegal Practices of the United States Courts.* Washington, D.C.: Government Printing office, 1890.
————. House and Senate. *Congressional Record.* Vols. 21–22. Fifty-first Congress.Washington, D.C.: Government Printing Office, 1889–1891.
————. Library of Congress. *Guide to the Benjamin Harrison Papers.* Washington, D.C.: Government Printing Office, 1964.
————. Library of Congress. *Guide to the Library of Congress Personal Papers.*Washington, D.C.: Government Printing Office, 1984.
————. *Report of the Commissioner of Indian Affairs to the Secretary of the Interior, 1890.* Washington, D.C.: Government Printing Office, 1891.
————. Senate. *Coinage Laws of the United States, 1792–1894.* Washington, D.C.: Government Printing Office, 1894.
————. Senate. *The Miscellaneous Documents of the Senate of the United States for the First Session of the Fifty-first Congress.* Washington, D.C.: Government Printing Office, 1891.
————. Senate. *Report of the United States Senate Committee to Inquire into Alleged Frauds and Violence in the Elections of 1878.* Washington, D.C.: Government Printing Office, 1879.

Newspapers:

Atlanta Constitution, 1890.
Biloxi (Mississippi) *Herald,* 1890–1891.
Boulder (Colorado) *County Herald,* 1890, 1893.
Boulder (Colorado) *County Herald Weekly,* 1886, 1889.
Boulder (Colorado) *News,* 1892.

Charleston (South Carolina) *News and Courier,* 1890.
Denver Daily News, 1893.
(Denver) *Rocky Mountain News,* 1889–1893.
Jackson Clarion–Ledger, 1889.
Jackson New Mississippian, 1887–1889.
Leavenworth (Kansas) *Advocate,* 1890.
Memphis Appeal–Avalanche, 1890.
Natchez Daily Democrat, 1890.
New York Herald, 1891.
Savannah Morning News, 1888–1891.
Woodville (Mississippi) *Republican,* 1891.

Contemporary Periodicals

Harper's Weekly, 1889–1891.
Literary Digest, New York, 1890–1891.
Literary World, New York, 1890.
Nation, New York, 1889–1891.
New England Historical and Genealogical Register, Boston, 1890.
New Nation, Boston, 1891.
Public Opinion, Washington, D.C., 1890–1891.
Puck, New York, 1887–1891.

Contemporary Articles:

Baynard, F. A. P. "The Degredation of Our Politics." *Forum* 9 (1890): 117–32.
Blackburn, Nathan A. "The Republican Platform." *Forum* 6 (1888): 10–18.
Bodington, Alice. "The Importance of the Race Question and Its Bearing on 'The Negro Question.'" *Westminster Review* (October 1890). Cited in *Literary Digest* 2 (1890): 34.
Bonaparte, Charles J. "The Strength and Weakness of Popular Government in the United States." *New Englander and Yale Review* 52 (1890): 284–92.
Boyesen, H. H. "What Shall the Public Schools Teach?" *Forum* 6 (1888): 92–100.
Breckinridge, C. P. "The Race Question." *Arena* 2 (1890): 39–56.
Brough, Charles H. "The Clinton Riot." *Publications of the Mississippi Historical Society* 10 (1902): 53–63.
Bryce, James. "A Word as to the Speakership." *North American Review* 151 (1890): 385–98.
Cable, George W. "A Simpler Southern Question." *Forum* 6 (1888): 392–403.
Calhoon, S. S. "Causes and Events That Led to the Calling of the Constitutional Convention of 1890." *Publications of the Mississippi Historical Society* 6 (1902):105–10.
Carlisle, J. G. "The Recent Election." *North American Review* 151 (1890): 641–49

———. "The Republican Program." *Forum* 7 (1889): 585–96.

———. "Republican Promise and Performance." *Forum* 9 (1890): 243–54.

Chamberlain, Daniel H. "Counting a Quorum." *New Englander and Yale Review* 52 (1890): 510–25.

———. "The Race Problem at the South." *New Englander and Yale Review* 52 (1890): 607–27.

Chandler, William E. "National Control of Elections." *Forum* 9 (1890): 705–18.

———. "Our Southern Masters." *Forum* 5 (1888): 508–20.

Clarkson, J. S. "The Politician and the Pharisee." *North American Review* 152 (1891): 613–23.

Colquitt, Alfred. "Is the Negro Vote Suppressed?" *Forum* 4 (1887): 268–78.

Dawes, Henry L. "The Chinese Exclusion Bill." *Forum* 6 (1889): 526–39.

———. "A Year of Republican Control." *Forum* 9 (1890): 24–35.

Edmunds, George F. "Corrupt Political Methods." *Forum* 7 (1889): 349–60.

Eustis, James B. "Race Antagonism in the South." *Forum* 6 (1888): 144–54.

Farwell, Willard B. "New Phases in the Chinese Problem." *Popular Science Monthly* 36 (1889): 181–91.

———. "Why the Chinese Must Be Excluded." *Forum* 6 (1888): 196–203.

Fenner, Charles B. "The Race Problem—The Negro Should Solve It." *Belford's Magazine* 5 (1890): 1–15.

Flint, Austin. "What Shall the Public Schools Teach?" *Forum* 5 (1888): 146–55.

Fortune, T. Thomas. "The Afro-American." *Arena* 3 (1891): 115–18.

———. "The Afro-American League." *The A.M.E. Zion Quarterly Review* (July 1890): 2–6.

Garner, Alfred W. "The Public Services of E. C. Walthall." *Publications of the Mississippi Historical Society* 9 (1906): 239–53.

Garner, James W. "Senatorial Career of J. Z. George." *Publications of the Mississippi Historical Society* 7 (1903): 245–56.

George, J. Z. "Demonetization of Silver." Political pamphlet. Washington, D.C.: Government Printing House, 1893.

Gilmore, Bishop R. "What Shall the Public Schools Teach?" *Forum* 5 (1888): 454–61.

Godkin, E. L. "The Republican Party and the Negro." *Forum* 7 (1889): 246–57.

Gulik, John Thomas. "Divergent Evolution through Cumulative Segregation." *Annual Report of the Smithsonian Institution, 1891*. Washington, D.C.: Government Printing Office, 1893.

Hale, Edward E. "Emigration and Immigration." *Cosmopolitan* 9 (1890): 254–56.

Halstead, Murat. "The Torrid Zone of Our Politics." *Forum* 4 (1888): 634–43.

Hamm, Walter C. "The Art of Gerrymandering." *Forum* 9 (1890): 538–51.

Hampton, Wade. "The Race Problem." *Arena* 2 (1890): 132–38.

———. "What Negro Supremacy Means." *Forum* 5 (1888): 383–92.

Harris, William T. "What Shall the Public Schools Teach?" *Forum* 4 (1888): 573–81.

Hart, Albert B. "Do the People Wish Reform?" *Forum* 9 (1890): 47–56.

Hearne, Thomas H. "The Race Problem—The Situation." *Methodist Review* 6 (1890): 690–705.

Hoadly, George. "Methods of Ballot Reform." *Forum* 7 (1889): 623–33.

Hoar, George F. "Are the Republicans in to Stay?" *North American Review* 149 (1889): 616–24.

———. "The Senate." *The Youth's Companion* 63 (1890): 620.

Howe, George. "The Last Slave-Ship." *Scribner's Magazine* 8 (1890): 113–28.

Hubbard, James M. "An Opportunity for the Negro." *North American Review* 152 (1891): 116–18.

Huxley, T. H. "On the Natural Inequality of Men." *The Nineteenth Century* 27 (1890): 1–23.

Jameson, John A. "National Sovereignty." *Political Science Quarterly* 5 (1890): 193–213.

Johnston, Frank. "The Public Services of Senator James Z. George." *Publications of the Mississippi Historical Society* 8 (1904): 201–26.

Judex. "The Speaker and His Critics." *North American Review* 151 (1890): 237–50.

Keatley, John H. "A New Race Problem." *Atlantic Monthly* 46 (1890): 207–11.

Kercheval, George T. "Fair Play for the Indian." *North American Review* 152 (1891): 250–53.

Langdon, W. Chauncy. "The Case of the Negro." *Political Science Quarterly* 6 (1891): 29–42.

Leonard, M. H. "The Meaning of the Pageant." *Independent* 42 (1890): 36–37.

Levermore, Charles H. "Impressions of a Yankee Visitor in the South." *New England Magazine* 3 (1890–1891): 311–19.

Lodge, Henry C. "The Coming Congress." *North American Review* 149 (1889): 293–301.

———. "Lynch Law and Unrestricted Immigration." *North American Review* 152 (1891): 602–12.

———. "The Restriction of Immigration." *North American Review* 152 (1891): 27–36.

Lodge, Henry C., and Terrence V. Powderly. "The Federal Election Bill." *North American Review* 151 (1890): 256–73.

Lowry, Robert. "The Needs of the South." *North American Review* 151 (1890). Cited in *Literary Digest* 1 (1890): 5–6.

Mathews, William. "The Negro Intellect." *North American Review* 149 (1889): 91–102.

Mayo, A. D. "The Progress of the Negro." *Forum* 10 (1891): 335–45.

———. "The Third Estate of the South." *New England Magazine* 3 (1890–1891): 299–311.

McKinley, William, Jr., et al. "What Congress Has Done." *North American Review* 151 (1890): 513–33.

McNeilly, J. S. "Climax and Collapse of Reconstruction in Mississippi, 1874–1896." *Publications of the Mississippi Historical Society* 11 (1910): 283–474.

———. "History of the Measures Submitted to the Committee on the Elective Franchise, Apportionment, and Election in the Constitutional Convention of 1890." *Publications of the Mississippi Historical Society* 6 (1902): 129–40.

———. "War and Reconstruction in Mississippi, 1863–1890." *Publications of the Mississippi Historical Society,* Centenary Series 2 (1918): 165–535.

Miles, Nelson A. "The Future of the Indian Question." *North American Review* 152 (1891): 1–10.

Mills, Roger Q. "Republican Tactics in the House." *North American Review* 149 (1889): 665–72.

Morgan, John T. "Federal Control of Elections." *Forum* 10 (1890): 23–36.

———. "The Race Question in the United States." *Arena* 2 (1890): 385–98.

———. "Shall Negro Majorities Rule?" *Forum* 6 (1889): 586–99.

Oldham, Edward A. "The Great Political Upheaval at the South." *Arena* 2 (1890): 629–33.

Palgrave, Reginald F. D. "The Recent Crisis in Congress." *North American Review* 151 (1890): 367–75.

Parkhurst, C. H. "What Shall the Public Schools Teach?" *Forum* 5 (1888): 47–56.

Pingrey, D. H. "The Right of the Federal Courts to Punish Offenders against the Ballot Box." *American Law Register.* Cited in *Literary Digest* 1 (1890): 426.

Pitman, R. C. "What Shall the Public Schools Teach?" *Forum* 5 (1888): 289–98.

Price, J. C. "Does the Negro Seek Social Equality?" *Forum* 10 (1891): 558–64.

Pryor, Roger A. "The Sufficiency of the New Amendments." *Forum* 9 (1890): 266–76.

Ray, D. Kinmount. "Notes and Comments: Stanley's Pygmies." *North American Review* 151 (1890): 253–54.

Reed, Thomas B. "Contested Elections." *North American Review* 151 (1890): 112–20.

———."A Deliberative Body." *North American Review* 152 (1891): 148–56.

———. "Obstruction in the National House." *North American Review* 149 (1889): 421–28.

———. "A Reply to X. M. C." *North American Review* 151 (1890): 228–36.

Richman, Irving B. "Citizenship of the United States." *Political Science Quarterly* 5 (1890): 104–23.

Rowland, Dunbar. "The Rise and Fall of Negro Rule in Mississippi." *Publications of the Mississippi Historical Society* 1 (1898): 189–99.

Sage, B. J. "Congressional Power on Education and Elections." *Belford Magazine* (May 1890). Cited in *Literary Digest* 1 (1890): 3–4.

Salvage, M. J. "What Shall the Public Schools Teach?" *Forum* 4 (1888): 460–71.

Sanford, Henry. "American Interests in Africa." *Forum* 9 (1890): 409–29.

Scarborough, W. S. "The Future of the Negro." *Forum* 7 (1889): 80–89.

———. "The Race Problem." *Arena* 2 (1890): 560–67.

Scomp, Henry A. "Can the Race Problem Be Solved?" *Forum* 8 (1890): 365–76.

Seiders, C. A. "The Race Problem: A Criticism of Senator Hampton's Paper." *Arena* 2 (1890): 633–35.

Shaffer, A. W. "A Southern Republican on the Lodge Bill." *North American Review* 151 (1890): 601–9.

Shaler, N. S. "The African Element in America." *Arena* 2 (1890): 660–73.

———. "The Nature of the Negro." *Arena* 3 (1891): 23–35.

———. "The Peculiarities of the South." *North American Review* 151 (1890): 477–88.

Smalls, Robert. "Election Methods in the South." *North American Review* 151 (1890): 593–600.

Snyder, John. "Prejudice against the Negro." *Forum* 8 (1890): 218–24.

Stanley, Henry M. "Stanley's Explorations." *Science* 15 (1890): 2–4.

Stetson, George R. "The New Basis of National Education." *Andover Review* (September 1890). Cited in *Literary Digest* 1 (1890): 595–96.

Super, O. B. "The Mission of the Anglo-Saxon." *Methodist Review* 6 (1890): 853–67.

Taylor, Hannis. "The National House of Representatives: Its Growing Inefficiency as a Legislative Body." *Atlantic Monthly* 45 (1891): 766–73.

Thompson, R. H. "Suffrage in Mississippi." *Publications of the Mississippi Historical Society* 1 (1898): 25–49.

Thomson, Joseph. "The Results of European Intercourse with the African." *Littel's Living Age* 185 (1890): 80–88.

Tourgee, Albion W. "The Right to Vote." *Forum* 9 (1890): 78–92.

———. "Shall White Minorities Rule?" *Forum* 7 (1889): 143–55.

Vest, George G. "The Hopes of the Democratic Party." *North American Review* 149 (1889): 539–49.

Ward, Herbert. "Life Among the Congo Savages." *Scribner's Magazine* 7 (1890): 135–56.

Ward, L. F. "What Shall the Public Schools Teach?" *Forum* 5 (1888): 574–83.

Watson, Tom. "The Negro Question in the South," *Arena* 6 (1892): 540-50.

Watterson, Henry. "The South and Its Colored Citizens." *Cosmopolitan* 9 (1890): 113–16.

White Albert S. "A Critical Inspection of the Social and Intellectual Condition of the Negro." *The A.M.E. Zion Quarterly Review* (July 1890): 42–46.

Contemporary Books

Altgeld, John P. *Live Questions.* Chicago: Donohue & Henneberry, 1890. Reprint, 3rd ed., Foundations of Criminal Justice Series, edited by Richard H. Ward and Austin Fowler. New York: AMS Press, 1973.

Alton, Edmund. *Among the Law-Makers.* New York: Charles Scribner's Sons, 1886.

The American Negro Academy Occasional Papers, 1–22. The American Negro: His History and Literature Series, ed. William Loren Katz. New York: Arno Press and the New York Times, 1969.

The Annual Reports of the American Colonization Society for Colonizing the Free

People of Colour of the United States, Vols. 64–91, 1881–1910. Reprint, New York: Negro Universities Press,1969.

Bancroft, Frederic, ed. *Speeches, Correspondence and Political Papers of Carl Schurz.* Vol. V. New York: Putnam's Sons, 1913.

Barrows, Isabel C., ed. *Mohonk Conference on the Negro Question.* Reprint, New York: Negro Universities Press, 1969.

Blassingame, John, and John R. McKivigan, eds. *The Frederick Douglass Papers— Series One: Speeches, Debates, and Interviews, Volume 5: 1881–95.* New Haven: Yale University Press, 1992.

Blyden, Edward W. *The African Problem and Other Discourses, Delivered in America in 1890.* London: W. B. Whittingham, 1890.

Boyd, James P. *Men and Issues of '92.* Publisher's Union, 1892.

Brown, George R., ed. *Reminiscences of Senator William M. Stewart of Nevada.* New York: Neale, 1908.

Bruce, Philip A. *The Plantation Negro as a Freeman: Observations of His Character, Conditions, and Prospects in Virginia.* New York: Putnam's Sons, 1889.

Bryce, James. *The American Commonwealth.* Vol. II. New York: McMillan, 1895.

Byars, William V., ed. *"An American Commoner": The Life and Times of Richard Parks Bland.* Columbia: Stevens, 1900.

Cooley, Thomas M. *A Treatise on the Constitutional Limitations Which Rest upon the Legislative Power of the States of the American Union.* 6th ed. Boston: Little, Brown, 1890.

Crummell, Alexander. *Africa and America: Addresses and Discourses.* Springfield, Massachusetts: Willey, 1891. Reprint, New York: Negro Universities Press, 1969.

Cullom, Shelby M. *Fifty Years of Public Service.* Chicago: McClurg, 1911.

Curry, J. L. M. *The Southern States of the American Union Considered in Their Relations to the Constitution of the United States and to the Resulting Union.* New York: Putnam's Sons, 1894.

Daniel, John W. Introduction to *Life and Reminiscences of Jefferson Davis.* Authored "By Distinguished Men of His Time." New York: Eastern, 1890.

Destler, Chester M., ed. *American Radicalism, 1865–1901: Essays and Documents.* Connecticut College, 1946. Reprint, New York: Octagon Books, 1963.

Dowd, Clement. *Life of Zebulon Vance.* Charlotte: Observer, 1897.

Dunn, Arthur W. *From Harrison to Harding: A Personal Narrative Covering a Third of a Century, 1888–1921.* Vol. I. New York: Putnam's Sons, 1922.

Field, Henry M. *Bright Skies and Dark Shadows.* 1890. Reprint, Freeport, New York: Books for Libraries Press, 1970.

Fisk, John. *Civil Government in the United States Considered with Some Reference to Its Origins.* Boston: Houghton Mifflin, 1890.

Follette, M. P. *The Speaker of the House of Representatives.* New York: Longmans, Green, 1896.

Foner, Philip S., ed. *The Life and Writings of Frederick Douglass, Vol. IV: Reconstruction and After.* New York: International Publishers, 1955.

Foner, Philip S, and Robert J. Branham, eds. *Lift Every Voice: African American Oratory, 1787–1900.* Tuscaloosa: University of Alabama Press, 1998.

Foraker, Julia B. *I Would Live It Again: Memories of a Vivid Life.* New York: Harper & Brothers, 1932.

Groves, Charles S. *Henry Cabot Lodge: The Statesman.* Boston: Small, Maynard, 1925.

Harlan, Louis R., ed. *The Booker T. Washington Papers.* Vol. III. 1889–1895. Urbana: University of Illinois Press, 1974.

Harris, Joel C. *Life of Henry W. Grady.* New York: Cassell, 1890.

Harrison, Benjamin. *This Country of Ours.* New York: Charles Scribner's Sons, 1911.

Hedges, Charles, ed. *Speeches of Benjamin Harrison.* 1892. Reprint, American History and Culture in the Nineteenth Century Series, ed. Martin L. Fausold. Port Washington, New York: Kennikat Press, 1971.

Herbert, Hilary A. *Why the Solid South? or, Reconstruction and Its Results.* Baltimore: Woodward, 1890.

Hoar, George F. *Autobiography of Seventy Years.* Vol II. New York: Charles Scribner's Sons, 1903.

Keller, Morton, ed. *The Art and Politics of Thomas Nast.* New York: Oxford University Press, 1968.

Knox, Thomas W. *The Republican Party and Its Leaders.* New York: Collier, 1892.

Langston, John M. *From the Virginia Plantation to the National Capitol.* Hartford: American, 1894. Reprint, New York: Johnson Reprint Corporation, 1968.

Lodge, Henry Cabot, and Charles F. Redmond, eds. *Selections from the Correspondence of Theodore Roosevelt and Henry Cabot Lodge, 1884–1918.* Vols. I and II. New York: Charles Scribner's Sons, 1925. Reprint, New York: Da Capo Press, 1971.

Lott, Davis N., ed. *The Inaugural Addresses of the American Presidents: From Washington to Kennedy.* New York: Holt, Rinehart and Winston, 1961.

Lowry, Robert, and William McCardle. *A History of Mississippi.* Jackson: Henry, 1891.

Lynch, John R. *The Facts of Reconstruction.* 1913; reprint, New York: Arno Press, 1968.

Macy, Jesse. *Our Government: How It Grew, What It Does, and How It Does It.* Boston: Ginn, 1891.

Marshall, Park. *A Life of William B. Bate: Citizen, Soldier, and Statesman.* Nashville: Cumberland Press, 1908.

Matthews, John M. *Legislative and Judicial History of the Fifteenth Amendment.* John Hopkins University Studies in Historical and Political Science. Baltimore: The John Hopkins Press, 1909.

McKinley, Carlyle. *An Appeal to Pharoah [sic]: The Negro Problem, and Its Radical Solution.* 3rd ed., with introduction by Gustavus M. Pinckney. New York: Fords, Howards, and Hulbert. 1907. Reprint, Westport, Connecticut: Negro Universities Press, 1970.

Morgan, John T., and John J. Ingalls. Introduction to Alexis de Tocqueville, *Democracy in America*, 1890 edition, in CD-ROM supplement to Robert Divine, et al., *America Past and Present*. 5th ed. New York: Addison-Longman-Wesley, 1999.

Otken, Charles H. *The Ills of the South.* New York: Putnam's Sons, 1894.

Paine, Albert B. *Th. Nast: His Period and His Pictures.* Pearson, 1904. Reprint, Gloucester, Massachusetts: Peter Smith, 1967.

Parker, George F., ed. *The Writings and Speeches of Grover Cleveland.* New York: Cassell, 1892. Reprint, New York: Kraus Reprint, 1970.

Platt, Thomas C. *The Autobiography of Thomas Collier Platt.* Edited by Louis J. Lang. New York: Dodge, 1910.

Riley, Franklin K. *School History of Mississippi.* Richmond, Virginia: Johnson, 1915.

Sherman, John. *John Sherman's Recollections of Forty Years in the House, Senate, and Cabinet: An Autobiography.* Vol. II. Chicago: Werner, 1895.

Shurter, Edwin D., ed. *The Complete Orations and Speeches of Henry W. Grady.* Norwood, Massachusetts: Norwood Press, 1910.

Storey, Moorfield. *The Negro Question: An Address Delivered Before the Wisconsin Bar Association.* New York: NAACP, 1918.

———. *Politics as a Duty and as a Career.* Questions of the Day, no. 58. New York: Putnam's Sons, 1889.

Turpie, David. *Sketches of My Own Times.* Indianapolis: Bobbs-Merrill, 1903.

Wallace, Lew, and George A. Townsend. *Lives of Harrison and Morton.* Philadelphia: Hubbard Brothers, 1888.

Watson, David K. *History of American Coinage.* 2nd ed. New York: Putnam's Sons, 1899.

Wilson, James G., and John Fiske, eds. *Appleton's Annual Cyclopedia of American Biography.* New York: Appleton, 1888–1889.

Secondary Sources

Articles

Ainsworth, Scott. "Electoral Strength and the Emergence of Group Influence in the Late 1800s: The Grand Army of the Republic." *American Politics Quarterly* 23 (1995): 319–38.

Coleman, James P. "The Origin of the Constitution of 1890." *Journal of Mississippi History* 119 (1957): 69–92.

Crofts, Daniel W. "The Black Response to the Blair Education Bill." *Journal of Southern History* 37 (1971): 41–65.

DeSantis, Vincent P. "The Republican Party and the Southern Negro, 1877–1897." *Journal of Negro History* 45 (1960): 71–87.

Dozer, Donald M. "Benjamin Harrison and the Presidential Campaign of 1892." *American Historical Review* 54 (1948): 49–77.

Edwards, Thomas S. "'Reconstructing' Reconstruction: Changing Historical Paradigms in Mississippi." *Journal of Mississippi History* 51 (1989): 165–80.

Ellam, Warren A. "The Overthrow of Reconstruction in Mississippi." *Journal of Mississippi History* 54 (1992): 175–202.

Evans, John W. "Catholics and the Blair Education Bill." *Catholic Historical Review* 46 (1960): 273–98.

Fishel, Leslie H. "The Negro in Northern Politics, 1870–1900." *Mississippi Valley Historical Review* 42 (1955): 466–89.

Fitzgerald, Michael W. "'We Have Found a Moses': Theodore Bilbo, Black Nationalism, and the Greater Liberia Bill of 1939." *Journal of Southern History* 63 (1997): 293–320.

Gatewood, Willard B., Jr. "North Carolina and Federal Aid to Education: Public Reaction to the Blair Bill, 1881–1890." *North Carolina Historical Review* 40 (1963): 465–88.

Going, Allen J. "The South and the Blair Education Bill." *Mississippi Valley Historical Review* 44 (1957): 267–90.

Hesseltine, William B., and Larry Gara. "Georgia's Confederate Leaders after Appomattox." *Georgia Historical Quarterly* 35 (1951): 1–16.

Hill, Daniel G. "The Negro in the Early History of the West." *The Iliff Review* 3 (1946): 132–42.

Lewis, Ronald L. "From Peasant to Proletarian: The Migration of Southern Blacks to the Central Appalachian Coalfields." *Journal of Southern History* 55 (1989): 77–102.

Logan, Frenise A. "The Movement of Negroes from North Carolina, 1876–1894," *North Carolina Historical Review* 33 (1956): 54–63.

Morgan, H. Wayne. "Western Silver and the Tariff of 1890." *New Mexico Historical Review* 35 (1960): 118–28.

Mothershead, Harmon. "Negro Rights in Colorado Territory (1859–1867)." *Colorado Magazine* 40 (1963): 212–23.

Robison, Dan M. "Governor Robert L. Taylor and the Blair Education Bill in Tennessee." *Tennessee Historical Magazine,* Series II, 2 (1931): 28–49.

Sinkler, George. "Benjamin Harrison and the Matter of Race." *Indiana Magazine of History* 65 (1969): 197–214.

Stiff, Cary. "Nash Walker's Answer to Jim Crow," *Empire Magazine,* 26 October 1969, 37.

Upchurch, Thomas Adams. "The Butler Emigration Bill of 1890 and the Path Not Taken in Southern Race Relations." *Southern Studies* IX (1998): 37–68.

———. "Senator John Tyler Morgan and the Genesis of Jim Crow Ideology, 1889–1891." *Alabama Review* 57 (April 2004): 110–31.

Wayne, George H. "Negro Migration and Colonization in Colorado—1870–1930." *Journal of the West* 1 (1976): 102–20.

Welch, Richard E., Jr. "The Federal Elections Bill of 1890: Postscripts and Prelude." *Journal of American History* 52 (1965): 511–26.

Wellborn, Fred. "The Influence of the Silver-Republican Senators, 1889–1891." *Mississippi Valley Historical Review* 14 (1928): 462–80.

Young, Bradley J. "Silver, Discontent, and Conspiracy: The Ideology of the Western Republican Revolt of 1890–1901." *Pacific Historical Review* (1995): 243–65.

Books

Alexander, De Alva S. *History and Procedure of the House of Representatives.* Boston: Houghton Mifflin, 1916.

Anderson, James D. *The Education of Blacks in the South, 1860–1935.* Chapel Hill: University of North Carolina Press, 1988.

Angell, Stephen W. *Bishop Henry McNeal Turner and African-American Religion in the South.* Knoxville: University of Tennessee Press, 1992.

Ayers, Edward. *The Promise of the New South: Life after Reconstruction.* New York: Oxford University Press, 1992.

Baker, Richard A. *The Senate of the United States: A Bicentennial History.* The Anvil Series, ed. Louis L. Snyder. Malabar, Florida: Krieger, 1988.

Barnes, James. *John G. Carlisle: Financial Statesman.* American Political Leaders Series, ed. Allen Nevins. New York: Dodd, Mead, 1931.

Barnes, Kenneth C. *Who Killed John Clayton? Political Violence and the Emergence of the New South, 1861–1893.* Durham: Duke University Press, 1998.

Barrows, Chester L. *William M. Evarts: Lawyer, Diplomat, Statesman.* Chapel Hill: University of North Carolina Press, 1941.

Bass, Herbert J. *"I Am a Democrat": The Political Career of David Bennett Hill.* Syracuse: Syracuse University Press, 1961.

Bay, Mia. *The White Image in the Black Mind: African-American Ideas about White People, 1830–1925.* New York: Oxford University Press, 2000.

Beer, Thomas. *Hanna.* New York: Alfred A. Knopf, 1929.

Bensel, Richard F. *Sectionalism and American Political Development, 1880–1980.* Madison: University of Wisconsin Press, 1984.

Berkhofer, Robert F., Jr. *The White Man's Indian: Images of the American Indian from Columbus to the Present.* New York: Alfred A. Knopf, 1978.

Berry, L. L. *A Century of Missions of the African Methodist Episcopal Church, 1840–1940.* New York: Gutenberg, 1942.

Betts, Raymond F. *The False Dawn: European Imperialism in the Nineteenth Century.* Minneapolis: University of Minnesota Press, 1975.

Binder, Sarah A. *Minority Rights, Majority Rule: Partisanship and the Development of Congress.* Cambridge, England: Cambridge University Press, 1997.

Blegen, Theodore C. *Minnesota: A History of the State.* Minneapolis: University of Minnesota Press, 1963.

Bond, Bradley G. *Political Culture in the Nineteenth-Century South: Mississippi, 1830–1900.* Baton Rouge: Louisiana State University Press, 1995.

Bracey, John H., ed. *Black Nationalism in America.* Indianapolis : Bobbs-Merrill, Co., 1977.

Brock, William H. *The United States, 1789–1890: The Sources of History.* Studies in the Uses of Historical Evidence Series, ed. G. R. Elton. Ithaca: Cornell University Press, 1975.

Brooks, Roy L. *Integration or Separation? A Strategy for Racial Equality.* Cambridge: Harvard University Press, 1996.

Brotz, Howard, ed. *African-American Social and Political Thought, 1850–1920.* Basic Books, 1966. Reprint, New Brunswick, New Jersey: Transaction Publishers, 1992.

Brown, Dee. *Bury My Heart at Wounded Knee: An Indian History of the American West.* New York: Henry Holt, 1970.

Buck, Paul H. *The Road to Reunion, 1865–1900.* Boston: Little, Brown, 1937.

Burdette, Franklin L. *Filibustering in the Senate.* Princeton: Princeton University Press, 1940.

Burnham, W. Dean. *Presidential Ballots, 1836–1892.* Baltimore: Johns Hopkins Press, 1955.

Burton, Theodore E. *John Sherman.* Boston: Houghton Mifflin, 1906.

Calhoun, Charles W. *Gilded Age Cato: The Life of Walter Q. Gresham.* Lexington: University Press of Kentucky, 1988.

Callcott, Margaret Law. *The Negro in Maryland Politics, 1870–1912.* John Hopkins University Studies in Historical and Political Science Series. Baltimore: John Hopkins Press, 1969.

Castel, Albert, and Scott L. Gibson. *The Yeas and the Nays: Key Congressional Decisions, 1774–1945.* Self-published, 1975.

Chandler, David L. *The Natural Superiority of Southern Politicians: A Revisionist History.* Garden City, New York: Doubleday, 1977.

Clanton, O. Gene. *Congressional Populism and the Crisis of the 1890s.* Lawrence: University Press of Kansas, 1998.

———. *Populism: The Humane Preference in America, 1890–1900.* Boston: Twayne Publishers, 1991.

Clymer, Kenton. *John Hay: The Gentleman as Diplomat.* Ann Arbor: University of Michigan Press, 1975.

Connelly, William E. *The Life of Preston B. Plumb, 1837–1891.* Chicago: Browne & Howell, 1913.

Coolidge, Louis A. *An Old-Fashioned Senator: Orville H. Platt of Connecticut.* Vol. II. 1910. Reprint, American History and Culture in the Nineteenth Century Series, ed. Martin L. Fausold. Port Washington, New York: Kennikat Press, 1971.

Cooper, John M., Jr. *Walter Hines Page: The Southerner as American, 1855–1918.* The Fred W. Morrison Series in Southern Studies. Chapel Hill: University of North Carolina Press, 1977.

Cresswell, Stephen. *Multi-Party Politics in Mississippi, 1877–1902.* Jackson: University Press of Mississippi, 1995.

Crunden, Robert M. *Ministers of Reform: The Progressives' Achievement in American Civilization.* Urbana: University of Illinois Press, 1982.

Current, Richard N. *Pine Logs and Politics: A Life of Philetus Sawyer, 1816–1900.* Madison: State Historical Society of Wisconsin, 1950.

Currie, James T. *The United States House of Representatives.* The Anvil Series, ed. Louis L. Snyder. Malabar, Florida: Krieger, 1988.

Daniel, Pete. *Standing at the Crossroads: Southern Life in the Twentieth Century.* Rev. ed. Baltimore: Johns Hopkins University Press, 1996.

Daniels, Roger. *Not Like Us: Immigrants and Minorities in America, 1890–1924.* Chicago: Ivan R. Dee, 1997.

Dann, Martin E., ed. *The Black Press, 1827–1890: The Quest for National Identity.* New York: Capricorn Books, 1972.

Davidson, Donald. *The Attack on Leviathan: Regionalism and Nationalism in the United States.* Chapel Hill: University of North Carolina Press, 1938.

Davis, Allen F. *Spearheads for Reform: The Social Settlements and the Progressive Movement.* New York: Oxford University Press, 1967.

Davis, Harold E. *Henry Grady's New South: Atlanta, A Brave and Beautiful City.* Tuscaloosa: University of Alabama Press, 1990.

Dearing, Mary R. *Veterans in Politics: The Story of the G.A.R.* Baton Rouge: Louisiana State University Press, 1952.

DeSantis, Vincent P. *Republicans Face the Southern Question: The New Departure Years, 1877–1897.* The Johns Hopkins University Studies in Historical and Political Science, vol. LXXVII, no 1. Baltimore: Johns Hopkins University Press, 1959.

———. *The Shaping of Modern America: 1877–1920.* 2nd ed. Wheeling, Illinois: Forum Press, 1989.

Dewey, Davis R. *National Problems, 1885–1897.* The American Nation: A History, vol. XXIV, ed. Albert B. Hart, New York: Harper & Brothers, 1907.

Dinnerstein, Leonard, Roger L. Nichols, and David M. Reiners. *Natives and Strangers: Blacks, Indians, and Immigrants in America.* 2nd ed. New York: Oxford University Press, 1990.

Dippie, Brian W. *The Vanishing American: White Attitudes and U.S. Indian Policy.* Middletown, Connecticut: Wesleyan University Press, 1982.

Dobson, John M. *Politics in the Gilded Age: A New Perspective on Reform.* New Perspectives in American History Series, ed. James P. Shenton. New York: Praeger, 1972.

Donaldson, Gary A. *The Second Reconstruction: A History of the Modern Civil Rights Movement.* The Anvil Series, ed. Hans L. Trefousse. Malabar, Florida: Krieger, 2000.

Donovan, Timothy P., and Willard B. Gatewood, Jr., eds. *The Governors of Arkansas: Essays in Political Biography.* Fayetteville: University of Arkansas Press, 1981.

Dorset, Phyllis F. *The New Eldorado: The Story of Colorado's Gold and Silver Rushes.* New York: Macmillan, 1970.

Dyer, Brainerd. *The Public Career of William M. Evarts.* New York: Da Capo Press, 1969.

278   Bibliography

Dyer, John P. *"Fightin' Joe" Wheeler*. Baton Rouge: Louisiana State University Press, 1941.

Eaton, Clement. *A History of the Old South: The Emergence of a Reluctant Nation*. 3d. ed. Prospect Heights, Illinois: Waveland Press, Inc., 1975.

Eckert, Ralph L. *John Brown Gordon: Soldier, Southerner, American*. Baton Rouge: Louisiana State University Press, 1989.

Elliott, Russell R. *History of Nevada*. Lincoln: University of Nebraska Press, 1973.
———. *Servant of Power: A Political Biography of Senator William M. Stewart*. Reno: University of Nevada Press, 1983.

Ellis, Elmer. *Henry Moore Teller: Defender of the West*. Caldwell, Idaho: Caxton Printers, 1941.

Ellison, Mary. *The Black Experience: American Blacks Since 1865*. London: B. T. Batsford, 1974.

Escott, Paul D., et al., eds. *Major Problems in the History of the American South, Volume II: The New South*. Boston: Houghton Mifflin, 1999.

Faulkner, Harold U. *Politics, Reform, and Expansion: 1890–1900*. The New American Nation Series, ed. Henry S. Commager and Richard B. Morris. New York: Harper & Brothers, 1959.

Fierce, Milfred C. *The Pan-African Idea in the United States, 1900–1919: African-American Interest in Africa and Interaction with West Africa*. New York: Garland, 1993.

Filler, Louis, ed. *Democrats and Republicans: Ten Years of the Republic* (Selections from Harry T. Peck, *Twenty Years of the Republic*). New York: Capricorn Books, 1964.

Foner, Eric. *Free Soil, Free Labor, Free Men: The Ideology of the Republican Party before the Civil War*. New York: Oxford University Press, 1970.

Fowler, Dorothy Ganfield. *John Coit Spooner: Defender of Presidents*. New York: University Publishers, 1961.

Franklin, John H., and Alfred E. Moss, Jr. *From Slavery to Freedom: A History of African Americans*. 7th ed. New York: McGraw-Hill, 1994; 8th ed., Boston: McGraw-Hill, 2000.

Frederickson, George M. *The Black Image in the White Mind: The Debate on Afro-American Character and Destiny, 1817–1914*. New York: Harper & Row, 1971.

Fry, Joseph A. *John Tyler Morgan and the Search for Southern Autonomy*. Knoxville: University of Tennessee Press, 1992.

Gaither, Gerald H. *Blacks and the Populist Revolt: Ballots and Bigotry in the New South*. Tuscaloosa: University of Alabama Press, 1977.

Garraty, John A. *Henry Cabot Lodge: A Biography*. New York: Alfred A. Knopf, 1965.
———. *The New Commonwealth: 1877–1890*. The New American Nation Series, ed. Henry S. Commager and Richard B. Morris. New York: Harper & Row, 1968.

Gaston, Paul M. *The New South Creed: A Study in Southern Mythmaking*. New York: Alfred A. Knopf, 1970.

Gentry, Claude. *Private John Allen: Gentleman, Statesman, Sage, Prophet*. Decatur, Georgia: Bowen Press, 1951.

Gerber, David A. *Black Ohio and the Color Line, 1860–1915*. Urbana: University of Illinois Press, 1976.

Going, Allen J. *Bourbon Democracy in Alabama: 1874–1890*. Tuscaloosa: University of Alabama Press, 1951.

Goodwyn, Lawrence. *Democratic Promise: The Populist Moment in America*. New York: Oxford University Press, 1976.

Gossett, Thomas F. *Race: The History of an Idea in America*. New York: Oxford University Press, 1963. Reprint, New York: Oxford University Press, 1997.

Gould, Lewis L. *Reform and Regulation: American Politics, 1900–1916*. Critical Episodes in Amerian History Series, ed. Robert A. Divine. New York: John Wiley & Sons, 1978.

Grantham, Dewey W. *The Democratic South*. Athens: University of Georgia Press, 1963.

Grob, Gerald N., and George A. Billias, eds. *Interpretations of American History: Patterns and Perspectives*. Vols. I and II. 6th ed. New York: Free Press, 1992.

Gross, Theodore L. *Albion W. Tourgee*. New York: Twayne Publishers, 1963.

Gyory, Andrew. *Closing the Gate: Race, Politics, and the Chinese Exclusion Act*. Chapel Hill: University of North Carolina Press, 1998.

Hale, Grace E. *Making Whiteness: The Culture of Segregation in the South, 1890–1940*. New York: Pantheon Books, 1998.

Harris, William C. *The Day of the Carpetbagger: Republican Reconstruction in Mississippi*. Baton Rouge: Louisiana State University Press, 1979.

Hatch, Louis C. *A History of the Vice-Presidency of the United States*. New York: American Historical Society, 1934.

Haws, Robert, ed. *The Age of Segregation: Race Relations in the South, 1890–1945*. Jackson: University Press of Mississippi, 1978.

Haynes, George H. *The Senate of the United States: Its History and Practice*. New York: Russell & Russell, 1960.

Hicks, John D. *The Populist Revolt: A History of the Farmers' Alliance and the People's Party*. Minneapolis: University of Minnesota Press, 1931.

Hietala, Thomas R. *Manifest Design: Anxious Aggrandizement in Late Jacksonian America* . Ithaca, N.Y. : Cornell University Press, 1985.

Hill, Adelaide C., and Martin Kilson, eds. *Apropos of Africa: Afro-American Leaders and the Romance of Africa*. Garden City, New York: Doubleday, 1971.

Hirshson, Stanley P. *Farewell to the Bloody Shirt: Northern Republicans & the Southern Negro, 1877–1893*. Bloomington: Indiana University Press, 1962.

Hochschild, Adam. *King Leopold's Ghost: A Story of Greed, Terror, and Heroism in Colonial Africa*. Boston: Houghton Mifflin, 1998.

Hofstadter, Richard. *The Age of Reform: From Bryan to F. D. R.* New York: Vintage Books, 1955.

———. *Social Darwinism in American Thought*. Rev. ed. New York: George Brazillier, 1955.

Holt, Thomas C., and Elsa Barkley Brown, eds. *Major Problems in African-American*

History, Volume II: From Freedom to "Freedom Now," 1865–1990s. Boston: Houghton Mifflin, 2000.

Jacobs, Wilbur R. *On Turner's Trail: 100 Years of Writing Western History.* Lawrence: University of Kansas Press, 1994.

Jarrell, Hampton M. *Wade Hampton and the Negro: The Road Not Taken.* Columbia: University of South Carolina Press, 1950.

Josephy, Alvin M., Jr. *The Congress of the United States.* New York: American Heritage, 1975.

Kantrowitz, Stephen. *Ben Tillman and the Reconstruction of White Supremacy.* Chapel Hill: University of North Carolina Press, 2000.

Katz, William L. *The Black West.* Garden City, New York: Doubleday & Company, 1971.

Kehl, James A. *Boss Rule in the Gilded Age: Matt Quay of Pennsylvania.* Pittsburgh: University of Pittsburgh Press, 1981.

Keller, Morton. *Affairs of State: Public Life in Late Nineteenth Century America.* Cambridge, Massachusetts: Belknap Press, 1977.

Kent, Frank R. *The Democratic Party: A History.* New York: Century, 1928.

Kenworthy, Leonard S. *The Tall Sycamore of the Wabash: Daniel Wolsey Voorhees.* Boston: Bruce Humphries, 1936.

Key, V. O. *Southern Politics in State and Nation.* New York: Alfred A. Knopf, 1949.

Killian, Lewis M. *White Southerners.* New York: Random House, 1970.

Knoles, George H. *The Presidential Campaign and Election of 1892.* Stanford University Publications Series: History, Economics, and Political Science, vol. V, no. 1. Stanford: Stanford University Press, 1942.

Kousser, J. Morgan. *The Shaping of Southern Politics: Suffrage Restriction and the Establishment of the One-Party South.* New Haven: Yale University Press, 1974.

Kovel, Joel. *White Racism: A Psychohistory.* New York: Vintage Books, 1970.

Kraus, Michael. *Immigration, The American Mosaic: From Pilgrims to Modern Refugees.* The Anvil Series, ed. Louis L. Snyder. Huntington, New York: Krieger, 1955. Reprint, Huntington, New York: Krieger, 1979.

Kraut, Alan M. *The Huddled Masses: The Immigrant in American Society, 1880–1921.* The American History Series, ed. John Hope Franklin and Abraham S. Eisenstadt. Arlington Heights, Illinois: Harlan-Davidson, 1982.

Krislov, Samuel. *The Negro in Federal Employment: The Quest for Equal Opportunity.* Minneapolis: University of Minnesota Press, 1967.

Krock, Arthur, ed. *The Editorials of Henry Watterson.* Louisville: Louisville Courier–Journal, 1923.

Lambert, John R. *Arthur Pue Gorman.* Baton Rouge: Louisiana State University Press, 1953.

Langford, Paul. *The Excise Crisis: Society and Politics in the Age of Walpole.* Oxford: Clarendon Press, 1975.

Lee, Gordon C. *The Struggle for Federal Aid, First Phase: A History of the Attempts to Obtain Federal Aid for the Common Schools, 1870–1890.* New York: Bureau of Publications, Teachers' College, Columbia University, 1949.

Lewis, David L., ed. *W. E. B. DuBois: A Reader.* New York: Henry Holt & Company, 1995.

Lewis, Oscar. *The Big Four: The Story of Huntington, Stanford, Hopkins, and Crocker, and of the Building of the Central Pacific.* New York: Alfred A. Knopf, 1938.

Limerick, Patricia N., Clyde A. Milner, and Charles E. Rankin, eds. *Trails: Toward a New Western History.* Lawrence: University of Kansas Press, 1991.

Litwack, Leon F. *North of Slavery: Free Blacks in the Free States, 1790–1860.* Chicago: University of Chicago Press, 1961.

Litwack, Leon F., and August Meier, eds. *Black Leaders of the Nineteenth Century.* Urbana: University of Illinois Press, 1988.

Logan, Rayford W. *The Betrayal of the Negro: From Rutherford B. Hayes to Woodrow Wilson.* London: Collier-Macmillan, 1965.

———. *The Negro in American Life and Thought: The Nadir, 1877–1901.* New York: Dial Press, 1954.

Lyman, Stanford M. *Chinese Americans.* Ethnic Groups in Comparative Perspective, ed. Peter I. Rose. New York: Random House, 1974.

Lynch, Dennis T. *Grover Cleveland: A Man Four-Square.* New York: Horace Liveright, 1932.

Lynch, Hollis R. *Edward Wilmot Blyden: Pan-Negro Patriot, 1832–1912.* West African History Series, ed. Gerald S. Graham. London: Oxford University Press, 1967.

Mandle, Jay R. *Not Slave, Not Free: The African American Economic Experience Since the Civil War.* Durham: Duke University Press, 1992.

Marcus, Robert D. *Grand Old Party: Political Structure in the Gilded Age, 1880–1896.* New York: Oxford University Press, 1971.

Marks, Henry S., and Marsha K. *Alabama Past Leaders.* Huntsville: Strode Publishers, 1982.

Matthews, Donald R. *U.S. Senators and Their Words.* Chapel Hill: University of North Carolina Press, 1960.

Mayer, George H. *The Republican Party: 1854–1964.* New York: Oxford University Press, 1964.

McElroy, Robert M. *Levi Parsons Morton: Banker, Diplomat, Statesman.* New York: Putnam, 1930. Reprint, New York: Arno Press, 1975.

McLemore, Richard A., and Nannie Pitts, eds. *A History of Mississippi.* Vol. II. Hattiesburg: University and College Press of Mississippi, 1973.

McMath, Robert C., Jr. *American Populism: A Social History, 1877–1898.* New York: Hill and Wang, 1993.

McMillen, Neil R. *Dark Journey: Black Mississippians in the Age of Jim Crow.* Urbana: University of Illinois Press, 1989.

McPherson, James M. *The Abolitionist Legacy: From Reconstruction to the NAACP.* Princeton: Princeton University Press, 1975.

———. *Ordeal by Fire: The Civil War and Reconstruction.* 3rd ed. Boston: McGraw-Hill, 2001.

McWilliams, Tennant S. *Hannis Taylor: The New Southerner as an American.* Tuscaloosa: University of Alabama Press, 1978.

Meier, August. *Negro Thought in America, 1880–1915: Racial Ideologies in the Age of Booker T. Washington.* With a New Introduction. Ann Arbor: University of Michigan Press, 1988.

Merrill, Horace S. *Bourbon Leader: Grover Cleveland and the Democratic Party.* Boston: Little, Brown, 1957.

Mezerik, A. G. *The Revolt of the South and West.* New York: Duell, Sloan, and Pearce, 1947.

Miller, Floyd J. *The Search for a Black Nationality: Black Colonization and Emigration, 1787–1863.* Urbana: University of Illinois Press, 1975.

Minor, Henry. *The Story of the Democratic Party.* New York: Macmillan, 1928.

Moos, Malcolm. *The Republicans: A History of Their Party.* New York: Random House, 1956.

Morgan, H. Wayne. *From Hayes to McKinley: National Party Politics, 1877–1896.* Syracuse: Syracuse University Press, 1969.

———, ed. *The Gilded Age.* Rev. ed. Syracuse: Syracuse University Press, 1970.

Moses, Wilson J. *Alexander Crummell: A Study of Civilization and Discontent.* New York: Oxford University Press, 1989.

———, ed. *Destiny and Race: Selected Writings, 1840–1898, of Alexander Crummell.* Amherst: University of Massachusetts Press, 1992.

Mosley, Mrs. Charles C., Sr. *The Negro in Mississippi History.* Rev. ed. Jackson: Purser Brothers, 1969.

Muzzey, David S. *James G. Blaine: A Political Idol of Other Days.* New York: Dodd, Mead, 1935.

Myers, William S. *The Republican Party: A History.* Rev. ed. New York: Century, 1932.

Nevins, Allen. *Grover Cleveland: A Study in Courage.* New York: Dodd, Mead, 1933.

———. *Hamilton Fish: The Inner History of the Grant Administration.* American Political Leaders Series, ed. Allen Nevins. New York: Dodd, Mead, 1937.

———, ed. *Letters of Grover Cleveland, 1850–1908.* Boston: Houghton Mifflin, 1933.

Nixon, Raymond B. *Henry W. Grady: Spokesman of the New South.* New York: Alfred A. Knopf, 1943. Reprint, New York: Russell & Russell, 1969.

Nolen, Claude H. *The Negro's Image in the South: The Anatomy of White Supremacy.* Lexington: University of Kentucky Press, 1967.

Oberholtzer, Ellis P. *A History of the United States Since the Civil War.* Vol. V. New York: Macmillan, 1937.

Oldfield, J. R., ed. *Civilization and Black Progress: Selected Writings of Alexander Crummell on the South.* Charlottesville: University of Virginia Press, 1995.

Olsen, Otto H. *Carpetbagger's Crusade: The Life of Albion Winegar Tourgee.* Baltimore: Johns Hopkins University Press, 1965.

Painter, Nell Irwin. *Exodusters: Black Migration to Kansas after Reconstruction.* New York: Alfred A. Knopf, 1977.

———. *Standing at Armageddon: The United States, 1877–1919.* New York: Norton, 1987.

Palmer, Bruce. *"Man Over Money": The Southern Populist Critique of American Capitalism.* Chapel Hill: University of North Carolina Press, 1980.

Parker, William B. *The Life and Public Services of Justin Smith Morrill.* The American Scene: Comments and Commentators Series, ed. Wallace D. Farnham. Boston: Houghton Mifflin, 1924. Reprint, New York: Da Capo Press, 1971.

Parks, Joseph A. *Joseph E. Brown of Georgia.* Baton Rouge: Louisiana State University Press, 1977.

Perman, Michael. *Struggle for Mastery: Disfranchisement in the South, 1888–1908.* Chapel Hill: University of North Carolina Press, 2001.

Phillips, Margaret I. *The Governors of Tennessee.* Gretna, Louisiana: Pelican, 1978.

Ponton, M. M. *Life and Times of Henry M. Turner.* Atlanta: Caldwell, 1917. Reprint, Westport, Connecticut: Greenwood Press, 1970.

Proctor, Ben H. *Not Without Honor: The Life of John H. Reagan.* Austin: University of Texas Press, 1962.

Quillen, Frank U. *The Color Line in Ohio: A History of Race Prejudice in a Typical Northern State.* Ann Arbor: University of Michigan Press, 1913.

Rabinowitz, Howard N. *Race Relations in the Urban South, 1865–1890.* New York: Oxford University Press, 1978.

Ray, Nicol C. *Southern Democrats.* New York: Oxford University Press, 1994.

Redkey, Edwin S. *Black Exodus: Black Nationalist and Back-to-Africa Movements, 1890–1910.* New Haven: Yale University Press, 1969.

Rhodes, James F. *History of the United States: From the Compromise of 1850 to the End of the Roosevelt Administration.* Vol. VIII. New York: McMillan, 1919.

Richardson, Leon B. *William E. Chandler: Republican.* American Political Leaders Series, ed. Allen Nevins. New York: Dodd, Mead, 1940.

Rigby, Gregory A. *Alexander Crummell: Pioneer in Nineteenth-Century Pan-African Thought.* Westport, Connecticut: Greenwood Press, 1987.

Robinson, William A. *Thomas B. Reed: Parliamentarian.* American Political Leaders Series, ed. Allen Nevins. New York: Dodd, Mead, 1930.

Rogers, William W., Jr. *Black Belt Scalawag: Charles Hays and the Southern Republicans in the Era of Reconstruction.* Athens: University of Georgia Press, 1993.

Rolle, Andrew F., ed. *Helen Hunt Jackson, A Century of Dishonor: The Early Crusade for Indian Reform.* Gloucester, Massachusetts: Peter Smith, 1978.

Rothman, David J. *Politics and Power: The United States Senate, 1869–1901.* Cambridge: Harvard University Press, 1966.

Rudwick, Elliott M. *W. E. B. DuBois: Propagandist for the Negro Protest.* Studies in American Negro Life Series, ed. August Meier. New York: Atheneum, 1969.

Rutland, Robert A. *The Democrats: From Jefferson to Clinton.* Columbia: University of Missouri Press, 1995.

———. *The Republicans: From Lincoln to Bush.* Columbia: University of Missouri Press, 1996.

Sage, Leland L. *William Boyd Allison: A Study in Practical Politics.* Iowa City: State Historical Society of Iowa, 1956.

Schriftgeisser, Karl. *The Gentleman from Massachusetts: Henry Cabot Lodge*. Boston: Little, Brown, 1944.

Schwartz, Bernard. *A Basic History of the U.S. Supreme Court*. The Anvil Series, ed. Louis L. Snyder. Huntington, New York: Krieger, 1979.

Seip, Terry L. *The South Returns to Congress: Men, Economic Measures, and Intersectional Relationships, 1868–1879*. Baton Rouge: Louisiana State University Press, 1983.

Sievers, Harry J. *Benjamin Harrison: Hoosier President*. Indianapolis: Bobbs-Merrill, 1968.

Silbey, Joel. *The United States Congress in a Nation Transformed, 1896–1963*. The Congress of the United States, 1789–1989 Series, vol. I. Brooklyn: Carlson, 1991.

Simkins, Francis B. *Pitchfork Ben Tillman: South Carolinian*. Baton Rouge: Louisiana State University Press, 1944.

Sinkler, George. *The Racial Attitudes of American Presidents: From Abraham Lincoln to Theodore Roosevelt*. Garden City, New York: Doubleday, 1971.

Socolofsky, Homer E., and Allan B. Spetter. *The Presidency of Benjamin Harrison*. American Presidency Series, ed. Donald R. McCoy, et al. Lawrence: University Press of Kansas.

Spicer, Edward H. *A Short History of the Indians of the United States*. The Anvil Series, ed. Louis L. Snyder. Malabar, Florida: Krieger, 1969. Reprint, Malabar, Florida: Krieger, 1983.

Sproat, John G. *"The Best Men": Liberal Reformers in the Gilded Age*. New York: Oxford University Press, 1968.

———. Introduction to *The Liberal Republican Movement* by Earle D. Ross, 1910. Seattle: University of Washington Press, 1970.

Staudenraus, Philip J. *The African Colonization Movement, 1816–1865*. New York: Columbia University Press, 1961.

Steinfeld, Melvin. *Our Racist Presidents: From Washington to Nixon*. San Ramon, California: Consensus Publishers, 1972.

Stephenson, Nathaniel W. *Nelson W. Aldrich: A Leader in American Politics*. New York: Charles Scribner's Sons, 1930.

Stern, Clarence A. *Republican Heyday: Republicanism Through the McKinley Years*. Ann Arbor: Edwards Brothers, 1962.

Stokes, Melvyn, and Rick Halpern, eds. *Race and Class in the American South Since 1890*. Oxford: Berg, 1994.

Summers, Mark W. *The Gilded Age: or, The Hazard of New Functions*. Upper Saddle River, New Jersey: Prentice Hall, 1997.

Takiki, Ronald. *Iron Cages: Race and Culture in Nineteenth-Century America*. New York: Oxford University Press, 1990.

Taylor, Quintard. *In Search of the Racial Frontier: African Americans in the American West, 1528–1990*. New York: Norton, 1998.

Thomas, John L. *Slavery Attacked: The Abolitionist Crusade*. Englewood Cliffs, New Jersey: Prentice-Hall, Inc., 1965.

Thornbrough, Emma Lou. *T. Thomas Fortune: Militant Journalist*. Chicago: University of Chicago Press, 1972.

Tindall, George B. *The Disruption of the Solid South*. Athens: University of Georgia Press, 1972.

———, ed. *A Populist Reader: Selections from the Works of American Populist Leaders*. New York: Harper & Row, 1966.

Towne, Ruth W. *Senator William J. Stone and the Politics of Compromise*. National University Publications Series in Political Science. Port Washington, New York: Kennikat Press, 1979.

Trefousse, Hans L. *Reconstruction: America's First Effort at Racial Democracy*. 2nd ed. The Anvil Series, ed. Hans L. Trefousse. Malabar, Florida: Krieger, 1999.

Tucker, Glenn. *Zeb Vance: Champion of Personal Freedom*. Indianapolis: Bobbs-Merrill, 1965.

Viorst, Milton. *Fall from Grace: The Republican Party and the Puritan Ethic*. New York: New American Radio, 1968.

Walls, William J. *Joseph Charles Price: Educator and Race Leader*. Boston: Christopher, 1943.

Wang, Xu. *The Trial of Democracy: Black Suffrage and Northern Republicans, 1860–1910*. New York: Oxford University Press, 1998.

Washington, Nathaniel J. *Historical Development of the Negro in Oklahoma*. Tulsa: Dexter, 1948.

Webb, Walter P. *Divided We Stand: The Crisis of a Frontierless Democracy*. New York: Farrar & Rinehart, 1937.

Weinstein, Alan. *Prelude to Populism: Origins of the Silver Issue, 1867–1878*. New Haven: Yale University Press, 1970.

Weinstein, Maurice A., ed. *Zebulon B. Vance and "The Scattered Nation."* Charlotte: Wildacres Press, 1995.

Welch, Richard E. *The Presidencies of Grover Cleveland*. American Presidency Series, ed. Donald R. McCoy, et al. Lawrence: University of Kansas Press, 1988.

Wharton, Vernon L. *The Negro in Mississippi: 1865–1890*. New York: Harper & Row, 1947.

White, Leonard D. *The Republican Era: A Study in Administrative History, 1869–1901*. New York: Free Press, 1958.

Wiebe, Robert H. *The Search for Order, 1877–1920*. The Making of America Series, ed. David Donald. New York: Hill and Wang, 1967.

Wilhelm, Sidney M. *Who Needs the Negro?* New York: Doubleday, 1971.

Williams, Burton J. *Senator John James Ingalls: Kansas' Iridescent Republican*. Lawrence: University Press of Kansas, 1972.

Williamson, Joel. *The Crucible of Race: Black-White Relations in the American South Since Emancipation*. New York: Oxford University Press, 1986.

———, ed. *The Origins of Segregation*. Boston: Heath, 1968.

———. *A Rage for Order: Black/White Relations in the American South Since Emancipation*. New York: Oxford University Press, 1984.

Woodward, C. Vann. *Origins of the New South.* Baton Rouge: Louisiana State University Press, 1951.

————. *The Strange Career of Jim Crow.* 3rd rev. ed. New York: Oxford University Press, 1974.

Wyeth, Newton. *Republican Principles and Policies: A Brief History of the Republican National Party.* Chicago: Republic Press, 1916.

Wynes, Charles E. *Forgotten Voices: Dissenting Southerners in an Age of Conformity.* Baton Rouge: Louisiana State University Press, 1967.

————, ed. *The Negro in the South Since 1865: Selected Essays in American Negro History.* Tuscaloosa: University of Alabama Press, 1965.

Dissertations

Anders, James M. "The Senatorial Career of John Tyler Morgan." Ph.D. Diss., George Peabody College for Teachers, 1956.

Crofts, Daniel W. "The Blair Bill and the Election Bill: The Congressional Aftermath of Reconstruction." Ph.D. Diss., Yale University, 1968.

Reference Works

African American Materials Project Staff of North Carolina Central University. *Newspapers and Periodicals by and about Black People: Southeastern Library Holdings.* Boston: Hall, 1978.

Bacon, Donald C., et al., eds. *The Encyclopedia of the United States Congress.* Vol. II. New York: Simon & Schuster, 1995.

Garraty, John A., and Mark C. Carnes, eds. *American National Biography.* New York: Oxford University Press, 1999.

Hopkins, Joseph G. E., et al., eds. *Concise Dictionary of American Biography.* New York: Charles Scribner's Sons, 1964.

Lowery, Charles D., and John F. Marszalek, eds. *The Greenwood Encyclopedia of African-American Civil Rights: From Emancipation to the Twenty-First Century.* (1st ed. 1992). Rev. and enl. ed. Westport, Connecticut: Greenwood Press, 2004.

Powell, William S., ed. *Dictionary of North Carolina Biography.* Vol. II. Chapel Hill: University of North Carolina Press, 1986.

Smith, Dwight L., ed. *Afro-American History: A Bibliography.* Clio Bibliography Series, ed. Eric H. Boehm. Santa Barbara: ABC-Clio, 1974.

Stubbs, Walter. *Congressional Committees: A Checklist, 1789–1982.* Westport, Connecticut: Greenwood Press, 1985.

Thomas, Joseph, ed. *Universal Pronouncing Dictionary of Biography and Mythology.* 5th ed. Philadelphia: Lippincott, 1930.

Webster's Biographical Dictionary. Springfield, Massachusetts: G & C Merriam, 1943.

Index

Abbot, Lyman, 13

"A bill to promote mendicancy," 49

abolition, 7, 14, 37, 68, 78, 87, 93–94, 115, 127, 141, 187, 193, 209

abolitionists. *See* abolition

Abraham and Lot, 33

accomodationism, 220

Africa, 24–32, 34–40, 43, 45, 184, 197, 199, 201–2

African Americans, xi; and Africans, 202; argue elections are more important than education, 65; and argument for dispersion over colonization, 31, 34; and backlash against GOP, 214; and black press and Blair Education Bill, 50; and building the United States, 45; called "a mass of ignorance," 57, 60; and citizenship, 209, 210; and colonization plans 24–27; comprised the largest of minority groups, 83; and criticism of the emigration movement, 43; demanded to stay in America and gain equal rights, 30–31; and destiny to return to Africa, 37; and disillusion with GOP, 21–22; education attempts since 1865 for, 47; and election of Benjamin Harrison, 20; and European immigrants, 188–89; forced to wait on civil rights movement, 165, 168, 171; and Fourteenth Amendment, 174; migration an alternative for, 44; migration into cotton states by, 40; and need of economic relief, 211; no help from Congress for, 218–19; and path of least resistance, 220, 229n33; rejection of Blair Education Bill is denial of social justice for, 62–63; seen by many to need vocational education over academics, 49; and Senate substitute bill, 125, 134, 141, 148, 154; and Social Darwinism, 121; and social deficiency, 198–99; and status in America, 2–3, 12–13; and status quo versus equal rights, 206; a tool for the GOP, 15, 193, 196; urged to return to Africa as Christian missionaries, 28–29, 36, 39; victim syndrome of, 203; and voter fraud in the South, 77, 86; and West, 175; and white superiority, 201

African Methodist Episcopal Church (AME), 20–21, 36, 38

Afro-American Colonization Society, 34

Afro-American Congress, 35–36

Afro-American League, 44, 205

Alabama, opposed Blair Bill, 47

Albany Argus, 210

287

Democratic National Convention, 126
Democratic Party, xi, 2; and adoption
of a cloture rule, 215; and alliance
with Silverites, 164–69; and
arguments against force bill, 102–
5, 108, 110; and arguments for
white superiority, 208–9; charged
GOP with discrimination, 113;
charged GOP with fomenting
sectional strife, 88–89; charged
GOP with gerrymandering, 76–
78; charged GOP with GOP
election fraud, 159–60; charged
with bypassing the Constitution,
61; charged with corruption and
profligacy, 7; charged with
Southern election abuse, 86; and
congressional election of 1890,
121–23; in deep South favored
migration, 34, 45, 47, 49, 55;
denounced marriage of Republicans and blacks, 22; and destruction of GOP civil rights agenda,
184; and divisiveness over blacks,
101; and election of 1888, 17–19;
feared move back to British
empire, 70; and filibustering,
156–58, 160–64; said GOP did
not care about blacks, 210; honest
in their views, 220, 227n20,
228n24, 230n40; members from
the South and denial of citizenship to minorities, 183; minority
party had more votes than GOP,
71–72; and nicknaming Fifty-first
Congress, 8; and overreaction to
Federal Elections Bill, 212, 214;
pointed out GOP hypocrisy
concerning Indian affairs, 177;
pushed for emigration of blacks,
23–24, 29; recounted horrors of
Reconstruction, 75; and resistance
to black southerners, 3, 5–6; and

resistance to GOP issues, 9;
resisted GOP efforts to help
blacks in 1874–1886, 73–74; and
strategy against force bill, 90–98;
and strengthened resistance to
Federal Elections Bill, 123–28,
130–39, 140–44; and success in
debate over Federal Elections Bill,
149–50; and support of independent press and public, 217–18;
and threat of filibuster, 67, 106–7;
and "tyranny of the majority," 69,
145; under-represented in North,
145; and voter fraud, 79–80; and
voter qualifications, 114–15, 119;
weapons against GOP majority, 8;
and white rule and defense, 99–
100
Democrats. See Democratic Party
Detroit Tribune, 39
Devens, Charles J., 137
devil, 81, 98, 139
disfranchisement, xi, 4, 24, 83, 86, 91,
96, 111, 136, 145, 218, 223,
248n41
Dolliver, Jonathan P., 117
Dolph, John N., 10, 129, 141–42, 162,
179, 182–83
Donnelly, Ignatius, 172
doughface, 119, 127, 147, 218
Douglass, Frederick, 31, 36–37, 43, 50,
87, 107, 142, 196, 206–7, 213–14,
218, 257n29
DuBois, W.E.B., 43
Dudley, Thomas U., 47, 258n43
Dudley, William, and "Dudley Affair,"
79–80, 159–60
Dunning, William A., 105

East, the, 251n13
Eden, 43
Edmunds, George, 106, 143, 164
egalitarianism. See egalitarians